TECHNIQUES

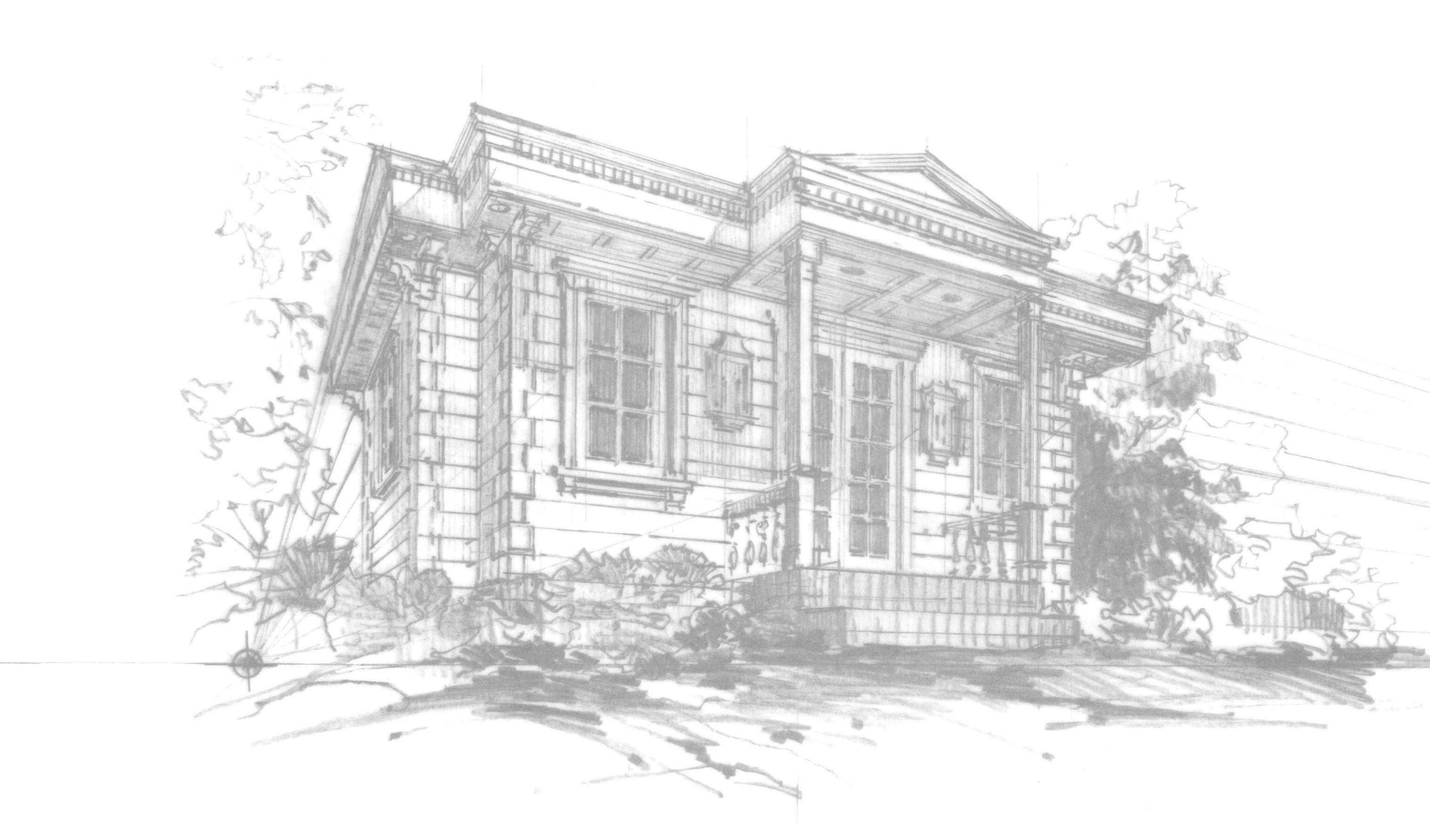

PHOTOGRAPHIC PERSPECTIVE DRAWING TECHNIQUES

Sid DelMar Leach, ASID

McGRAW-HILL PUBLISHING COMPANY

New York St. Louis San Francisco Auckland Bogotá
Caracas Hamburg Lisbon London Madrid Mexico
Milan Montreal New Delhi Oklahoma City
Paris San Juan São Paulo Singapore
Sydney Tokyo Toronto

Library of Congress Cataloging in Publication Data

Leach, Sid DelMar.
Photographic perspective drawing techniques / Sid DelMar Leach.
p. cm.
ISBN 0-07-036814-7
1. Photography, Architectural. 2. Perspective. 3. Architectural drawing. I. Title.
TR659.L42 1990
720'.28'4—dc20 89-12369
CIP

234567890 KPKP 976543210

ISBN 0-07-036814-7

The editor for this book was Joel E. Stein, the designer was Naomi Auerbach, and the production supervisor was Suzanne Babeuf. It was set in Auriga by Progressive Typographers.

Printed and bound by Halliday Lithographers.

I wish to dedicate this book to a few important people instrumental in its realization: to Donna, who gave me the encouragement to write the first version, to the doctors at Children's Hospital and at Stanford, who saved my life, and to April, who brought me back to what life should be, took care of me, and inspired me to refine this work to what it is now.

CONTENTS

PREFACE

Using the techniques of photographic perspective drawing and other companion visualizing techniques found in this book the designer of remodeled spaces can create three-dimensional design drawings that are visually correct and in scale with an existing building.

This approach to design drawing allows designers, architects, and other professionals to use the lines of perspective found in the photograph to bypass the conventional "constructed" methods of design visualization.

Home owner–builders, contractors, cabinetmakers, and furniture makers, as well as the design professional, can benefit greatly from this time-saving approach. Quick sketches and design studies are a snap when using the step-by-step photographic methods based on the author's many years of experience as a designer of commercial and residential interiors, cabinet work, and fine furniture.

Unlike some books on perspective drawing that give glimpses of techniques, this book takes the reader through each process thoroughly and completely, using subject matter that carries each project through from the initial photograph to the final presentation drawing. The over 300 photographs and illustrations clearly show the various drawing methods used to aid in the design development stages as well as construction phases of projects ranging from the simplest bath addition to a resort hotel remodel. In conjunction with photography the importance of sketching construction methods using both the photographic perspective method as well as isometric drawings and remodeled elevations and details — each, an invaluable on-the-job communication tool — is stressed.

Sid DelMar Leach

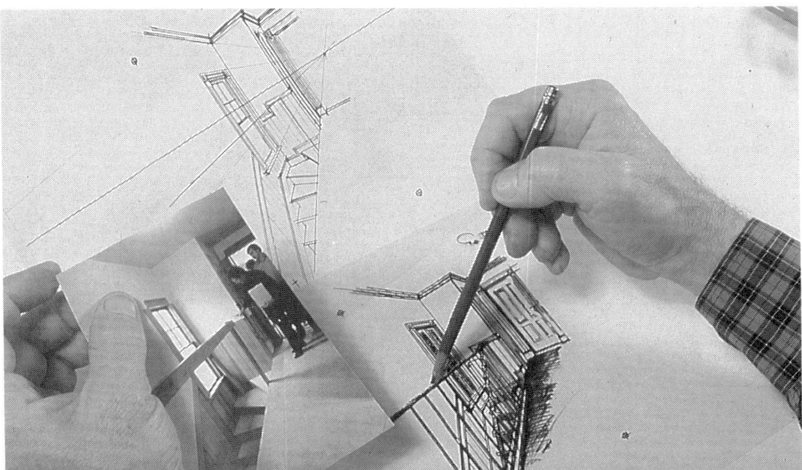

INTRODUCTION

A blank sheet of paper can be intimidating. For those involved in the building profession, much time and much energy are spent laboring over drawings. Idea sketches are created, reworked, and refined; details are elaborated upon; and plans and elevations are drawn. Finally, from this lengthy, often arduous process, a three-dimensional perspective drawing is born.

For professionals — be they architects, designers, or builders — who are trying to communicate ideas to a potential client, what is drawn on those blank sheets of paper can mean the difference between winning or losing a job.

Once a job is won, drawings can provide workers on the job with vital information that words alone can't convey, making the difference between a job well done or a costly hit-and-miss affair. It's as simple and as important as that.

Once you have mastered them, the techniques described in this book will enable you to consistently produce quality drawings with a minimum of headaches. With these techniques in your portfolio, you'll be able to assemble three-dimensional perspective drawings without using ponderous projection methods, even if you have only minimal artistic training. Soon you will be easily translating your ideas to paper, unhindered by worries about your artistic drafting ability.

Key among the techniques in this book is a method that has been developed for creating professional perspective drawings, a method that uses photographs as the starting point. This technique is called *photolinear perspective,* and it could become the single most important technique in your design drawing repertoire — and in your work as well.

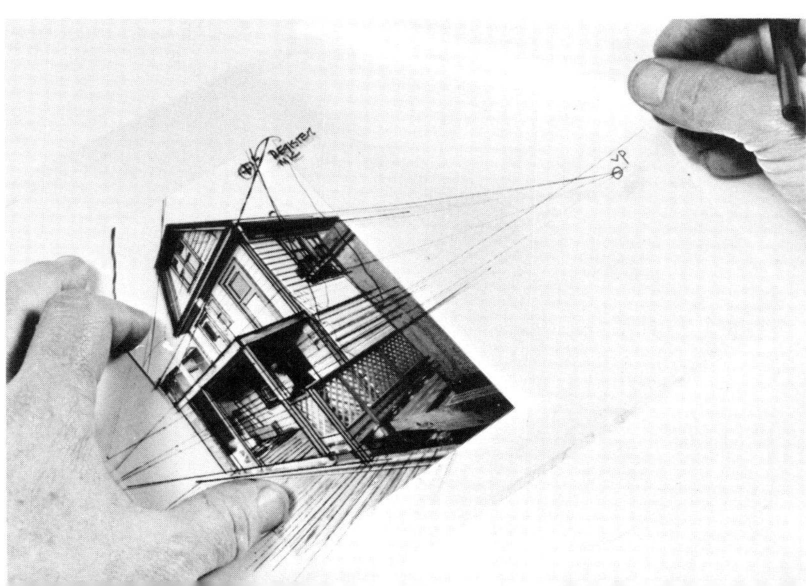

CHAPTER 1

THE PHOTOLINEAR PERSPECTIVE METHOD: AN OVERVIEW

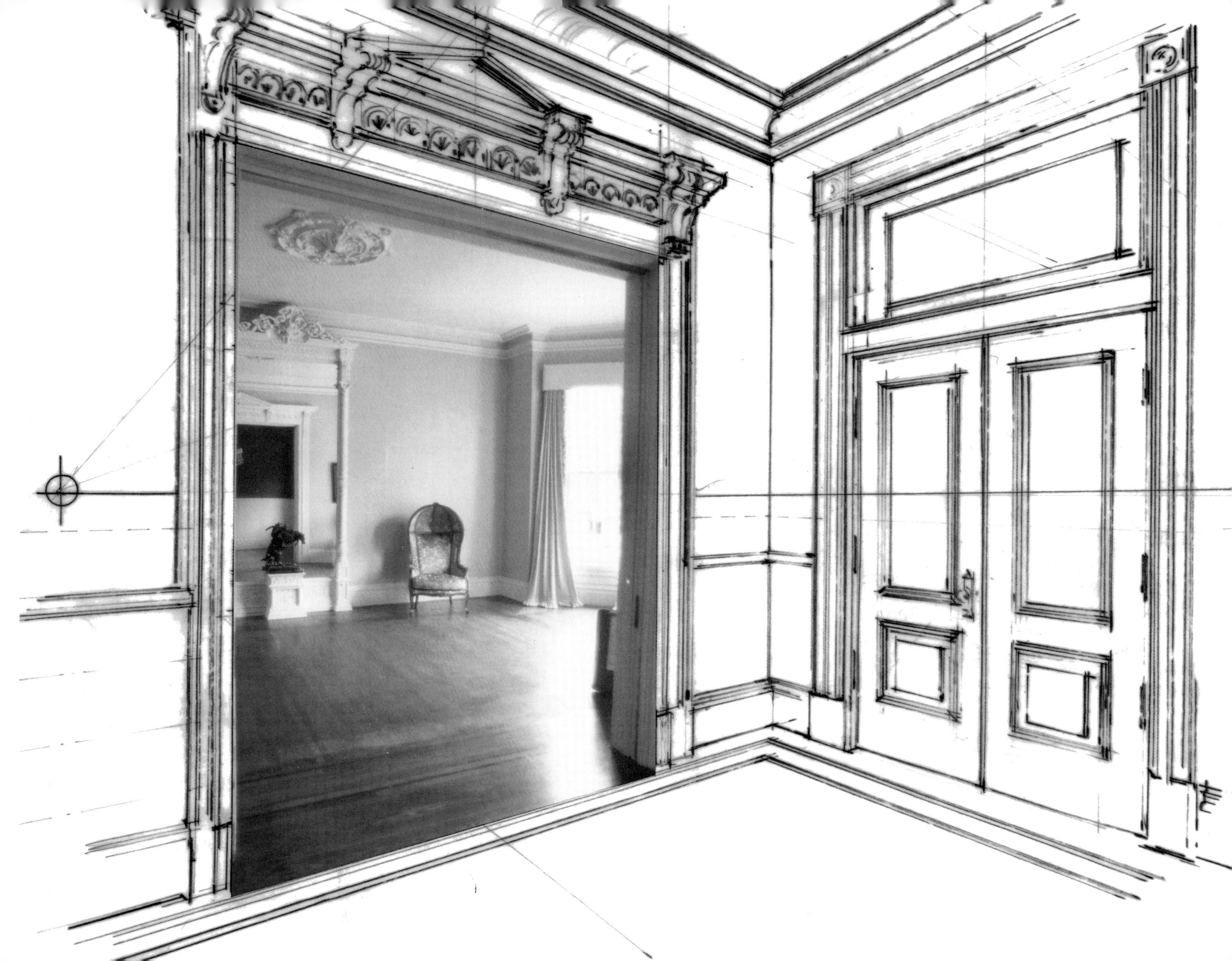

Renovation Design and Illustration

This book is a photographic approach to remodeling illustration. Before photographs, measurements, designs, or sketches are considered, however, there must be a project complete with a client and an existing building. The step-by-step processes shown in this book are based on existing buildings and three-dimensional objects.

Current input as well as design criteria are assumed to be established in all exercises shown here, because this book is not about renovation design, but about renovation design presentation drawing.

The Sketch as a Tool for Visualization

One of the designer's and architect's most important and valuable aids to design and communication is the three-dimensional sketch or perspective rendering. These two-dimensional representations of three-dimensional objects allow the creator to visualize design ideas and communicate these to clients, associates, contractors, and builders.

The speed and accuracy with which sketches can be made depend greatly on the method used to create them. A sketch employs height, width, and depth in the same way as a photograph portrays a three-dimensional object on a two-dimensional surface. This principle of implied three-dimensional realism, found within the photograph, is used in this book to create design sketches and renderings that are visually pleasing as well as dimensionally and proportionally accurate. See Figure 1.1.

The Photolinear Perspective Method of Design Illustration

The method developed here, called *photolinear perspective,* gives you the tools to translate ideas to three-dimensional graphic form, without requiring extensive schooling in art, by using a photograph as the starting point.

◀ **FIGURE 1.1** The photolinear perspective method begins with a photograph. The lines of perspective within the photograph are traced along with the total linear representation of the subject on an overlay sheet of tracing paper. From this line drawing you can add to or subtract from the subject, using the methods shown in this book.

Here the limited format of this photograph has been enlarged to incorporate a greater viewing area than that of the photograph. From this you can create a presentation drawing in scale with the original photograph without having to use laborious mechanical projection methods of perspective.

CHAPTER 1

THE PHOTOLINEAR PERSPECTIVE METHOD: AN OVERVIEW

By tracing over a photograph, you can create a rapid perspective drawing without using the tiresome projection methods and grid underlays traditionally employed in architecture and design schools. Then all that is needed is a mastery of some basic drafting techniques, including a range of pencil and pen techniques, to create professional, three-dimensional drawings.

By using photographs as the basis for drawings that show proposed remodeling work, you are immediately starting out with an existing structure and volume of space.The following steps are covered in detail, and you should study each example carefully, paying special attention to the step-by-step illustration and techniques shown.

Steps of Renovation Design in the Photolinear Perspective Method

1. *Examine the building* (both the interior and the exterior) to establish existing conditions and design possibilities, and obtain input from the client as necessary.

2. *Take photographs of both the interior and the exterior of the building* keeping vertical lines within each image vertical. At the same time, document all pertinent physical building information.

3. *Specify all pertinent building measurements,* both interior and exterior, on roughly drawn plans and elevations.

4. *Draw scaled plans and elevations* to reflect existing building conditions.

5. *Select photographs that will be used to portray areas of new designs* and their adjacent related environment.

6. *Enlarge photographs to workable size,* using photocopy or traditional enlargement techniques.

7. *Establish lines of perspective and vanishing points within each photograph* by tracing the existing structure and extending the major horizontal elements.

8. *Translate existing known measurements of each photographic image* onto a tracing-paper overlay.

9. *Divide and extend planes of the traced photograph image,* using established lines of perspective and vanishing points as a guide and proportional geometric division methods.

10. *Establish revised plane relationships that will portray new design concepts* to their best advantage.

11. *Draw lines defining new designs* on newly constructed planes, using additional registered tracing-paper overlay sheets for each area concerned.

12. *Combine all pertinent information from progressive overlay sheets* onto one final overlay. This drawing will become the underdrawing that will show all existing and redesigned portions of the building as well as landscaping and the surrounding environment.

13. *Create a value study* on a clean tracing-paper overlay to establish light and dark areas as well as shade and shadows, which will give the final drawing an implied third dimension.

14. *Establish the extent or boundaries of the new sketch* that will be delineated on drafting vellum or frosted acetate drafting medium.

15. *Lay in all pencil or pen ''wash'' strokes* that will, when combined with variable-weight linear strokes, create the final three-dimensional drawing.

16. *Print and mat* the drawing for presentation.

Finding Perspective within a Photograph of an Existing Building

Examination of the building Once a client has hired an architect or designer to renovate an existing building and has conveyed design criteria and considerations, the building must be physically examined by the design team. It is during this phase of any project that photographic and measuring documentation should be planned. Without proper documentation, accurate design representation of any form is impossible.

Photographic images are far superior to thumbnail sketches because all elements are faithfully recorded. But photographs without backup physical measurements are of little use in the overall design process. Lines of perspective that can be found within a photograph of an existing building can be used to create sketches showing proposed architectural changes and additions. Unlike the case of some drawings created with the traditional perspective methods, proportional dimen-

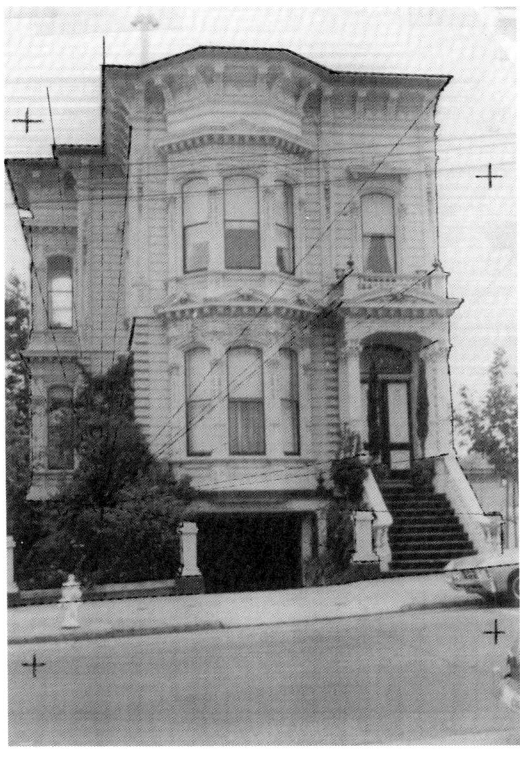

FIGURE 1.2a This is an example of a good photograph for the photolinear perspective method. Vertical lines are vertical, and the subject is sharp and clear. The lines of perspective have been traced from the eaves and porch roof, and these lines intersect at one point, the vanishing point. This is an example of a one-point perspective. The point of intersection when the photograph is traced is the position of the camera.

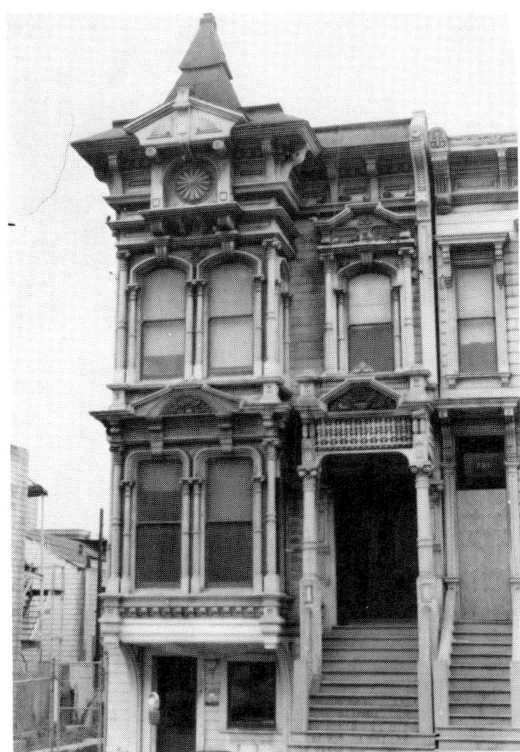

FIGURE 1.2b This photograph of a Victorian house entrance does not meet the requirements for photolinear perspective. The subject is out of perpendicular, and the "vertical" lines, if traced, would meet at a point above the page. Vertical lines must be photographed as vertical for the methods shown in this book.

sions can always be shown accurately, in the photolinear perspective method, if all the steps listed here are followed.

Once major elements and other items in the photograph are established, remodeling sketches and drawings can be created in scale with each photograph and presented to a client to show what the proposed scheme will look like.

The importance of good photographs Good photographs are the foundation on which the whole process rests. The first step, therefore, involves learning how to take architectural photographs—knowing what to look for and what to be aware of. See Figure 1.2.

The photographs taken must provide basic documentation for the project and must serve as the foundation upon which you can create "instant" perspective drawings for the purposes of remodeling. The photographs also serve as a pictorial checklist when you are away from the site, helping you to remember important details of a project. Also the initial photographs can later serve as dramatic "before" pictures, to be held up next to the "after" pictures showing the finished project.

Take lots of photographs By taking lots of photographs, you are focusing the eye and camera on every detail, both large and small, of the initial project. In this process the eye is being trained to see more clearly than before, and the camera becomes the third eye, revealing elements in new ways.

The Type of Photographs to Be Taken

Photographs taken of buildings or parts of buildings to be remodeled are used later in the creation of perspective drawings. The close-up photographic details that highlight texture, shapes, light, and shade will be used as a reference to help in refining the basic perspective drawing and to bring it to life. Additional photographs of details aid in the informational architectural drawing process and, if taken properly, will help in the creation of professional remodeling drawings, without the need for constant visits to the job site.

Together, the photographs will provide a pictorial encyclopedia of the project. See Figure 1.3.

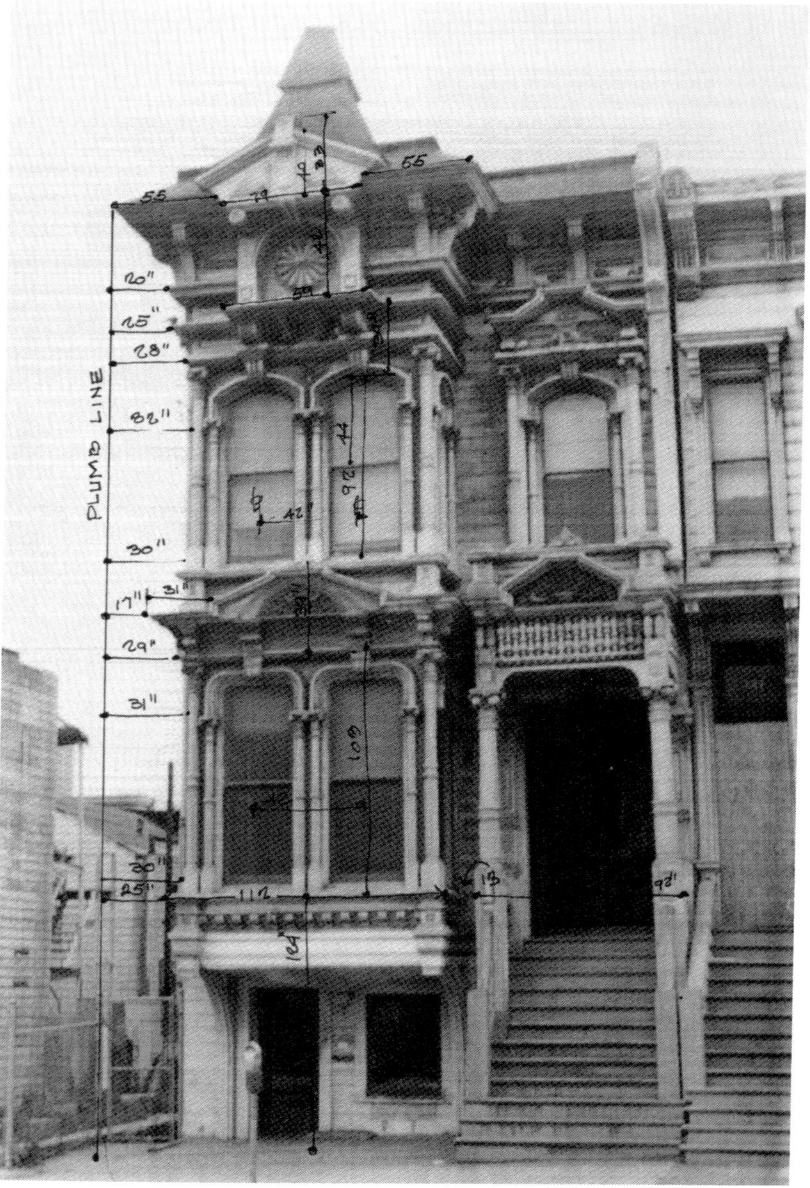

1.3a

FIGURE 1.3a and b The measured elevation in (b) of the house shown in (a) clearly reveals the underlying geometric centerline relationship of major architectural elements. Note that similar elements appear at each centerline. The projection of the left bay is noted on the side view, "Elevation of Bay Windows," and contains the same window elements as the primary elevation. The measured drawings created from photographs and on-site dimension notations, which were required in this instance for replacement of trim and windows, determined to have deteriorated beyond repair, include ¼" = 1'0" scale drawings in (b) and 3" = 1'0" size details such as in (c) and (d). Complete and accurate photographs and on-site measurements are needed to create detail drawings such as this one. To this effect refer also to Figures 1.7 and 1.8a, b, and c.

TURNED CAP FINIAL
SHAPED CEDAR SHINGLE ROOF
FRIEZE
CARVED CAPITAL
REEDED COLONETTES
PROJECTING BAY
LEAD FLASHED SILL
GRADE at SIDEWALK
1737
TAR and GRAVEL ROOF
Second FLOOR
First FLOOR
20'-0"
24'-0"
3'-0"
24'-0"
71'-0"
Varies
EXTERIOR DETAILS
from the Residence at . . .
1737 WEBSTER ST.
SAN FRANCISCO
CALIFORNIA
MEASURED AND DRAWN BY SID DELMAR LEACH A.S.I.D.
STYLE: STICK-EASTLAKE
DATE BUILT: 1886
BUILDER: NEWSOM BROTHERS
PARLOR
ENTRY FOYER
PROJECTING BAY
PLAN of ENTRANCE
SCALE of FEET
0 1 2 3 4 5 10 15 20
ELEVATION of BAY WINDOWS
ELEVATION of PRIMARY FACADE
SECTION through ENTRANCE

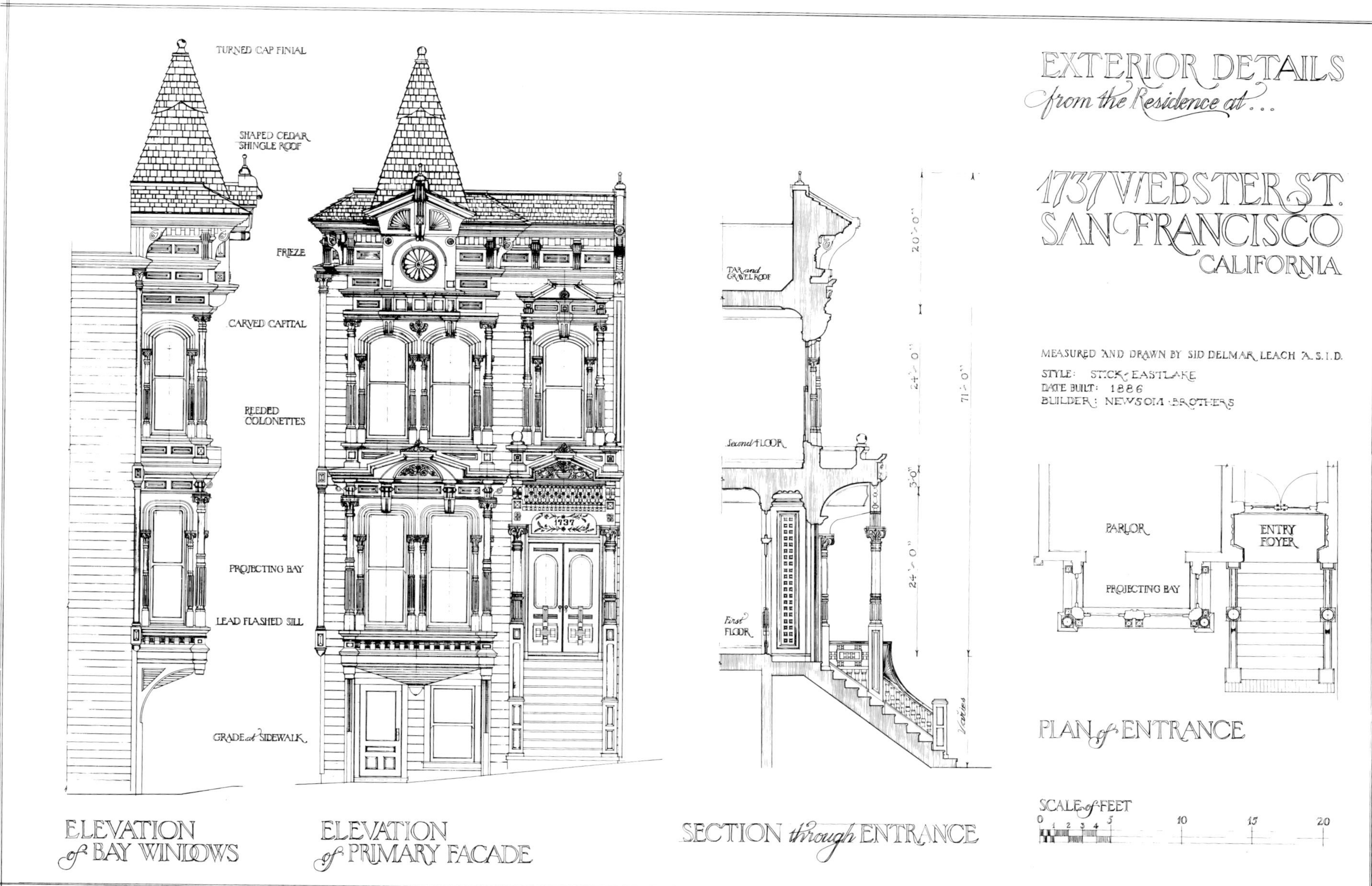

1.3b

FIGURE 1.3c This 3″ = 1′0″ scale drawing of an upper bay window with column trim shows clearly not only dimensionally rendered elevated details, but also cross sections (shown shaded) that are drawn as part of the informational drawing. The principles of "conventional" light (see Chapter 5) are applied to an elevation by using shade and shadow to make the two-dimensional drawing appear as three-dimensional as possible. See also "Rendered Elevations" in Chapter 7.

FIGURE 1.3d In this drawing of the upper projecting bay pediment of the house in Figure 1.3a, it becomes apparent how many geometric shapes are involved in the makeup of some highly decorated structures.

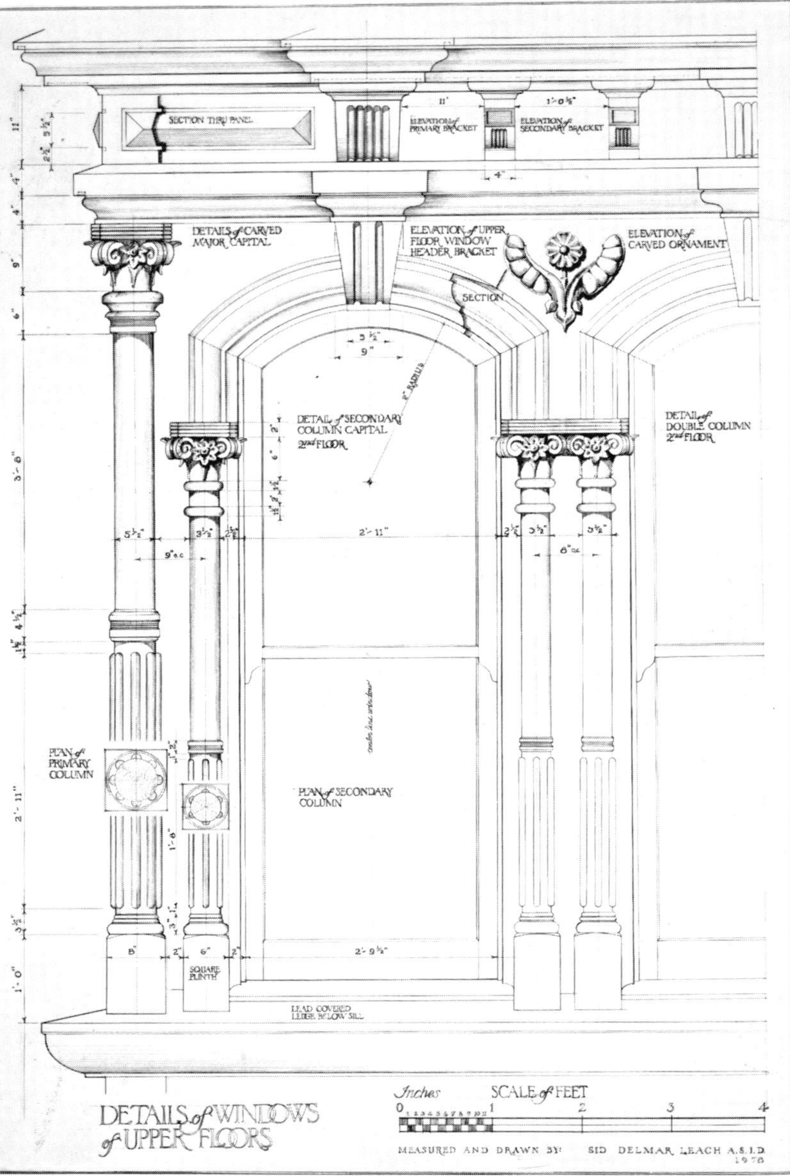

1.3c

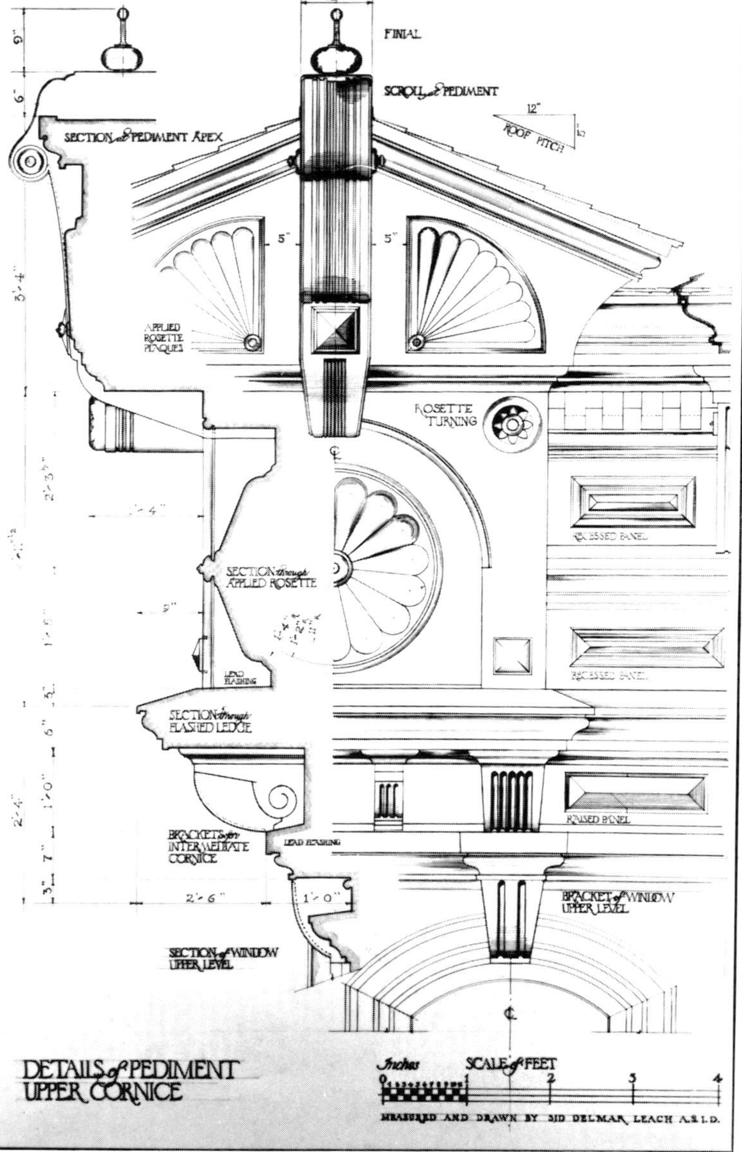

1.3d

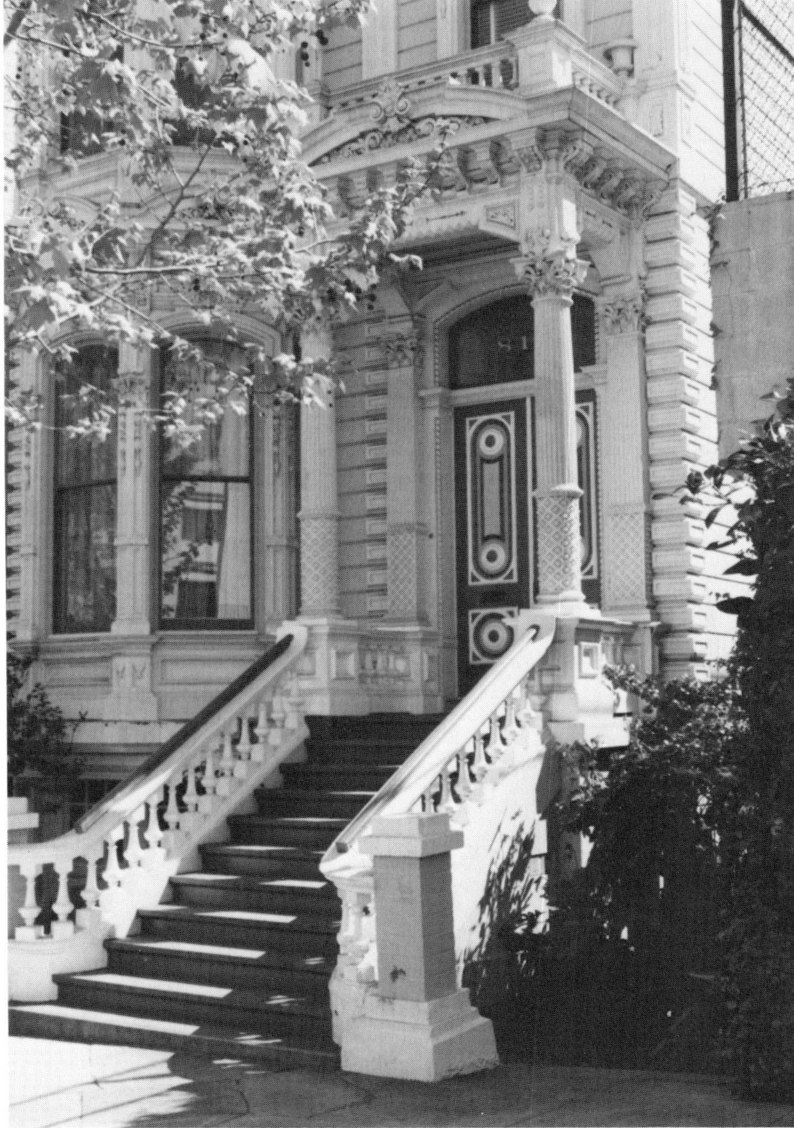

1.4a

Photographing and Measuring an Exterior to Aid in the Creation of Three-Dimensional Perspective Drawings: What to Look For

Learning to see architecture in terms of geometric elements Looking at the exterior of a building, the eye takes in many elements at once. The eye is alternately beguiled by colors, textures, and details, until finally the brain processes all the information into a general picture which can be recognized as a house. See Figure 1.4.

The first step, therefore, is to learn to see clearly. In using the photolinear perspective method, you will begin to see the building as a combination of the most basic of geometric elements, i.e., cubes, cylinders, cones, and pyramids. (See Figure 1.5). Being able to see a building as a combination of geometric solids is fundamental to the whole process. A gable roof becomes an equilateral triangle, a projected bay becomes a cube, a wood turning becomes a series of connected cylinders, and moldings are made up of many shapes combined. When you organize a volume of space into smaller units, each unit becomes easier to comprehend. See Figures 1.6 and 1.7.

As well as looking for the building's underlying geometry, you must take photographs of details from all angles.

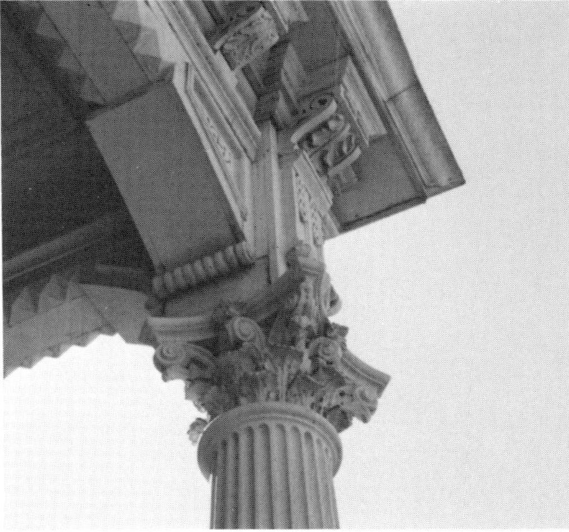

1.4b

FIGURE 1.4 This enlarged detail (b) of the entry to the house in Figure 1.2a shows how turnings and geometric shapes are used to create a total overall image. In the process of breaking the overall picture into individual geometric solids, it is often possible to see the symmetry and rational layout of a structure.

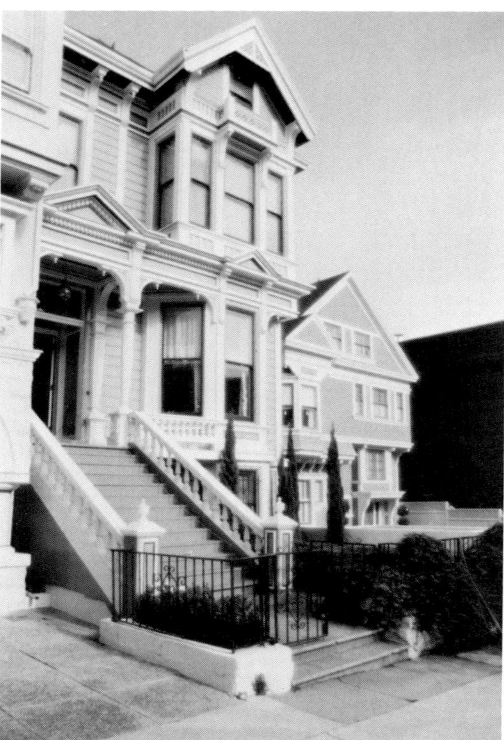

1.5a

FIGURE 1.5 Early Victorian houses such as this 1887 structure (a) are comprised of decorative elements (b) which could be ordered in those times from any number of stocking dealers specializing in architectural ornamentation. When documenting a house such as this, *you cannot take too many photographs.* These images are very helpful for general information purposes and for drawing perspectives, elevations, or details of the structure.

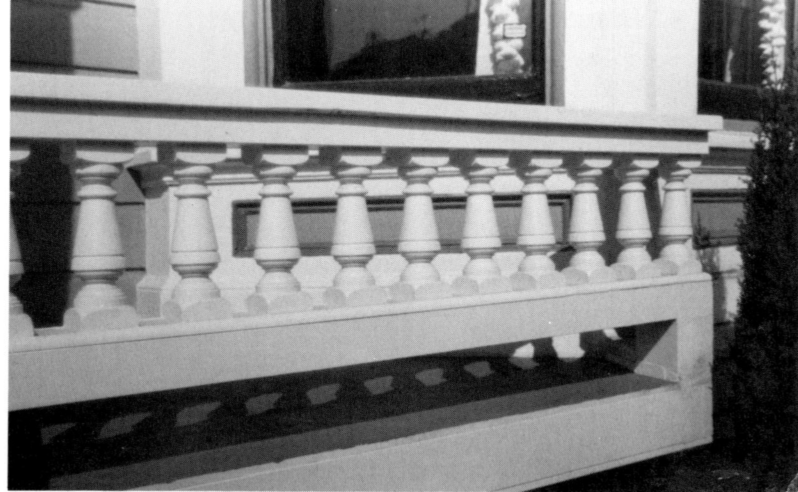

1.5b

FIGURE 1.6 An enlarged photocopy of the photograph in (a), chosen to create the illustration of the garage addition shown in (b), was traced and oriented to vertical before the illustration underdrawing was made. The suggestion of trees overhanging the driveway has been used to frame the subject and to draw attention to the center of the drawing.

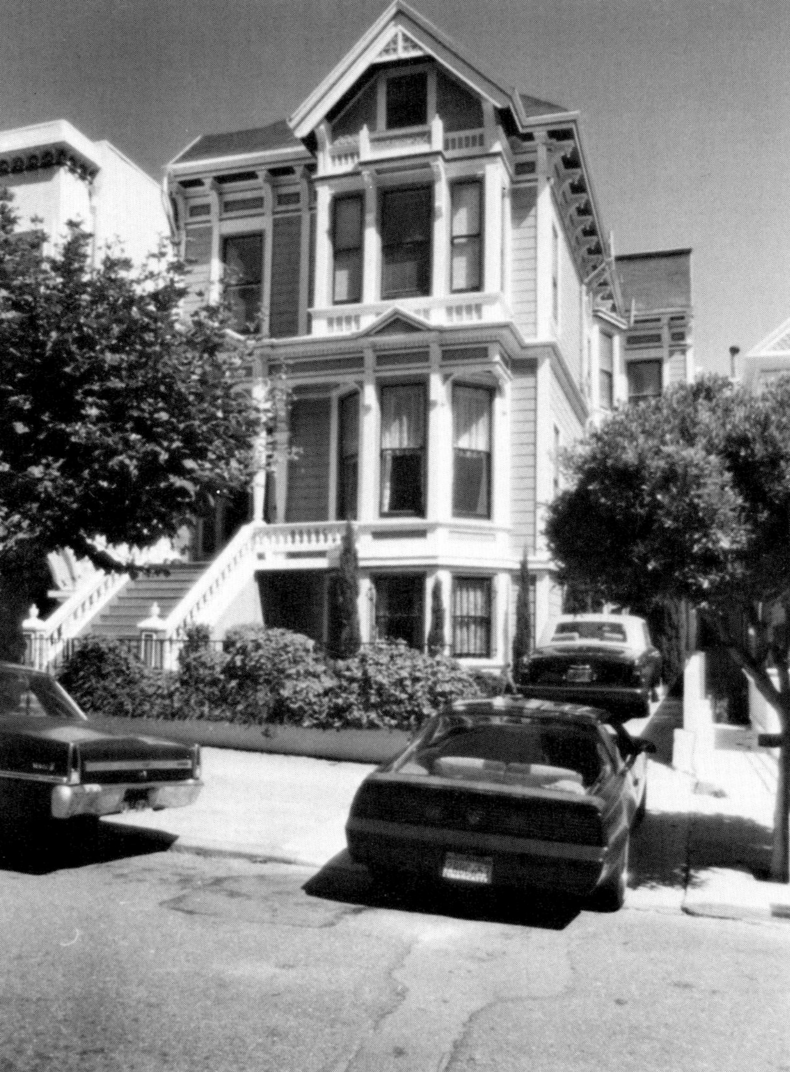

1.6a

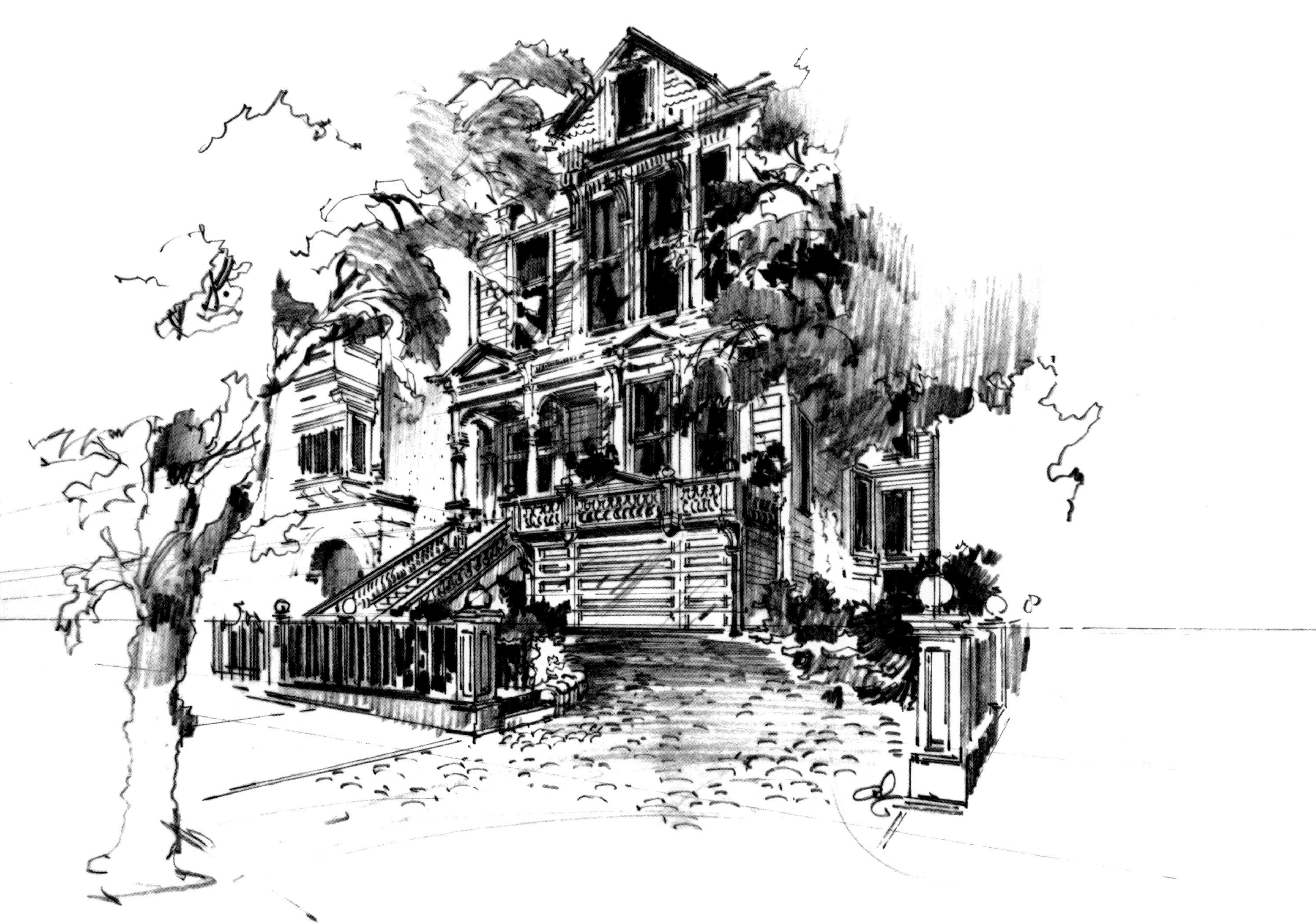

1.6b

Photographic Details: A Way to Record and Organize Information

While you are measuring, details should be photographed with a Polaroid or any instant-print camera. The advantage of taking Polaroids is that you have an instant picture on which you can write the corresponding dimensions. As you go about with your tape measure, measuring elements on the actual building, you can write these dimensions on the prints.

If you have assistants with you, get them to paste up your Polaroids on an 8″ × 10″ cardboard sheet, using rubber cement. Then these can be cut to fit a 3″ snap-ring binder that you can slip around your wrist, to carry while you are climbing about the building or measuring from a tall ladder. See Figures 1.7 and 1.8.

If scaffolding is already in place, you can gain access to the upper stories to measure eaves and corbels from there. If not, there is really no good method of measuring details, although a telephoto lens will enable you to get good photographs of upper elements.

It is always a good idea to measure with an assistant, since your first few times on a scaffold can be daunting. An alternative to climbing on the scaffolding when you are working on a lower building is to use a ladder. In either case, if your are unsure about climbing scaffolding and ladders, get someone experienced to do the measuring for you.

Be sure to give that person detailed instructions about what to photograph and measure. Above all, make sure it is someone whose accuracy you trust, since you will be working from these measurements when you do the scale drawings.

Always attach a cord to your camera and tape measure to make sure they won't fall to the ground should they slip out of your hand. It is also a good idea to keep about five pencils clipped to your shirt pocket.

How to Use Your Photographs as an Alternative to Measuring

An alternative to measuring the roof pitch from scaffolding (shown in Figure 1.8) is to plot it from a shot photographed flat on as an elevation.

When to Photograph

Photographs showing surface texture are very important. The sun casts shadows of varying intensity, depending on the time of day and the weather. It is often best to wait until the sun creates the greatest contrast between light and shadow before you photograph your subject. However, photographs taken at various times of the day are also needed for general remodeling information.

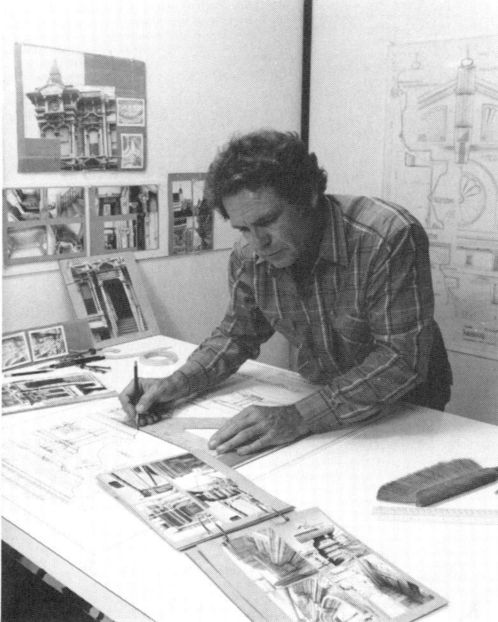

FIGURE 1.7 When remodeling drawings are required for a complex architectural structure such as this one, photographs from all angles are needed to show full elevations and close-up details. Note the Polaroid photographs glued to the ring binder on the table. With this handy over-the-wrist measuring and documentation aid, the risk of dropping photographs from a ladder or scaffold is minimized.

Take photographs of all sides of the building, exercising care to show any projecting architectural elements. Also take elevated photographs from the roof or scaffolding if it exists. These will allow you to verify the footprint of the building as well as later plot gardens, driveways, porches, steps, and the like.

Photograph Your Subject in an Orderly Manner

Remember, you can never take too many photographs when documenting a project.

To photograph a building, in this case a three-story Victorian edifice, divide the building into segments and photograph each segment individually. Then take photographs encompassing the entire elevation.

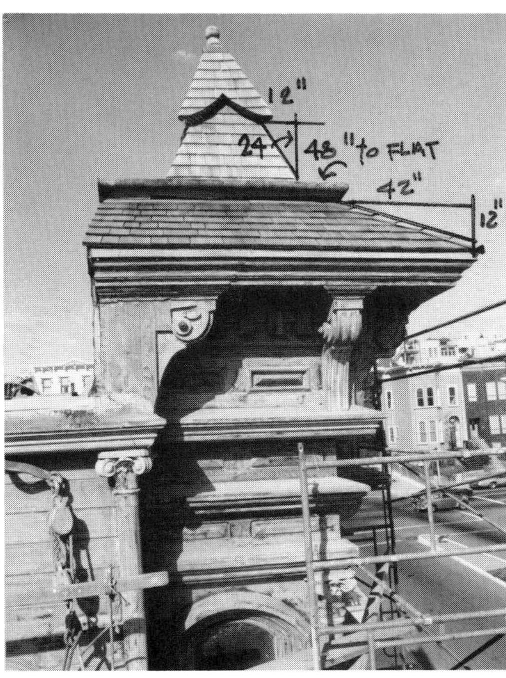

FIGURE 1.8a If you cannot reach the roof to measure the slope, often you can measure this angle and its relation to the horizontal approximately from a photograph that shows the profile of the roof. Use a scale rule, and draw both a "horizontal" line and a line to follow the pitch. These two lines should cross at one point. Next measure the vertical rise, using the same scale to measure the run. (Any scale will do, as long as it corresponds to the size of image on the photograph.)

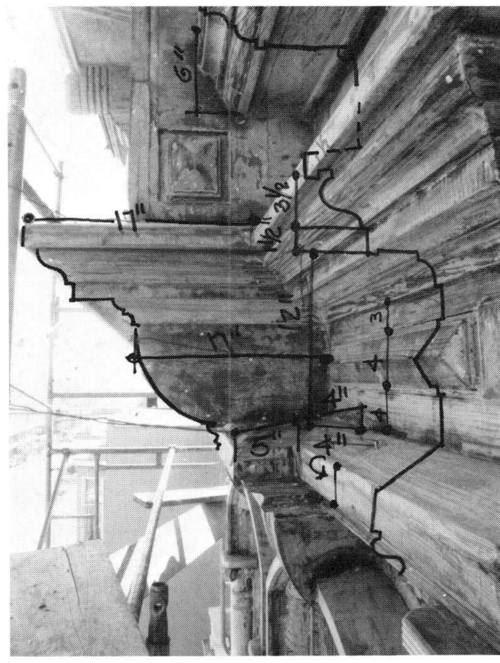

FIGURE 1.8b Be sure to show the profile and size of each molding or group of moldings on the informational detail photographs. These photographs were taken with a 35-mm camera and placed in a ring binder, and the dimensions were added at the site. Note the ink line denoting the cross section of the molded area on the right of the photograph. This was used to define a profile where the photograph was unclear.

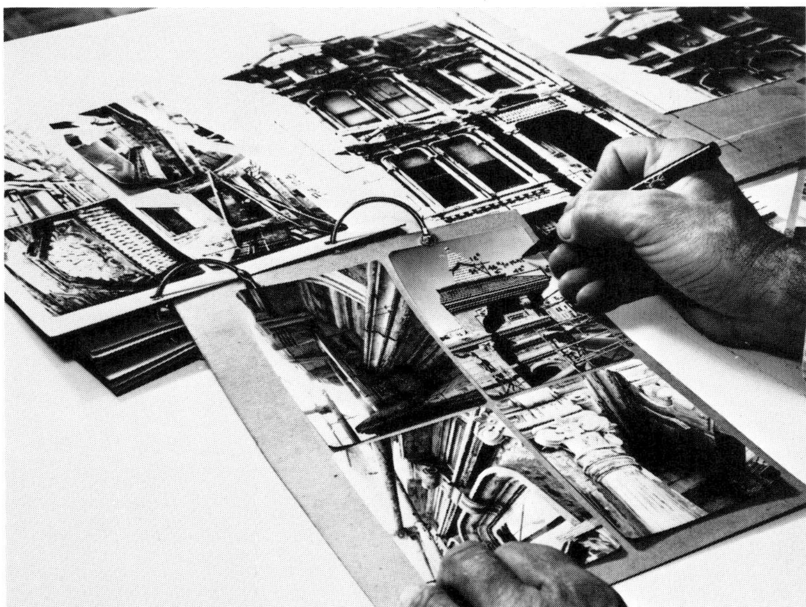

FIGURE 1.8c When details are photographed with a Polaroid or 35-mm-format camera and you add the dimensions to the prints on location, little is left to the imagination when you are away from the job site. See the roof pitch in the middle photograph, noting the horizontal "run" of the roof slope, which is 42", and the "rise" of the slope, which is 12". The roof slope in this case is 1/3.5—a very uncommon slope by today's standards. If a true elevation photograph is taken of elements such as this, accurate dimensions and angles can be measured and calculated directly from the photographic image.

Where to position yourself Pointing the camera upward to include the roof of the building often makes the sides of the top of the building appear to slope inward, since the picture planes of the film and of the building are no longer parallel. See Figure 1.9a and b.

How to avoid distortion Distortion can be avoided by photographing from a height, by standing on a ladder or positioning yourself either in a window or from the balcony of a building opposite. In addition, a perspective correction lens for a 35-mm camera can be used to keep the image vertical.

Keep the measuring corner vertical Remember, the entire structure should be comprehensively documented, with attention paid both to details and to the overall structure.

All this proper preplanning during the photograph process will help you to better translate your ideas onto paper later. Remember, *pictures are taken both to aid in the creation of perspective drawings and to provide detailed information about the project in the form of close-up shots.* You are taking photographs that will provide the cornerstone for the perspective drawings you will later create. The examples shown are of Victorian structures, which have been included for their visual complexity but which are geometrically simple.

How to Set Up Exterior Shots

If you can climb onto the roof or scaffolding, you can drop a white cotton rope (weighted with a piece of cast-iron sash weight) from the eaves, thereby establishing a vertical reference point that can be used to measure the projections from the primary plane.

If you mark off the cord at 1′ intervals, allowing for the stretch created by the sash weight, you can later calculate the height of the roof from the photographs by counting the divisions and projecting these back to the primary *true measuring corner* (TMC) of the building.

In the case of a two-point perspective, this major building corner will be the key vertical axis in the drawing, dividing the structure into right and left planes. For purposes of continuity, in this book planes which recede to the *vanishing point right* (VPR) are designated as primary and secondary planes A, A^1, A^2, and so on. In the illustrations that follow, all planes that diminish to the *vanishing point left* (VPL) are planes B, B^1, B^2, and so on.

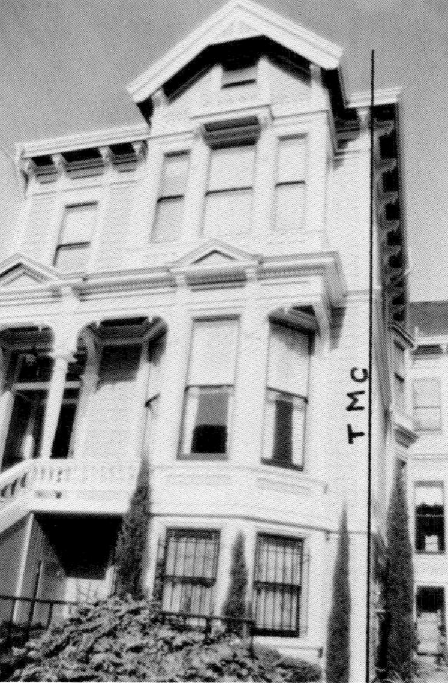

1.9a

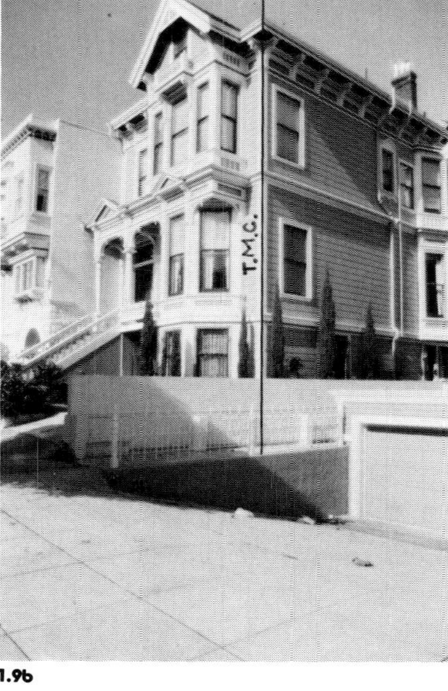

1.9b

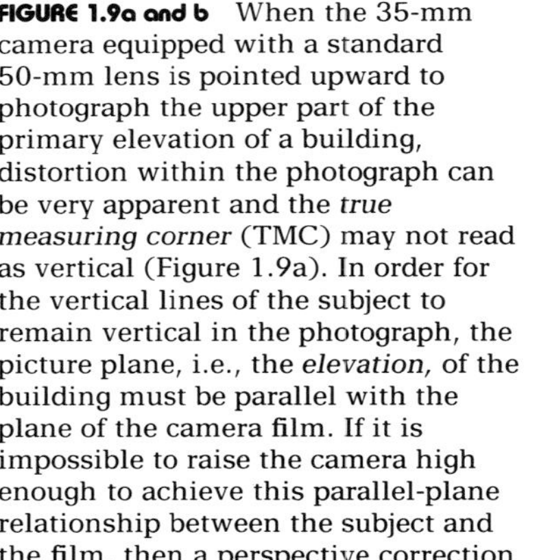
FIGURE 1.9a and b When the 35-mm camera equipped with a standard 50-mm lens is pointed upward to photograph the upper part of the primary elevation of a building, distortion within the photograph can be very apparent and the *true measuring corner* (TMC) may not read as vertical (Figure 1.9a). In order for the vertical lines of the subject to remain vertical in the photograph, the picture plane, i.e., the *elevation*, of the building must be parallel with the plane of the camera film. If it is impossible to raise the camera high enough to achieve this parallel-plane relationship between the subject and the film, then a perspective correction lens must be used to bring the two planes into parallel and to ensure vertical lines in the final photograph.

A 24- to 28-mm wide-angle lens will allow you to be closer to the subject while photographing for verticality, but even then it is difficult to include a building of three to four stories completely within the picture without incurring some vertical distortion.

If you cannot get vertical extremities into the picture without distortion, try to keep the chosen TMC vertical (Figure 1.9b) and adjust the other corners of the building to vertical during the tracing process. See also Figure 1.9f.

The Importance of the TMC in Photographs

It is important for later reference to photograph the chosen primary building corner so that it will be seen in both front and side views. The TMC in most cases is the corner nearest the viewer. In a one-point

FIGURE 1.9c, d, e, and f The Victorian shown in these images has been photographed with a 35-mm camera fitted with a 24-mm wide-angle lens. In this instance because of the width of the street in front of the house, it was not possible to position the camera far enough from the base of the building to allow complete verticality in the photograph without distortion to at least one corner of the structure.

The photograph in (e) was chosen from the three shown of this subject to be used to create the tracing in (f). The traced overlay shows both primary and secondary planes and how the vertical distortion was corrected to create a satisfactory tracing. By using a T square and triangle during tracing, all "vertical" lines were brought to a true vertical, in order to create a satisfactory underdrawing.

The TMC in this photograph was chosen as the major building corner nearest the photographer. All other vertical lines were drawn as vertical on the tracing paper, even though they slope inward on the upper part of the photograph. It is best to choose a starting point at the uppermost corners of intersecting planes when you are drawing the vertical lines. As these lines are brought down toward the ground in the tracing process, an adjustment must be made so that the main definitive lines of the structure "read" in the final tracing and underdrawing.

perspective where the primary plane approaches a true elevation, the TMC is a strong vertical axis on either the right or the left side of this plane.

The TMC will aid in establishing verticality and scale in the photograph. As we will see when we discuss photographic techniques further, all vertical elements in the photograph must be approaching absolute vertical in order to later create an accurate perspective drawing. As long as one corner of the building reads as absolute vertical, corrections can be made during tracing. See Figures 1.16 and 1.17.

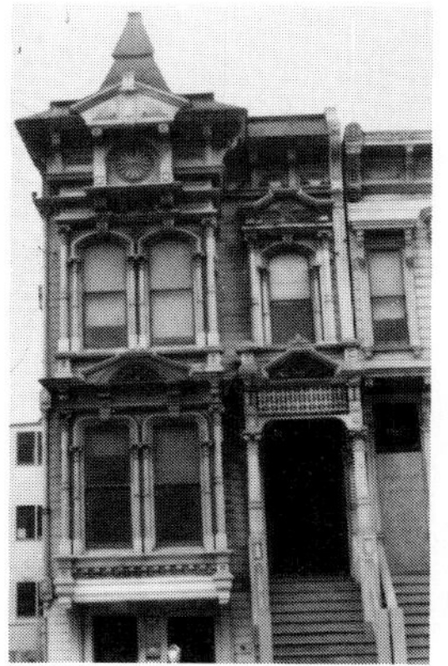

1.9c

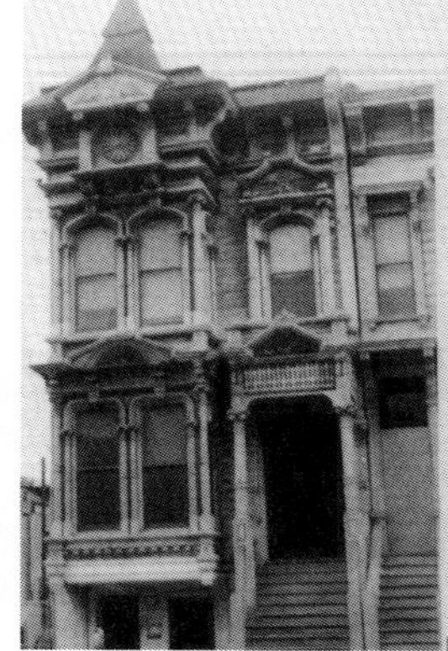

1.9d

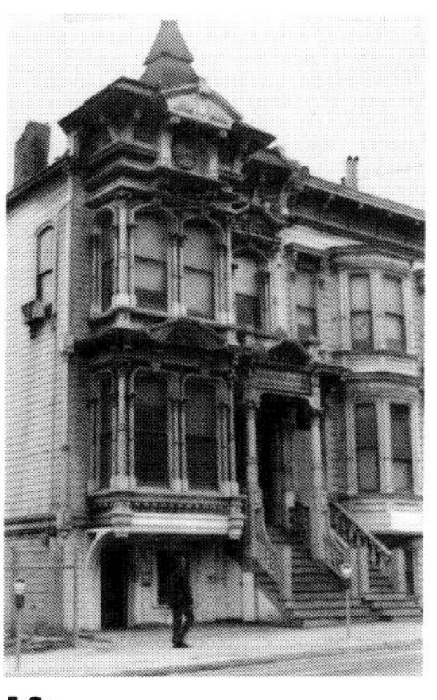

1.9e

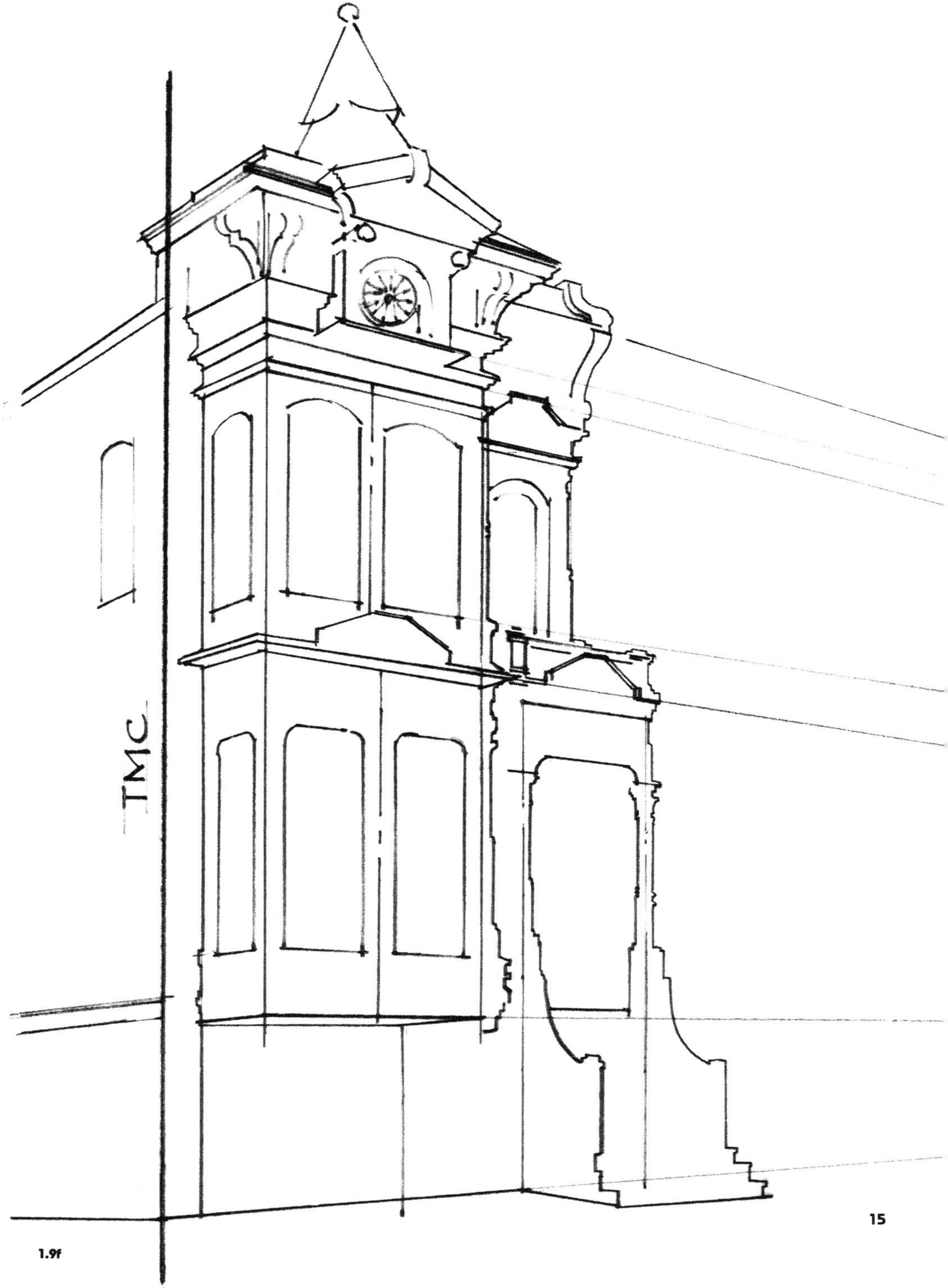

TMC

1.9f

Proper Preplanning Prevents Poor Performance: Build Dimensions into Your Photography

When you are preparing the subject to be photographed, whether it is a house elevation or a one- or two-story structure, a four-story Victorian house, or any interior view, some secondary measurements other than the total roof-to-ground or floor-to-ceiling dimension should be noted which can later be "read" in the photograph. This will enable you to calculate certain dimensions on the final drawing. Include items of known dimension that have a strong horizontal quality. See Figure 1.10.

When photographing a subject for the creation of a two-point perspective drawing, you must remember that the vertical TMC will divide the structure or portions of the structure into *A* and *B* planes, some having secondary planes such as A^1 and A^2 or B^1 and B^2. All "horizontal" lines extending along both primary and secondary planes *A* will recede to the right; similarly, lines along *B* planes will recede to the left.

That point where the extensions of major *horizontal* traced building lines intersect to the left is the VPL (see Figure 1.10a and b); the point where they intersect to the right is the VPR.

By joining the two "found" vanishing points, you create the horizon line. This should read as a horizontal line from which all vertical lines will be perpendicular in both the photograph and the resulting sketch.

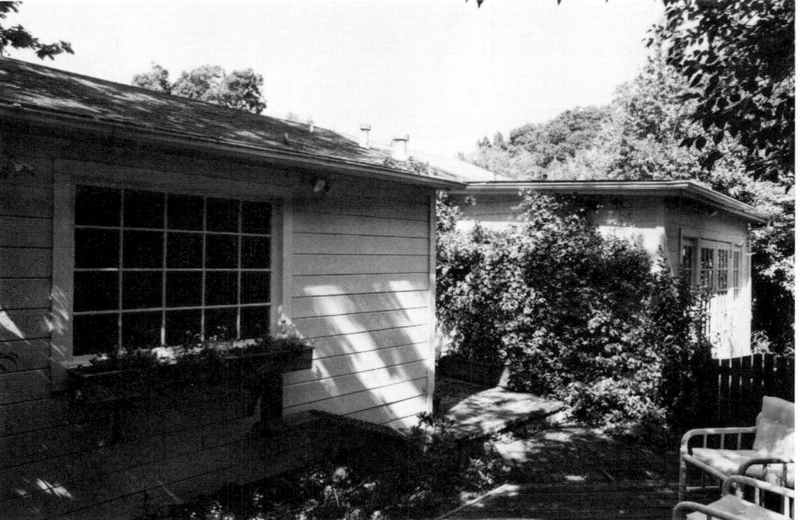

1.10a

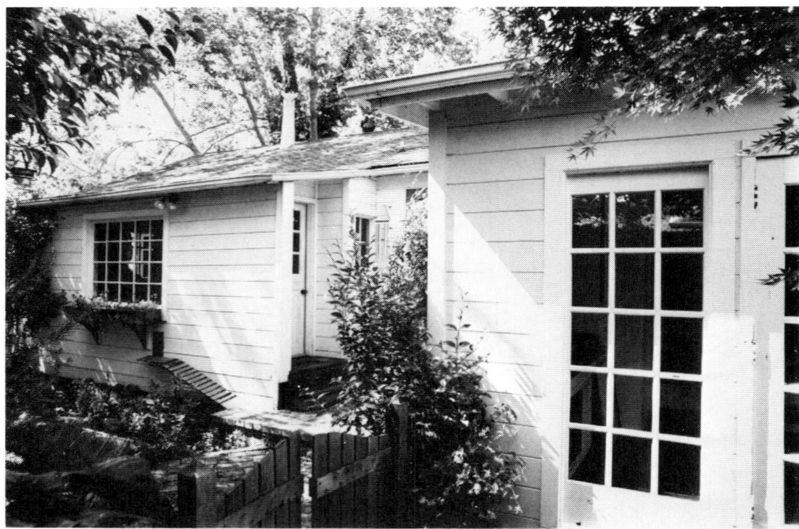

1.10c

FIGURE 1.10a through d The two photographs in (a) and (c) of the same subject, taken from different locations, and their respective overlay tracings in (b) and (d) clearly illustrate the photolinear perspective theory.

The corner chosen on this cottage as the TMC shows clearly in each photograph, and the siding forms visual, evenly spaced, 7″-high vertical divisions.

Linear representations of all parallel horizontal lines (i.e., roof ridge, eaves, window head, windowsill, and all siding), when extended, cross at either the VPL or the VPR. *Note:* The sloping edge of the shed roof does not conform because it is not parallel to all other horizontal lines.

The TMC in these photographs was chosen as the corner that represents the leading vertical corner dividing planes *A* and *B* of the building, and the siding acts as a vertical tape measure to verify the height on the photographs.

The photographs have been covered with tracing-paper overlays onto which all major horizontal lines of the cottage have been traced. Note the TMC, *BC*, where vertical reference has been established by using the 7″ measure of the siding dimensions as a scale of reference at the TMC. The VPR and VPL have been plotted, and their horizontal connection (the horizon) has been shown in each case. All major vertical edges of windows and doors along with primary building corners read as vertical.

The 7″ spacing of horizontal siding multiplied by the number of siding planks on the walls denotes a vertical height of 8′2″ plus approximately 2″ of trim exposed at the uppermost point.

Door, window head, and windowsill heights can be accurately measured on the photograph by using the siding as a guide. Note also that the TMC separates primary planes *A* and *B*.

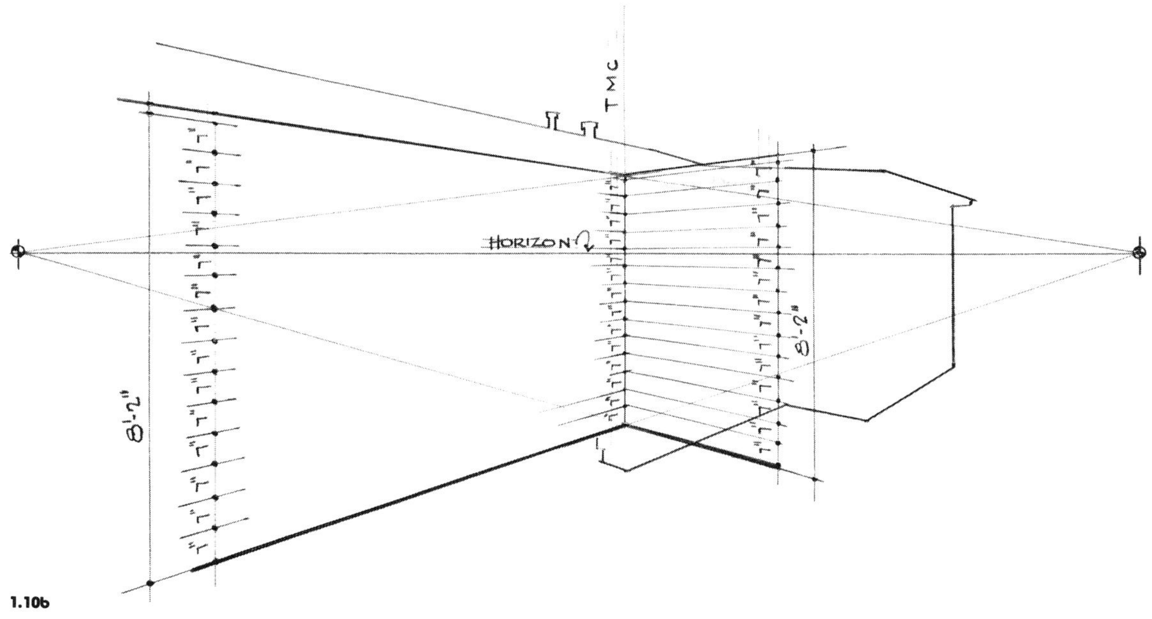

1.10b

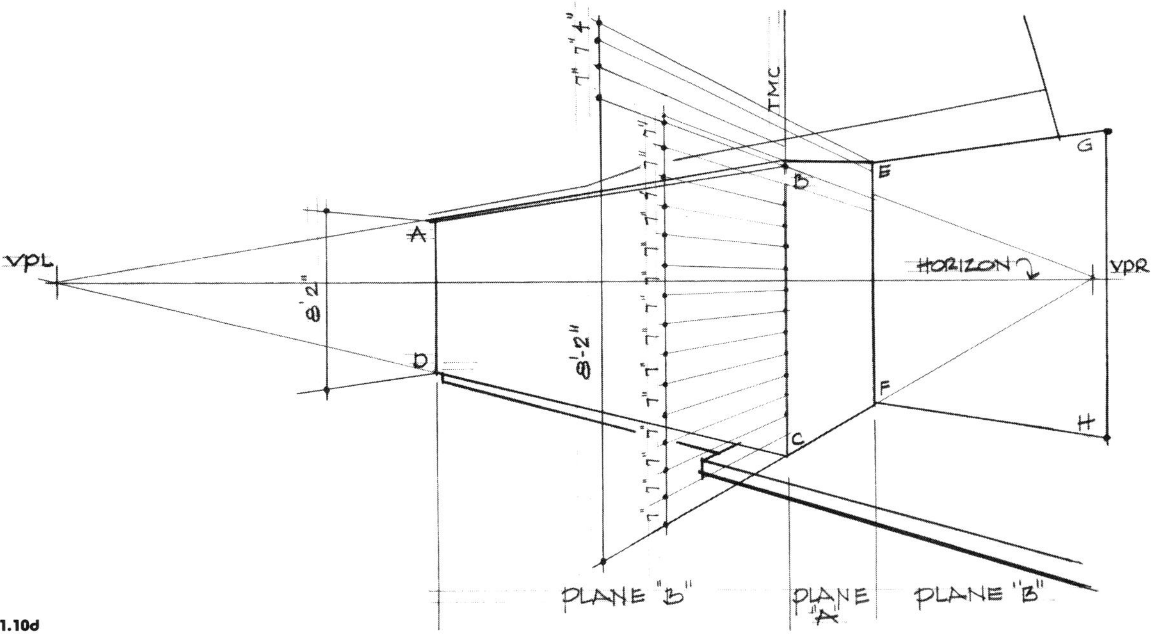

1.10d

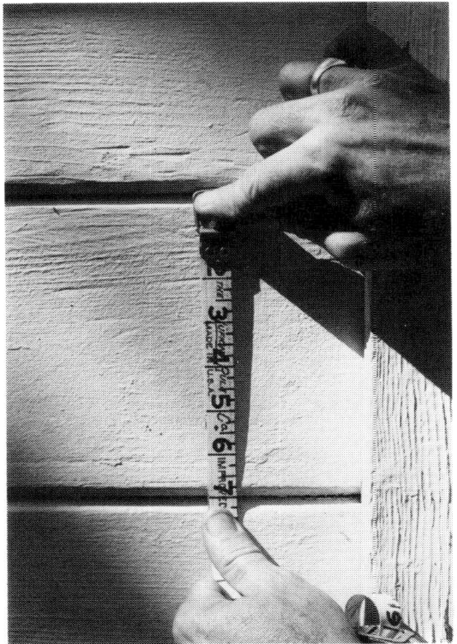

FIGURE 1.10c Easily read photographic notations such as this siding dimension are valuable in later calculations you may make away from the job site.

The Story Pole: Another Way to Include Dimensions in Photographs

The photograph that includes a ''story pole'' or other visual vertical-division indicator can later be traced over, and the vertical divisions of this axis noted on the drawing. From this, other measurements can be calculated visually.

The ''pole,'' made of *polyvinyl chloride* (PVC) pipe and sold at most do-it-yourself stores, is marked as a tape measure with black at 1′0″ intervals.

Propped up against the structure, this pole will allow you to roughly figure vertical dimensions on the photograph. Laid horizontally, this visual measuring device can aid in the calculation of horizontal dimensions. If you photograph a person holding this story pole, you can also establish the human scale, thus giving a realistic sense of proportion when drawing the three-dimensional remodeling sketches.

Example Figure 1.11 shows a ¾″-diameter pole positioned vertically on the front of a hotel and leaned against the building at the upper windowsill. With the pole accurately marked so that each division can be seen in the photograph, you can transfer the dimensions onto your drawing directly from the photograph.

Figure 1.12a shows a different kind of story pole being held horizontally. The horizontal reference line is shown to create a measured height line. Unlike in the previous example, the scale in this photograph is established by both the 2″ × 4″ × 6′ board and the human element. Later while the drawing of the iron railing and gate in Figure 1.12c is created, proportional dimensions can be geometrically calculated and used to complete the sketch.

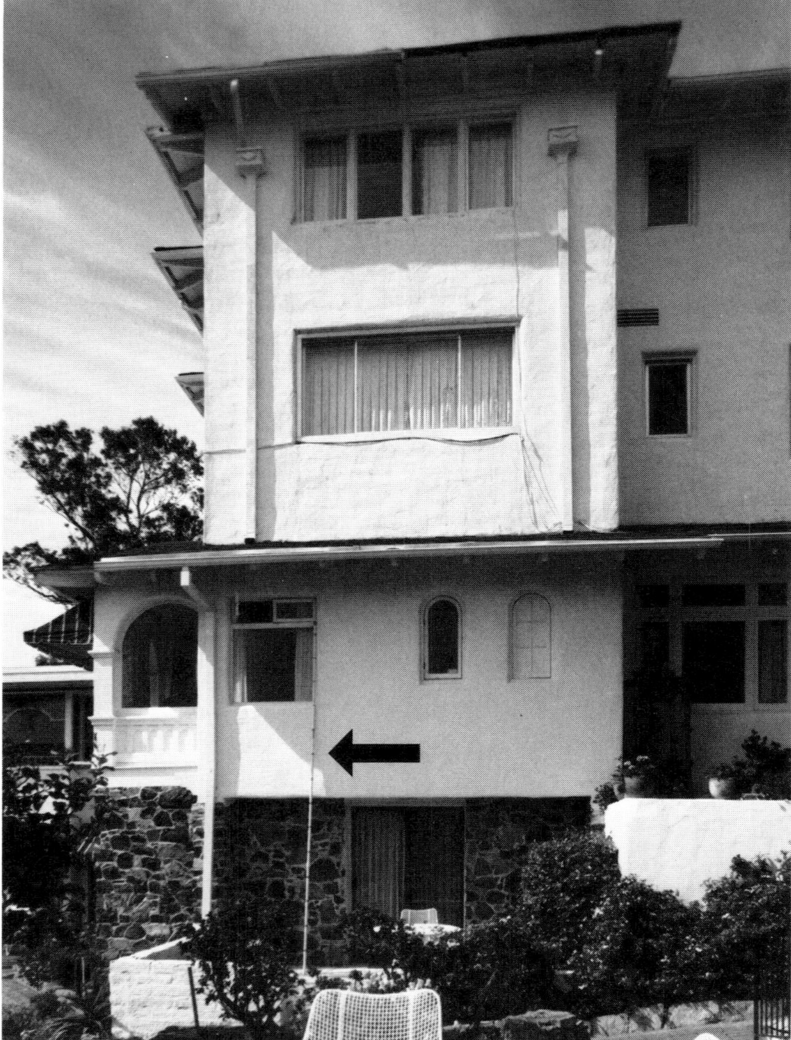

FIGURE 1.11 The story pole shown here is a ¾″ white PVC pipe wrapped at 12″ intervals with black electrical tape in order to provide a photographic height notation of a portion of this hotel (seen again in Chapter 8). Note that some portions of the pole are obscured by the planting and the low-slump stone wall in the photograph.

If certain elements of the building or the story pole measuring aid is hidden by shrubbery, these can be reestablished visually on an overlay sheet of tracing paper or Mylar by tracing visible building lines and approximating those lines hidden behind shrubbery and trees.

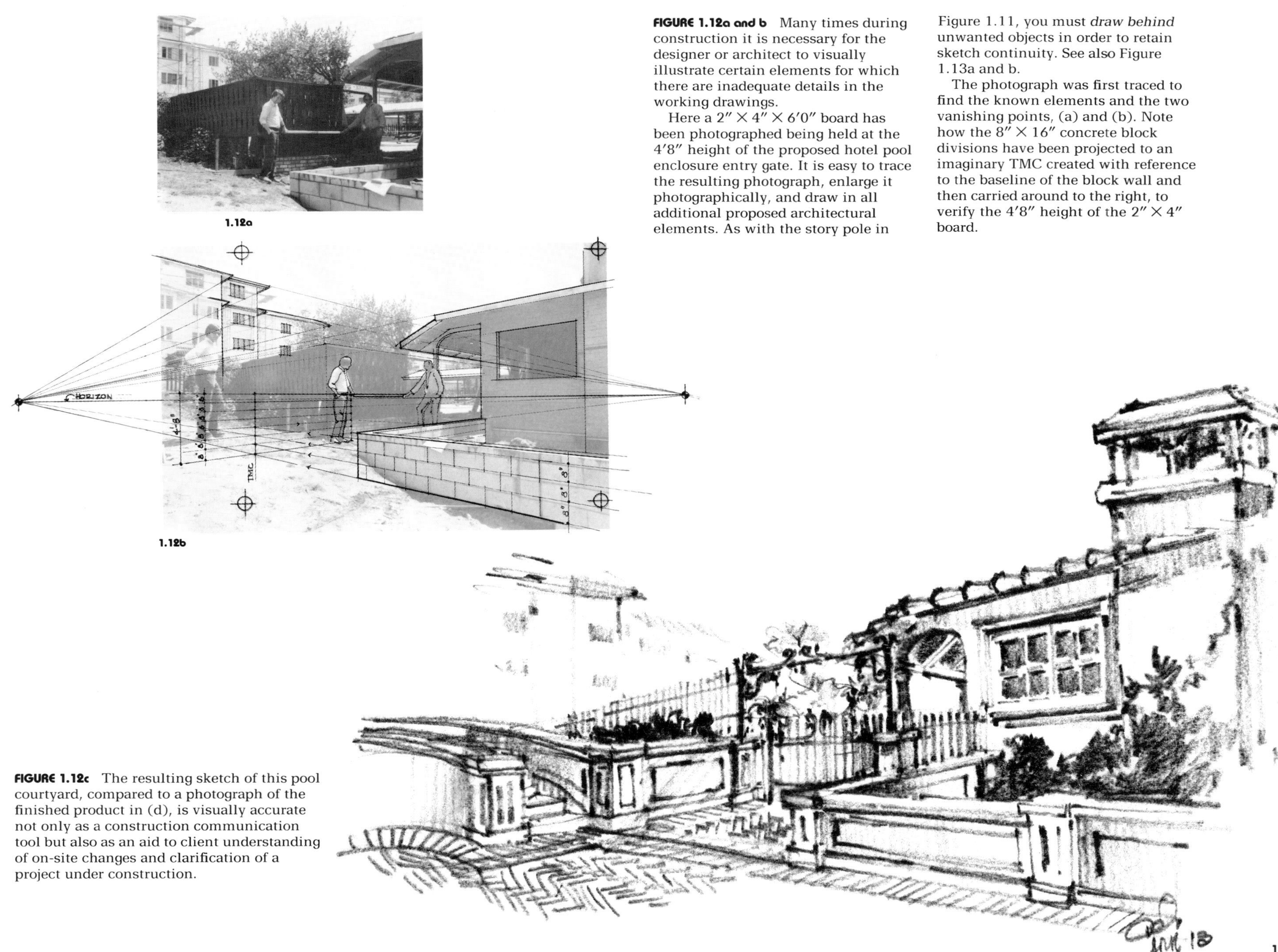

1.12a

1.12b

FIGURE 1.12a and b Many times during construction it is necessary for the designer or architect to visually illustrate certain elements for which there are inadequate details in the working drawings.

Here a 2″ × 4″ × 6′0″ board has been photographed being held at the 4′8″ height of the proposed hotel pool enclosure entry gate. It is easy to trace the resulting photograph, enlarge it photographically, and draw in all additional proposed architectural elements. As with the story pole in Figure 1.11, you must *draw behind* unwanted objects in order to retain sketch continuity. See also Figure 1.13a and b.

The photograph was first traced to find the known elements and the two vanishing points, (a) and (b). Note how the 8″ × 16″ concrete block divisions have been projected to an imaginary TMC created with reference to the baseline of the block wall and then carried around to the right, to verify the 4′8″ height of the 2″ × 4″ board.

FIGURE 1.12c The resulting sketch of this pool courtyard, compared to a photograph of the finished product in (d), is visually accurate not only as a construction communication tool but also as an aid to client understanding of on-site changes and clarification of a project under construction.

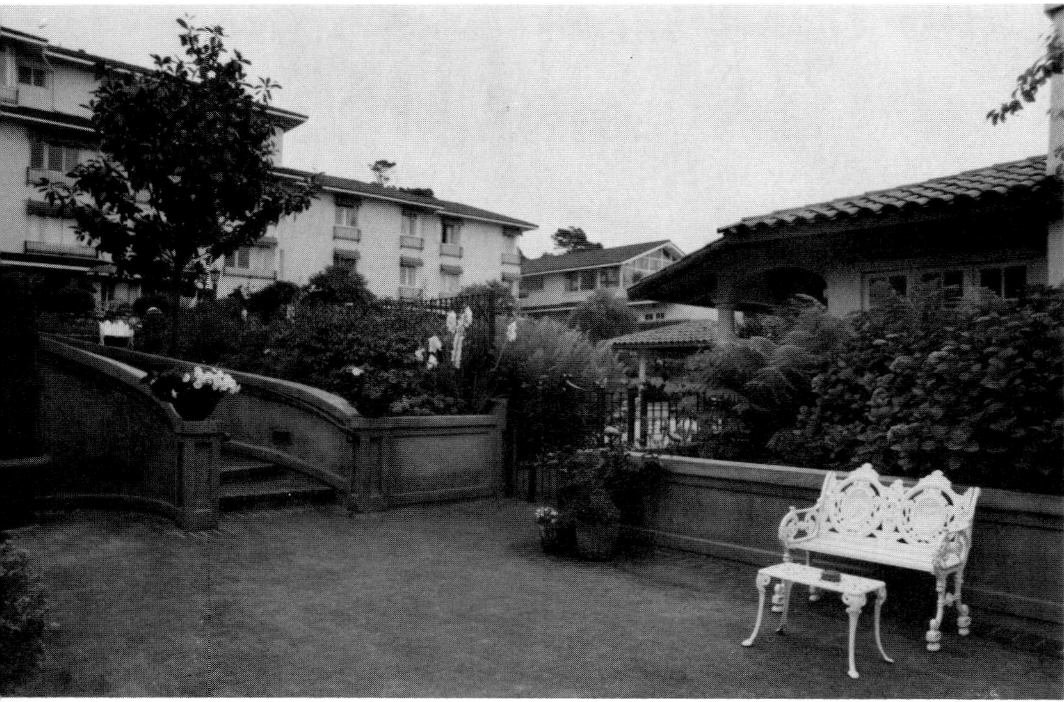

FIGURE 1.12d
SUBJECT: The lower pool courtyard of the LaPlaya Hotel in Carmel by the Sea, California
PROJECT DESIGNER: The author
PRODUCTION ARCHITECTS: Keeble and Rhoda.
INTERIOR CONSULTANT: Elizabeth Burnstein

Trees and things in the way If you know that you are going to have to work around existing natural elements on a particular job, remember to include these in your photographs. Shoot these from several angles so that you can draw around these elements when doing the sketch. See Figure 1.13.

FIGURE 1.13a, b, and c The author's studio shown in the photograph in (a) and the line tracing in (b) was photographed from a very low angle, and it is partially obscured with foliage. In the photograph note that the upper width of the structure (below the projected overhang) appears to be less than that at the base of the building. This is because the camera was pointing up, causing the picture plane to be out of parallel with the plane of the subject. See also Figure 1.9a through f. The subject was traced so that all "vertical" elements would read as vertical (as seen in the adjusted line tracing). The procedure for this is as follows:

1. Cover the photograph with tracing paper.

2. Find the vanishing points to the left and right by tracing the major building lines to the point of convergence. These lines should intersect at or very near one point for each plane *A* and *B*. (The VPR will terminate all *A* planes, and the VPL will terminate all *B* planes.)

3. Continue the upper wall line from the VPL through point *A* to the right, to approach point *B* behind the foliage.

4. Approximate the positions of points *B, C,* and *D* by comparing them visually with the left side of the building.

5. Drop vertical lines from points *A* and *B* to points *D* and *C* below.

The siding lines, windowsills, and window heads will be traced in their shown positions, except this time the jambs will be traced as vertical for the sketch (instead of following their obvious out-of-vertical character in the original photograph).

Once the primary plane of the building has been traced, the overlay at the upper building line can be brought to the same perpendicular position atop perpendicular walls.

If the tracing is done carefully, as if the foliage did not exist, the viewer will not be aware that the photographic perspective has been altered in the final sketch.

H, F, and 2B pencils were chosen as the drawing medium to be used on Clearprint 1000H tracing paper for the final drawing. The addition of decorative trim enhances the overall presentation of the subject (Figure 1.13c). Corner quoins, corbels, and a small railing are used to enhance the pediment-accentuated entry. Note also the absence of foliage in the final sketch. It was purposely left out to show more detail. The construction lines have been left in for clarity; however, these would not appear in a presentation drawing.

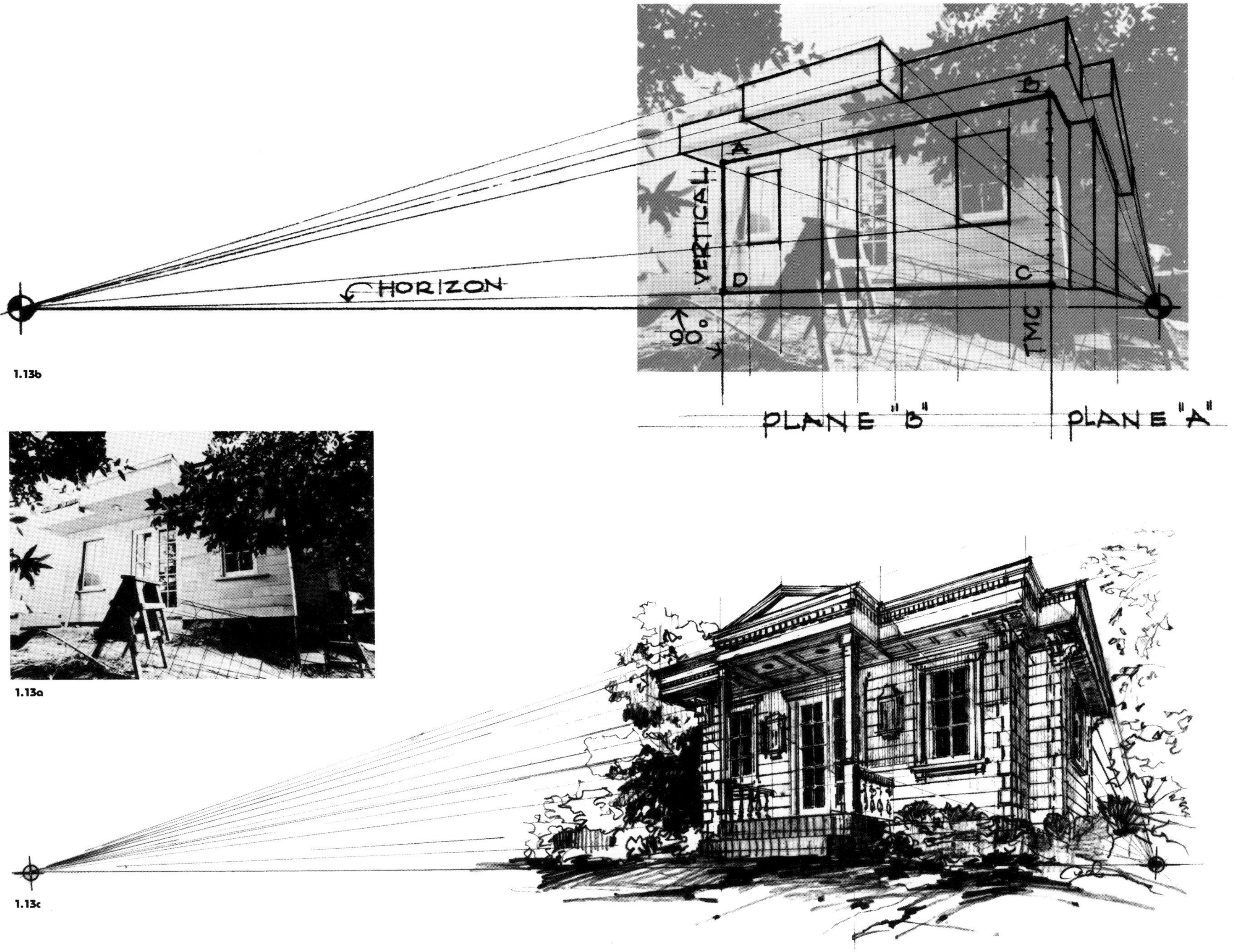

1.13b

1.13a

1.13c

Documenting and Photographing an Interior

Interiors, of course, are much easier to photograph and document than exteriors, but where ceilings are particularly high, a stepladder may be necessary.

Before you take any interior photographs, first you must do a scale plan drawing of the space from measurements taken at the site. The usual scale of ¼″ = 1′0″ will give a satisfactory scale drawing that represents all the room's dimensions. Graph paper divided into increments of ¼″ can aid in this on-site process where you must depend on freehand drawing methods.

The On-Site Rough Floor Plan and Elevations

When measuring an interior, you begin by drawing a floor plan of each room, one room per sheet. Be sure to extend your measurements to door and window openings, and indicate the adjacent room by name, using a common doorway as a reference. Either you can draw the plans freehand and work out the dimensions later, or you can do it on site, using ¼″-scale graph paper, which takes more time initially but saves work later. When measuring, you should note the overall ceiling height, door heights, windowsill and window head heights, fireplace opening height and width, mantel height and width, crown mold and base dimensions, wainscot height, stairs (number of treads, rise, and total run), countertops, plumbing fixtures, and anything else pertinent to the space. The same principles discussed earlier for exteriors apply to interiors.

Take the dimensions of the room, and draw up a floor plan to scale, using a sheet of tracing paper or graph paper. See Figure 1.14a through c.

Don't be afraid to take lots of photographs to show the interior from the different vantage points. You should take corner shots, showing ceiling and floor lines, as well as shots showing the vertical and horizontal wall lines. The aim is to have enough shots to form a collection of photographs that project the overall "feeling" of the room's space. A good way to do this is to stand in the center of a room and turn in a circle to photograph the room in its entirety.

In measuring an interior space, it is important to draw each wall in elevation, showing windows, doors, and cabinets with their approximate sections. Sections allow you to show in close-up detail how each room relates to the next vis-à-vis door-head heights, ceiling height, floor height, stairs, and so on. From the rough plan and elevations, it is a simple matter to create a final ¼″ = 1′0″ floor plan.

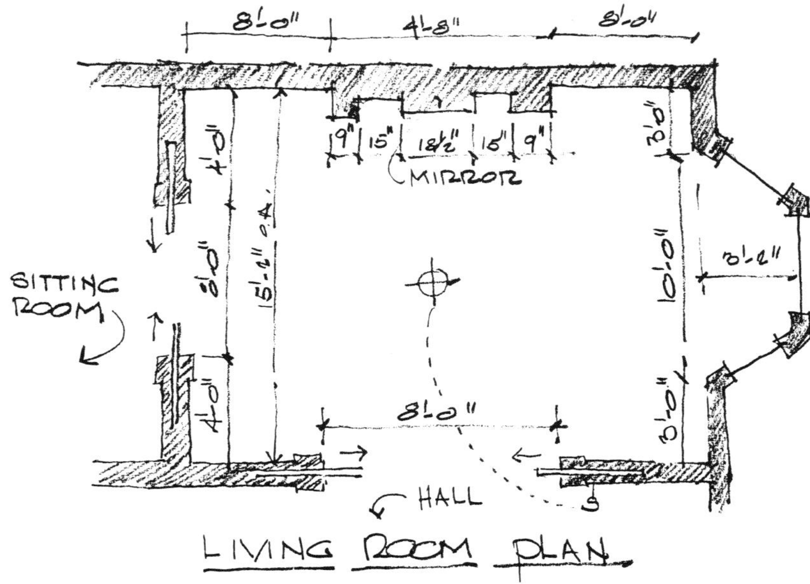

FIGURE 1.14a This roughly sketched plan of a living room shows wall elements as though a knife were used to cut through walls above the windowsill height. Note the dimensions on the sketched plan as you measure around the room, starting in any corner and systematically recording all necessary figures and notations. Be certain to note adjacent rooms by name at all common-door openings.

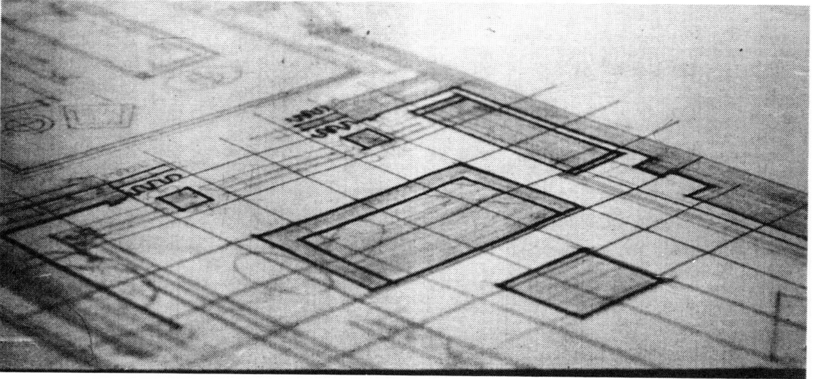

FIGURE 1.14c This completed ¼″ = 1′0″ plan incorporates all measures taken and noted on the freehand drawing of the primary features of the room (Figure 1.14a).

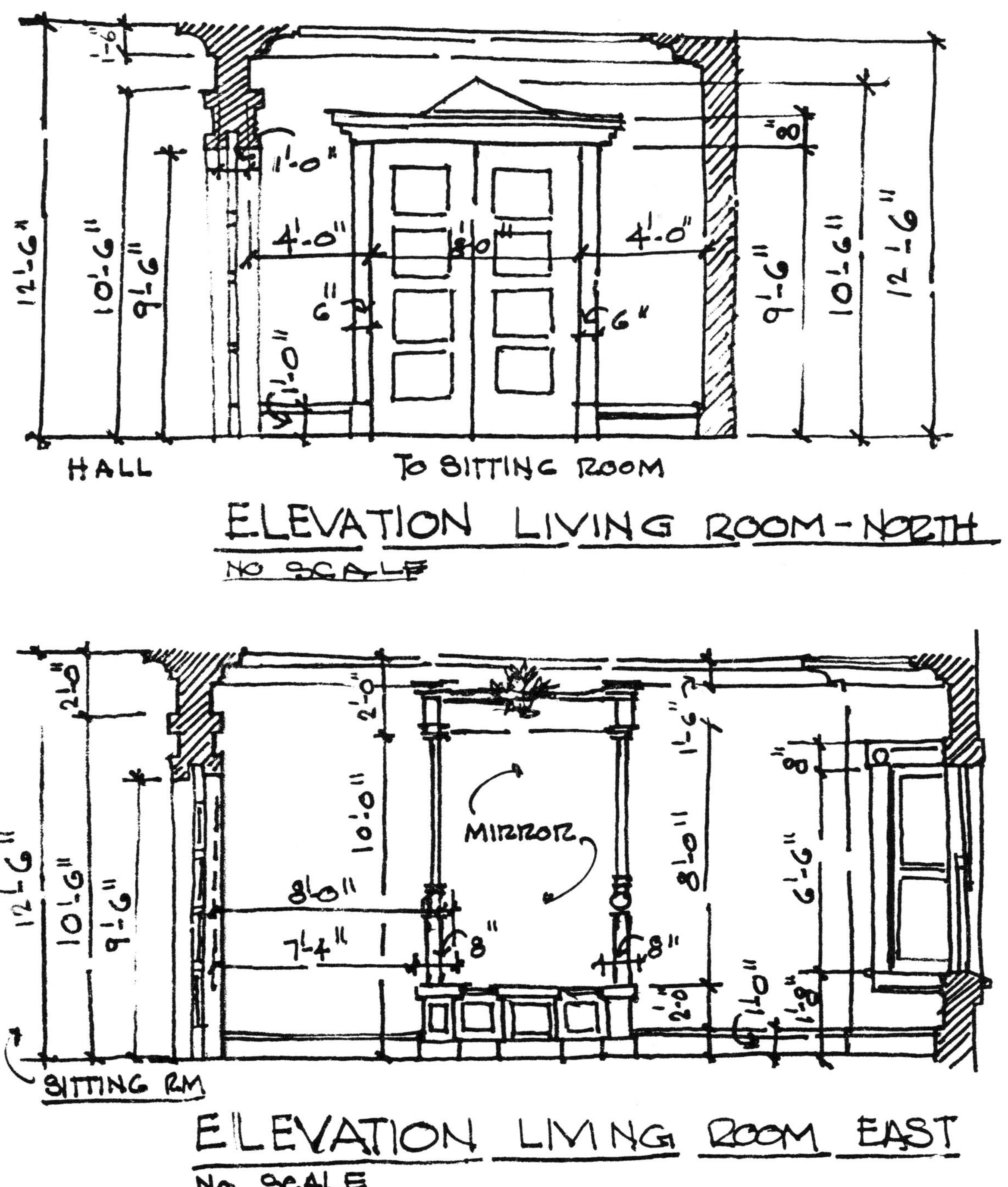

FIGURE 1.14b Elevations of complicated walls should be drawn at the same time as the floor plan and should be keyed to it. Sections should be included to show wall thickness, ceiling heights, cornice sections, cabinet sections, and other important associated dimensions.

Each elevation of a complex space should be roughly drawn, noting all vertical dimensions as well as any horizontal measures and notations that cannot be shown on the floor plan. Each elevation or section should show related architectural features found on walls that intersect the elevated wall to the right and left. It is on these sections that door and window opening heights, ceiling heights, cabinets, and cornice sections can be graphically shown and their dimensions noted.

Picking the TMC for the Photograph

Two-point perspective: Interior In this progressive illustration (Figure 1.15) the near wall has been chosen as the TMC. The position from which the photograph is taken must therefore permit inclusion of this vertical line, as the photographer has done here.

Then, in tracing over the chosen corner within the photograph, the line drawn over the TMC can later be marked off into even vertical divisions, by using the slanted-scale method in Chapter 2 and block divisions drawn on the wall, pilasters, and columns. In Figure 1.15a through e, the TMC is created by the edge of the wall to the right of the right-hand column. To begin, a shot of the area to be remodeled is taken, showing the rough staircase, wall, opening, and bare column. By using the corner of the opening closest to the bare cast-concrete column as the TMC, a height measurement is established. This value can be marked off in equal measurements, in this case to create the height of the "stone building blocks," and can be located by projection from the elevation, a process described in Chapter 4. By tracing over the base and ceiling lines in the photograph, the VPR and VPL are established. Connections can then be drawn from these two points, marking each increment on the TMC, to the vanishing points, so that the block work, cornice, and base may all be drawn to scale and rendered visually accurate.

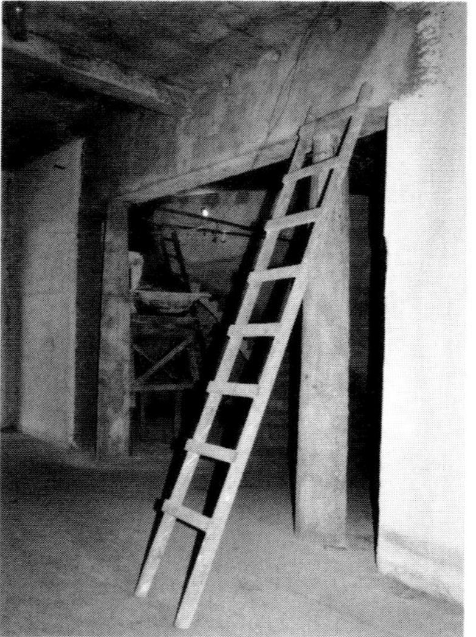

1.15a

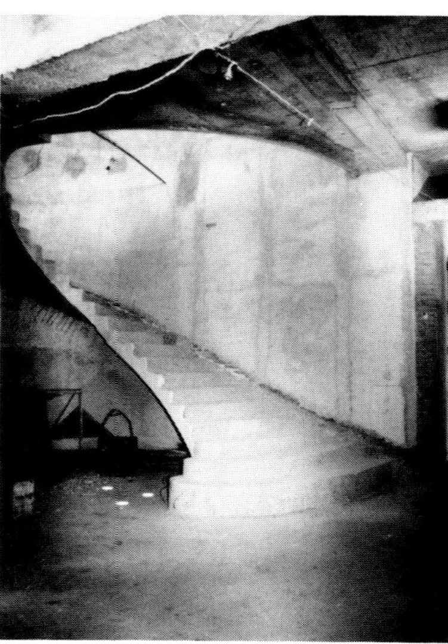

1.15b

FIGURE 1.15a and b The photograph in (a) of two structural columns at the entry to a grand staircase has been taken to aid in the creation of a final drawing, to show plaster block indications, new pilasters, a grand curving staircase, and an elaborate cornice. The ladder shown in the photograph will be left out of the tracing, of course, and the staircase seen beyond in (b) will be accentuated in the final sketch. A measured plan and elevation (Figure 1.15c) will be used to establish architectural elements in the space.

FIGURE 1.15d The round columns to be constructed of cylindrical stone blocks were first drawn as vertical stacked cubic solids around a centerline; each has a top and a bottom plane whose outlines project to the vanishing points of the perspective drawing. Note that the top and bottom of each cylinder look like an ellipse and that the ellipse becomes less round as it gets closer to the horizon. One looks down on each ellipse below the horizon line and up at the ellipse above the horizon line. The ellipse becomes a line *only* at the horizon.

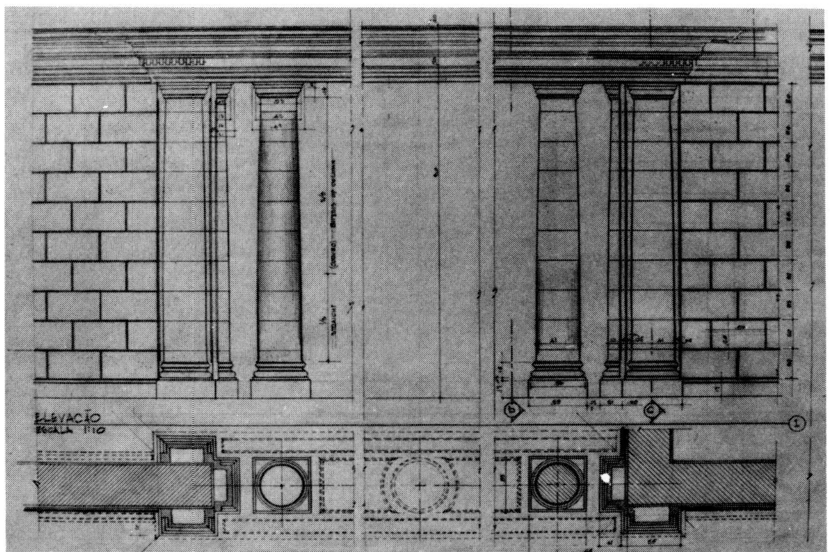

FIGURE 1.15c The elevation was drawn using the metric system at 1 : 20 and includes the plan of the columns and pilasters. All block outlines and base and cornice details are shown in this dimensional elevation.

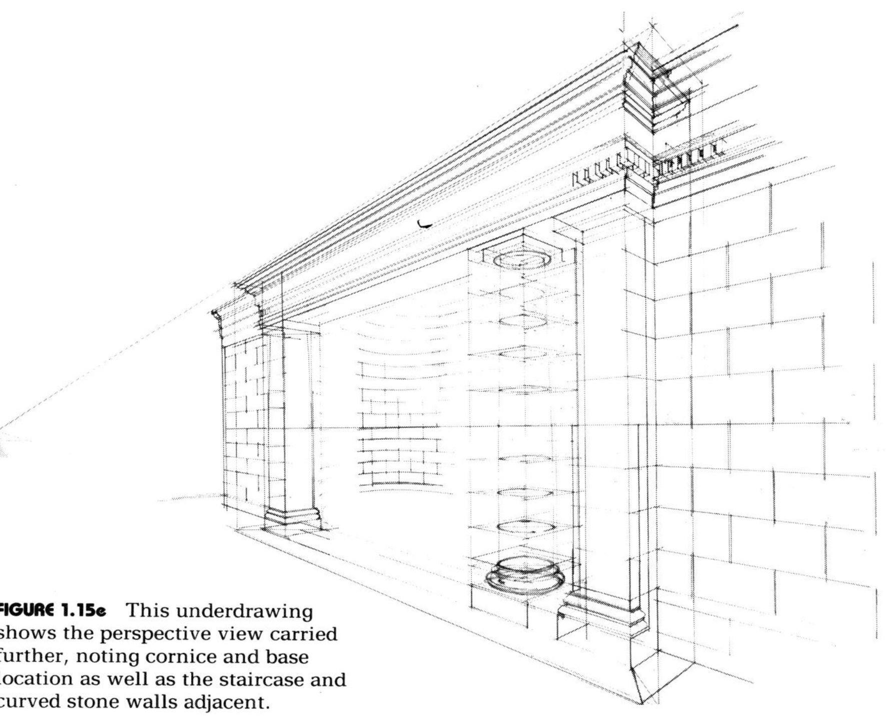

FIGURE 1.15e This underdrawing shows the perspective view carried further, noting cornice and base location as well as the staircase and curved stone walls adjacent.

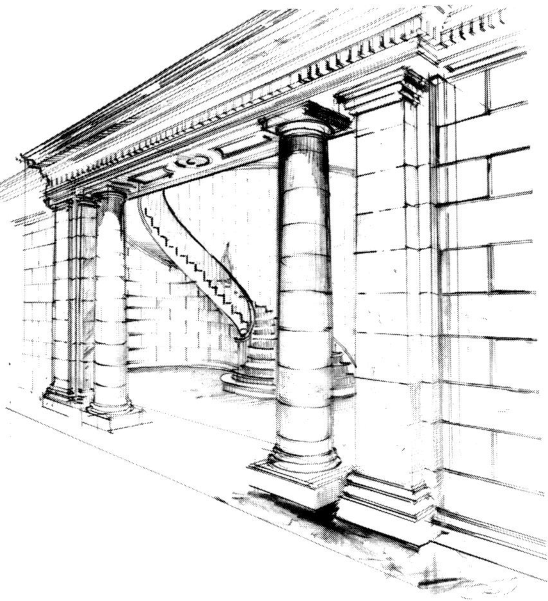

FIGURE 1.15f The finished drawing shows the area delineated in pencil. Note the roundness of each column as well as the implied *entasis*—a slight convexity beginning at the base one-third of the way up each column and continuing to the top—that is apparent on both the columns and pilasters.

One-point perspective: Interior When you are photographing a subject flat on to create a one-point perspective (see Figures 1.16 and 1.17), try to pick one strong element to establish the center of interest. In Figure 1.17, the columns provide a strong central vertical thrust to the photograph. All lines representing horizontal structural elements in this one-point perspective picture, when traced, converge to a *single* vanishing point to the right of these columns instead of the VPR and VPL shown in most of the two-point perspective illustrations so far.

Similarly, in any interior or exterior photograph, whether you are shooting from a central or a side position, you must be sure to establish verticality for the TMC. If, however, lines on the resulting photograph are not absolutely vertical, they can be corrected on the tracing overlay.

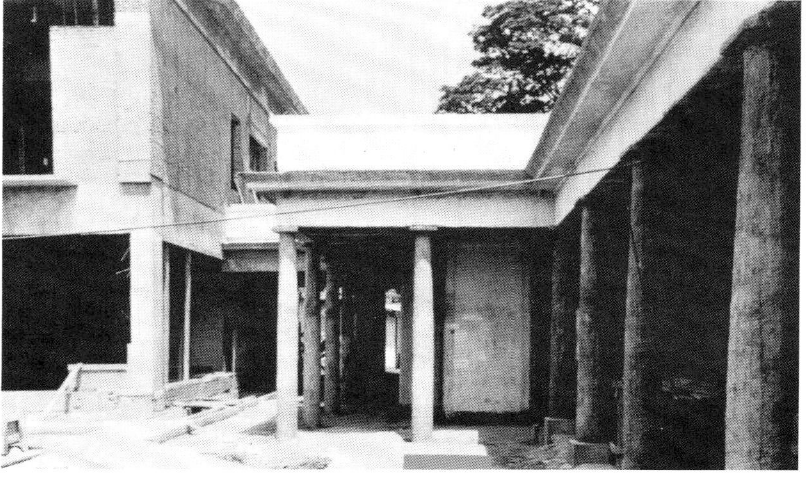

1.17a

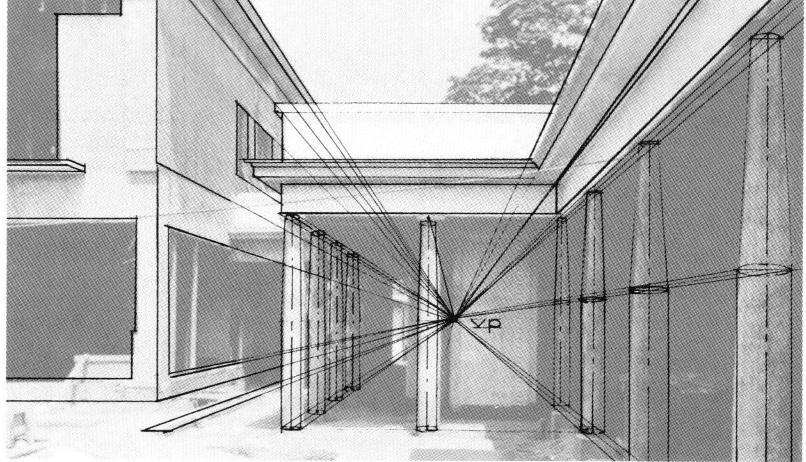

1.17b

FIGURE 1.17 This interior-exterior of a pool cabana (a) under construction has been photographed so as to create a one-point perspective with the rear plane created by the columns in elevation.

This overlay (b) was drawn over a screened 8½″ × 11″ photocopy enlarged from a 35-mm standard-size print.

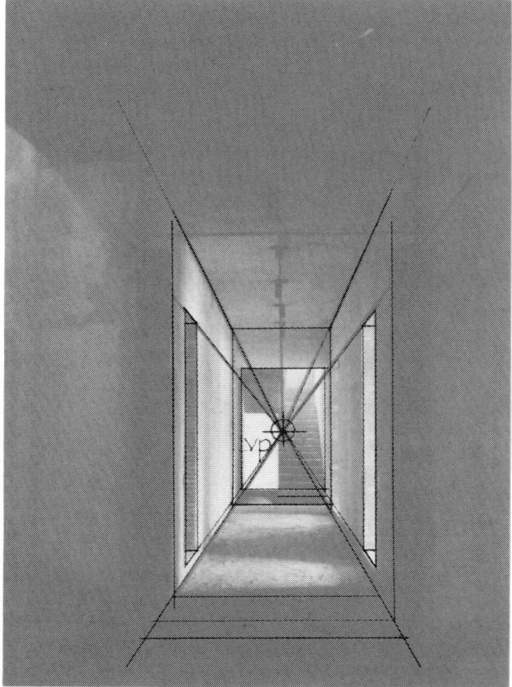

FIGURE 1.16 This photograph of an interior wall was taken as a one-point perspective. The rear wall is in elevation, and vertical lines are vertical. The TMC can be located on either the right or the left vertical foreground line of the overlay tracing.

Visual Aids

Another trick in photographing for remodeling purposes is to mark the site with colored or masking tape, or string, to show the floor plan elements or boundaries of the proposed work. In Figure 1.18a and b, the edge of the deck to be extended outward from the house is marked with white rope. The boundary line for the extension, in this case a semicircular deck, is established by photographing the rope that follows a 12′0″ radius line marked on the ground.

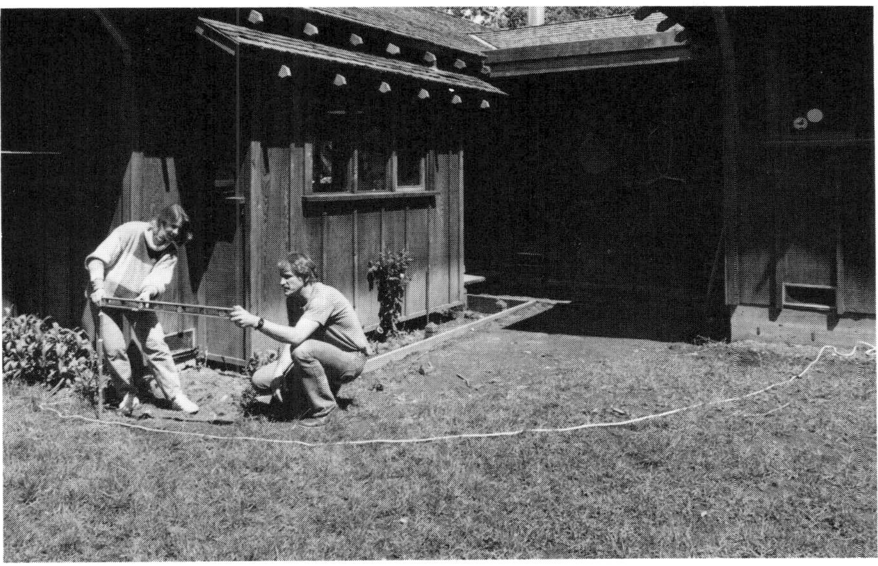

FIGURE 1.18 The deck perimeter line has been marked with a white rope. The semicircular shape marked on the ground and noted on the tracing overlay is, in reality, a one-quarter circle with its radius at the house wall at a point that lines up with the wall to the right rear. The radius point has been marked in the photograph with a pipe driven into the ground. The one-quarter circular shape on the grass was struck with a sharp stick attached to a 12′0″ length of rope with one end looped over the pipe at the radius point. Next the outline of the circular deck was marked with white rope that would be visible in the photograph. The carpenter's level is positioned relating to the vertical height divisions marked on the pipe driven into the ground at the left front of the deck, as shown. In this way an accurate height scale, as well as human scale, has been introduced. Note that the level is being held at the proposed height of the horizontal picket supports for the railing.

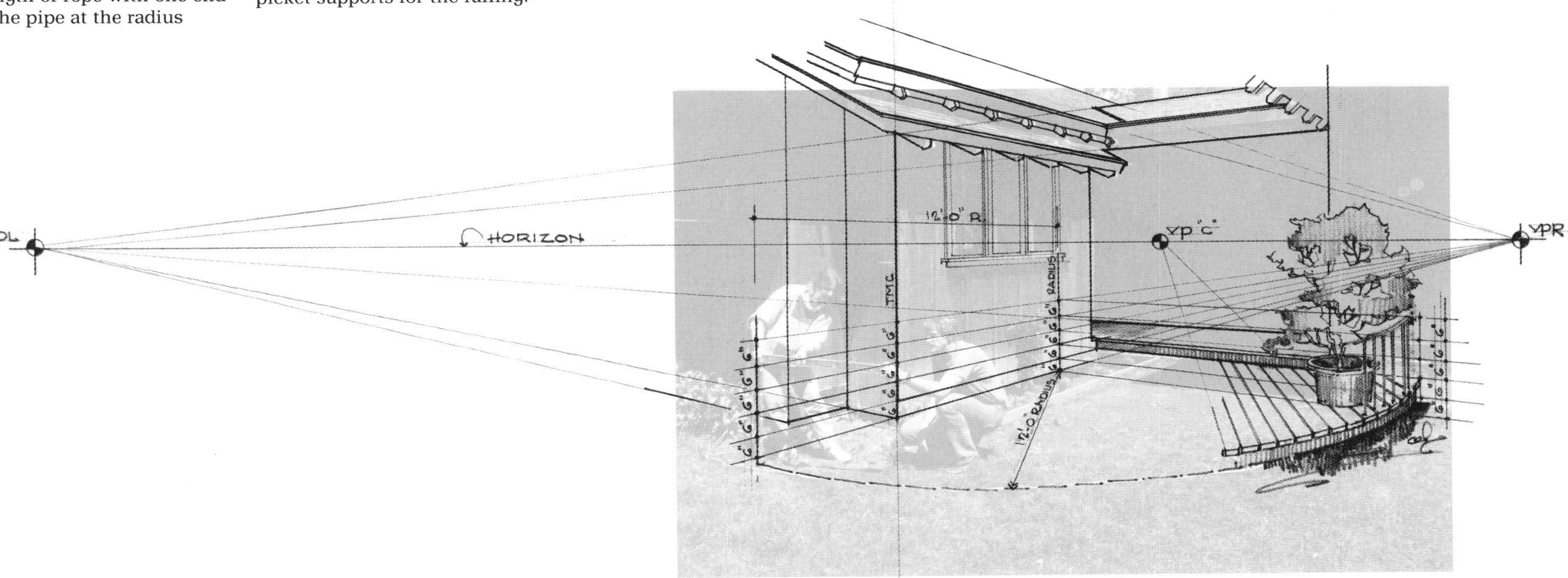

For an interior shot, the dimensions of proposed construction work, if known, can be marked with masking tape, both on the walls and on the floor. You can also lay tape on the floor to describe furniture position and size, if placement is known at the time. Once the photograph has been taken that shows the taped outline on the floor, it is a simple matter to draw onto a tracing of the photograph the projected furniture, by using the resulting floor plan in perspective as the basis for the placement of each piece. Vertical measures can, of course, be projected from the TMC to determine the height of each piece. See Figure 1.19a through d and Figure 3.3j as well.

FIGURE 1.19 Figure 1.19c shows in full size the layout of proposed furniture for this Victorian house, and the resulting sketch in (d) is taken from the photograph in (a). To make this marking approach and photographic expansion successful, consider the following:

1. A ¼″ floor plan of the existing walls and windows and a furniture layout must be made from which to work.

2. Furniture corners (as well as radius points in the case of curved furniture) should be located, first on the ¼″-scale plan, with dimensions from each wall shown. Then, it is a simple matter to recreate these *coordinates* full size and to mark them with tape on the floor.

3. There should be little or no furniture in place when the site is photographed.

4. Placement of furniture should be outlined on the floor, full size, and photographed (Figure 1.19c).

5. The masking tape should be lightly *tacked* in place by pressing it with the fingers every 8″ to 10″.

6. Of course, one must try to photograph the full-size plan from eye level and be careful to keep vertical lines vertical, including as much in the photograph as the camera lens will allow.

7. The tape must be removed as soon as photographs are taken and never left overnight — it can pull the finish from the floor if it is left in place too long, for heat and sunlight can make masking tape extremely difficult to remove.

8. The photograph should be traced to find the vanishing points.

9. The photograph tracing should be expanded (Figure 1.19b) by including the walls, floor, and door of the entry hall. One should use the same vanishing points as were found on the original photograph (Figure 1.19a) to accomplish this.

The drawing has thus been enhanced by increasing the viewing angle to include an entry hall as well as the living room. Although the 24-mm-wide lens was used for the original photograph, the viewing angle was limited by the width of the entry hall, which controlled the distance from which the photograph could be taken. Photographs of the entry hall were necessary to aid the author in the creation of this expanded line drawing. Rugs, paintings, drapery, and other decorative items that make the sketch look inviting have been added in the final pencil sketch (Figure 1.19d). Note again the visible limits of the original photograph and how photographic expansion was used to create a more desirable ambiance for the final drawing.

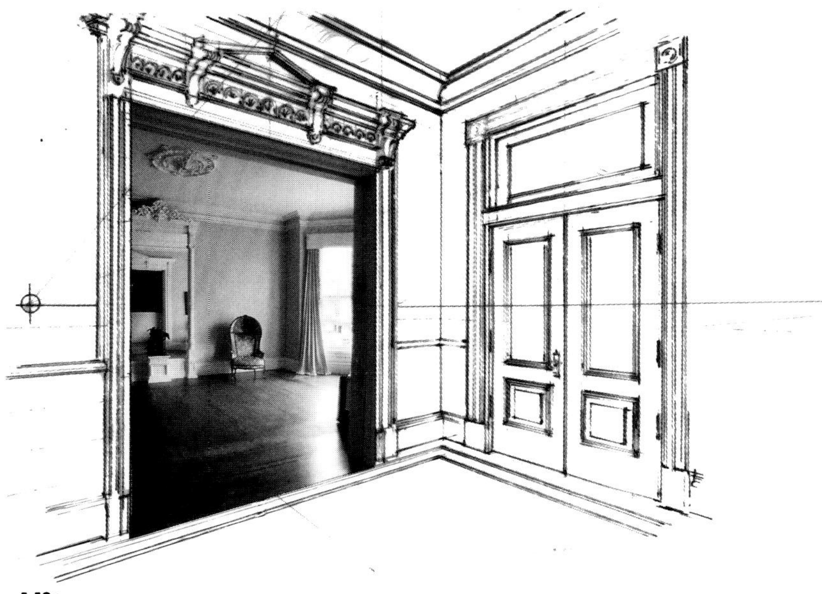

1.19a

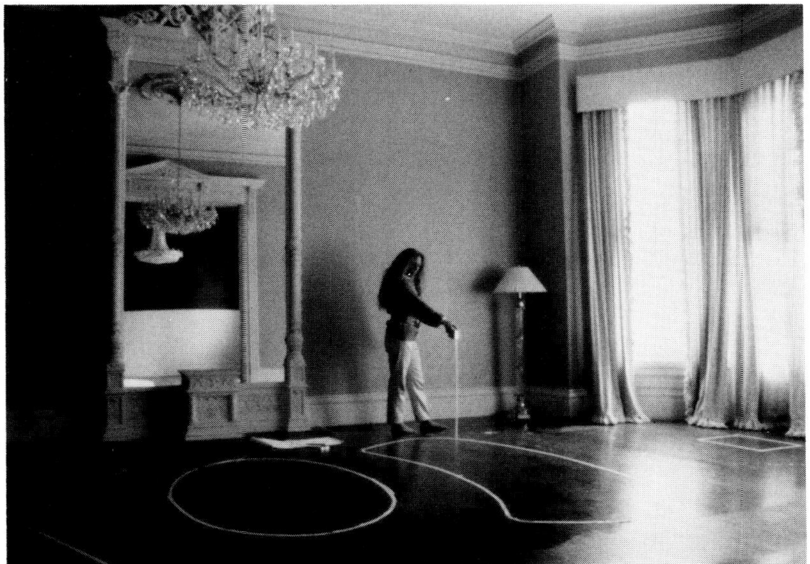

1.19c

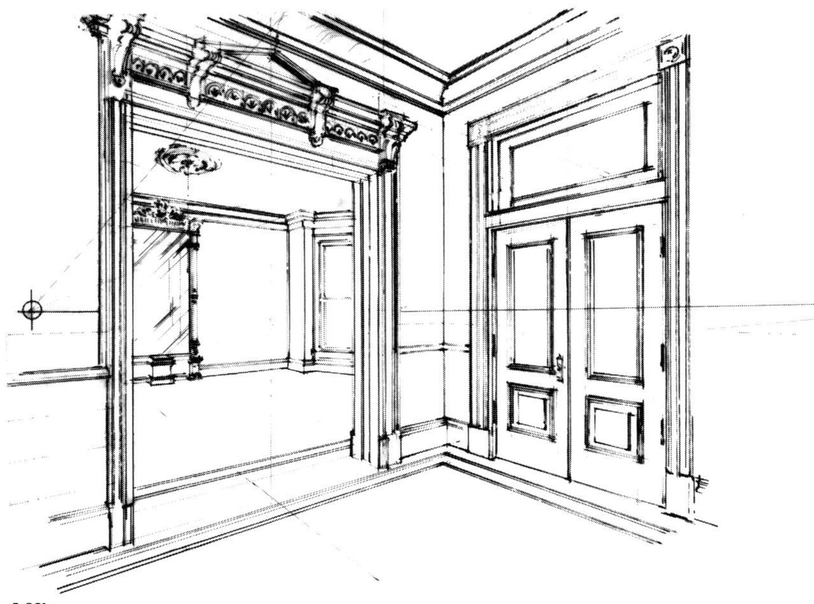

1.19b

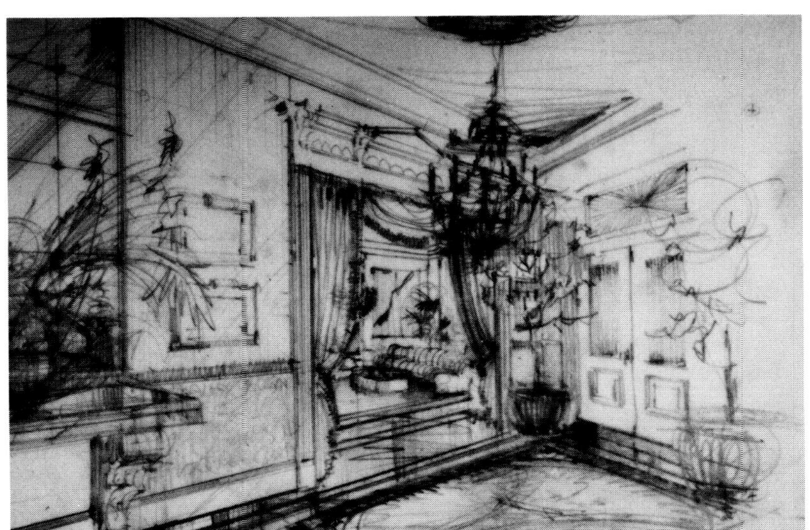

1.19d

CHAPTER 2

DIVIDING SPACE WITHOUT MEASURING

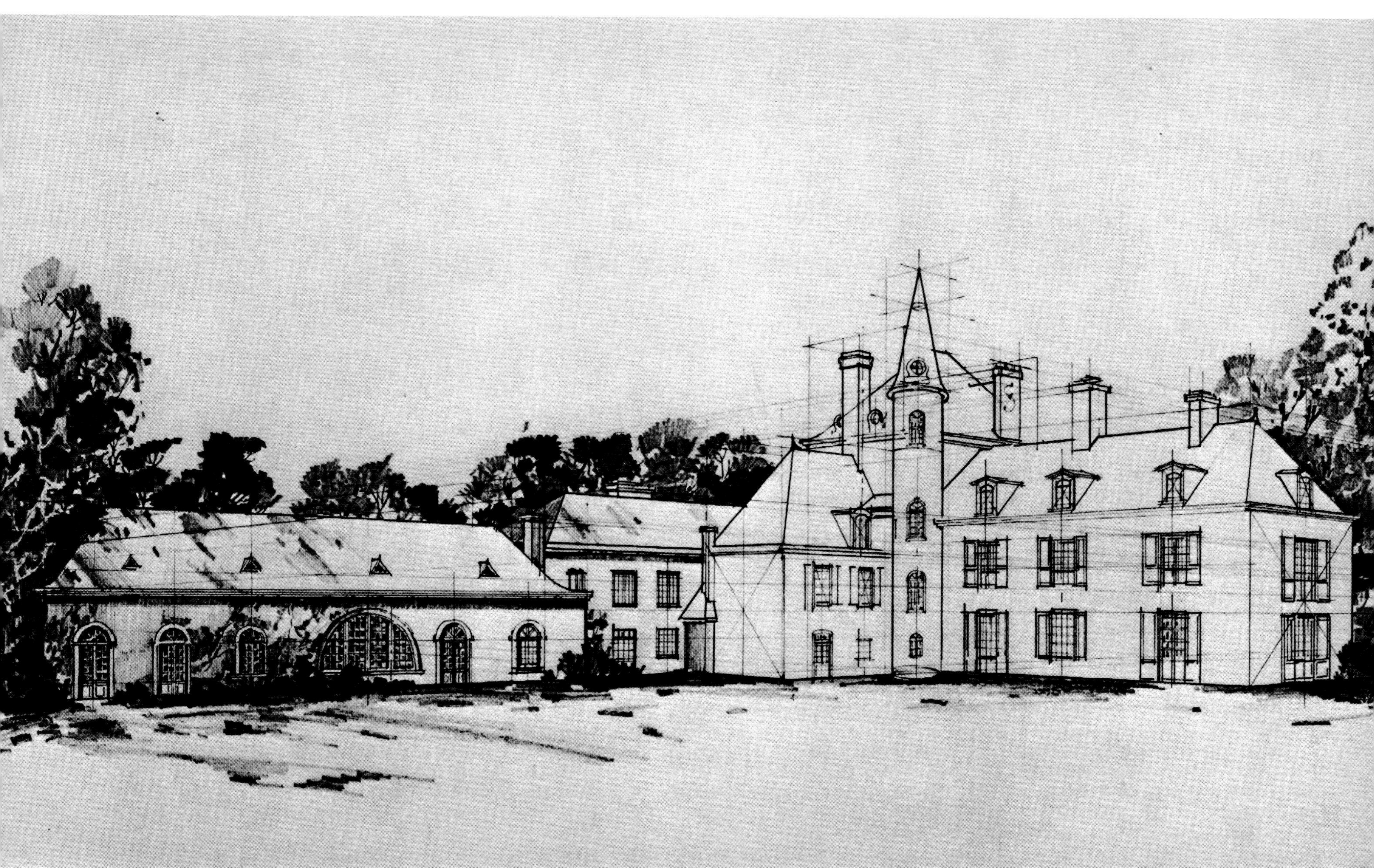

The Two-Dimensional Photograph

A photograph of a building, either exterior or interior, can be thought of as a two-dimensional representation of a three-dimensional volume of space. A simple house can be thought of as one or more or a combination of cubic solids, i.e., cubics, and rectangular, triangular, conic, and cylindrical solids as well as solids that have as their base parallelograms, circles, and free-form shapes.

Anything can be put into a box (see illustration, facing page). We see it every day. Regardless of its shape, an object can be surrounded by a rectangular box. If the rectangular box were big enough, theoretically it could contain a house or any building. If the surfaces of the box or *cubic solid* were thought of as transparent, we could see the object, house, or building within the box.

The boxes are used to group three-dimensional elements and to control scale. The photolinear perspective method advances this theory one step further by combining these outline drawings with photographs.

When a photograph is taken of the exterior of any cubic solid, only those surfaces that are visible from the single vantage point of the camera lens are recorded on the two-dimensional film. Those parts of objects that are behind the visible surfaces are only implied in the photograph; but if one begins to think of all surfaces of the object as being transparent, the unseen surfaces and plane divisions can be visualized. For example, if two connecting rooms are carefully photographed from one vantage point, it is possible to trace the resulting photograph and to draw in only the desired lines. If the wall between the rooms is not drawn, the second room can be added to the first in the tracing. It is not easy to think of walls as being transparent in order to see beyond them into adjacent spaces; but when this information is combined with floor plans, elevations, and sections, it is not impossible to do so, and in most cases this visualization is highly probable.

To draw a revision for an existing building with visual accuracy, one must have accurate photographs, a plan of the existing space, measured and drawn elevations of all architectural elements as well as sections through the structure (to record ceiling heights), and a roof plan, if work is to be done on the exterior of a building or if space is to be added to a freestanding structure.

Three-Dimensional Thinking

The designer wishing to combine areas, delete walls, and add space to or delete space from any structure shown in a drawing can visually

CHAPTER 2

DIVIDING SPACE WITHOUT MEASURING

perform these tasks on paper, using simple geometric exercises. One can, for example, subdivide a volume, add to it, and plot a grid on most any surface. This grid can then be used to plot the position of doors, windows, fireplaces, bath and kitchen cabinets, and other architectural elements as well as the placement of furniture.

Once the cubic solid has had a geometric grid placed on its surface, this grid can be used to divide the entire three-dimensional box into smaller cubes much like a three-dimensional map where any point within the volume can be located by height, width, and depth coordinates. Computer technology has electronically perfected this principle to create three-dimensional graphics that can visually approximate anything of a two- or three-dimensional nature with photographic accuracy.

Simple Three-Dimensional Graphics

The drawings in this section show simplified methods of division on planes of implied three-dimensional forms. This information, when combined with photographs, can be used to create design drawings with visual three-dimensional accuracy. Before working with photographic representations of volumes of space, however, you must learn how to impose a geometric grid over a simple cube.

We use the simple cube only to illustrate the proportional division of visible surfaces on a three-dimensional form. The position of the viewer of these simple cubes has been established at a constant height. *If the height of the viewer changes, the drawing must change accordingly. If the position of the viewer changes, the drawing must change also.*

Dividing the Vertical Space

In Chapter 1 we saw the importance of establishing a vertical true measuring corner (TMC) in the photograph and how, when traced to create a perspective drawing of limited scope, this vertical division line divides portions of the structure into both primary and secondary planes *A* and *B*. From there, we saw how to establish the horizon line, the vanishing points, and vertical divisions of the TMC. The drawings thus created are the basis for the photolinear perspective method.

Measuring within a Photograph

The goal is to be able to proportionally measure and draw three-dimensional elements within a photograph. This can be accomplished by imposing a geometric perspective grid with accurate visual scale over portions of the photograph, after first tracing over the main existing lines of perspective. This goal, as you will see, is accomplished in a similar manner to imposing a geometric grid over a simple cube. Once this proportional measuring grid has been created on any two planes of a building, the grid can be expanded to provide a reference within which to plot additions or alterations to the structure.

With this method, we can complement the usually tedious and often inaccurate architectural projection process used to illustrate new structures, one that is based on plans and elevations. Although this method is taught in most design and architectural schools, it is not a satisfactory answer to remodeling related three-dimensional drawings.

The TMC

As we saw in Chapter 1, connecting equally spaced points along the TMC to the vanishing points (or point) creates a series of lines that represent horizontal lines (vertical space divisions). As these lines approach the TMC, they are spaced farther apart, and they diminish to converge at the vanishing point(s). Because of the lines of perspective within the photograph, we know that, although to the eye and on the photograph the lines appear to converge, the physical measurement between them actually remains the same—and their vertical height division measures the same as the marks along the TMC.

Assigning Scale to the TMC

If we have divided the TMC on the tracing at a scale of 1′ for each mark, then the space between each horizontal line projected from these marks to the vanishing points represents 1′ all the way to the vanishing point or points. Similarly, if we partition the TMC into any other equal number of divisions, say 7″ apart such as the siding lines on the cottage in Figure 1.10a, then lines extended to each of the two vanishing points represent lines on the plane of the building that in reality will be 7″ apart.

Adding or Subtracting Height within a Photograph

Using the vertical space division of the TMC, we can begin to add vertical height to or subtract vertical height from our subject to scale with the photograph.

Proportional Measurement of Horizontal Space

We have examined how to divide vertical space within a drawing and have seen how vertical dimensions on a perspective drawing can be approximated. However, before we discuss how to do remodeling drawings and sketches for an actual building, let's take a closer look at the geometric principles and techniques that apply to horizontal space or *visual depth* which cannot be measured, but can be proportionally and geometrically divided.

Almost any building is made up of a combination of geometric solids such as cubes, cones, and cylinders. We need to know, therefore, how to divide up these volumes and shapes into the desired measurements, both horizontal and vertical, and how to add to and subtract from them. Thus the designer can calculate the desired projections, additions, and recesses visually proportional to a building's existing scale.

The Cube as the Basic Volume

In this chapter, the division and extension of the volume of a basic cube, seen from an eye level of approximately one-third the height of the TMC, are examined by two methods. The first relies on the use of *intersecting diagonal lines* to subdivide planes of the cube into even multiples only; the second method employs the *slanted-scale approach* to line division. By using the latter technique, the TMC on the cube (or on a photograph of a cubic volume) can be partitioned into any number of divisions, either odd or even. This technique, when combined with corner-to-corner diagonal lines, can be used to subdivide surface planes of the cube into an even or odd number of divisions that are equal in both height and depth.

Once the division of lines and planes on the visual surfaces of a cube in perspective is understood, further divisions and extensions of the volume of the cube are possible with either method or with a combination of the two. By using the two methods of plane division and extension, divisions on the planes of the cubic volumes can be carried into the volume and transferred to the object within. An example is the house created from the cube in Figure 2.13a through k.

With this knowledge, it is possible to subdivide as well as extend and delete portions of the interior or exterior planes of a three-dimensional cubic volume. A building is, of course, much more than just a cubic volume of space with planes that form exterior boundaries. But if you can begin with these exercises, using the study of simple cubes shown here as examples, it should not be too difficult for you to adapt the principles to a house or other building. This requires much study and practice in applying and adapting the simple principles described here. You must, of course, acquire the knowledge of the architectural elements that make up our three-dimensional environments.

The following comparative examples take you from the surface division of two planes of a cube, as seen from a height of one-third of the height of the TMC, through the extension of the cubic solid. The last part of the example takes the divided cube through each successive step in elevation and perspective until the illusion of a house emerges and a finished illustration of that house may be seen.

Then in Chapter 3 you will be shown how to use these spatial division techniques on an interior space that has been traced directly from photographs.

Bisecting a Plane with Intersecting Diagonal Lines

Step 1. Figure 2.1a shows the standard way to divide a plane surface of a cube or a rectangular elevation into two evenly spaced parts by using diagonal lines. Figure 2.2a shows that by continuing the process, each half of cube elevation plane *A* can be further halved through the use of intersecting diagonals. The result is four equally spaced *depth* divisions.

Step 2. Figure 2.1b shows how plane *A*, now seen in perspective, may be divided into two equal *depth* divisions by using intersecting diagonals, just as was done for the elevation view. In Figure 2.2b, intersecting diagonals are used to divide each half of plane *A* of the three-dimensional cube into two more equal parts, making a total of four equal divisions, as was done for the elevation (Figure 2.2a). By repeating steps 1 and 2, each division can be halved as many times as desired.

FIGURE 2.1a and 2.2a How to Divide an Elevation into Two Equal Parts by Using Diagonal Lines To find the center of any square or rectangle, opposing diagonal lines are drawn from corner to corner. This technique works with only an *even* number of divisions, that is, 2, 4, 8, 16, and so on.

1. Draw diagonals from opposing corners of plane *ABCD,* that is, from *A* to *C* and from *B* to *D*.

2. The diagonals cross at *O*, which is the center of the plane.

3. Each area can be divided further by drawing a vertical line from the baseline at *F* up through *O* to the top line at *E*. This creates equal plane divisions *AEFD* and *EBCF*.

4. When this procedure is used, the number of divisions increases as each segment is further divided in half. See Figure 2.1b for the perspective application.

FIGURE 2.1b and 2.2b How to Divide a Plane in Perspective into Two Equal Horizontal Divisions by Using Diagonal Lines Note that the same principle of space division, i.e., placement of diagonal lines across the plane, holds true for dividing a plane in perspective as for one in elevation. There are two primary differences: The top and bottom *horizontal* lines for planes *A* and *B* converge to the VPR and VPL, and the divisions of space on the face of the plane appear to be getting smaller as they approach the vanishing point. In a two-point perspective, each plane is the projection from a single *vanishing point;* i.e., plane *A* will have lines that converge at the VPR, and all lines on plane *B* will converge at the VPL.

To further divide the horizontal space of plane *A*, refer to the elevation in Figure 2.2a; and follow the same procedure to create the equally divided plane *A* in perspective, as in Figure 2.2b.

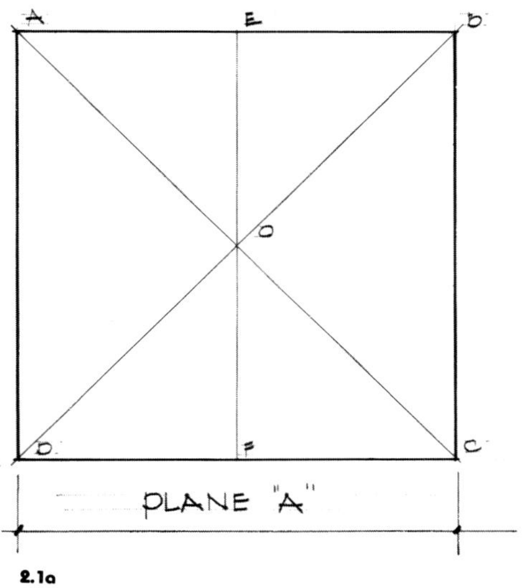

2.1a

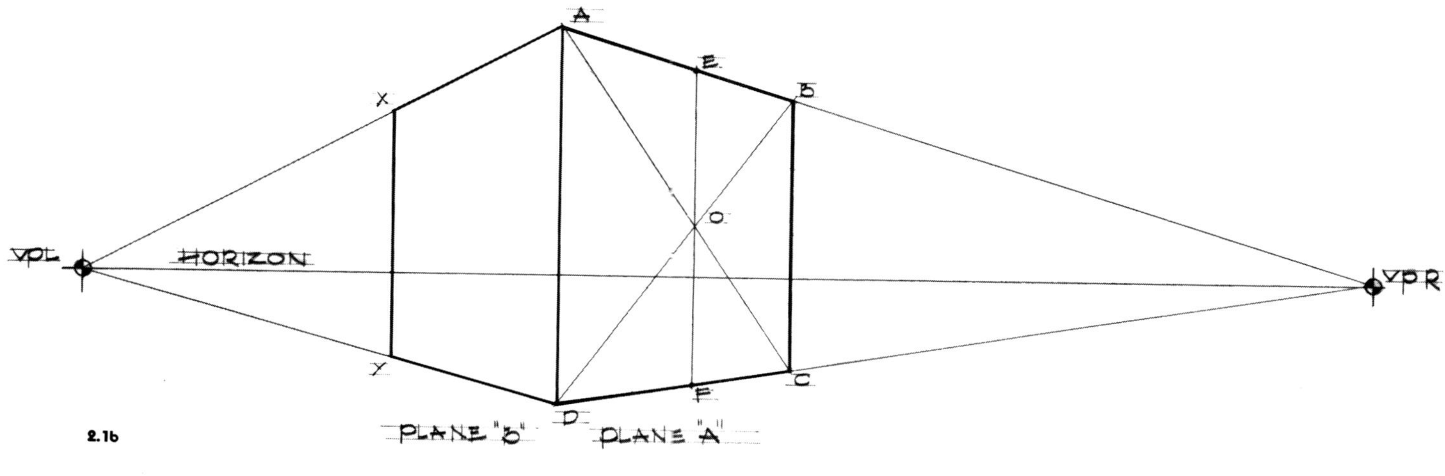

2.1b

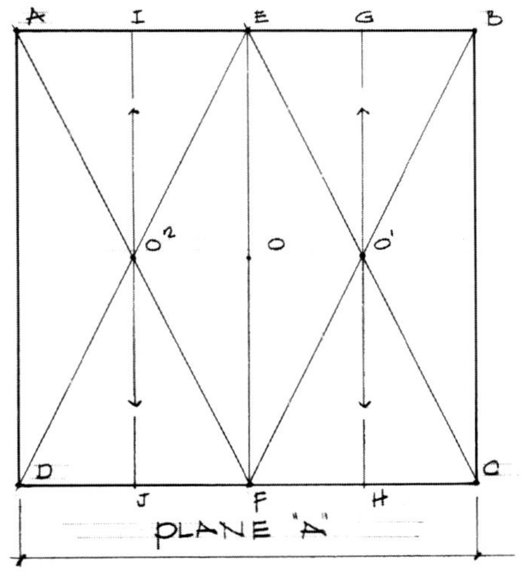

2.2a

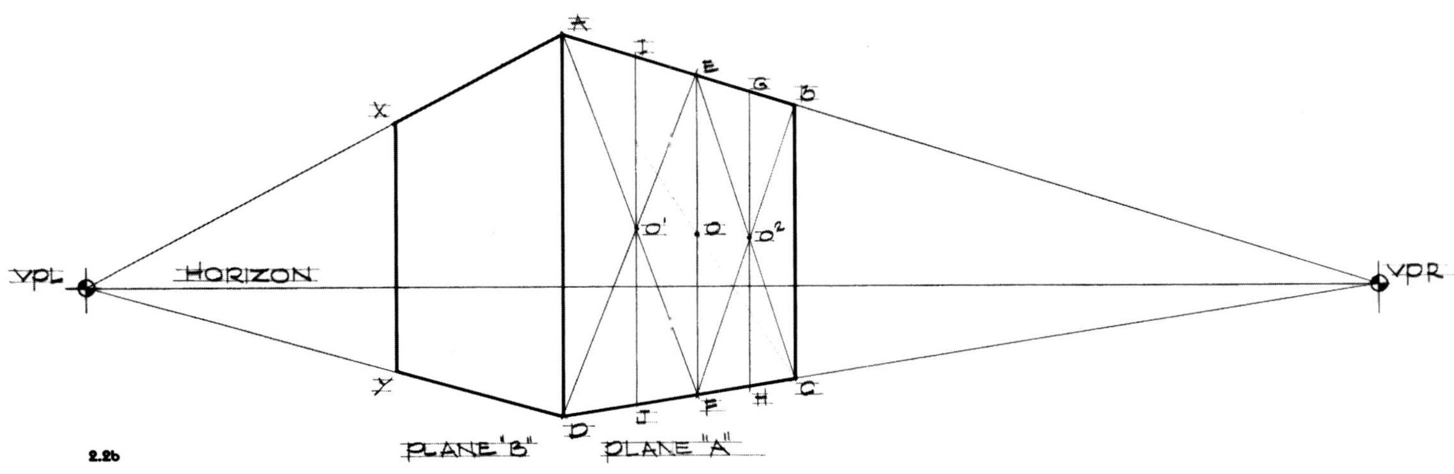

2.2b

Step 3. To continue the process, plane *A* can be divided into a grid of 16 equal squares, as shown progressively in elevation views (Figures 2.3a, 2.4a, and 2.5a) and their companion perspectives (Figures 2.3b, 2.4b, and 2.5b).

Step 4. Plane *B* can be divided into a 16-square grid in both elevation and perspective by using a similar method. See Figure 2.6a and b.

FIGURES 2.3, 2.4, 2.5, and 2.6 Creating a Grid on a Plane in Elevation and Perspective

1. Four equal divisions have been created within a square plane. This is illustrated in both elevation (Figure 2.3a) and perspective (Figure 2.3b).

2. Draw diagonal *AC* (Figure 2.4a and b).

3. The three vertical divisions *IJ*, *EF*, and *GH* intersect diagonal *AC* at points *K*, *O*, and *L*, respectively. Draw horizontal lines through *K*, *O*, and *L* (Figure 2.5a).

4. In Figure 2.5b diagonal *AC* is used to create the grid in perspective.

5. Now plane *ABCD* should be divided into 16 equal squares in both elevation and perspective. *Note:* The horizontal lines intersecting diagonal *AC* at points *K*, *O*, and *L*, when drawn in perspective, appear to be getting closer together as they approach and finally converge at the VPR.

6. Figure 2.6a and b shows the grid on two visible planes of the cube.

7. If the cube is drawn as transparent, these same principles apply to the placement of an equal grid on any surface. Here the grid designations have been omitted for the balance of the cube surfaces, to lessen confusion.

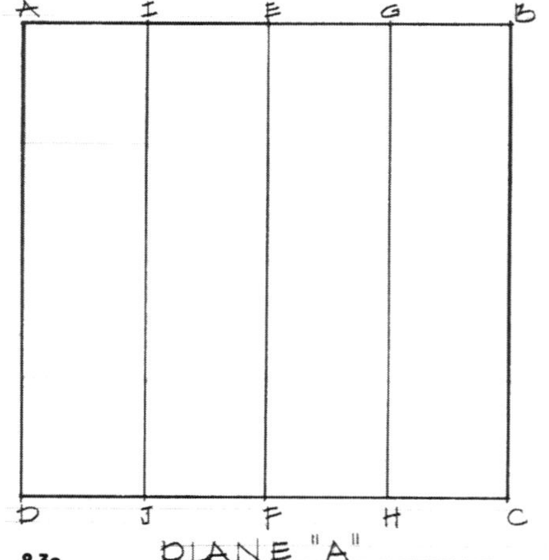

2.3a

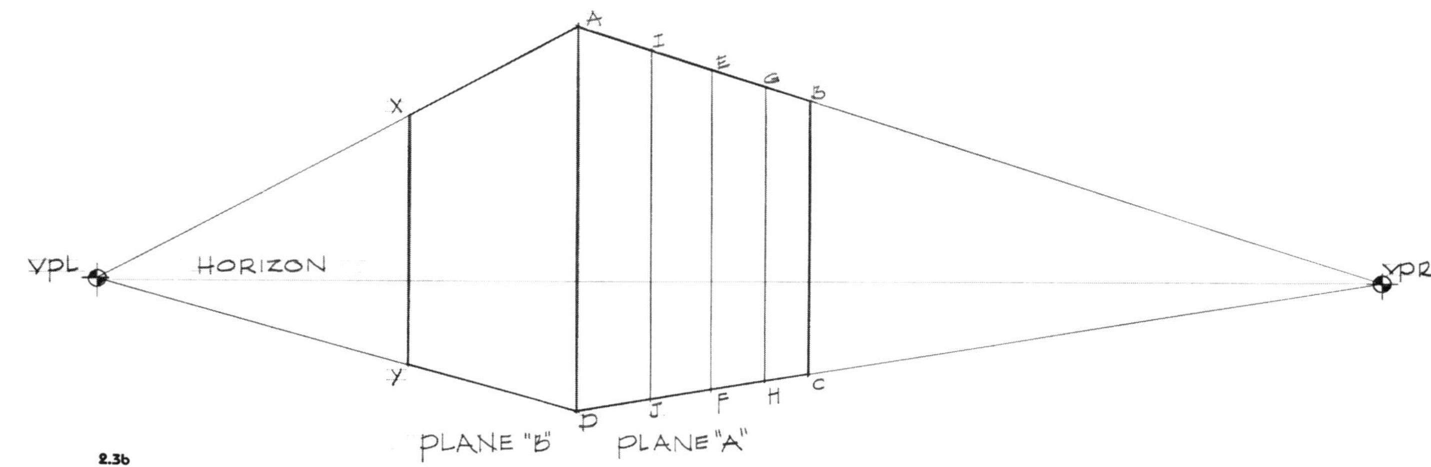

2.3b

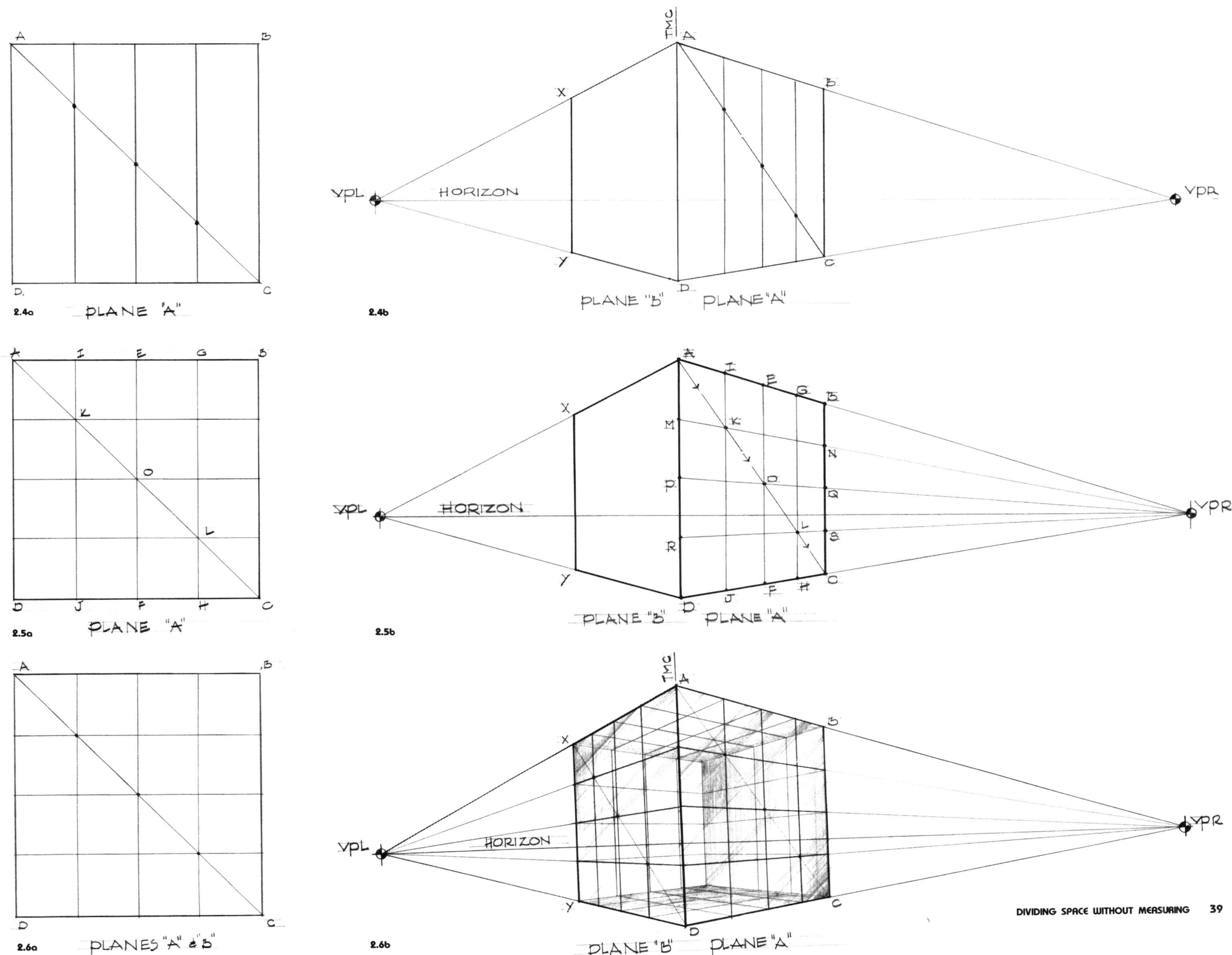
A
B
D
C
2.4a
PLANE "A"
TMC
A
X
B
VPL
HORIZON
VPR
Y
C
D
PLANE "B"
PLANE "A"
2.4b
A
I
E
G
B
K
O
L
D
J
F
H
C
2.5a
PLANE "A"
A
I
E
G
B
X
M
K
N
VPL
HORIZON
P
O
Q
VPR
R
L
S
Y
C
D
J
F
H
PLANE "B"
PLANE "A"
2.5b
A
B
D
C
2.6a
PLANES "A" & "B"
TMC
A
B
X
VPL
HORIZON
VPR
Y
C
D
PLANE "B"
PLANE "A"
2.6b

Divide a Plane by Using the Slanted-Scale Method

This example partitions plane *A* into 36 equal divisions (6 on each side) by employing the slanted-scale method. First the TMC must be divided into six equal height divisions, and then corner-to-corner diagonal lines are added to complete the process (Figures 2.7 through 2.9). Division in this manner can be accomplished for any number of units (odd or even) and is not limited to even division, as is the intersecting-diagonal method shown in Figures 2.1 through 2.6.

Step 5. Plane *B* can now be divided into 36 equal squares by using these same principles, thus creating a grid on all exposed faces of the cube in both elevation and perspective (Figure 2.10a and b).

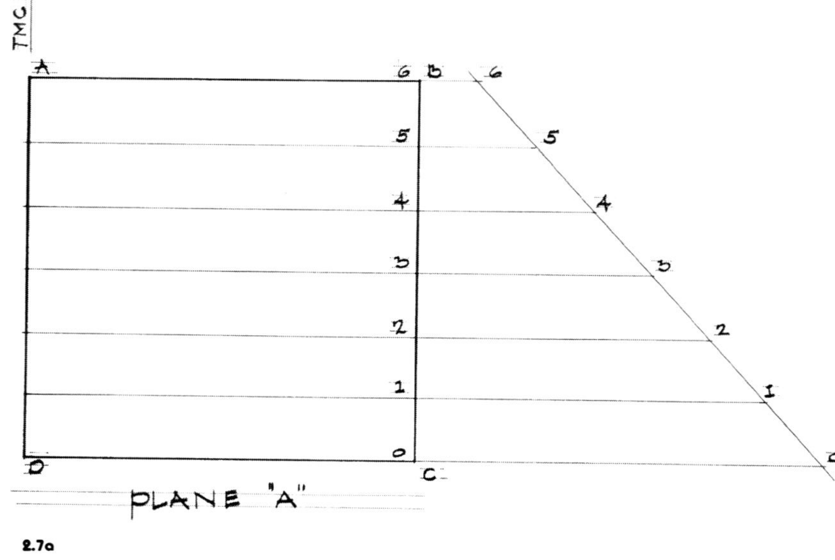

2.7a

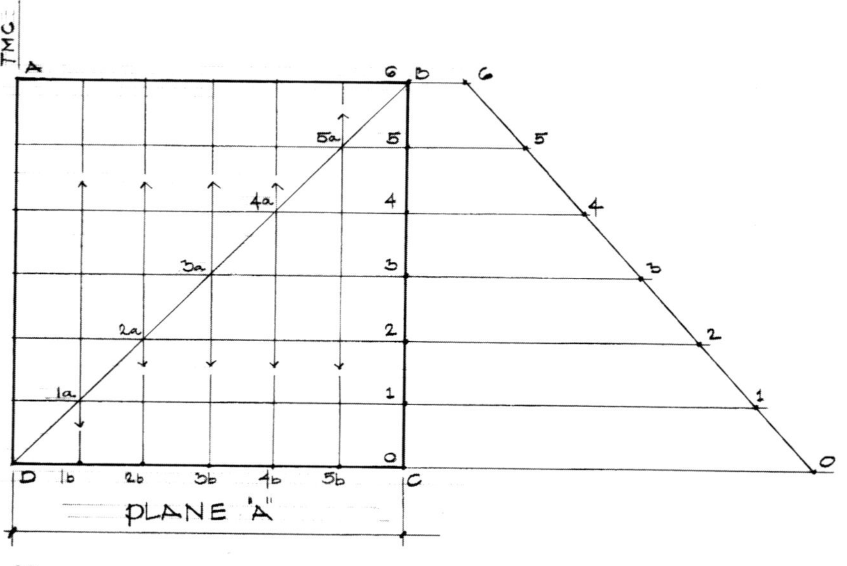

2.8a

FIGURE 2.7, 2.8, 2.9, and 2.10 How to Create a Grid on Plane A in Elevation and Perspective. The slanted-scale method of line division can be used to partition the TMC, when it cannot be measured, into any equal number (odd or even) of divisions, in this case six equal height divisions. This is done as follows:

1. Extend horizontal lines *AB* and *DC* to the right or left of the TMC (line *AD* of plane *A*) a few inches, as in Figure 2.7a.

2. Now, using any equally marked scale, label the bottom extended line 0 and the uppermost line 6.

3. Draw a line along the calibrated edge of the scale, and put a tick mark on the line at each equal division of this diagonal line.

4. Use a *T* square to extend horizontal lines from each tick mark to the TMC (line *AD*), to divide this vertical line into six equal height divisions. A similar procedure is followed for either an elevation or a perspective drawing.

5. Once the TMC has been divided equally, the same procedure can be followed to create a grid on planes *A* and *B*, as in Figures 2.4 through 2.6.

TMC
A
B
F
6
5
4
3
2
1
VPL
HORIZON
VPR
E
C
D
PLANE "B"
PLANE "A"
2.7b

TMC
A
B
F
6
5
4
3
2
1
5a
4a
3a
2a
1a
VPL
HORIZON
VPR
E
1b
2b
3b
4b
5b
C
D
PLANE "B"
PLANE "A"
2.8b

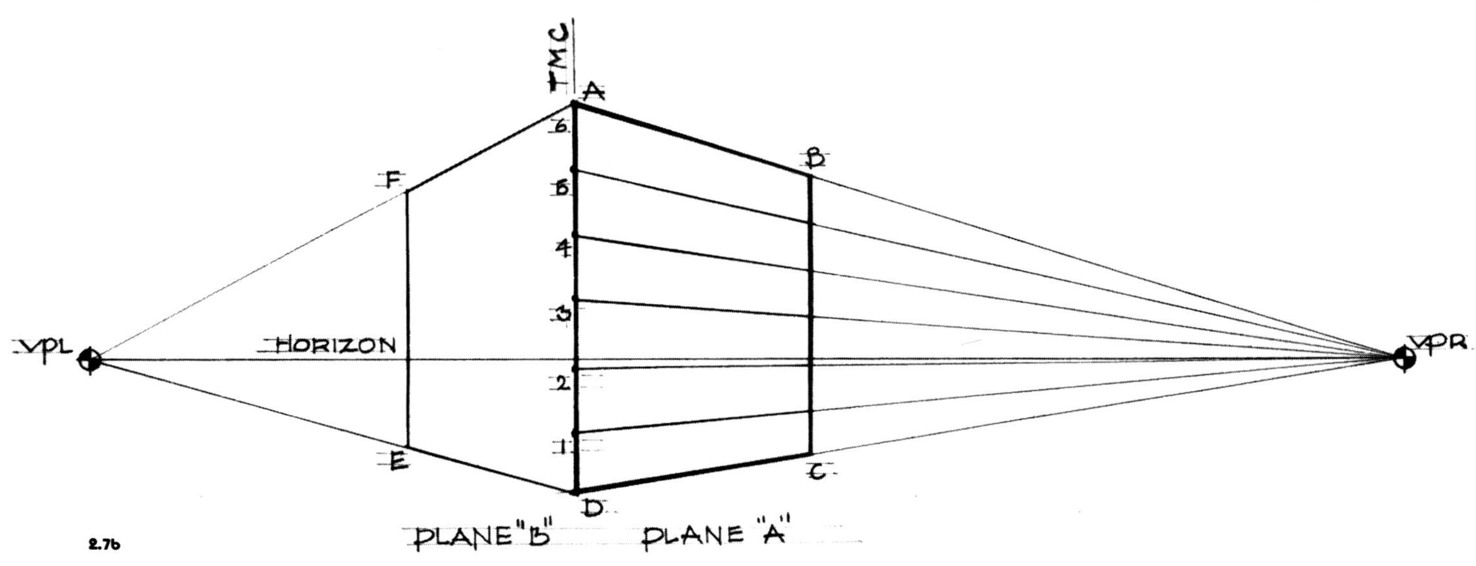

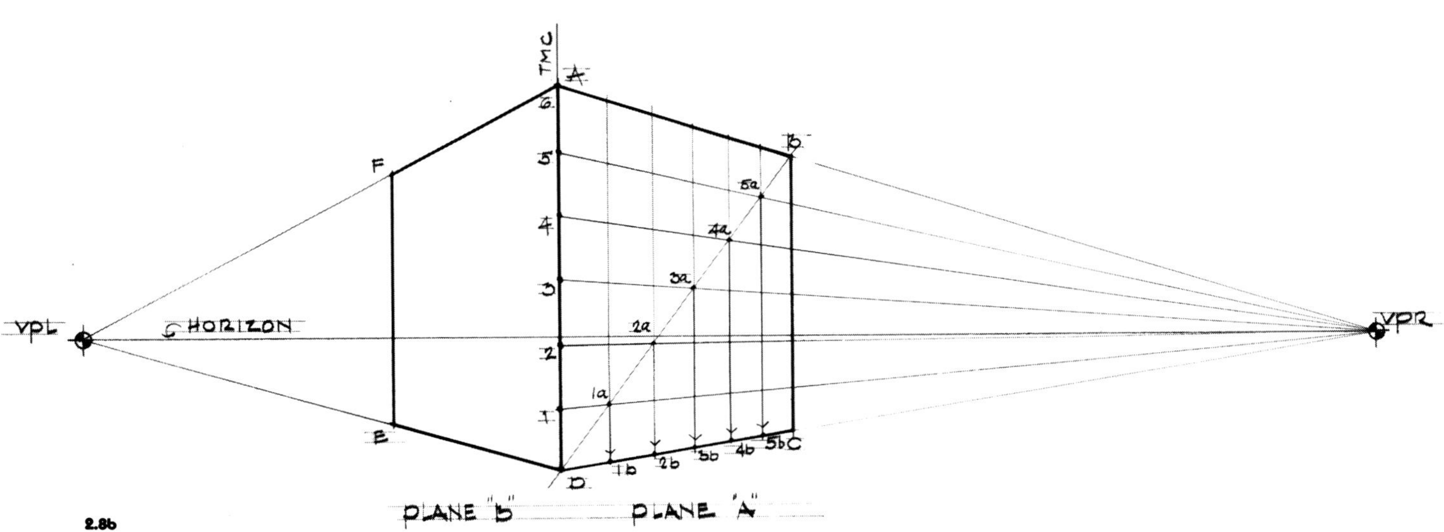

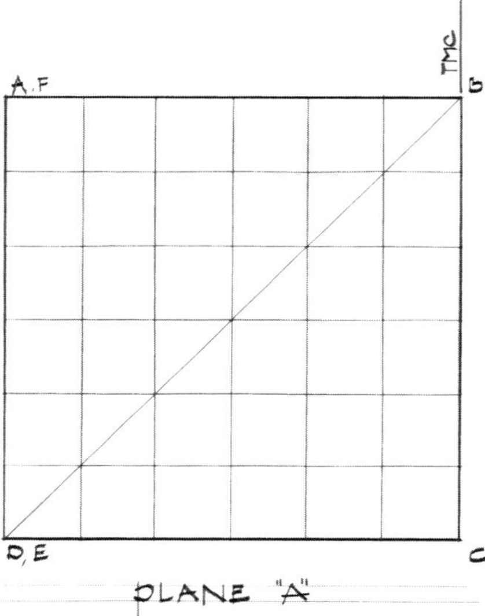

2.9a

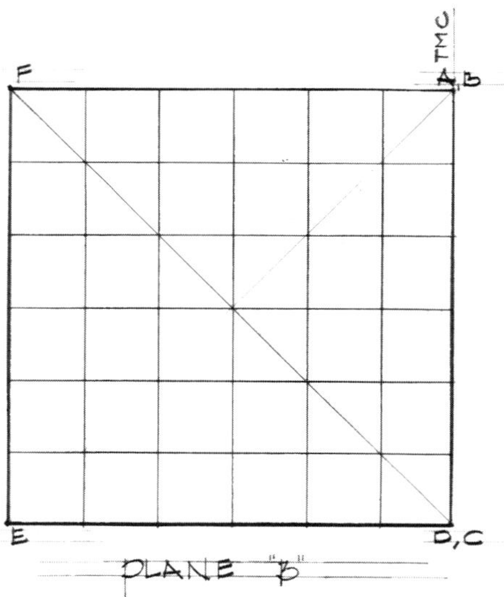

2.10a

TMC
A
B
F
VPL
HORIZON
VPR
E
C
D
PLANE "B"
PLANE "A"
2.9b

TMC
A
B
F
VPL
HORIZON
VPR
E
C
D
PLANE "B"
PLANE "A"
2.10b

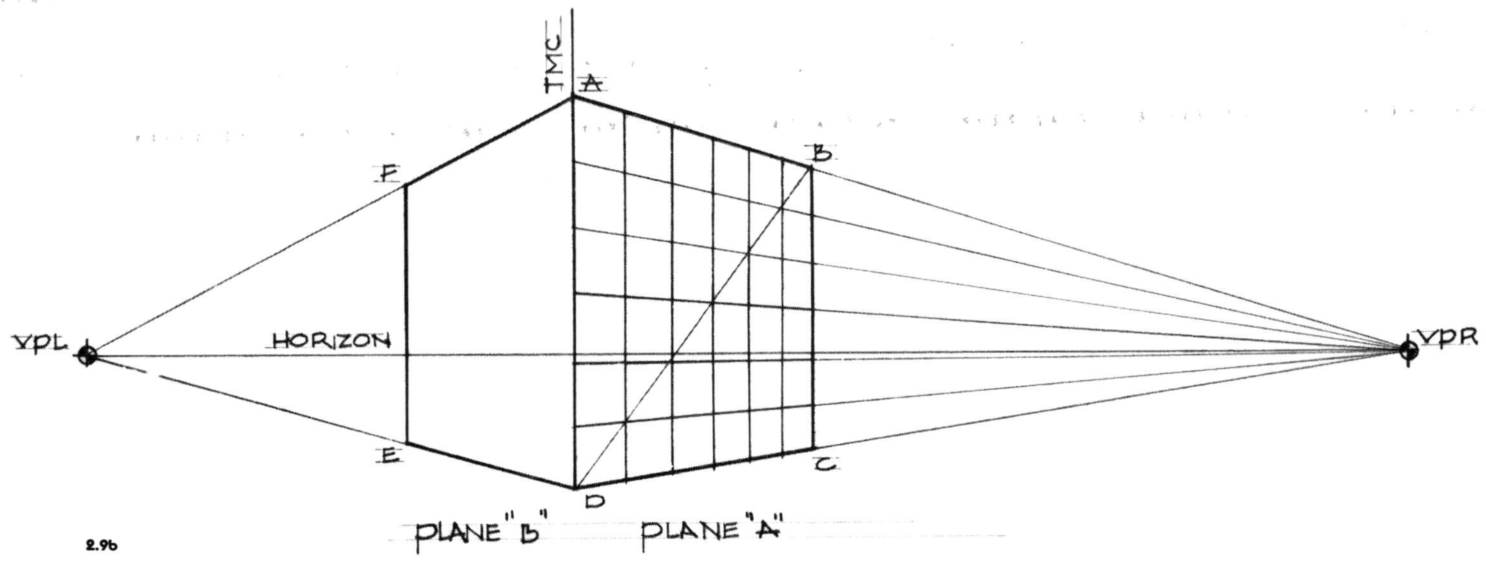

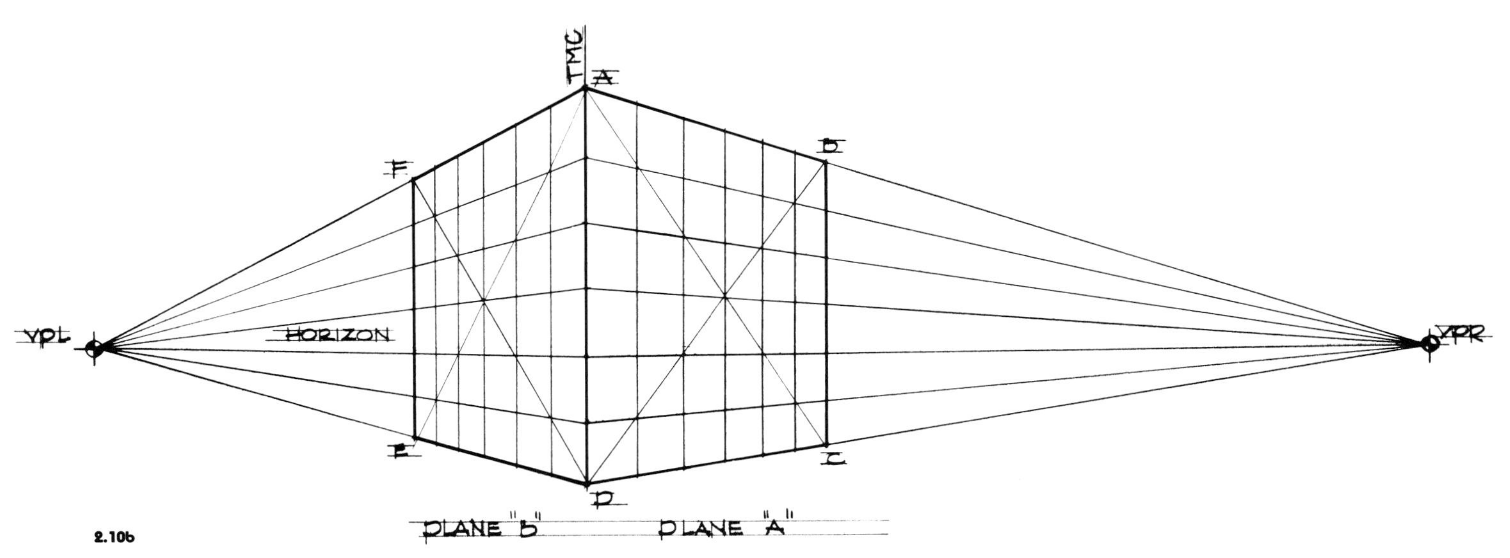

Extending the Grid of a Plane in Either Direction with the Use of Corner-to-Corner Diagonal Lines

The examples in Figures 2.11 and 2.12 are based on a cubic solid whose face planes have been divided into a grid of 16 equal squares (4 × 4) and whose TMC height is partitioned into four equal height divisions.

Let us examine Figure 2.11a (elevation) and b (perspective) to see how plane *A* may be extended away from the viewer and toward the vanishing point.

First we extend the top and bottom perimeter lines of the plane toward the vanishing point, and then we extend the grid toward the vanishing point (two divisions), using diagonal lines extended from the grid squares on the face of the cube, as in the proportional measuring method.

Figure 2.12a (elevation) and b (perspective) shows a cube with plane *A* extended toward the viewer. To do this, first extend the top and bottom perimeter lines of the plane toward the viewer, and then continue the grid forward, using extended diagonal lines drawn through the corners of two of the cubes' face divisions, as in Figure 2.11a and b, but this time away from the vanishing point. You have now seen how to extend plane *A* toward the vanishing point or away from it toward the viewer.

Plane *B* can also be extended in either direction by using a similar procedure. This simple geometric method allows you to start with a volume of space and extend it in any direction to create a larger space. By reversing the process, it is possible to *delete* a like amount from the cube as well.

FIGURES 2.11a and b and 2.12a and b How to Extend a Plane of the Cube in Perspective Away from the Viewer To extend plane *A* away from the viewer and toward the VPR, the division of this plane must be examined first in elevation and then in perspective.

In Figure 2.11a, plane *A*, that is, plane *ABCD*, has been divided into 16 equal squares by using diagonal *AC* to create the grid. To extend this plane to the right two divisions, a second diagonal is used.

1. Extend *parallel* lines *AB*, *MN*, *PQ*, *RS*, and *DC* to the right an undetermined amount (for the perspective see Figure 2.11b). These lines, if extended, will converge at the VPR.

2. Draw the second diagonal *EQ*, and extend it down and to the right until it crosses extended line *RS* at *U* and continues down to the baseline extension at C^1.

3. Draw a vertical line through intersection *U*, and darken in a new perimeter line B^1C^1.

4. You have now extended the cube in equal increments both in elevation and in perspective.

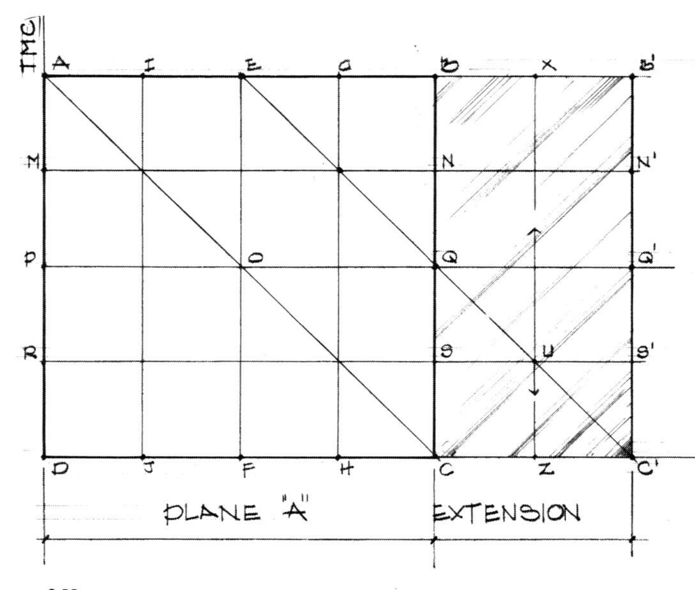

2.11a

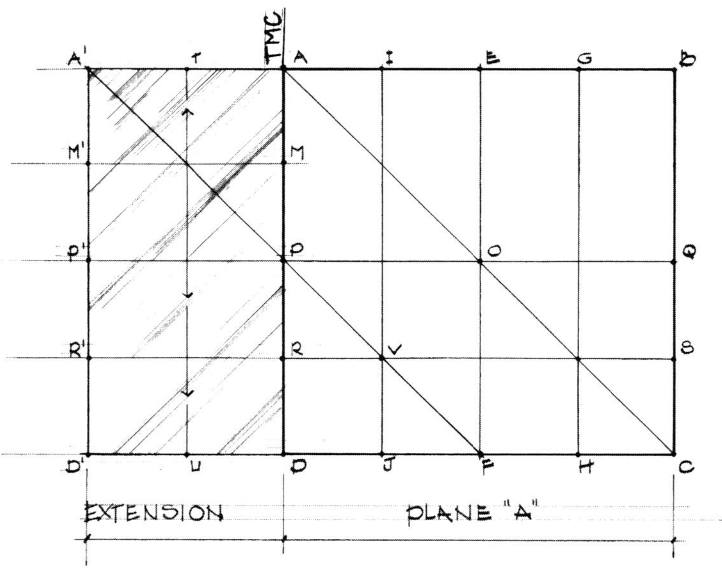

2.12a

5. You may repeat this procedure as many times as necessary to add as much area to the plane as is desired. The plane increases proportionally each time a new diagonal is drawn.

6. You can also use this method to decrease any plane of the cube or to increase any plane in any direction. See Figure 2.12a and b.

TMC
A
I
E
G
B
X
B'
M
N
N'
O
P
Q
Q'
VPL
HORIZON
VPR
U
R
S
S'
C
Z
C'
D
J
F
H
PLANE "B"
PLANE "A"
EXTENSION
A'
T
M'
P'
R'
D'
V
EXTENSION
PLANE "A"

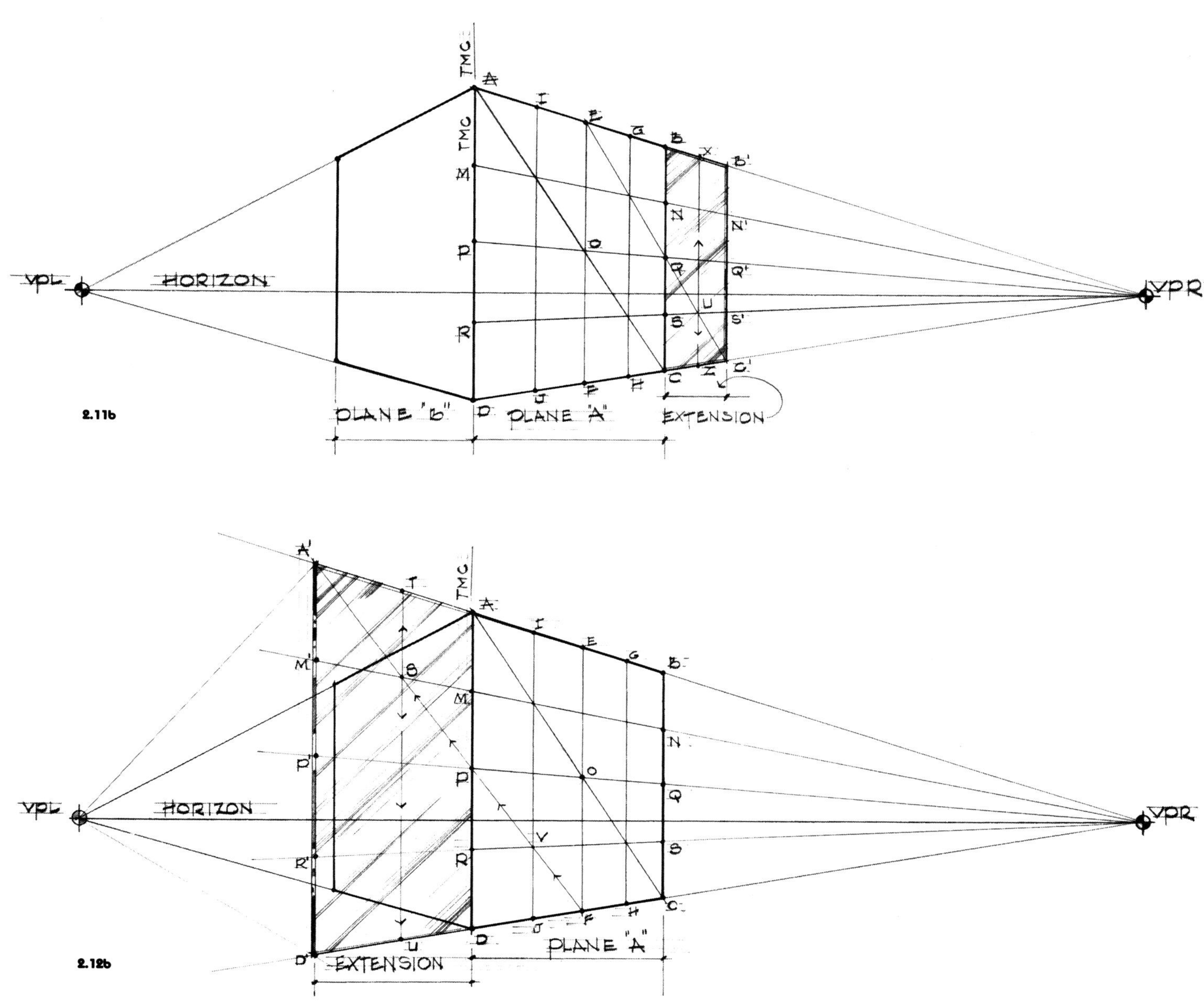

2.11b

2.12b

Practical application Figure 2.13a and b shows a cubic solid whose surface plane *B* is divided into 36 equal squares. The *B* plane has also been extended one division away from the vanishing point, forming plane *B′*, in order to create an addition to the cubic solid.

The cube and its extension will become the basis for the creation of a house, seen in Figure 2.13b through k.

Once the cubic solid in elevation and in perspective has been extended to the right one division, to create a cube extension, and the desired height divisions are chosen and extended around the cubical volume, then the TMC and the grid can be used to plot height on either desired vertical plane *A* or *B* (see the grid division lines in elevation in Figure 2.13c and d).

All "horizontal" lines on each *A* plane will, if extended, converge at the VPR, and all "horizontal" lines on *B* planes will converge at the VPL.

2.13a

FIGURE 2.13a and b How to Extend a Portion of a Cube Away from the Vanishing Point and toward the Viewer Refer again to Figure 2.10b, the cube in perspective that has each of its *A* and *B* planes divided into 36 equal squares.

1. Begin by extending plane *B* as in Figures 2.11b and 2.12b. See plane *B* of Figure 2.13a for the process in elevation.

2. Now connect top and bottom points *L* and *O* (on the new extended plane called B^1) to the VPR, to create a new plane A^1 (plane *LMNO*) in front of the original *A* plane (plane *ABCD*).

3. Using point designations A^1, B^1, C^1, and D^1 on the grid of plane *A*, extend these from the VPL to the new plane A^1 at points *P, Q, R,* and *S*. Darken these lines to distinguish them from the grid lines, or use an overlay of tracing paper for this step to lessen confusion (Figure 2.13b). The cube and its extension are now becoming visible in the perspective drawing.

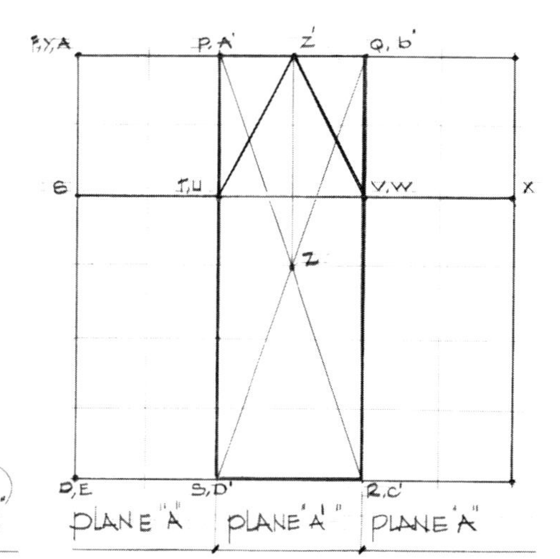

2.13c

FIGURE 2.13c and d From a Cubic Solid to a House The cube and its extension can be used as the basic form for what can become a house with a porch. (On the elevation in Figure 2.13c, note the designations of the front and side elevation planes *A* and A^1 as well as planes *B* and B^1 on the orthographic projection. The cube's division lines have been darkened, and connection lines have been drawn to denote roof apex and eave lines. Follow this procedure for the house drawing:

1. To draw eave lines around the cube and its extension, cover the drawing with a clean sheet of tracing paper and draw in the grid line denoting two horizontal divisions from the top of the cube.

2. Bisect the extended plane A^1 with intersecting diagonal lines, to find *Z* at the center of the extended plane. Similarly, bisect plane *B* to find *Y*.

3. Now draw a vertical line up from *Z* to find Z^1 on the upper perimeter line of plane A^1, and do similarly from *Y* to Y^1, also on the upper perimeter of the cubic solid.

VPL
HORIZON
VPR
PLANES "b & b'"
PLANES "A & A'"
VPL
HORIZON
VPR
PLANE "b"
"b'"
"A'"
PLANE
PLANE
PLANE "A"

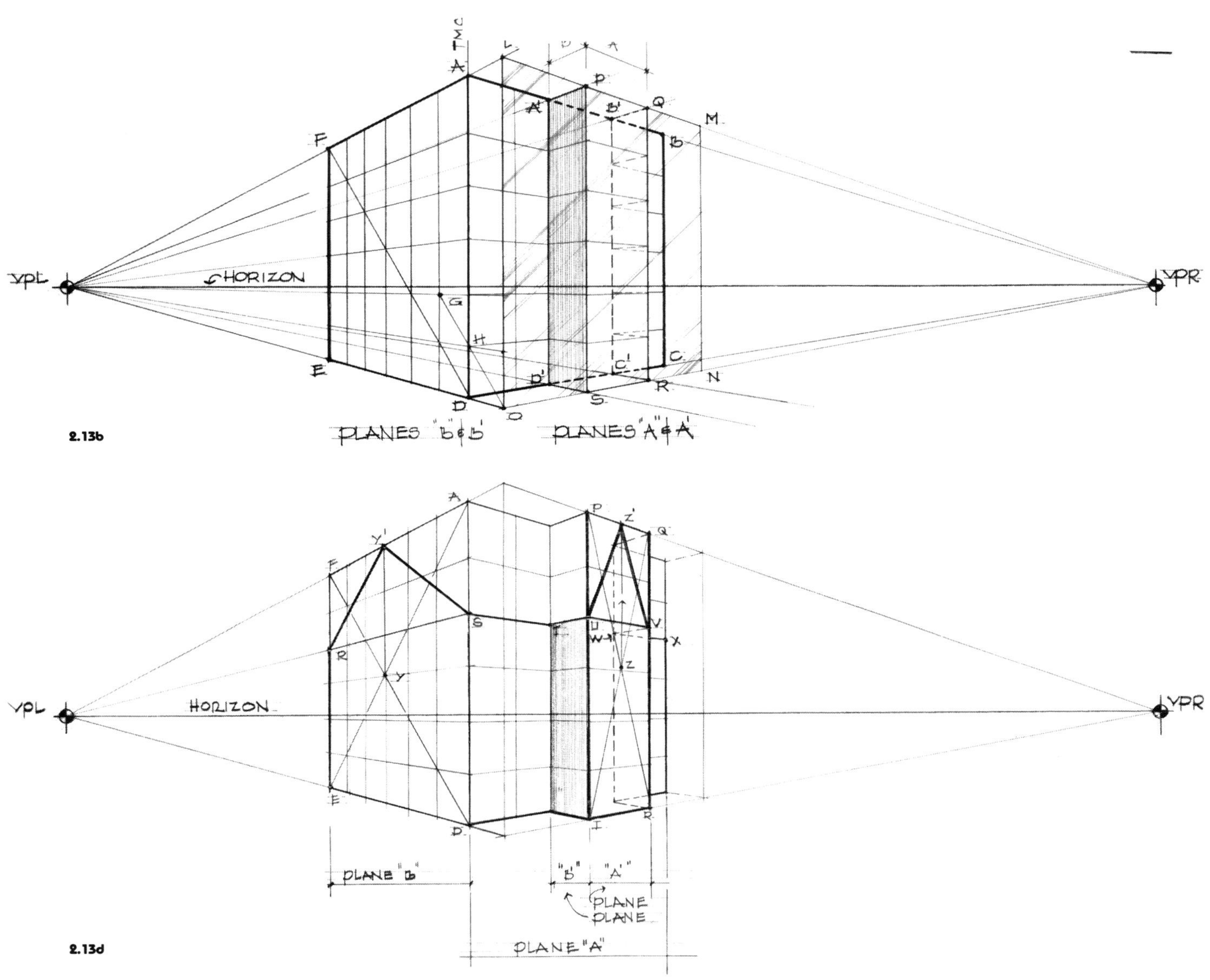

2.13b

2.13d

Eave and Gable Locations

As we continue the process, a house starts to emerge from the drawing. Darker lines indicating gable and eave placement are located and reinforced on the grid on the faces of the cube in perspective (Figure 2.13f) and in elevation (Figure 2.13e).

Windows

Window outlines located and darkened on the face of each plane in elevation can be transferred to the grid of each plane in the perspective, and these architectural elements can be defined.

Roof Apex and Ridge Lines

The roof apex is drawn next, by tracing ridge lines from the uppermost centerline of the gable ends of planes *A* and *B* toward the vanishing points.

Valleys

Where the two ridge lines intersect, a valley can be formed by connecting this intersection to the eave intersections. As this process continues, the house outline becomes clearer (Figure 2.13e and f).

The Human Scale

It is very important to include a ''people'' scale in any drawing, to visually establish the size of the structure. Representations of people do not have to be lifelike, but they must be drawn in scale with the building.

Linear Definition

The house in Figure 2.13g and h has dimension because of added line work. Each new three-dimensional element, such as the chimney, has both *A* and *B* planes (the *horizontal* lines of which project back to their respective vanishing points). The eaves, window jambs, railing posts, and applied trim all have planes *A* and *B*, and as we will see in Chapter 5, these planes can further be defined through the addition of shade and shadow. See Figure 2.13j and k.

FIGURE 2.13e and f

1. Referring to the grid overlay of the front and side elevation outline drawings (Figure 2.13e) and using another overlay of clean tracing paper for the perspective (Figure 2.13f), connect Y^1 to the VPR and Z^1 to the VPL. Where these two roof ridge lines intersect at Z^2, extend a line down to *T* on the eave line to form the valley of the roof of the house Z^2T.
2. On plane *B* connect points RY^1 and Y^1S to denote the gable end.
3. Similarly, on plane A^1 connect points UZ^1 and Z^1V. These form the gable ends of what will become the peaked roof over the porch, as shown on this extended plane.

As the house starts to emerge, note the placement of the scale figure used to aid the viewer in proportional relationship. This figure immediately allows the mind to associate the emerging drawing with that of a *house* rather than with the cubic solid from which it grew. The figure's eye level should be on the horizon, and the size of the figure is determined by how far it is placed from the ''house.''

FRONT ELEVATION
PLANE "A"
PLANE "A'"
PLANE "A"
SIDE ELEVATION
PLANE "B"
PLANE "B'"

2.13e

VPL
HORIZON
VPR
TMC
PLANE "B"
PLANE "B"
PLANE "A"
PLANE "A"

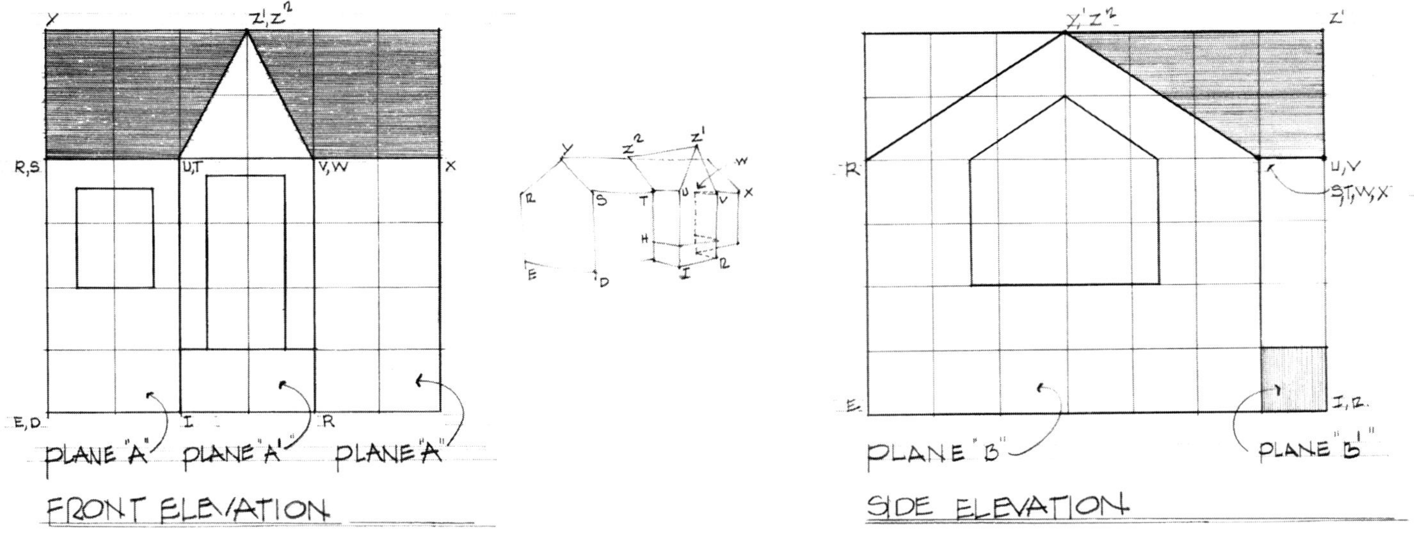

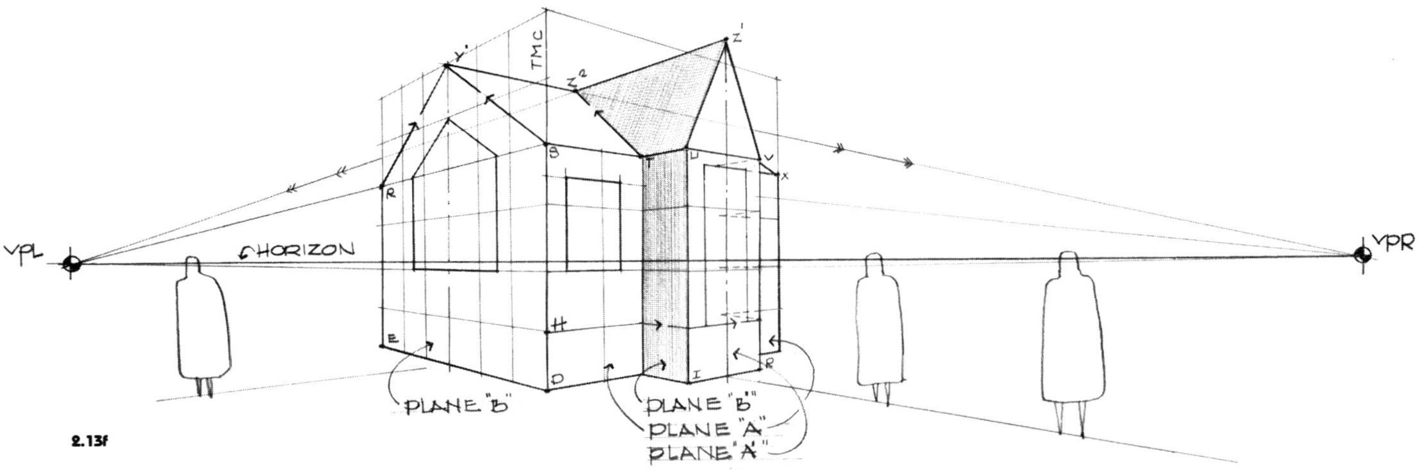

2.13f

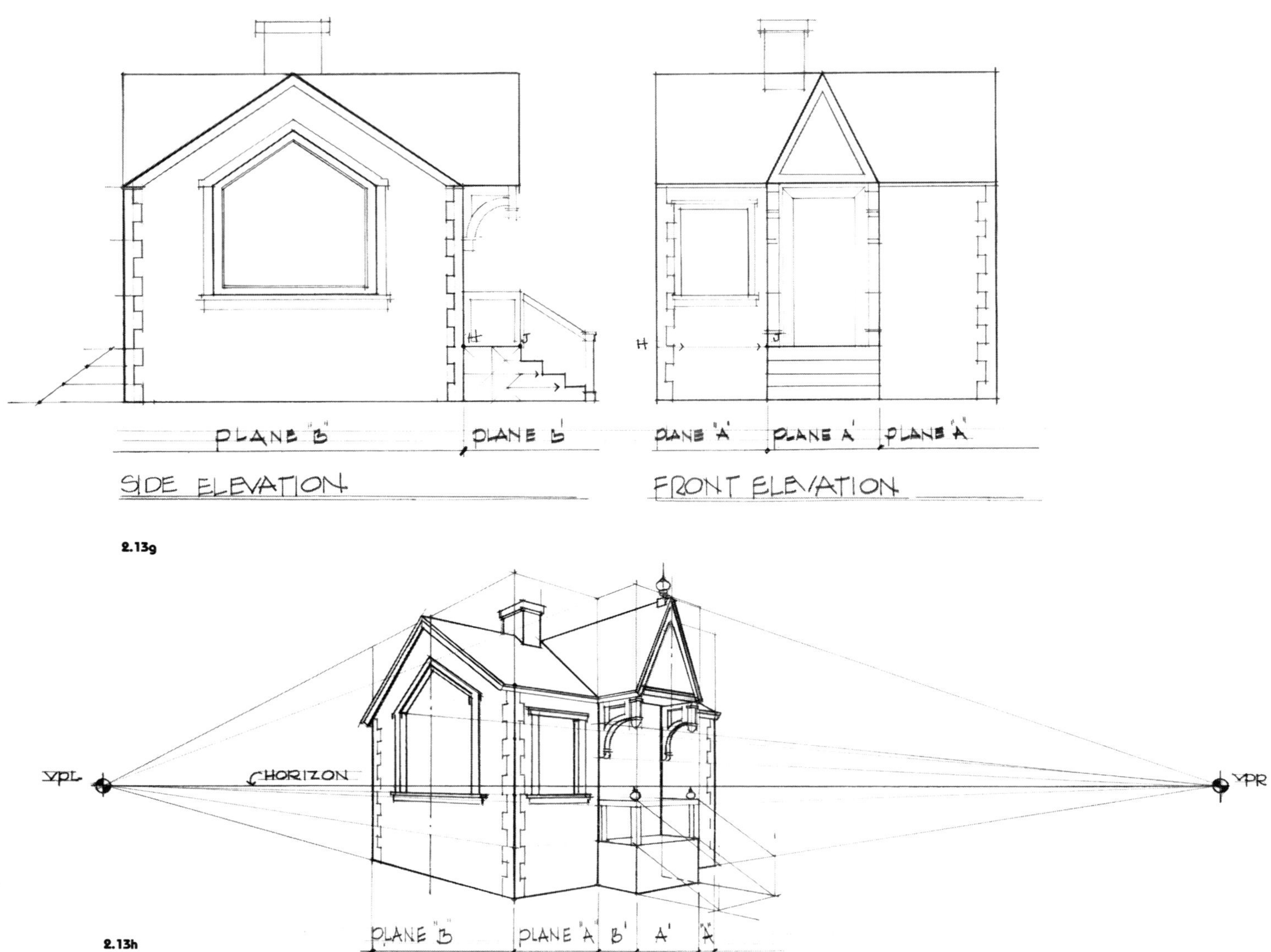

FIGURE 2.13g, h, and i In these illustrations, the roof gable and trim have been added as well as corner trim, porch trim, railings and a chimney, and decorative horizontal siding.

The Victorian trim for the porch has been plotted and lightly drawn in along with the porch railing, and its extension is forward from extended plane A^1.

Windows have been drawn by using as a guide the original equal horizontal and vertical grid divisions plotted on the elevation and perspective drawings.

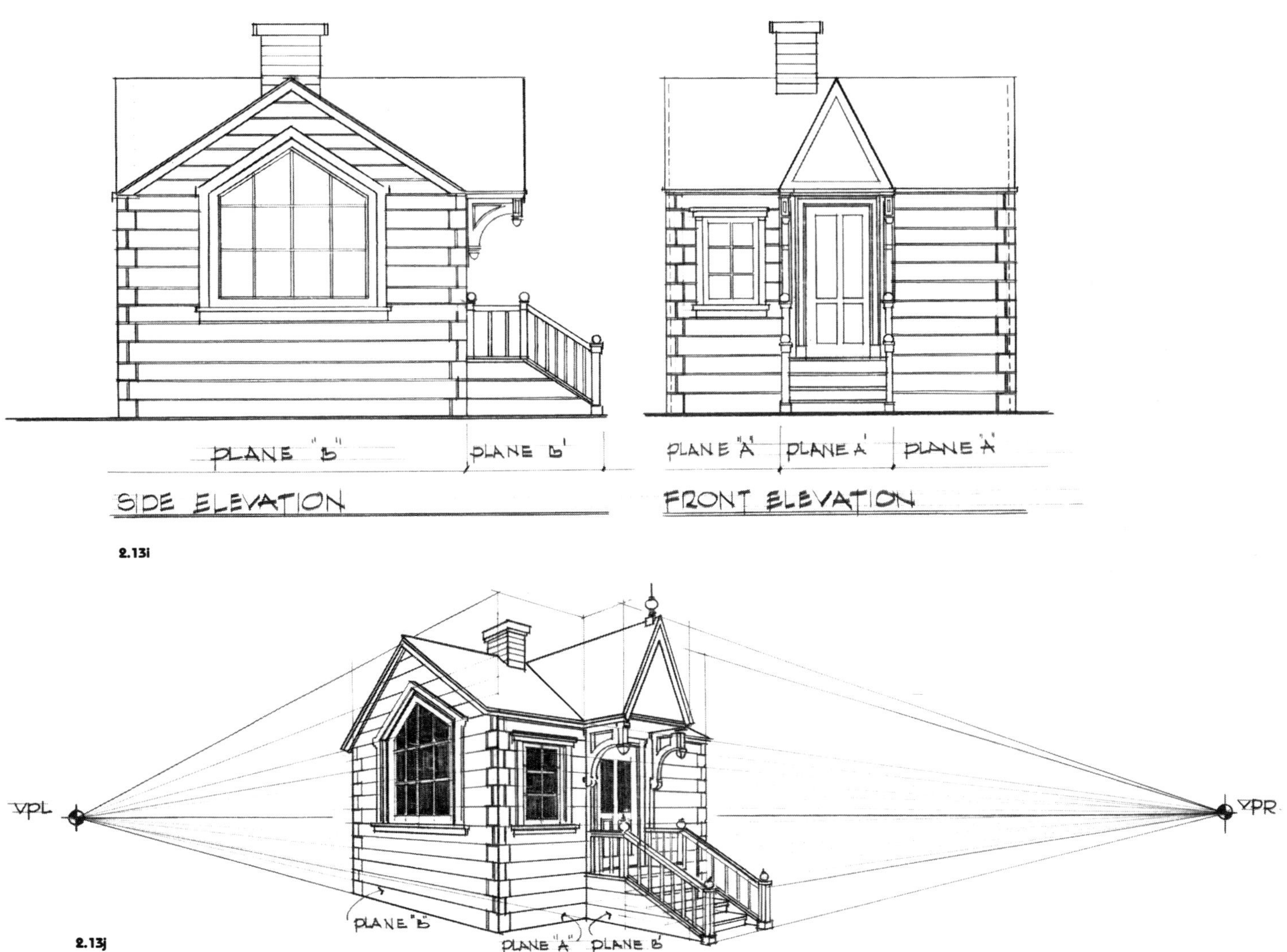

FIGURE 2.13j and k The original grid divisions have again been used as a guide in plotting the siding and corner trim on this final overlay, drawn on Clearprint 1000H tracing paper. The visual dimension has been plotted on all added decorative trim, and window areas have been darkened, leaving the thin mullions the white of the paper. All that is left to complete the illustration is the entrance path, entourage, and a suggestion of shade and shadow (explained at length in Chapter 5). Trees and plantings are used to silhouette the major outlines of the structure and to define its overall shape. Low shrubbery and a suggestion of a lawn complete the sketch.

Entourage

The original cube in Figure 2.10b has now been developed into the house in Figure 2.13j and k, and it is completed with the addition of trees and shrubbery.

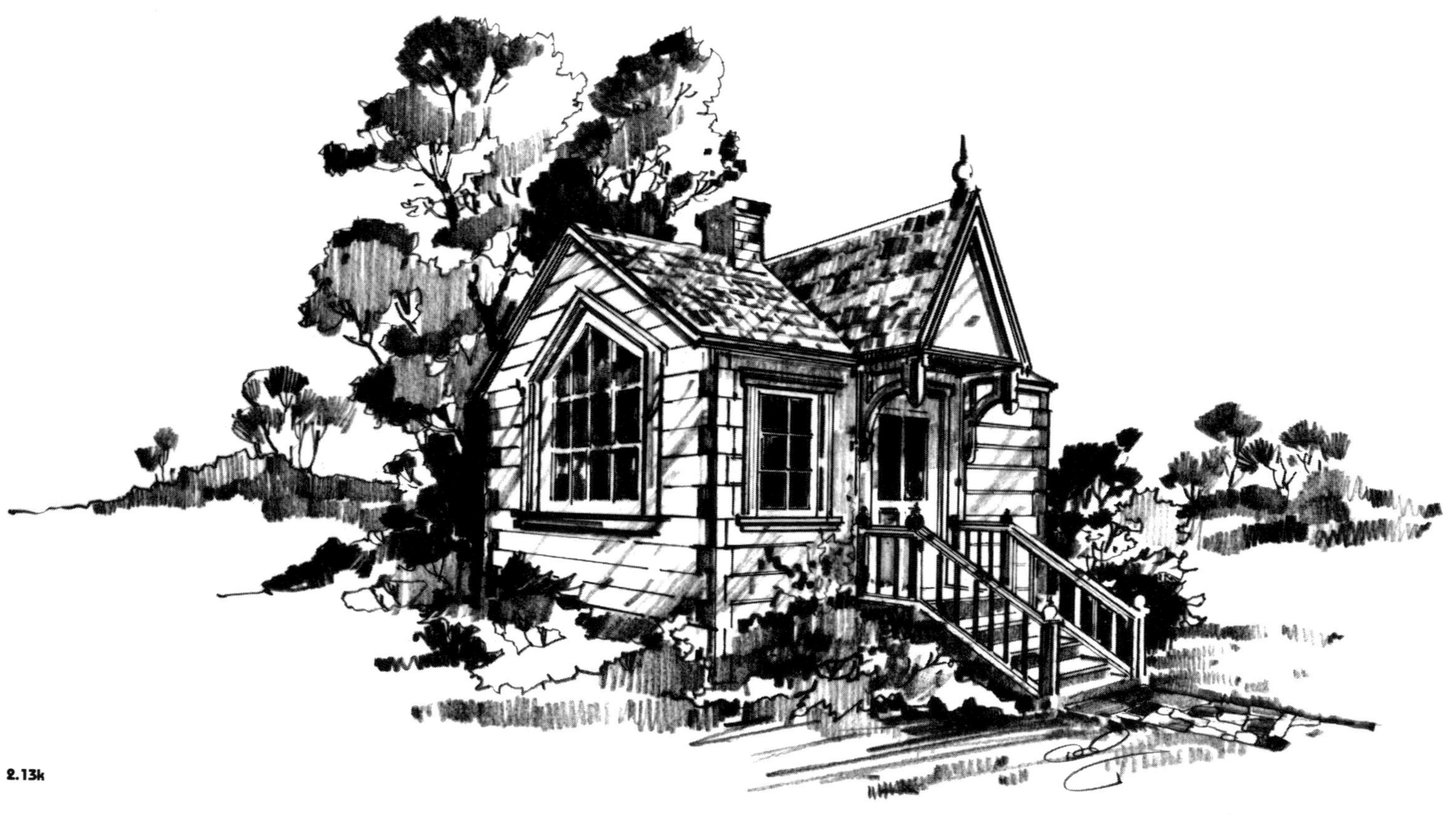

2.13k

Overview

In each step of the examples found in this chapter, the elevation view has played a large part in the layout and development of the perspective. All height divisions on the TMC were plotted by the intersecting diagonal, or slanted-scale, method. Then the face of each cube was divided into an equal grid overlay, from which all primary height divisions were located. [All major horizontal (depth) measurements were made by using intersecting diagonal lines.] As you can see from these examples, three-dimensional drawing becomes a matter of understanding a few basic principles, all of which are used in photolinear perspective exercises to follow.

These methods of proportional space division and multiplication comprise the basic preliminary steps that, when combined with photographs, will enable you to develop remodeling drawings in perspective that can show both additions to and subtractions from an existing structure, all in visually accurate scale. Horizontal scale in perspective can be plotted proportionally, but the accuracy is more visual than actual. Although it is impossible to accurately measure space that is receding to a vanishing point (one- or two-point perspective), it is possible, as you will see in Chapter 3, to create remodeling drawings and sketches that are proportionally and visually accurate.

How is this done? Again, let's continue looking at the methods that were employed on the exterior of a plain cube. But this time the principles will apply to the interior of a cube and how that interior can be viewed. We use an actual house renovation project to clearly illustrate the underlying geometry in the process.

CHAPTER 3

FROM THEORY TO PRACTICE

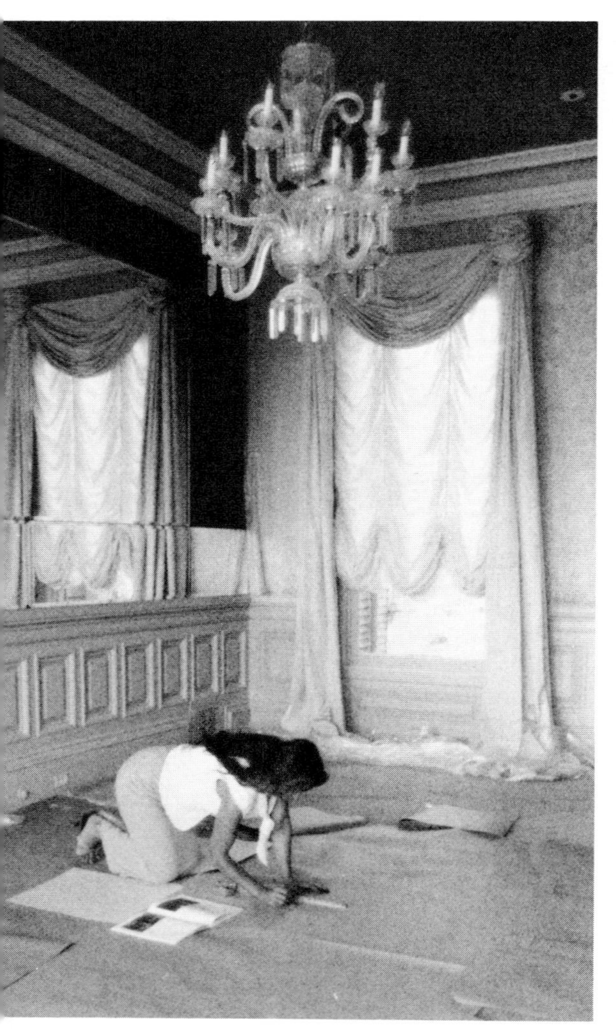

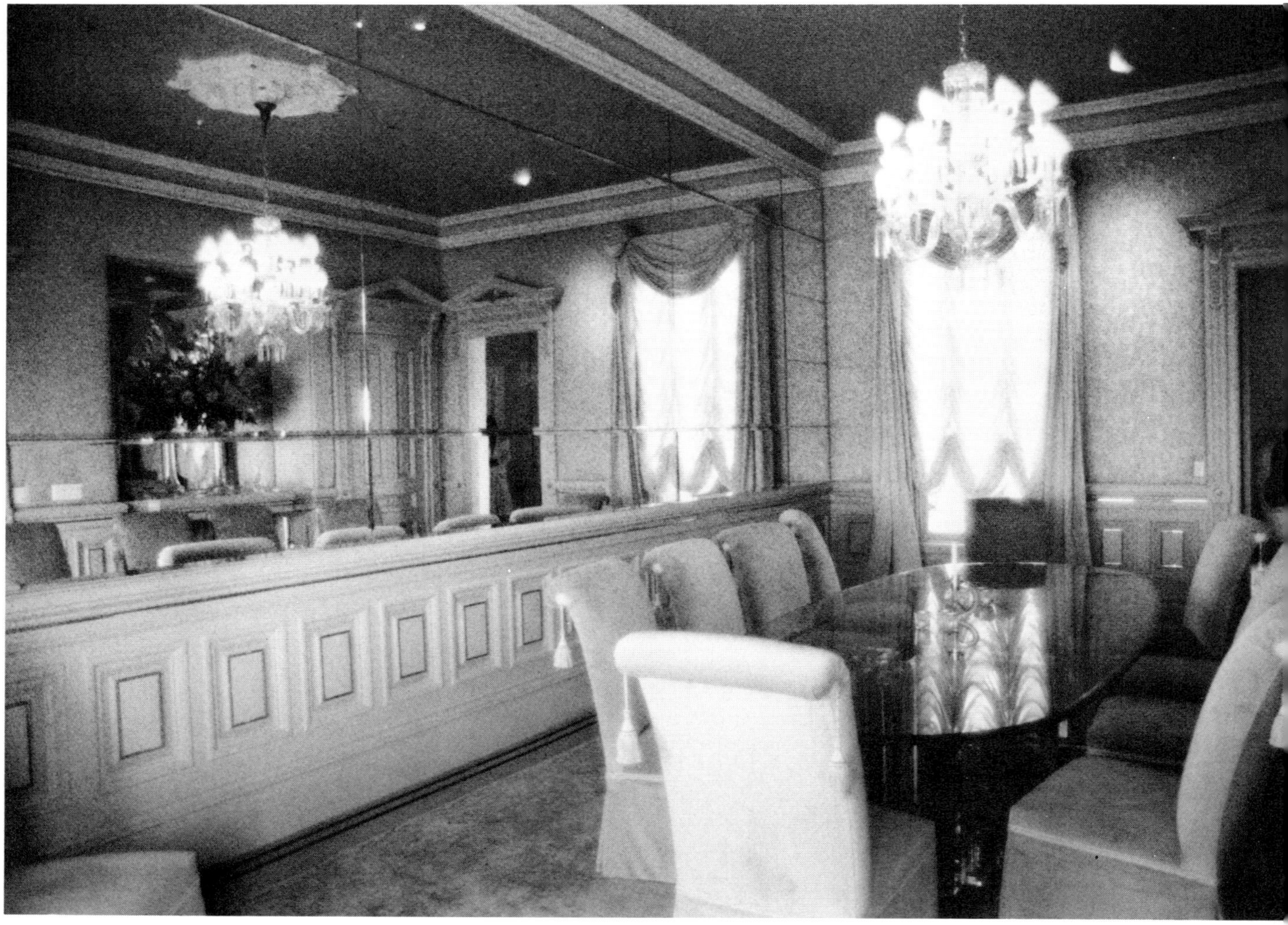

Working with Interior Space

Now that you have divided a cubic solid into equal parts by using the slanted-scale method and the method of intersecting diagonal lines, let's apply the process to some specialty conditions relating to interior photographs:

1. How to expand the area encompassed in an interior photograph for the purposes of a design sketch.
2. How to impose a grid on both the walls and the floor of the interior photograph in order to accurately place furniture or make sketches depicting architectural changes in sketches of the room.
3. How to combine two photographs of limited scope to create a single drawing that depicts a greater viewing area.
4. How to create measured floor plans and elevations that correspond to the photographs to be taken of an interior space.

Figure 3.1a and b are primary and secondary photographs taken with a 35-mm single lens reflex camera fitted with a 24-mm wide angle lens, showing the same corner of an ornate Victorian room, with each photograph encompassing only a small part of the room and each incorporating the corner of the room that is to be designated the TMC. Figure 3.2 is a line tracing of Figure 3.1 and includes the TMC, as noted.

A rough floor plan sketch and elevations of the room are shown in Figure 3.3a and b and in Chapter 1, 1.14a and b. Figure 3.1a and b shows the major elements of the room, i.e., the pediment parlor doorway to the sitting room and the full-height mirror of the living room. The roughly drawn floor plan (Figure 3.3a) and the roughly sketched perspective (Figure 3.3b) show the location and measurements of all architectural features. The placement of one arrangement of selected furniture is shown in the perspective plan view in Figure 3.3c.

The Floor Plan Grid in Perspective

To place a three-dimensional grid over the floor area within the combined photograph tracing (Figure 3.3e), you must have a starting point that can be used to cross-reference the floor plan to the photograph tracing. Furthermore, you must decide which photograph of the two shown is to be the primary photograph and used as the starting point (i.e., it will be traced to find its two vanishing points, which are used to create a final drawing). The collection of overlapping photographs,

CHAPTER 3

FROM THEORY TO PRACTICE

FIGURE 3.1a and b These two photographs, showing a Victorian living room and sitting room, will be used as the photographic beginning to the photolinear perspective theory for an interior illustration. Each photograph was taken with a 35-mm camera equipped with a 24- to 48-mm wide-angle zoom lens and includes a common inside corner (where two walls intersect). This vertical line will become the TMC for the illustrations to follow. Note the "curved" door jambs in these two photographs. This is caused by the photographer using a wide angle lens that is very close to the foreground vertical elements. This condition will be eliminated in the tracing process that follows.

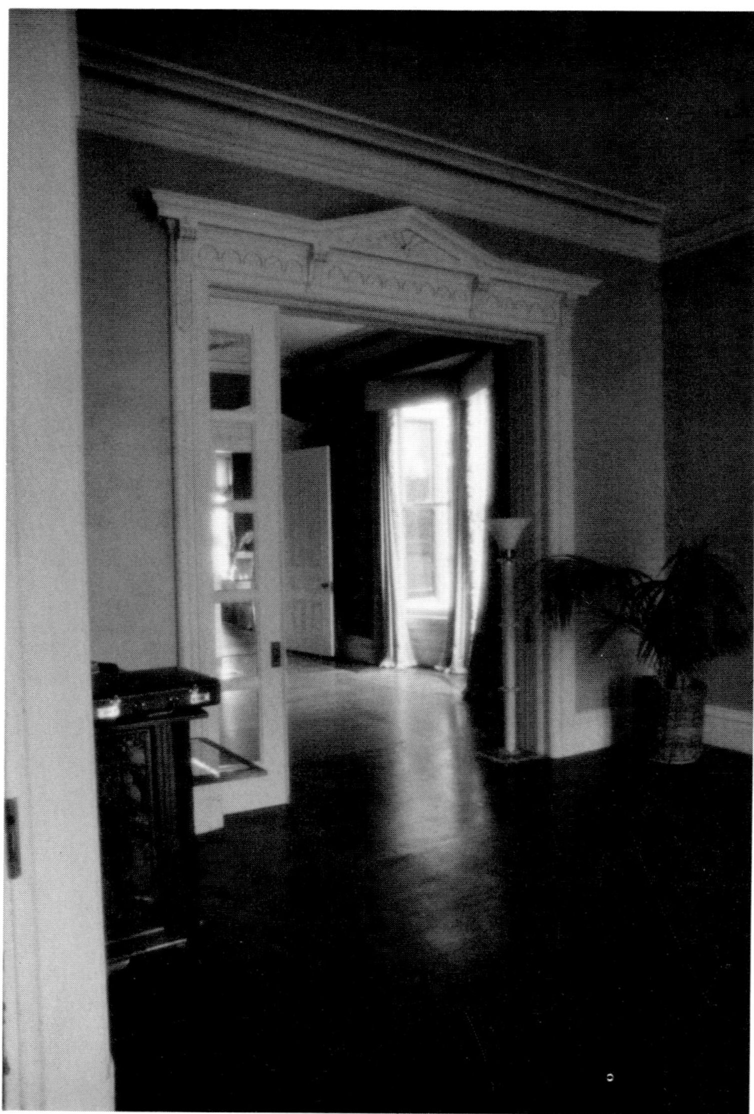

3.1a

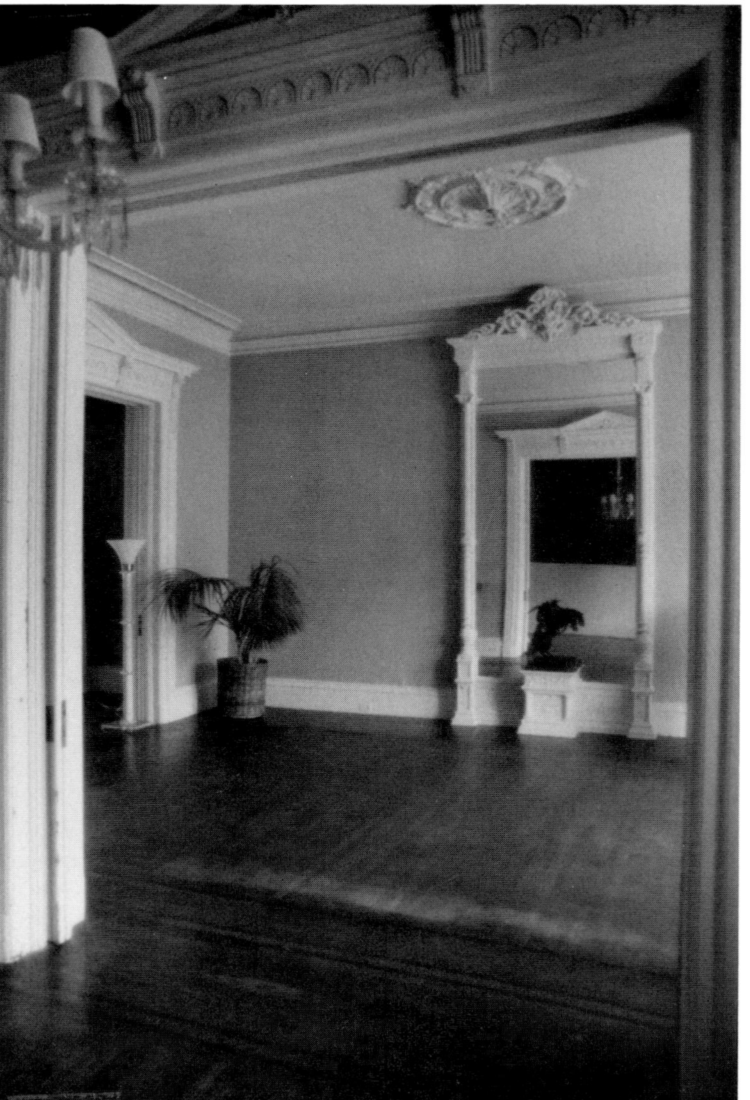

3.1b

FIGURE 3.2 This line tracing shows all the major outlines (linear representations) of the physical structure of the living room and sitting room seen in the photograph in Figure 3.1a. This tracing will be combined later, in Figure 3.3e, with the photograph in Figure 3.1b to include a representation of the living room mirror.

The intersection of the two primary living room wall planes is designated the TMC and has been photographed as vertical.

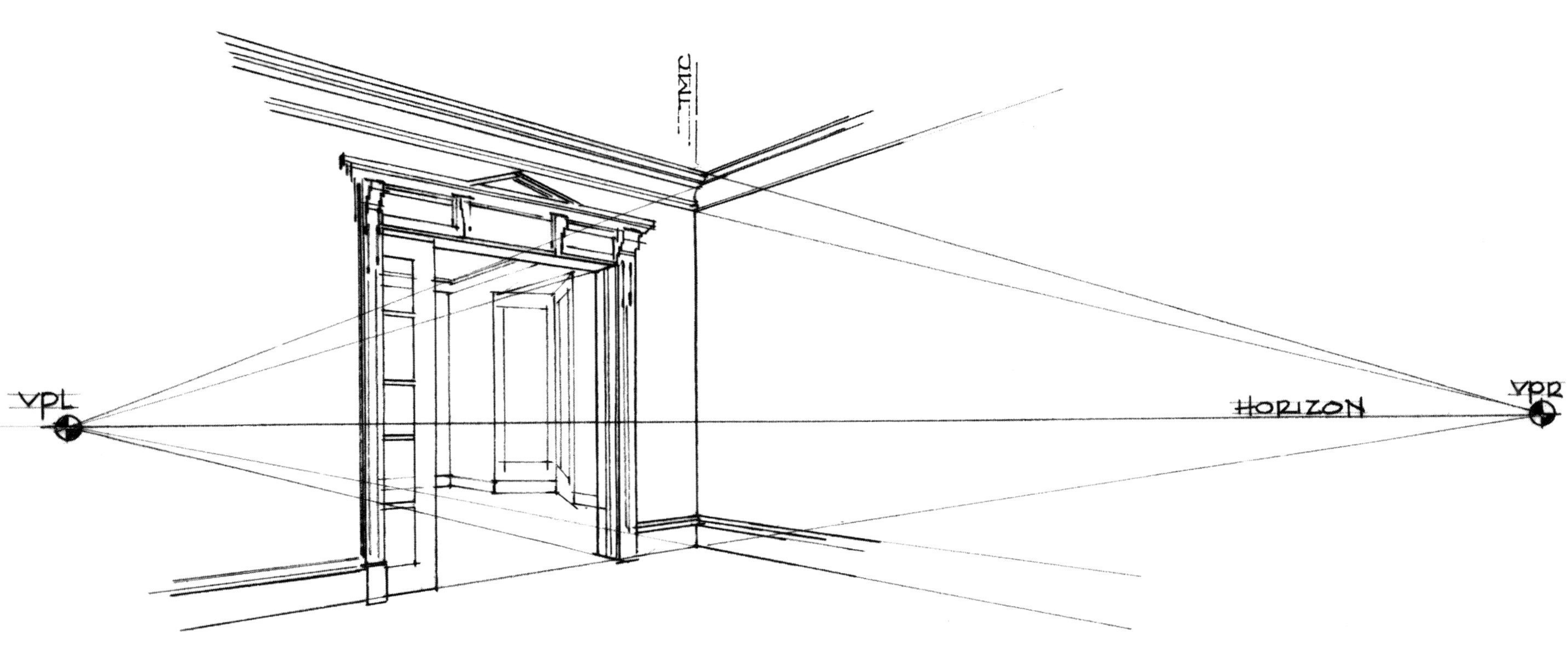

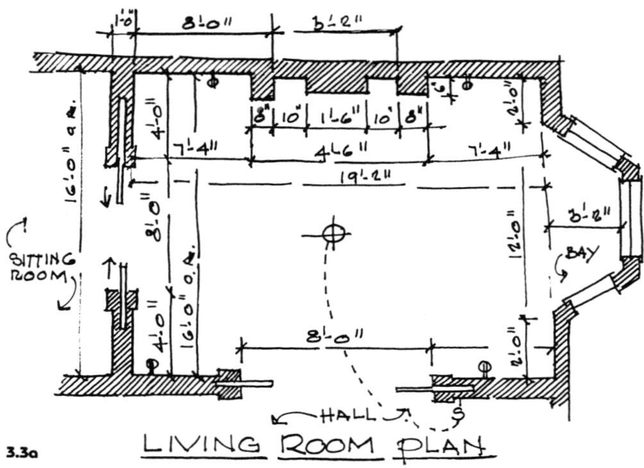

3.3a

FIGURE 3.3a and b The roughly sketched dimensioned floor plan (a) and three-dimensional line drawing (b) shown here roughly denote placement of major existing architectural features of the room so that dimensional notations may be shown. A three-dimensional drawing is much less confusing than the combined sketched plan and elevations shown in Figure 1.14b, which are necessary for noting all primary and secondary dimensions of a complex interior.

FIGURE 3.3c The drafted ¼″ = 1′0″ scale plan of the living room and partial sitting room depicted in Figure 3.1a and b is shown in perspective in Figure 3.3c, in order to achieve a realistic viewpoint of the floor plan. The camera height during photographing must be calculated in scale with the floor plan. The center of the camera lens is thus positioned 2″ (or 8 × ¼″) above the floor plan to achieve a visual vantage point that is 8′0″ above and in scale with the floor plan drawn at ¼″ = 1′0″. The furniture has been placed on the floor grid and has been darkened for clarity.

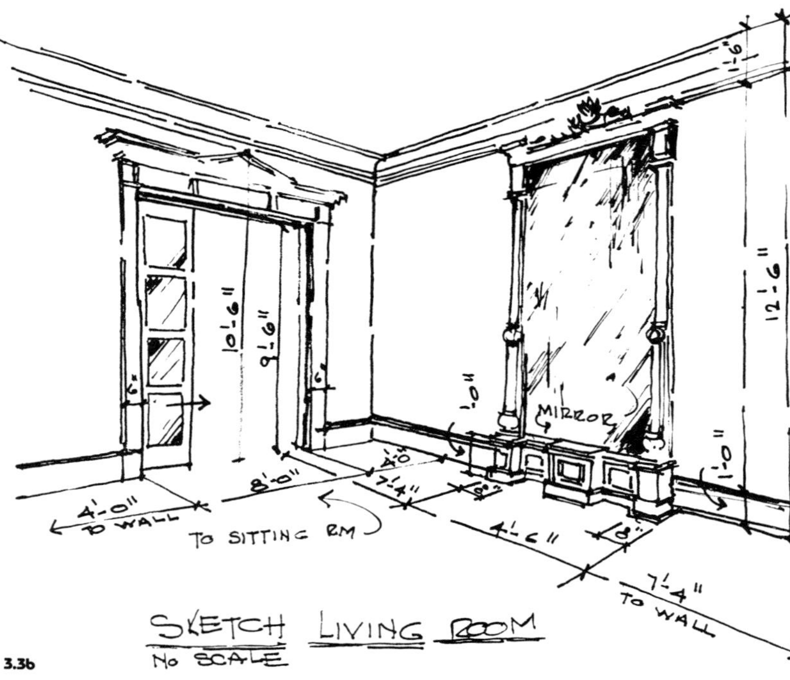

3.3b

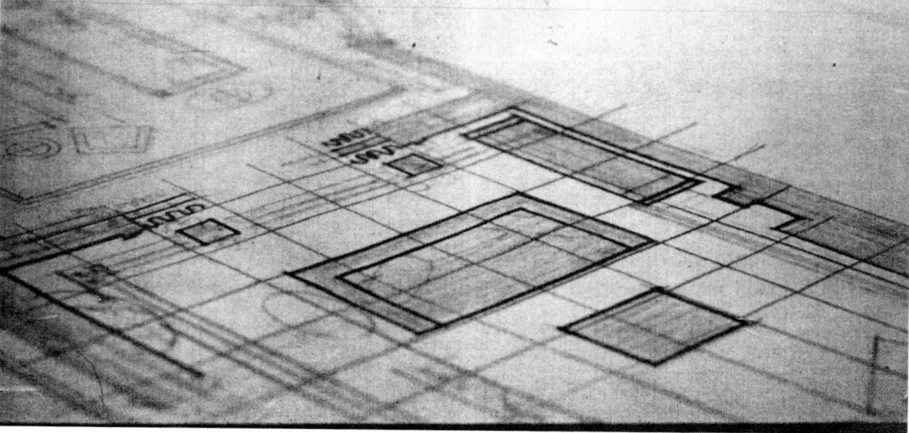

3.3c

taken from the same height and position in the room, will have the same horizon line but different sets of vanishing points (see Chapter 1, "Photographing the Interior"). Because of this, the two photographs cannot be "combined" simply by tracing elements; the final drawing must be built up from only one, by using the principles shown here. Figure 3.1a is designated the primary photograph.

Figure 3.3d shows how to divide the 8′0″ door opening by using intersecting diagonals. This technique locates floor divisions within the 8′0″ opening that are 2′0″ each. Then these divisions can be projected across the floor on an overlay of thin tracing paper. Refer to the drafted plan in perspective (Figure 3.3c) while doing this.

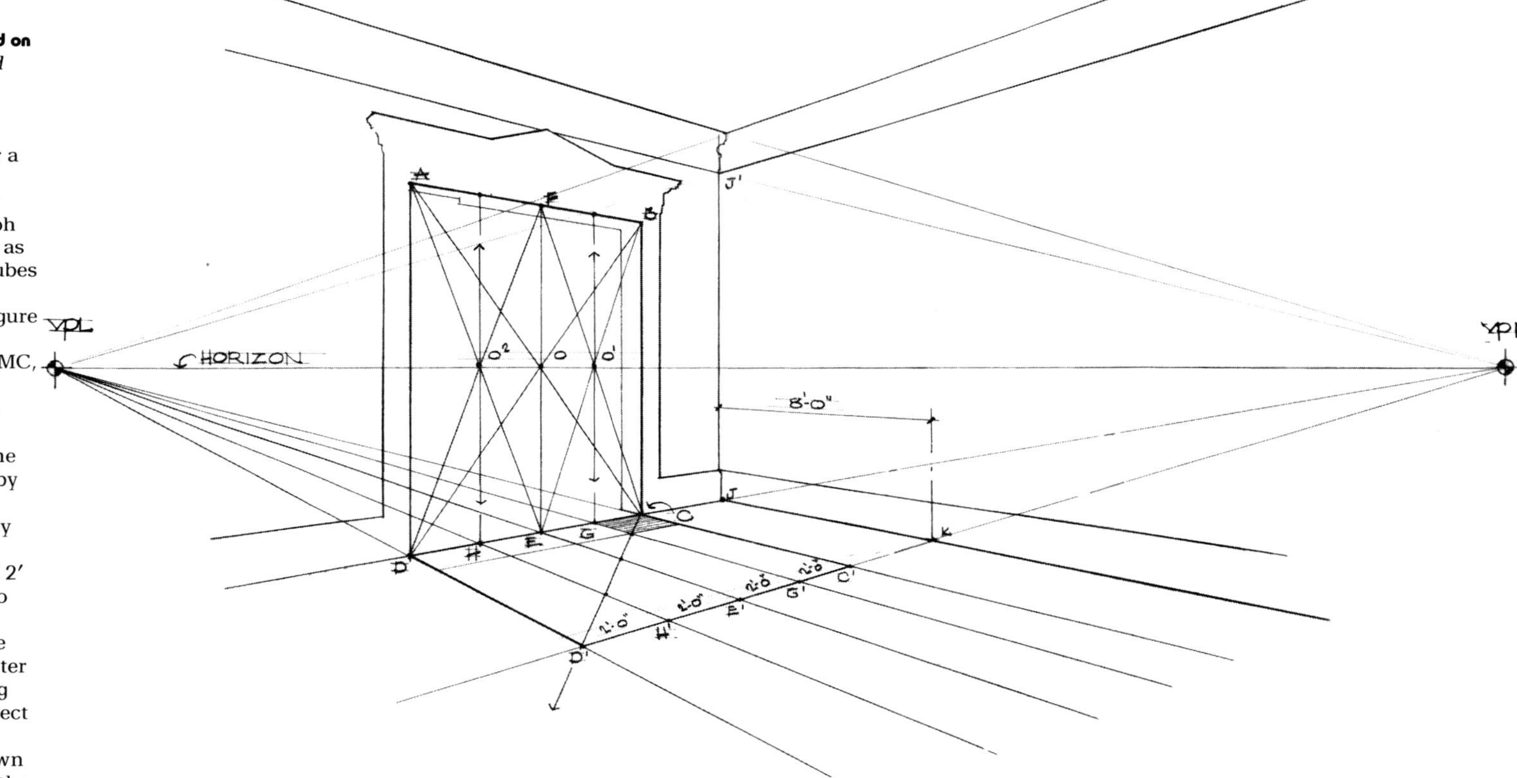

FIGURE 3.3d Creating a Perspective Grid on a Photograph *Defining the TMC and finding the vanishing points* To combine the elements in the photographs shown in Figure 3.1a (primary) and 3.1b (secondary) for a more encompassing drawing, you must first create a grid on the floor and walls of the primary photograph tracing. The same principles apply as were used to divide space on the cubes shown in Chapter 2.

Starting with the line tracing, Figure 3.1c, of the photograph shown in Figure 3.1a, you must assign the TMC, in this instance, JJ^1. This vertical plane division is later divided into vertical 1′0″ height increments.

Next, find the VPR and VPL of the primary photograph (Figure 3.1a) by tracing the main ceiling and floor lines and extending them until they intersect.

Place a ¼″ = 1′0″ reference 2′ × 2′ grid over the ¼″ floor plan. Refer to the plan in Figure 3.3c. Lay out a 2′ × 2′ floor grid on the perspective line tracing by *first* finding the center of the door opening via intersecting diagonals *AC* and *BD*. These intersect at *O*.

From *O* draw a vertical (both down and up) to intersect the floor at *E* (the center of line *DC* at the floor line) and *F*, which lies on the center of line *AB* at the door head.

Now bisect each half of the opening again by drawing diagonals *FC, BE, AE,* and *FD.* Where these diagonals intersect at O^1 and O^2, extend vertical lines down to the baseline *DC* at *G* and *H.*

The baseline has now been divided into four equal spaces in perspective, just as in the ¼″ = 1′0″ floor plan. It is also shown in perspective in Figure 3.3c.

Next extend lines an undetermined distance from the VPL through points *D, H, E, G,* and *C* across the floor to the right front of the viewer.

Refer again to the dimensioned sketch (Figure 3.3a) and perspective floor plan (Figure 3.3c). Plot a square on the floor to the right-hand base of the 8′0″ door opening that is visually square, i.e., as a floor tile would appear if viewed from the same angle (shown shaded). This is an approximate visual process that cannot be measured.

Draw a diagonal through two opposing corners of this "tile" from point *C* to the left front until it intersects the extended line from the VPL to *D* at D^1.

From *D*, which is 8′0″ across the floor from the base of the door opening *DC*, connect a line to the VPR. This will intersect the wall baseline at *K*, the approximate location of the wall-mounted decorative mirror frame and will intersect extended lines at *H, E, G,* and *C*.

Next, mark baseline *JK* on plane *B* (88″ + 8″ = 96″ or 8′0″).

The square CC^1D^1D now drawn on the floor is in scale with the photograph and is in direct relation to the floor plan. Each leg of the square is 8′0″ long.

Note: The mirror will be offset from the 8′0″ measure by 8″ (the width of the left mirror pedestal). Final placement of this architectural element is *visual* and can be easily approximated by using the 8′0″ dimension from plane *B* as a guide.

Next a 2′0″ square on the floor must be visually located (Figure 3.3d), to act as the starting point from which the grid may be established across the floor. Then the mirror taken from the second photograph (Figure 3.1b) can be located on the adjacent wall in its proper position.

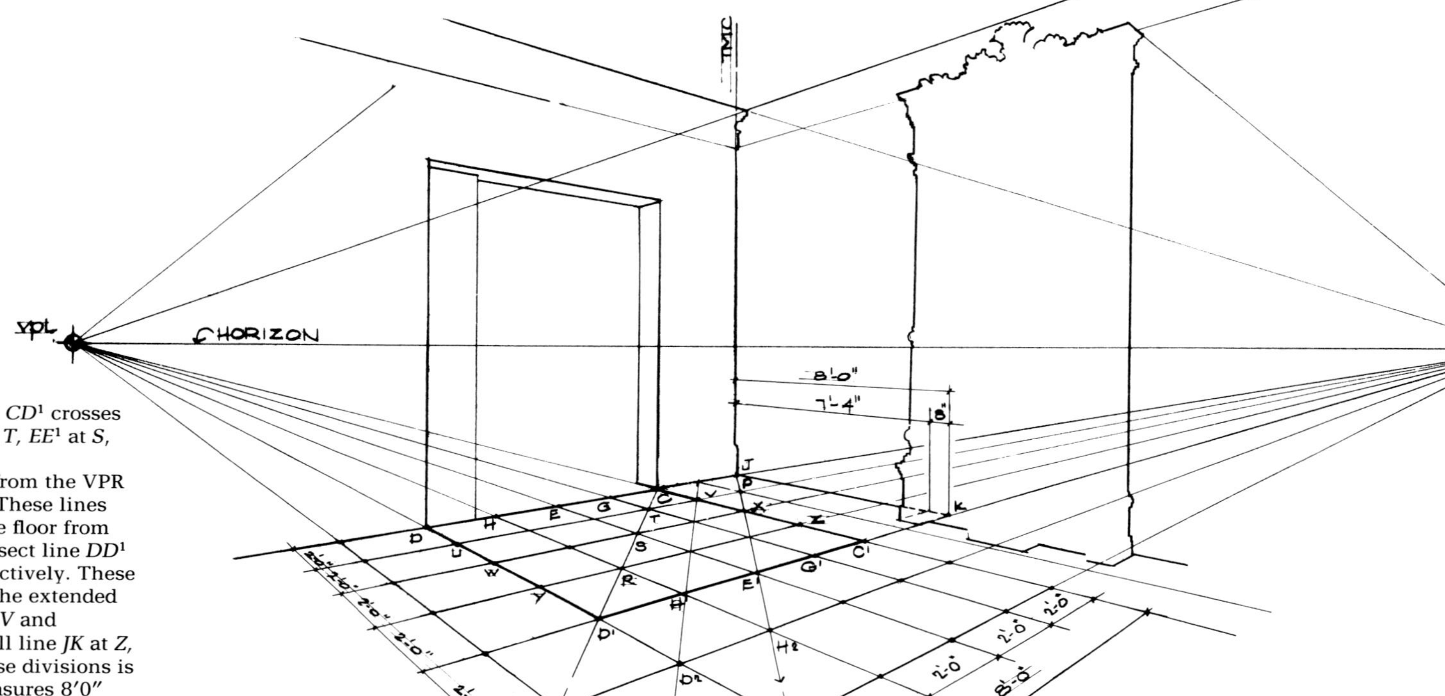

FIGURE 3.3e Diagonal CD^1 crosses extended line GG^1 at T, EE^1 at S, and HH^1 at R.

Next extend lines from the VPR through R, S, and T. These lines will extend across the floor from right to left and intersect line DD^1 at Y, W, and U, respectively. These lines will also cross the extended line CC^1 at Z, X, and V and intersect the base-wall line JK at Z, X, and V; each of these divisions is 2′0″. From J to K measures 8′0″ given the 8″ offset of the architectural mirror (refer again to the ¼″-scale floor plan in Figure 3.3c). Now square CC^1D^1D has been divided into 16 smaller squares each 2′0″ in each direction.

To extend the 2′0″ grid across the floor in any direction, we can extend a plane by using diagonals. Any diagonal will suffice, but for this illustration refer to diagonal XE^1.

Extend diagonal XE^1 forward toward the viewer. This will cross the extended line from the VPL to HH^1 at H^2 and the extended line from the VPL to DD^1D^2 at D^3.

Next draw extended lines back to the VPR from D^2 and D^3. When these lines cross extensions of all lines from the VPL, they form 2′0″ × 2′0″ squares across the floor (to the right front in this instance). You must be aware of distortion in the vicinity as these 2′0″ × 2′0″ grid squares approach the right front of the floor area.

This process can be continued in any direction to eventually cover the floor with a 2′0″ grid in scale with the photograph and relating directly to the ¼″-scale floor plan.

Once the 8′0″ extension from the door to the sitting room has been established, an outline drawing of the mirror frame seen in the secondary photograph (Figure 3.1b) can be included on the overlay. Again, this is a visual process, for the mirror cannot be traced directly since it has a different set of vanishing points from those in the primary photograph. However, the mirror can be easily drawn after its base is located with relation to the floor grid. (Note the 8″ encroachment of the mirror frame into the 2′0″ × 2′0″ grid laid out on the floor.)

First we enlarge the photograph of the mirror frame in (b) (using a photocopy process) until it is sized to the wall height at point K on the floor intersection with wall plane B (Figure 3.3a). The major height designations can then be traced from the left side of the mirror frame on the photographic enlargement and the balance drawn from visual reference within the photograph.

Once the mirror has been located and a 2′0″ grid has been projected across the living room floor as seen in the floor plan, it is a simple matter to continue this grid into the sitting room through the door opening (Figure 3.3f).

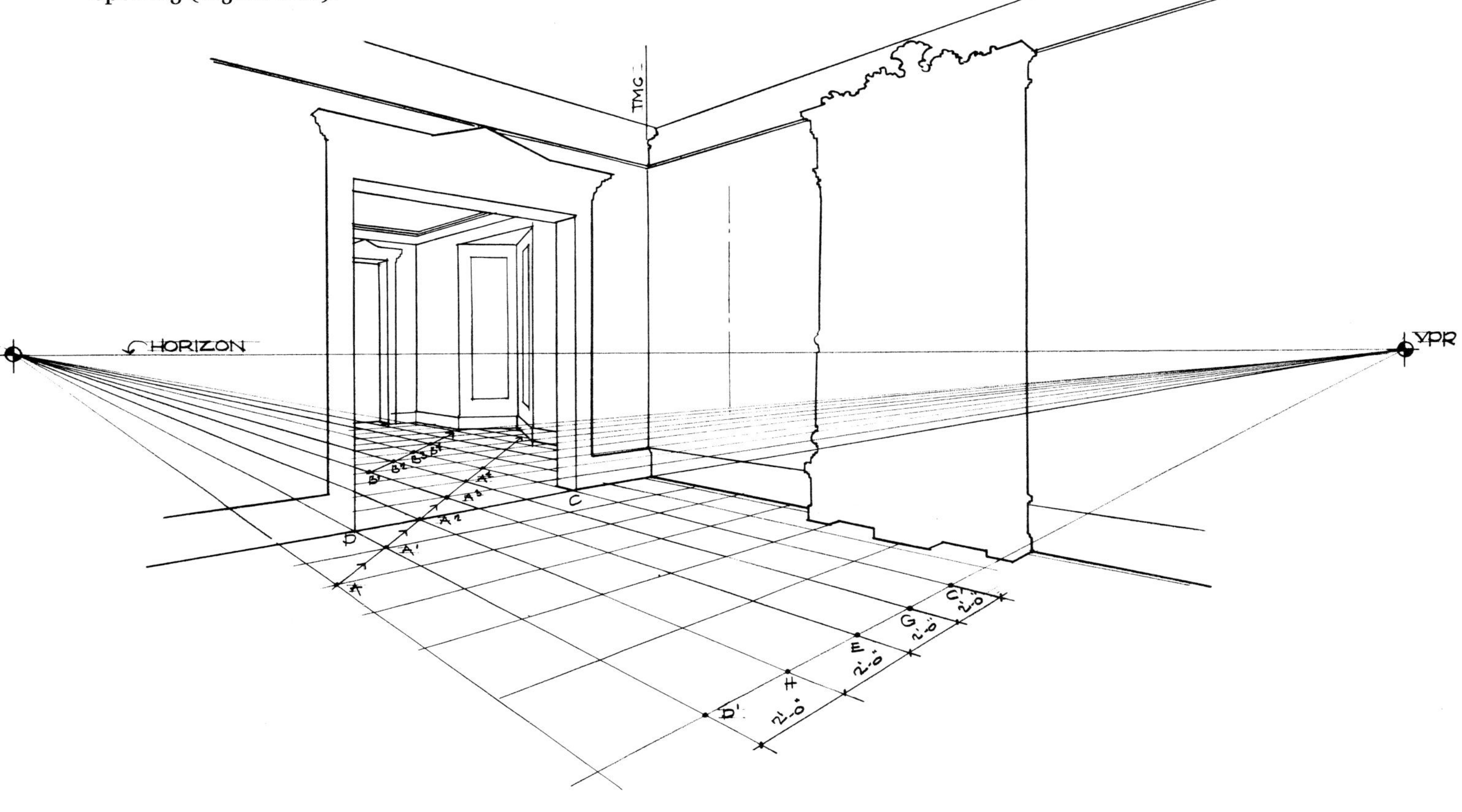

FIGURE 3.3f Once the grid has been established on the floor of the room in the foreground, it can be carried into the adjacent room, as seen through the door opening. The previous grid notations in the foreground floor area have been eliminated here for clarity.

To extend the grid into the adjacent room, begin by drawing diagonal AA^1 across the floor away from the viewer. This line will cross original extension lines from the VPL at A^2, A^3, A^4, and so on. The intersections of the original grid extension lines to the VPL create additional 2′0″ × 2′0″ squares.

By the same principle, the diagonal through B^1, B^2, B^3, *and* B^4 when repeated as many times as necessary in other areas of the floor creates a grid that covers the floor in both rooms in all directions with equal 2′0″ squares.

Combining the Two Photographs

The mirror frame outline can be drawn in visually by using the second photograph (Figure 3.1b) as a reference for size, position, and architectural detail. Remember, you will not be able to trace the mirror frame exactly as it appears in Figure 3.1b because it will have a different set of vanishing points from those located on the primary photograph (Figure 3.1a), but it is easy to approximate the details and the mirror outline. A separate overlay should be used for this and each successive step until the final drawing (Figure 3.3m) is completed.

Once the floor grid has been located and the mirror outline noted, the 2′0″ divisions that are marked on the floor can be projected up the walls to locate the division of horizontal space in scale with the photograph (Figure 3.3g).

FIGURE 3.3g Now that the entire floor grid has been established, it is easy to continue the divisions up the wall, in order to draw windows in the wall areas of plane *B* of the living room.

We begin by dividing the TMC into 1′0″ height designations, using the slanted-scale method shown in Chapter 2, for a total of 11′0″ (eleven 1′0″ units) to the underside of the cornice molding. *It is necessary to apply the grid to only the flat wall portions below the cornice molding.* Project these 1′0″ height divisions on the TMC across the wall to the right front, using lines that originate at the VPL.

The floor grid can now be extended up the wall by using the floor "tile" divisions as a guide and starting at V^1, X^1, and Z^1 and so on along the floor-wall line. These vertical extensions, when intersected by extended lines from the VPR through each vertical 1′0″ division on the TMC, will form a 2′0″ × 1′0″ grid on the wall area. This process can be repeated on the wall area to the right of the mirror after the floor grid has been extended to the right front.

Note the distortion that occurs as the floor and wall grids approach the area of the VPR to the right front of the drawing. This condition always occurs in a two-point perspective drawing if the picture area approaches the vanishing points too closely.

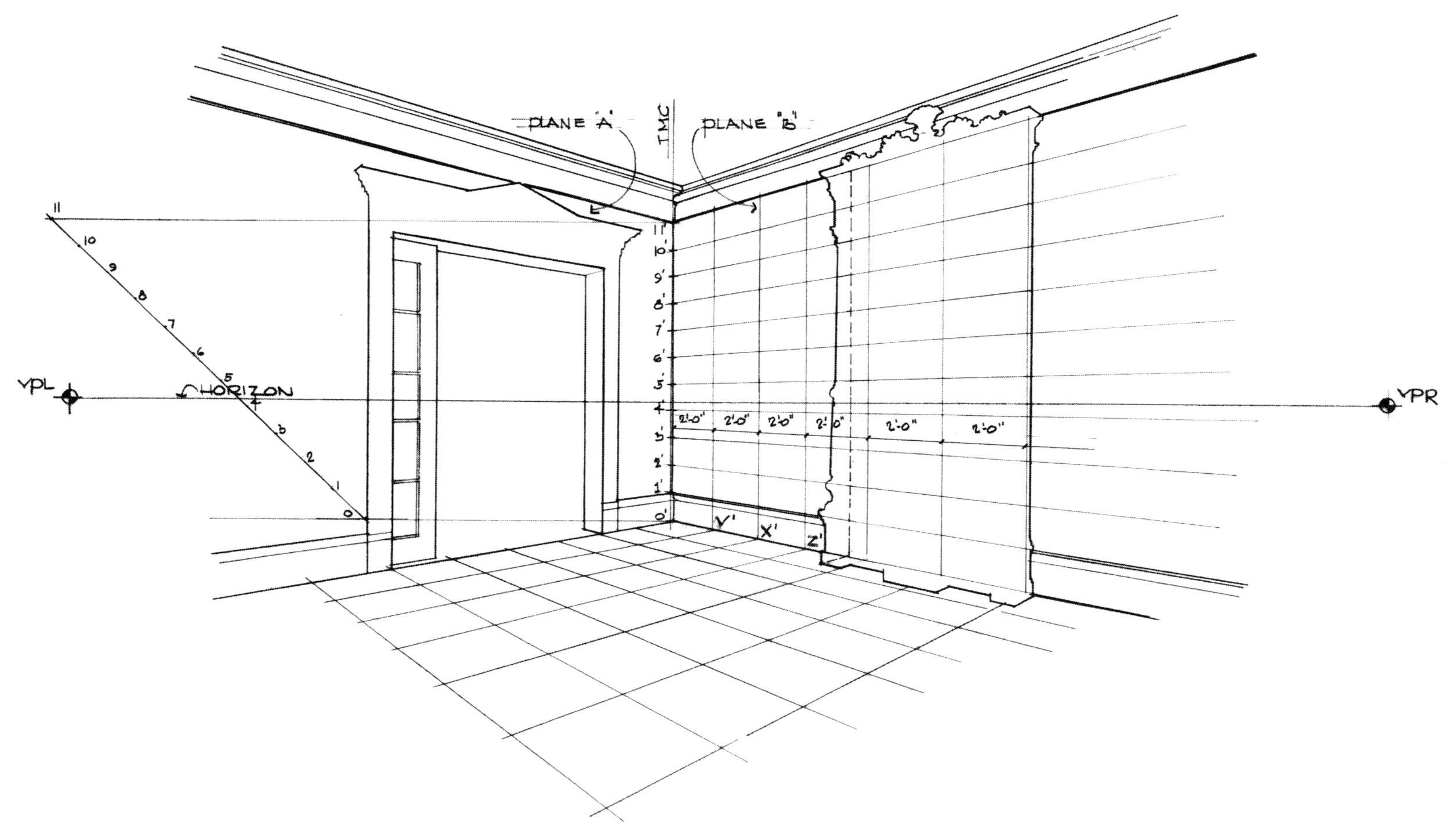

Vertical Height Division with the TMC as a Guide

Vertical 1′0″ height divisions must be located on the TMC, by using the slanted-scale method shown in Figure 2.7a. These division lines, when projected from the VP along the walls, will intersect the vertical lines projected up from the floor grid, to create visually accurate 1′0″ × 2′0″ grid designations on the wall surfaces. From this you will be able to establish the proposed new window locations, shown in Figure 3.3h and i.

Locating the New Windows

Windows, because they will be centered on the walls to each side of the mirror frame, can be located by either of two methods.

1. The windows can be located by using the vertical grid on the wall surface, as shown in Figure 3.3g.

2. The windows can be centered on the wall through the use of intersecting diagonals (Figure 3.3h).

Of course, the head and sill heights are projected from those found on the TMC. The distortion factor in the foreground must be considered, and the drawing must be stopped before those areas are reached. Figure 3.3h shows to what extent the viewing area must be contained to keep the foreground wall and floor areas as distortion free as possible.

Figure 3.3i shows an overlay drawing depicting the finished windows in position. Note the plane designations *A* and *B*, and remember that even the smallest three-dimensional objects within the drawing will have these two planes if the objects incorporate planes that are parallel or perpendicular to the primary wall surfaces.

Figure 3.3i was traced from Figure 3.3h to include only the major architectural features, both existing and proposed, of each room. Note also the absence of floor and wall grid lines (for viewing clarity) and the inclusion of the sitting room walls that were traced from the original photograph (Figure 3.1a), as seen through the door opening.

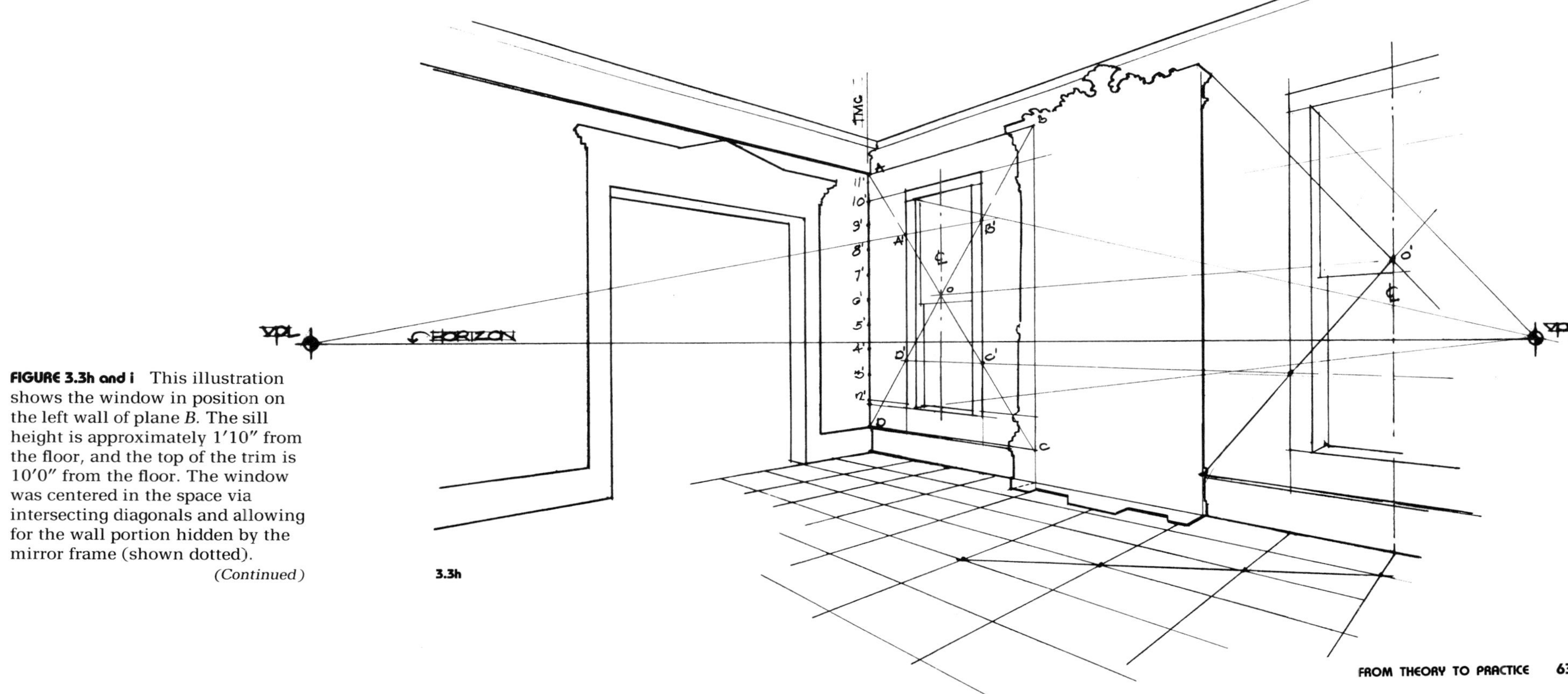

FIGURE 3.3h and i This illustration shows the window in position on the left wall of plane *B*. The sill height is approximately 1′10″ from the floor, and the top of the trim is 10′0″ from the floor. The window was centered in the space via intersecting diagonals and allowing for the wall portion hidden by the mirror frame (shown dotted).

(Continued)

The window to the right of the mirror cannot be shown in its entirety because of its location. It is too close to the VPR, creating distortion that is too great as the right front of the drawing is approached. Figure 3.3i shows the completed window to the left of the mirror and a suggestion of the window to the right of the mirror.

Note again the plane designations *A* and *B*.

Locating the Furniture

Once the floor grid, wall grid, and major architectural features are located on separate overlay sheets, the furniture shown on the floor plan (Figure 3.3c) can be drawn in. Using coordinates of the grid for easy location, find the floor area covered by each item of furniture and determine the height of the box onto which each piece can be drawn (see Figure 3.3j).*

* A more detailed description of this process can be found in Leach, *Techniques of Interior Design and Illustration* (New York: McGraw-Hill, Architectural Record Books, 1976).

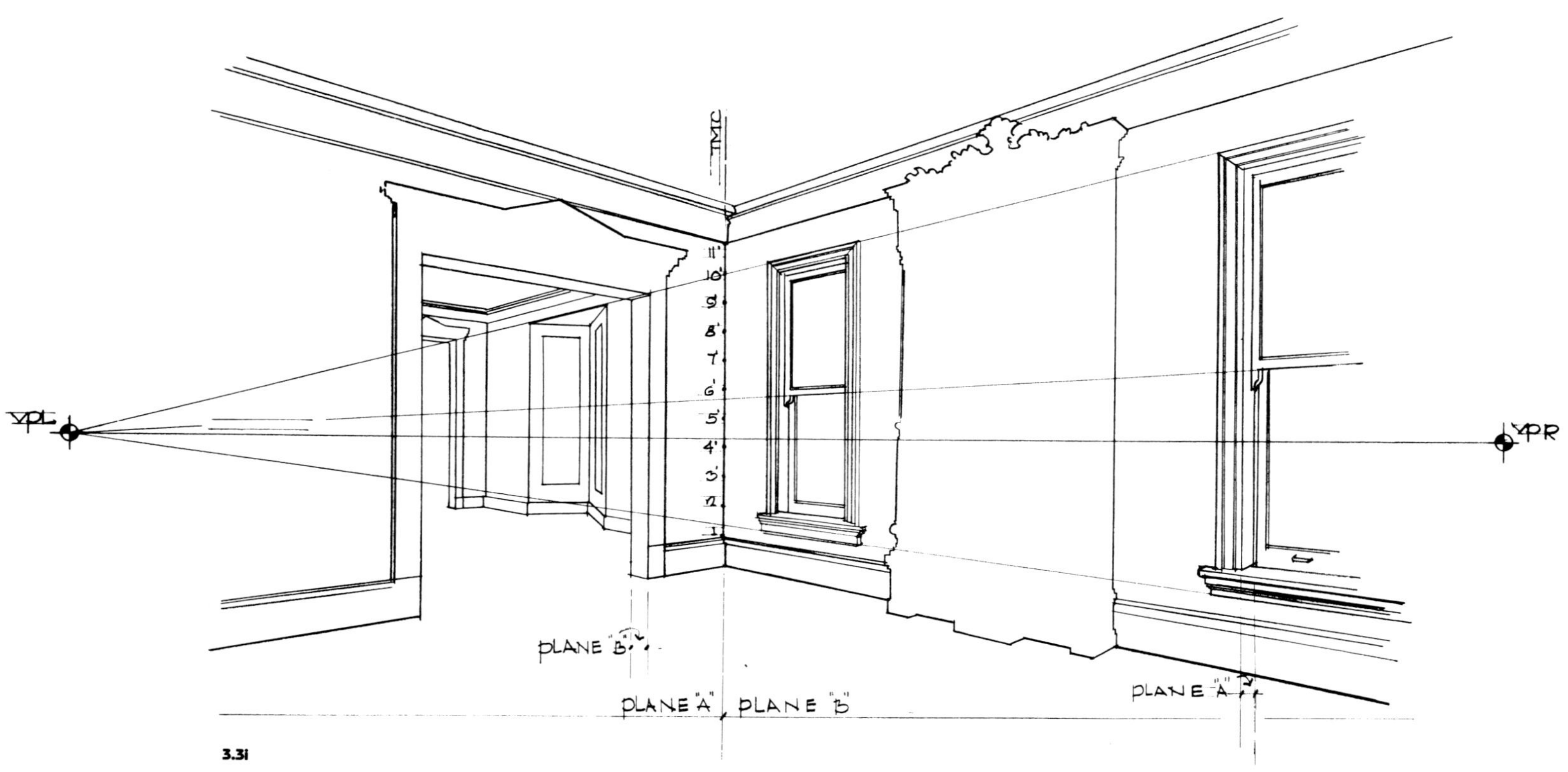

3.3i

FIGURE 3.3j Preparation for Final Illustration The final task in this illustration is the placement of the furniture as shown on the ¼″-scale plane in Figure 3.3c. Refer to the 2′ × 2′ grid placed on the plan to aid locating the furniture.

Locate the area covered by the sofa by counting grid sections from each wall and placing a dot at points *A*, *B*, *C*, and *D*. This is done by comparing the grid-covered floor plan and the perspective grid and by locating corresponding coordinates on each.

Next find the height of the box that is to contain the sofa (2′6″ high including pillows) by noting the 2′6″ height on the TMC at *H*.

Extend a line from the VPL through *H* along the wall at the 2′6″ height until the line intersects vertical line C^1H^1. Point C^1 is found by extending baseline *DC* of the sofa's cubic solid toward the VPR until it reaches the base-wall intersection at C^1. Vertical height C^1H^1 is the 2′6″ height noted on the TMC.

Now extend vertical lines up from the sofa baseline to intersect the height line extension (from the VPR to H^1) at C^1 and D^1.

Connect points D^1 and C^1 to the VPL to find the upper box corners A^1 and B^1.

The box has now been positioned on the floor grid in its proper relation to the ¼″-scale floor plan.

The small table to the left of the sofa can be located via the same procedure.

Accessories

Drapery suggestions, chandelier location, and definitive furnishings are drawn next on a separate overlay sheet (Figure 3.3k and l), with the rug position, pictures, and a lamp noted. Figure 3.3k shows an alternate sketch without windows. This is also drawn on a separate overlay sheet. Be sure to locate each tracing paper overlay with register marks in at least two opposite corners of the sheet. Of course, these marks will not be kept in the final drawing of the space.

The Final Drawing

Figure 3.3m shows how all overlay sheets are combined into one to create a presentation drawing. The final tracing was executed on Clearprint 1000H tracing paper. Plants, accessories, shade and shadow designations, and creative line work provide the viewer with an exciting, visually accurate drawing that had as its origin two combined photographs and a floor plan.

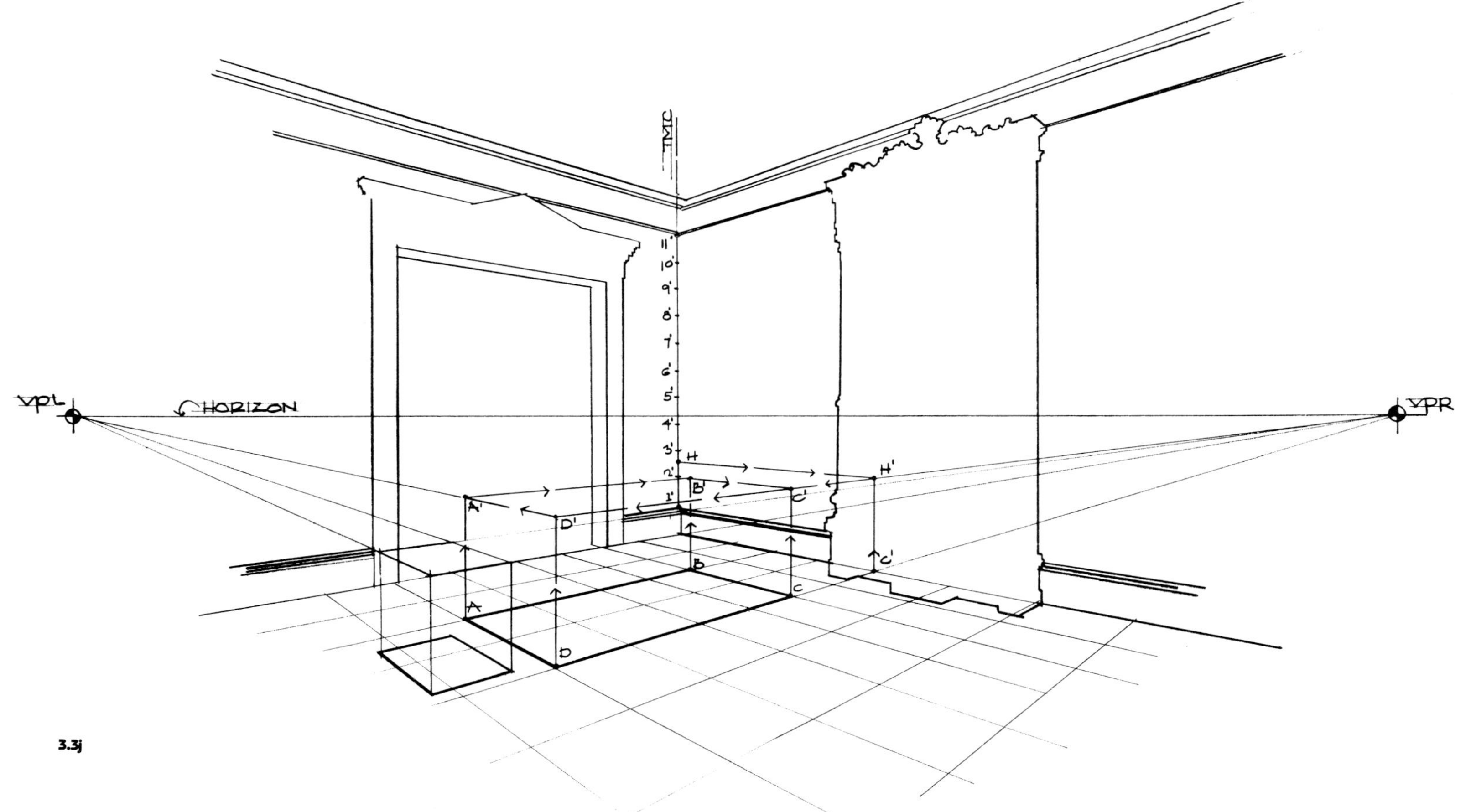

3.3j

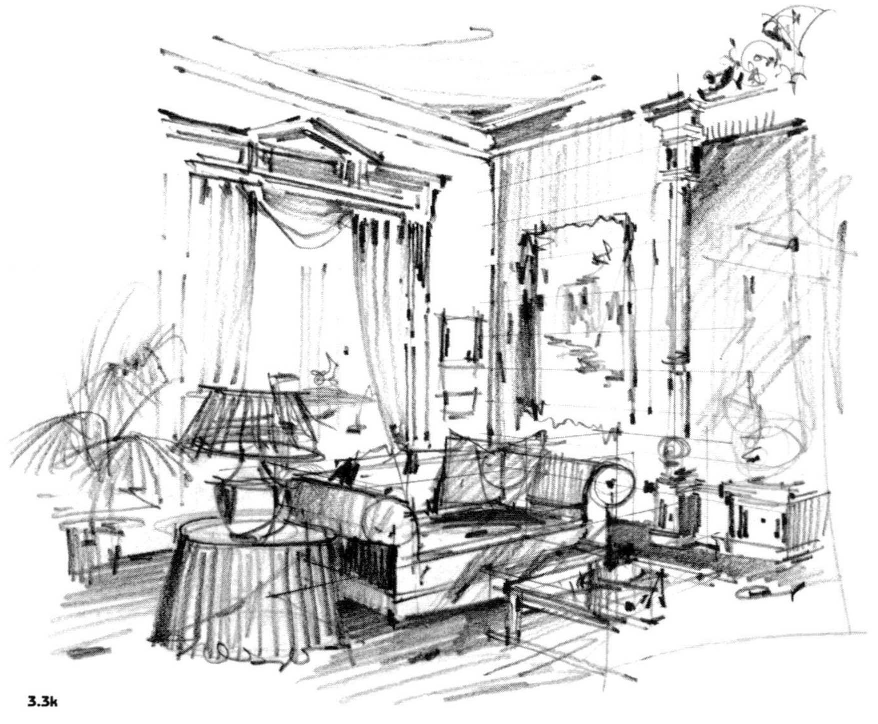

3.3k

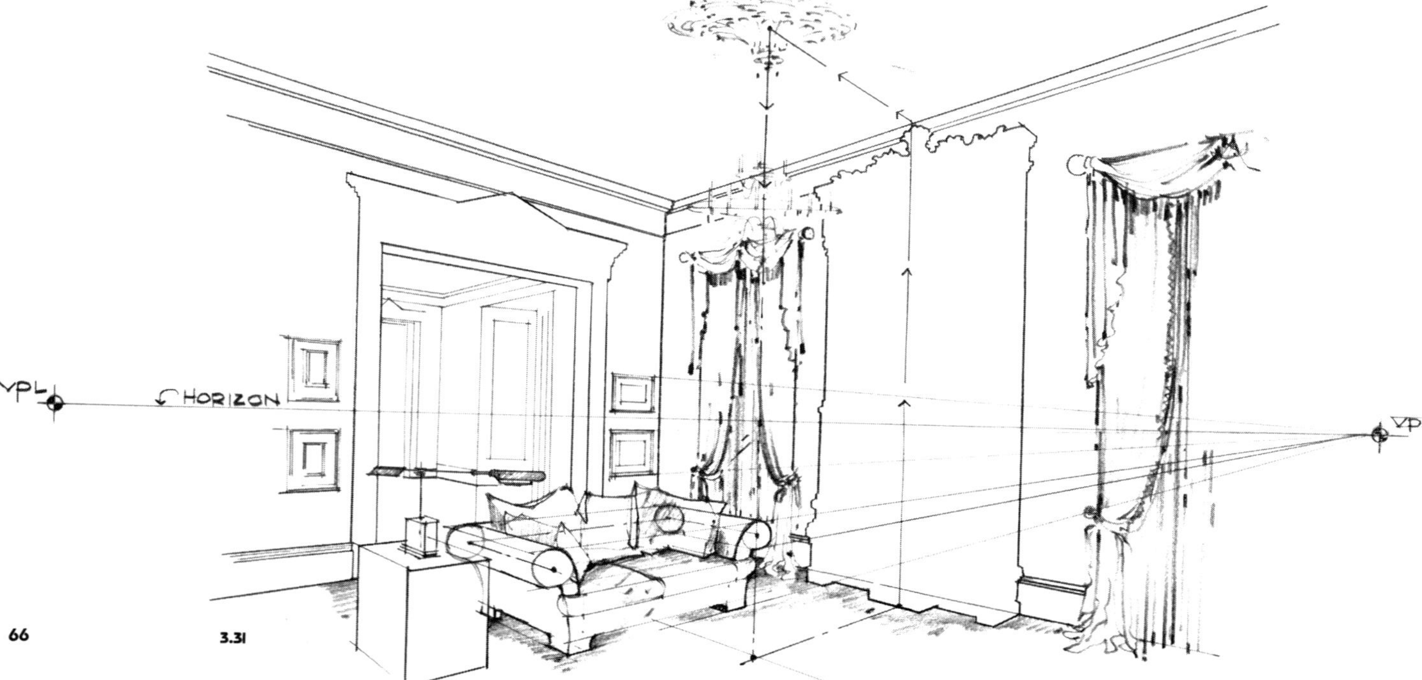

3.3l

FIGURE 3.3k to m Figure 3.3l shows the completed sofa with pillows contained in the box shown in Figure 3.3j. The addition of the traditional drapery, pictures, and chandelier is a final touch before the final drawing is begun.

Figure 3.3k shows an alternate design study scheme for this room without windows on both sides of the mirror. This view shows a very rough sketch of an alternate scheme and does not include a complete representation of the room. Note that all construction lines are visible in this study because the drawing is drawn as *transparent* until all overlays are registered and positioned for tracing onto either frosted Mylar or Clearprint 1000H tracing paper.

The final steps begin by combining all overlay sheets into one drawing. You must draw into this final presentation drawing only those elements that are to be retained, leaving out any unwanted areas, construction lines, horizon lines, vanishing-point designations, and all register marks.

Once the linear work is satisfactory, the suggestion of shade and shadow can be created on a value study and work on the final pencil drawing can begin. Figure 3.3l begins to show dimension on the furniture. This process, of course, has been carried to completion in Figure 3.3m. Note the careful pencil delineation of architectural elements such as the mirror and pediment doorway, furnishings, and, of course, the careful pencil application used to create the suggestion of shade and shadow based on the three-value system noted in Chapter 5.

The pencils used were of the 2H, H, F, and 2B varieties. The paper chosen was Clearprint 1000H tracing paper.

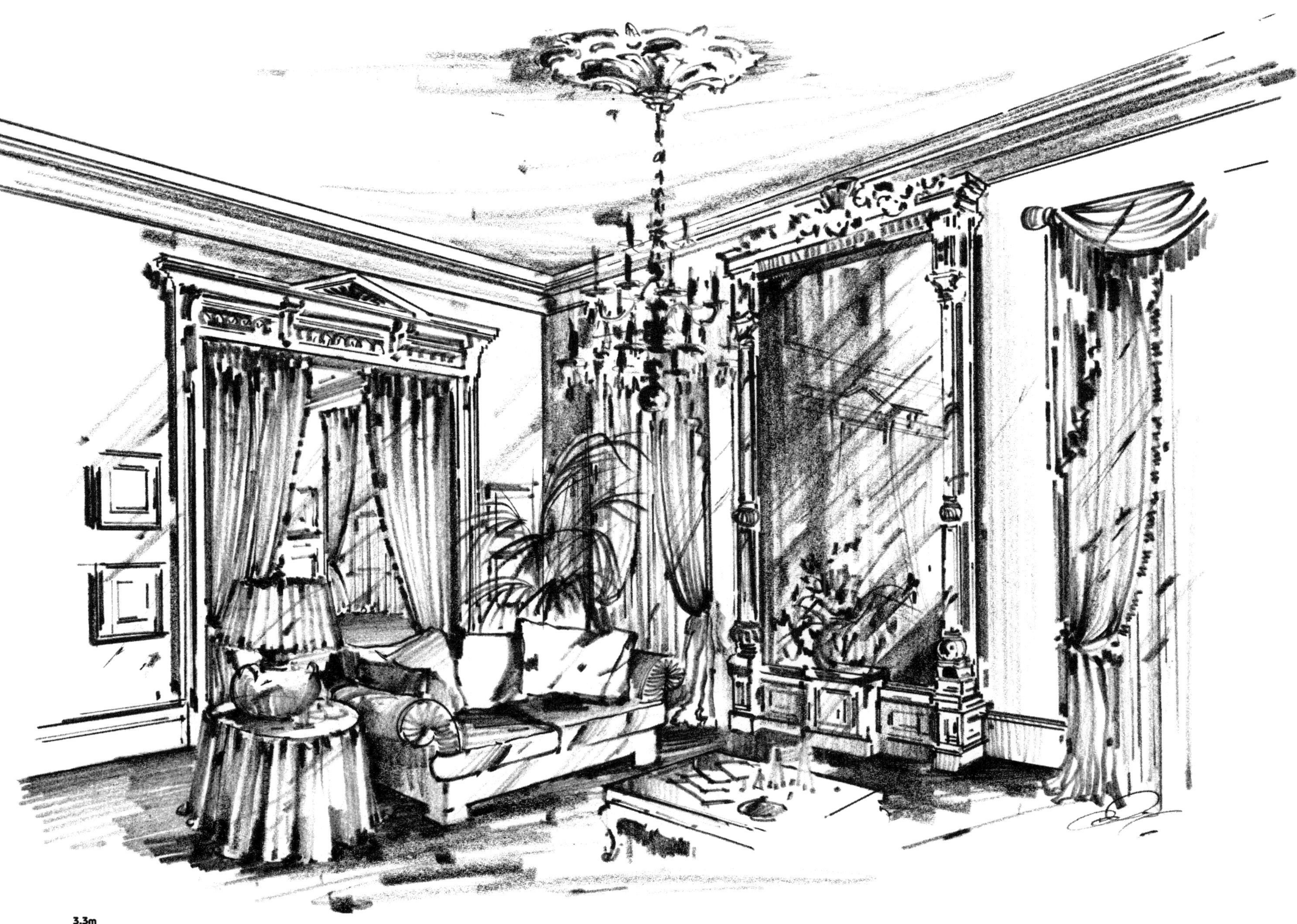

3.3m

Figure 3.3n and o shows two pencil renderings based on the combined photographs (Figure 3.1a and b). The alternate furniture layout was located first on a drafted floor plan, and then on the line tracing of the space, in a similar manner to that used for Figure 3.4d through m. Drapery was added to the design in Figure 3.3n to give the feeling of a more enclosed living area than that shown in Figure 3.3m, and the proposed windows were removed from the sketches as well.

FIGURE 3.3n and o These two illustrations show various furniture and drapery suggestions and alternate views of the same rooms as in Figure 3.3m. These views do not show windows to either side of the decorative mirror.

The strength of the intricate architectural detail in a period house such as this can be captured more economically in design sketches and presentation drawings if these complex elements can be traced directly from photographs, as was done here.

PROJECT: Residential remodel
PROJECT DESIGNER: The author
ASSISTANT DESIGNER: April Kinsburg

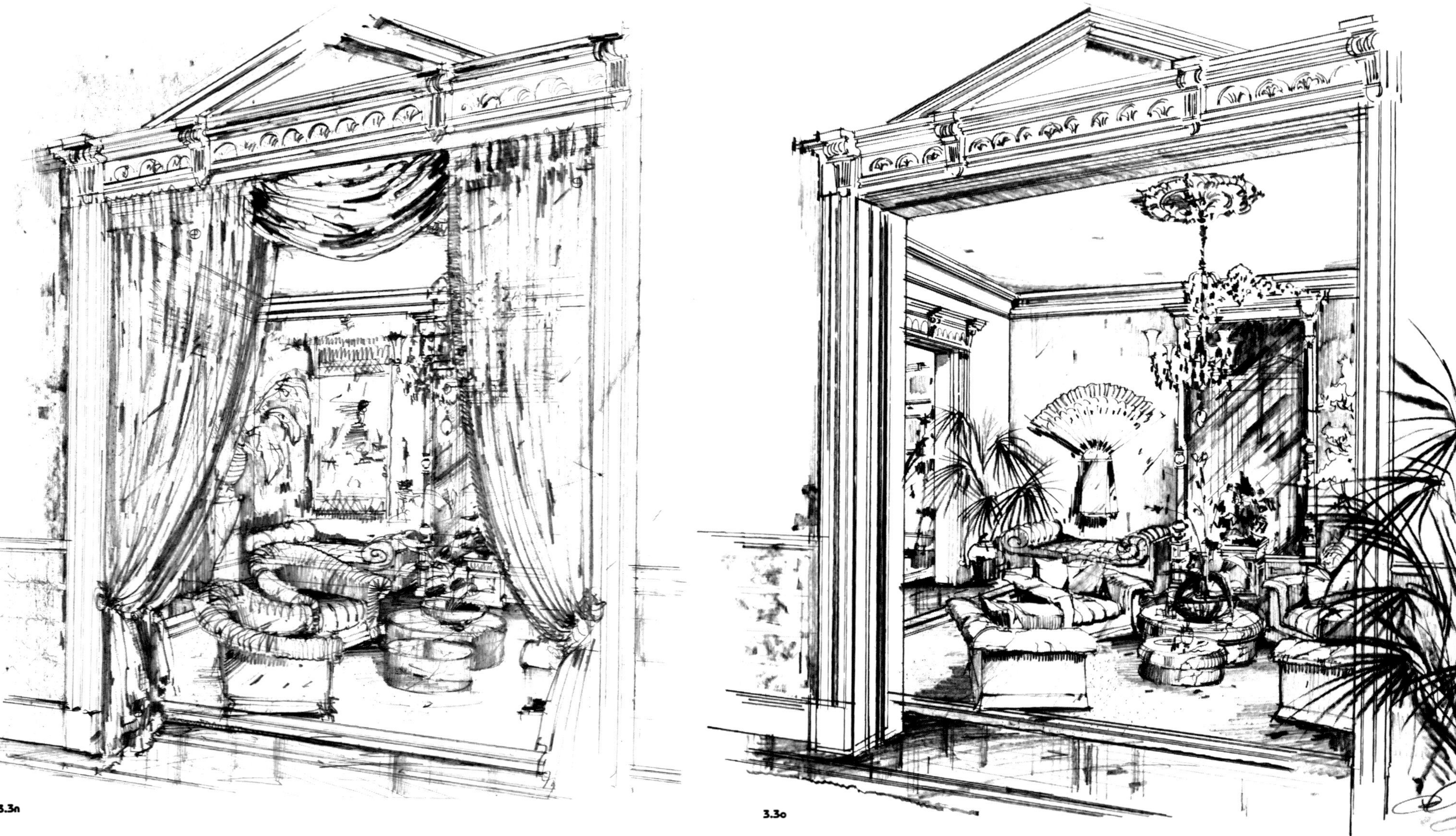

3.3n

3.3o

CHAPTER 4

THE PROJECTED ELEVATION: AN ALTERNATE METHOD OF SPACE DELINEATION

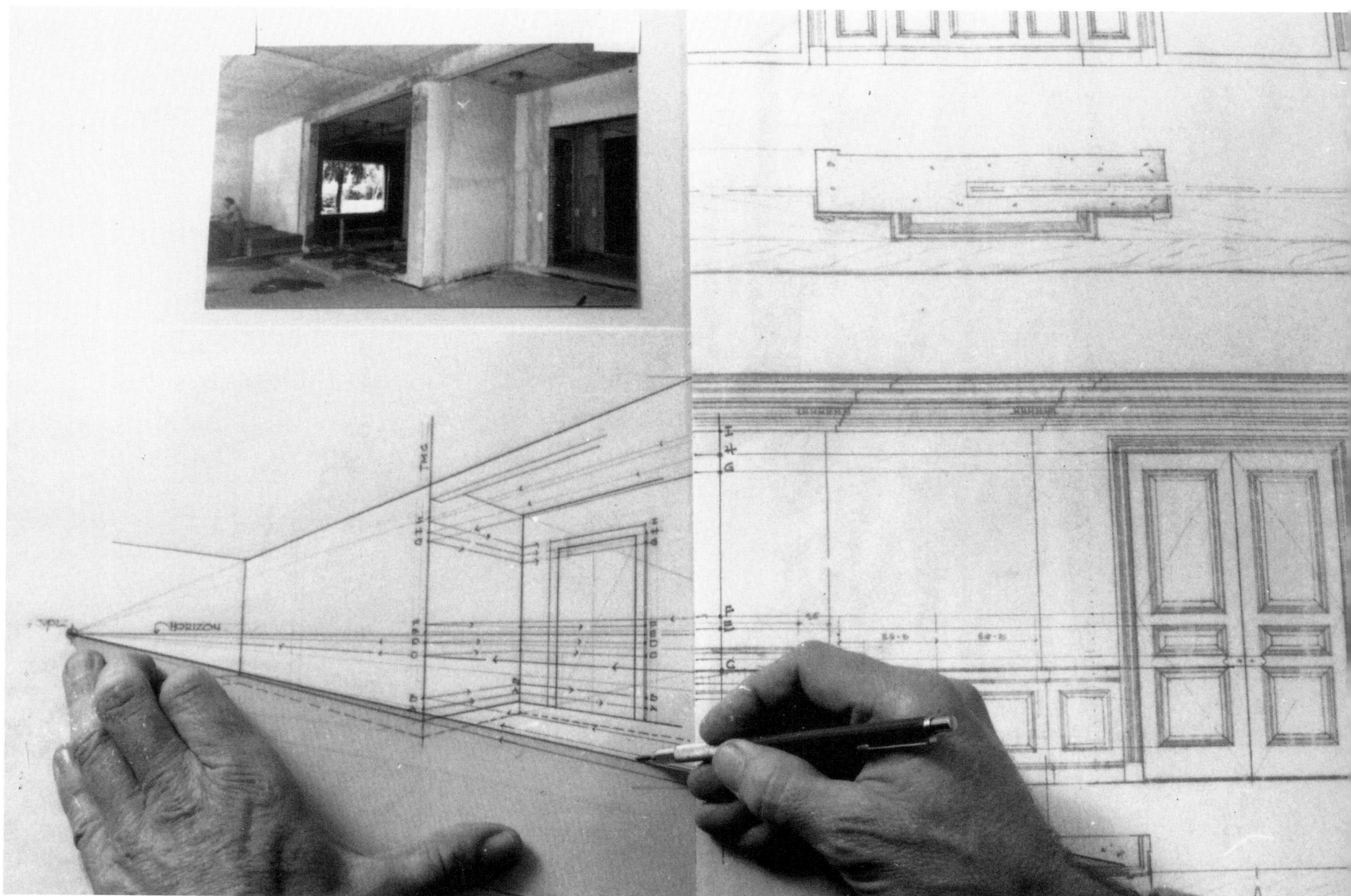
HORIZON

CHAPTER 4

THE PROJECTED ELEVATION: AN ALTERNATE METHOD OF SPACE DELINEATION

An alternate method of creating a design sketch from a traced photograph incorporates the projected elevation. In this method actual heights of all major architectural features are projected directly from an elevation of the space to the chosen TMC.

This system works well when the wall areas require a very complicated breakup of both horizontal and vertical space, as is found in the elevation of this stately living room wall (Figure 4.1a). This wall area is shown also in the photograph (Figure 4.1b) of the space under construction.

Tracing the Photograph and Assigning the TMC

The photograph of the basic building skeleton will be traced and used for the final drawing. However, the process requires a number of tracing-paper overlays to accomplish the task.

Figure 4.1c shows the line tracing of the photograph, with major lines traced to find the VPR and VPL. The TMC — located on the rear and foreground vertical corners of the room — will be divided into 10 equal height increments to help in dividing the major fireplace wall into 10 equal visually accurate horizontal spaces via the slanted-scale method shown in Figures 2.7 through 2.10. First, the height division was accomplished on the rear wall vertical intersection via the slanted-scale method, and then each division was projected forward from the VPL across the face of the fireplace wall, to create equal vertical height divisions on both the wall surface and the TMC.

Dividing the Wall Surface Using Intersecting Diagonal Lines

A diagonal line was drawn from opposite corners of the wall. Where this line intersects the 10 equal height divisions, lines were brought down to the baseline, partitioning the horizontal space into equal, visually accurate increments, all in scale with the photograph and the line perspective drawing (see Figure 4.1d).

The major wall extensions that form the projection for the chimneypiece were located merely by counting the designated wall divisions to the left of the TMC and darkening these lines. Refer to the elevation (Figure 4.1a) during this process.

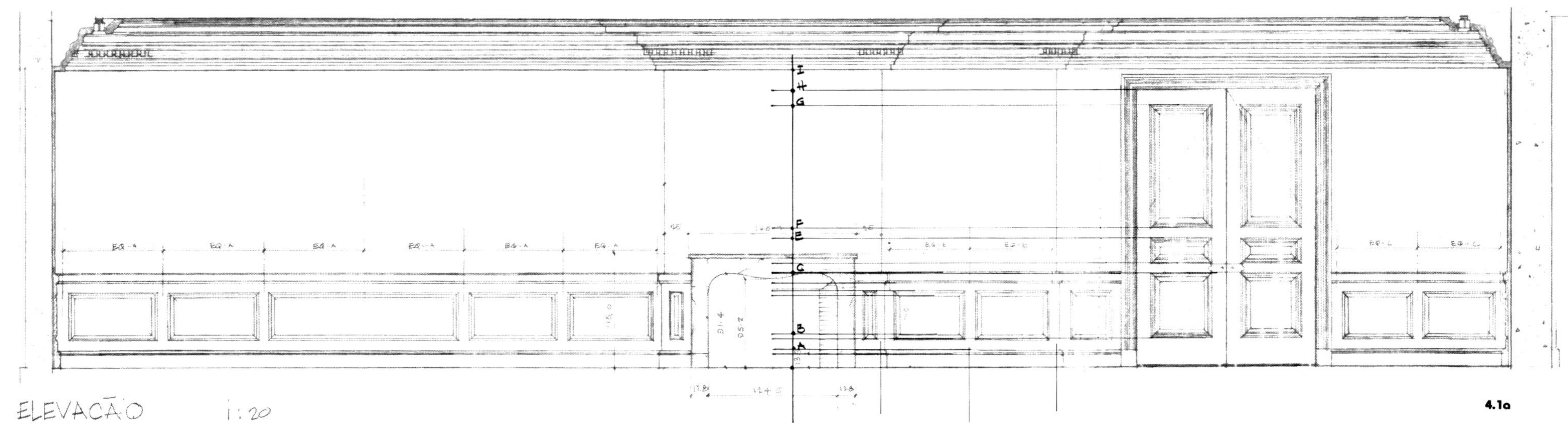

4.1a

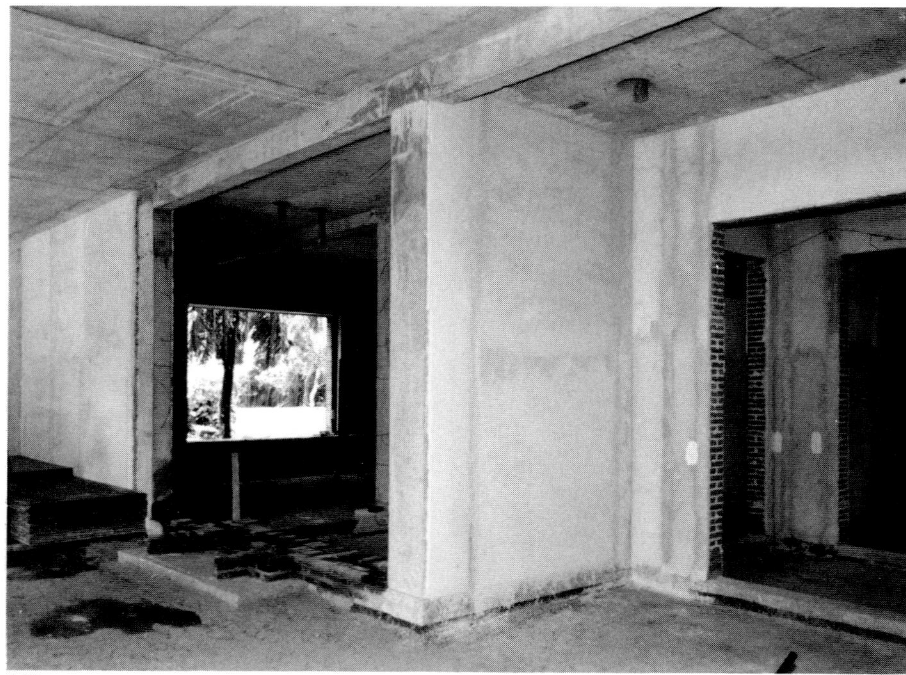

4.1b

FIGURE 4.1a to c The photograph in Figure 4.1b shows the basic construction skeleton of what is to become a formal living room complete with a paneled wainscot, a fireplace, paneled doors, and an elaborate cornice.

The procedure for this exercise will vary from the methods shown in Figure 3.1a through m in that an additional method of height division of the TMC will be shown that uses height projections taken directly from an elevation of the subject drawn at 1 : 20 metric scale (see Figure 4.1a).

1. Begin by tracing the lines of the photograph onto an acetate or tracing-paper overlay, noting all major lines of the basic concrete-and-brick skeleton. (The tracing is shown in Figure 4.1c.)

2. Extend major wall and ceiling lines in each direction to locate the VPL, VPR, and horizon line.

In the first part of this exercise, plane *B* is to be partitioned into equal horizontal divisions in order to approximately locate the fireplace projection and paneling on each side of the chimneypiece, as seen in the elevation. The method is similar to the division of planes on a cube in Figure 2.7a.

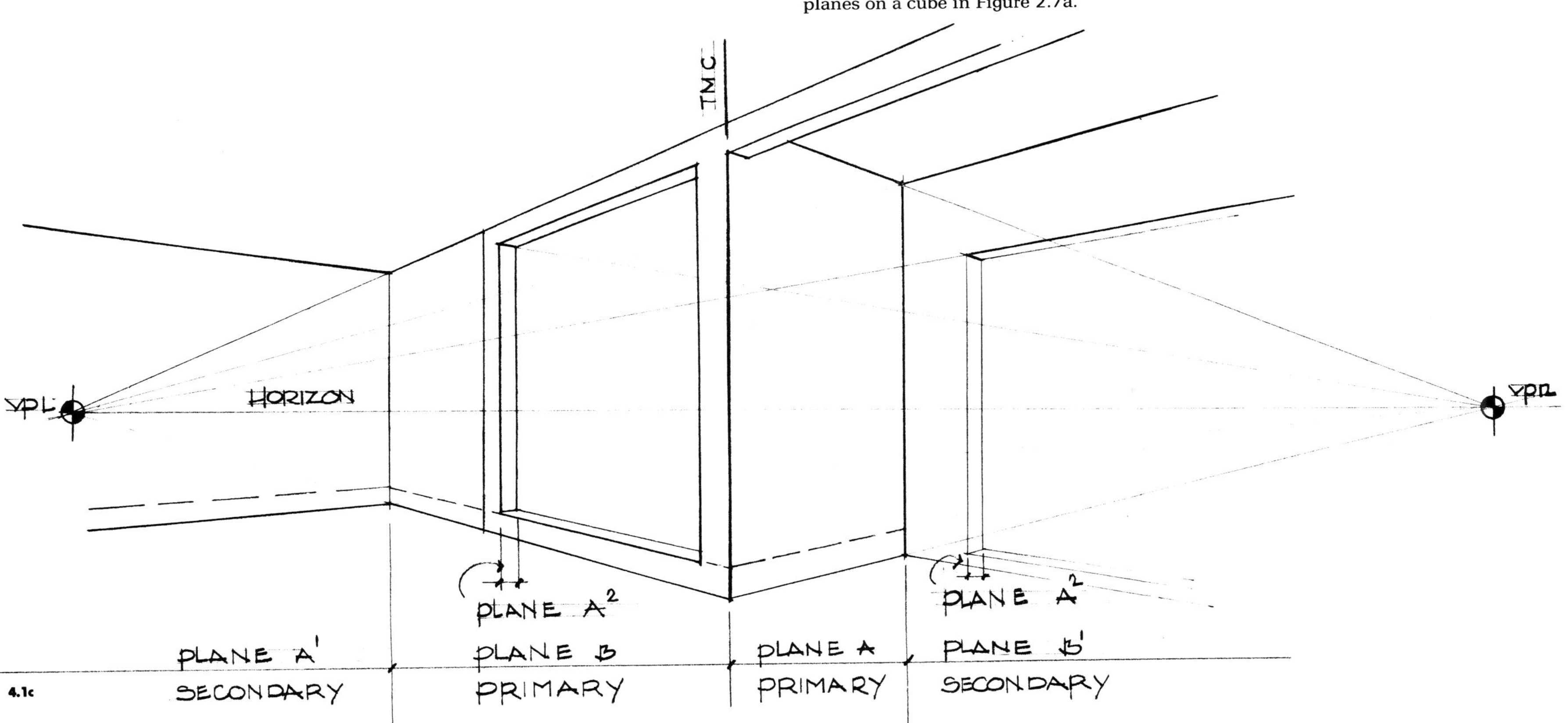

4.1c

FIGURE 4.1d Refer to the cube division exercise in Figures 2.7 through 2.10 that divided plane *A* and plane *B* into 36 equal divisions via the slanted-scale method. The division method noted here will be slightly different in that the rear wall intersection line is used to divide the TMC. To divide the TMC into 10 equal divisions:

1. Define plane *B*, that is, $A^1 A^2 B^2 B^1$, by darkening selected traced lines of Figure 4.1c.

2. Using the height at the back wall (instead of at the TMC), divide line A^1B^1 into 10 equal spaces, using the slanted-scale method.

3. Project lines from the VPL through each height division and across wall plane *B* until they intersect the TMC. Now the TMC, or A^2B^2, will also be divided into 10 equal height divisions.

4. Draw a diagonal from A^1 to B^2, and drop vertical lines to the baseline from where this line intersects the projected height line extensions. For clarity, these lines are shown in the area of the wainscot only. Darken full-height lines *FG* and *DE* to represent the approximate division lines representing the location of the fireplace projection shown in elevation (Figure 4.1a).

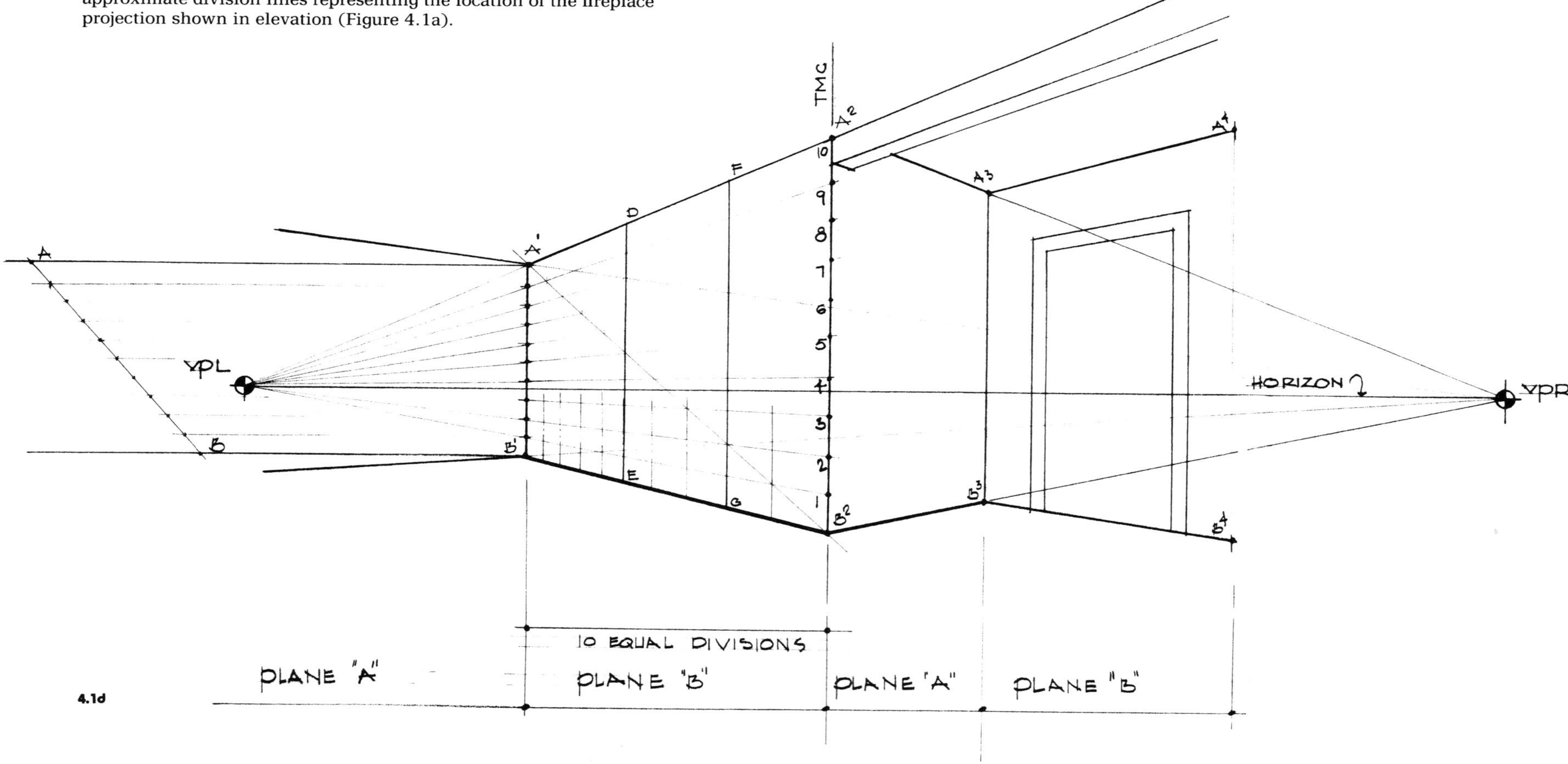

4.1d

Projections from the Primary Wall Plane

The fireplace secondary plane B^1 can be projected forward of primary plane *B*, as seen in the cube extension exercise in Figures 2.7 through 2.10.

The remaining wall divisions noted on this overlay will be used later to visually locate the wainscot paneling divisions to the left of the fireplace projection.

The Projected Elevation Process

Up to now this drawing has progressed by the use of techniques of dividing space equally that were developed in Chapter 2. Next, you will see how the adjusted photograph tracing (Figure 4.1d), which shows the wall plane *B* divided into 10 equal divisions, can be combined with the original elevation (Figure 4.1a) in order to plot the height of architectural elements such as base, paneling, wainscot, fireplace mantle, door panel and frames, and the cornice.

Place another overlay over the preceding drawing and trace only definitive wall and ceiling break lines. Next extend the ceiling-wall line as well as the floor-wall line of the major wall area, noted as plane *B*, to the right an undetermined distance, as shown in Figure 4.1e.

Fold the elevation (Figure 4.1a) (with the fold line vertical) at an area of the elevation that allows you to see most major horizontal lines on the elevations. Then extend the primary parallel horizontal plane height designations across the elevation to the fold line, using red or green ink so that lines are clearly visible on the elevation without obscuring the original drawing.

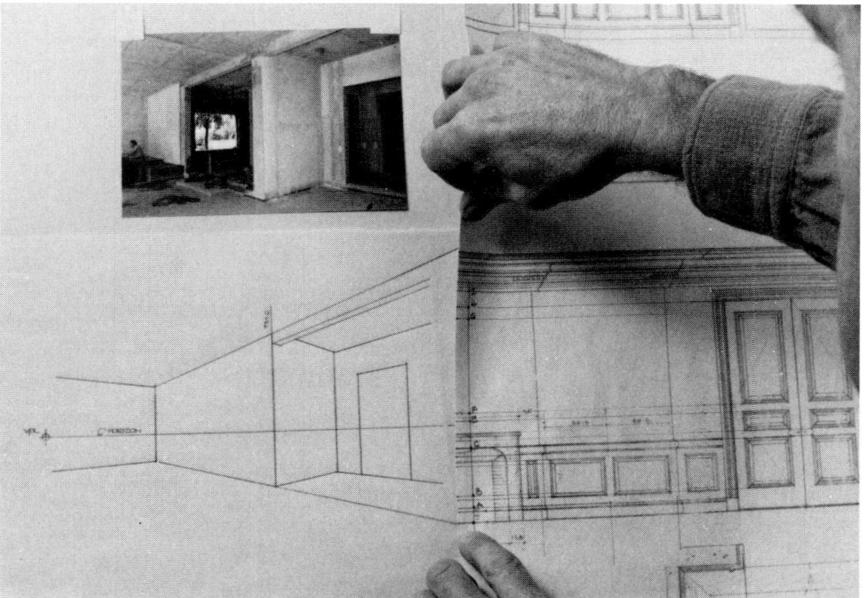

4.1e

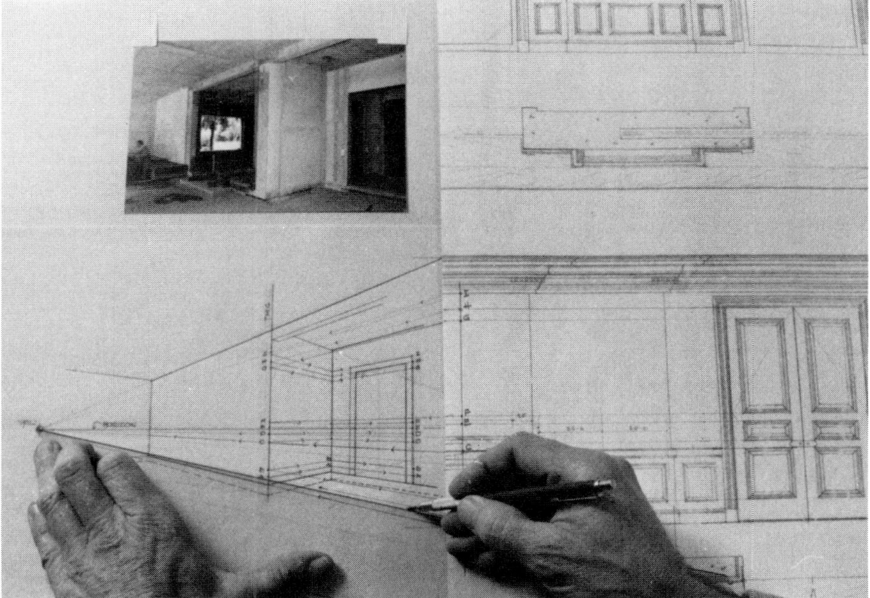

4.1f

FIGURE 4.1e to g *Note:* This portion of the drawing shows how a scaled elevation, when combined with a tracing of a photograph, can determine the height layout for all elements of the drawing, i.e., base, wainscot, door divisions, mantel height, chimneypiece, and cornice. For clarity of this portion of the process, a clean tracing-paper overlay is used, one that does *not* reflect the 10 equal height divisions on the TMC as well as the wainscot divisions.

1. Begin by dividing the elevation with a vertical line or folding the elevation as shown in Figure 4.1e. It is not important where this division is noted as long as all major height notations on the elevations are visible.

2. Extend major height lines on the folded elevation (preferably with a red-ink pen), and mark them with a dot and letter designation on a vertical reference line adjacent to the folded edge of the elevation. *(Continued)*

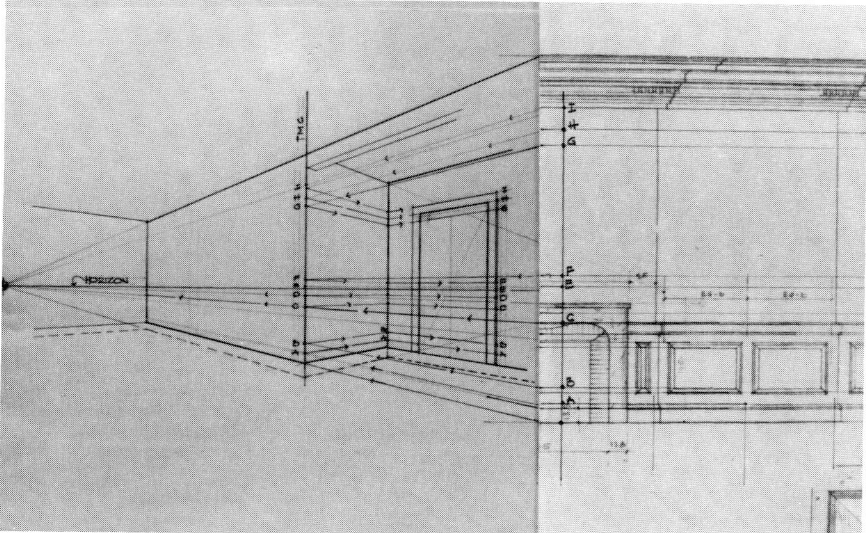

4.1g

Example. Base = A, lower wainscot rail and molding = B, wainscot height = C, door rail division = E and F, door top rail = G, door head = H, and cornice = I.

Now from each of these marked divisions on the folded elevation, on the perspective line tracing project toward the VPL lines that will intersect the TMC. Mark these divisions as well as all other primary horizontal lines with a corresponding letter projected directly from those noted on the vertical reference line and the folded edge of the elevation.

Now project each height notation from the TMC to the right across plane A toward the VPR until these intersect vertical wall line TU, and note each.

Next project lines, to the *right* away from the VPL, through each mark on vertical line TU across plane B^1 until they reach the right door opening frame. Projected lines noting base height, mantel height, wainscot height, cornice height, and other major height divisions are carried to the *left* from the TMC toward the VPL, and these lines determine the height of major woodwork and plaster features of the room, located on plane B.

After the leading corner intersections between primary wall planes A and B have been marked off in projected increments (the thickness of the floor should be noted as well as the position of the crown mold line at I, shown in the elevation section in Figure 4.1a), the wainscot height C and crown mold and door panel divisions at B, D, E, F, G, and the top of the door at H can be noted as the drawing progresses.

Note all plane designations and their respective vanishing points. The A planes converge at the VPR while all B planes converge at the VPL. Note also how strong vertical *inside* and *outside* corners clearly divide all A planes from B planes.

Follow the arrows from the folded elevation shown in (f) and (g) to review the process, noting the projected line direction and the height divisions as they are "walked" around the room. Also note how at each vertical break line between planes A and B the projected lines change direction from one vanishing point to the other. For example, the height of the wainscot at C has been carried to the left across primary plane B as well as to the right across primary plane A and then back to the right again across secondary plane B^1.

Remember that horizontal panel divisions, such as were shown in Figure 4.1d, and the chimneypiece position on plane B were approximated by dividing this wall into 10 equal divisions via both the slanted-scale method and a diagonal line. This division, seen in Figure 4.1h, approximates the panel layout of the wall plane.

Placement of the Folded Elevation

It is now a simple matter to position this fold line of the elevation vertically such that the top and bottom of the elevation line up with the projected wall-ceiling and wall-floor lines. Then you tape this reference elevation in place.

You may now project from this vertical fold line all major horizontal divisions to the left toward the VPL until they intersect the TMC as shown in Figure 4.1f. These lines connecting to the VPL will be projected from the folded elevation across the face of plane B to create the definitive height divisions of the paneling and chimneypiece. However, before that is done it is a good idea to "walk" the lines around the walls closest to the viewer, i.e., planes A and B. This will lessen the confusion created by overlapping lines that will occur unless each wall surface is drawn on a separate tracing paper overlay.

Where these lines carry around a corner on an A plane they may be connected to the VPR until they again intersect a B plane. There the lines are picked up by the VPL again, and may be projected back across a B plane to the right (see Figure 4.1g). In this manner these horizontal divisions may be located in perspective and in scale anywhere on planes A and B. It is in this manner that the paneling is formed.

Three-Dimensional Sections to Aid in the Development of a Sketch

Figure 4.1i shows the further refinement of the process after the elevation is removed from the drawing. Note that the cornice molding line has been projected around the ceiling line, and a three-dimensional representation of its cross section has also been drawn in perspective that refers to the section of the molding shown at each end of the elevation.

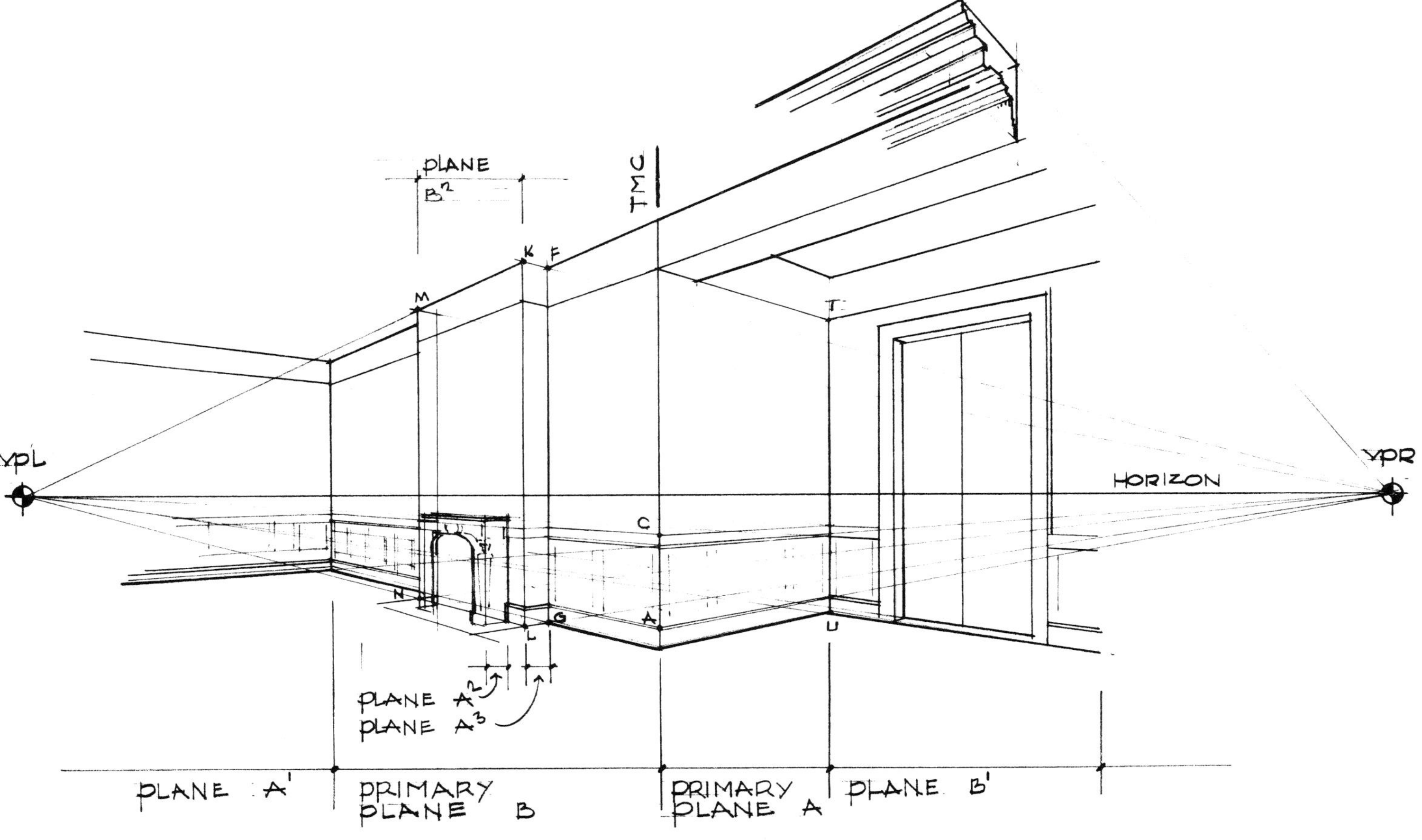

FIGURE 4.1h In this tracing overlay, the major architectural features of the room have been further defined to combine wainscot divisions (noted in Figure 4.1d) with their respective height divisions (Figure 4.1g).

Note that the cornice mold has been drawn in section (its cross section in perspective lies on an *A* plane) and that all lines denoting its linear extension are projected in the direction of the VPL until they reach an *A* plane. There their direction changes to the direction of the VPR, and so on.

The projection of the fireplace and its wall extension follows the cube extension theory discussed in Chapter 2, and the projection forms two secondary planes, *A* and *B*, each true to its respective vanishing points.

Overview

The completed dimensional drawing (Figure 4.1j) shows how the projected elevation technique, when combined with the slanted-scale method of division, has been used to create a visually accurate drawing that conveys the grand scale of the elaborately embellished three-dimensional interior appointments.

Note these facts for this drawing technique and its procedure:

1. The horizontal wainscot divisions of the fireplace wall are traced from the initial wall elevation shown in Figure 4.1a.

2. Wainscot divisions on primary plane *A* were visually located before border and panel height lines were projected across the fireplace wall, primary plane *B* (Figure 4.1f and g).

3. The cornice section was increased from that shown in Figure 4.1h to allow the structural beam to be hidden, creating a decorative support over the entrance to the secondary doorway (Figure 4.1i).

4. A four-value system has been used to roughly designate planes, panels, molding recesses, and extensions (Figure 4.1i).

5. The pencil-and-paper combination for this drawing was 2H, 2B, and F leads on Clearprint 1000H tracing paper.

PROJECT: Residence, Brazil
ARCHITECTURAL INTERIOR DESIGN: The Author

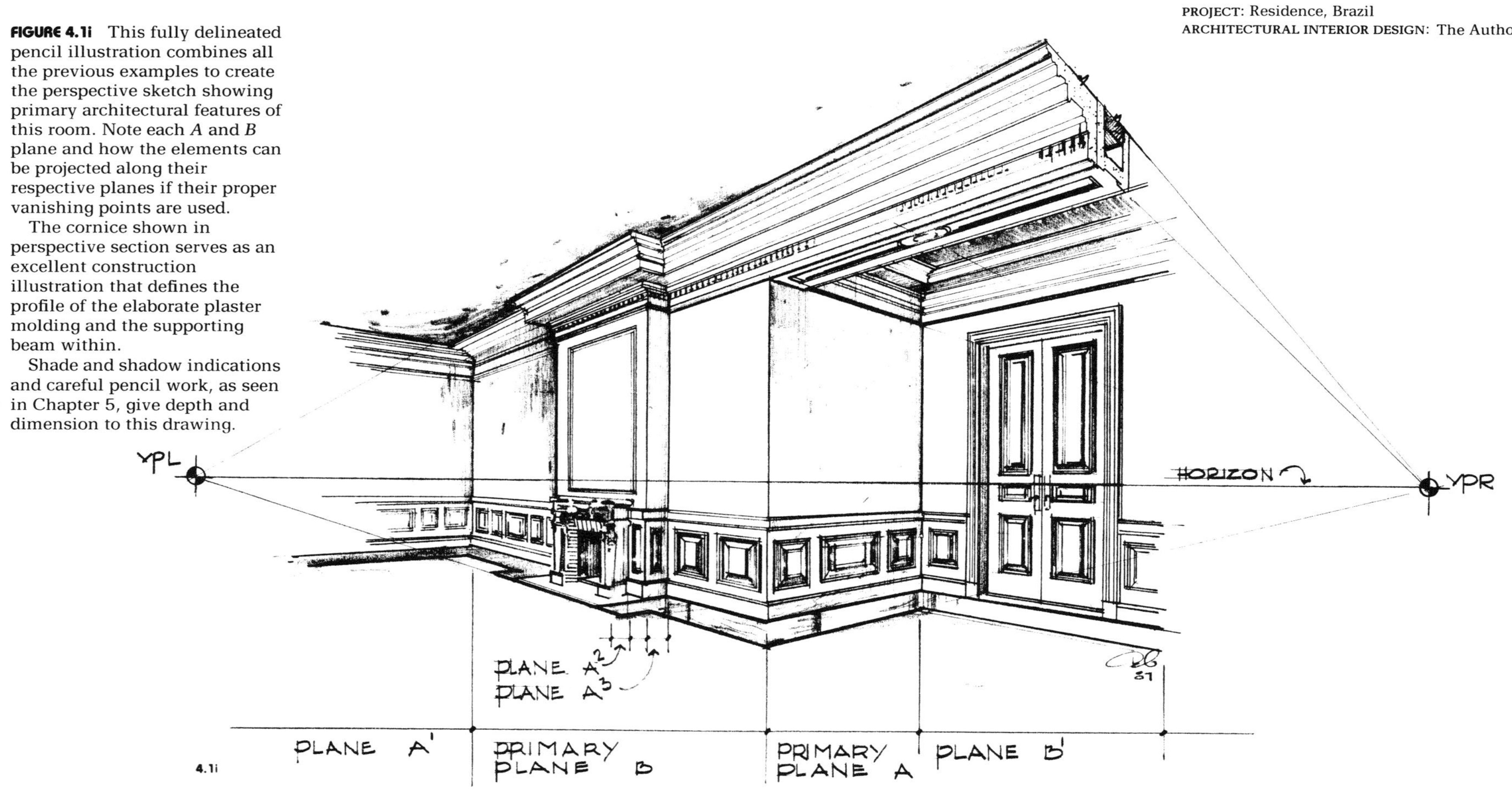

FIGURE 4.1i This fully delineated pencil illustration combines all the previous examples to create the perspective sketch showing primary architectural features of this room. Note each *A* and *B* plane and how the elements can be projected along their respective planes if their proper vanishing points are used.

The cornice shown in perspective section serves as an excellent construction illustration that defines the profile of the elaborate plaster molding and the supporting beam within.

Shade and shadow indications and careful pencil work, as seen in Chapter 5, give depth and dimension to this drawing.

Additional Examples of the Projected Elevation

Figures 4.2 and 4.3 illustrate how this technique can be adapted to develop both a one-point perspective drawing from an elevation and a three-dimensional view of a piece of furniture that has been projected from its elevation.

FIGURE 4.2 The Projected Elevation: One-Point Perspective. Major points defining the chimneypiece depicted in Figure 4.2c have been projected forward from a point on the elevation shown in (a) toward the viewer in (b) to create the perspective drawing shown in (c). Lines were projected forward from this chosen point on the primary *A* plane of the wall to create secondary planes which form the projections and recesses of the finished mantelpiece shown in the final installation (Figure 8.4c).

The overlay in (b) shows how all primary lines converge at one vanishing point, the *station point* or position of the viewer.

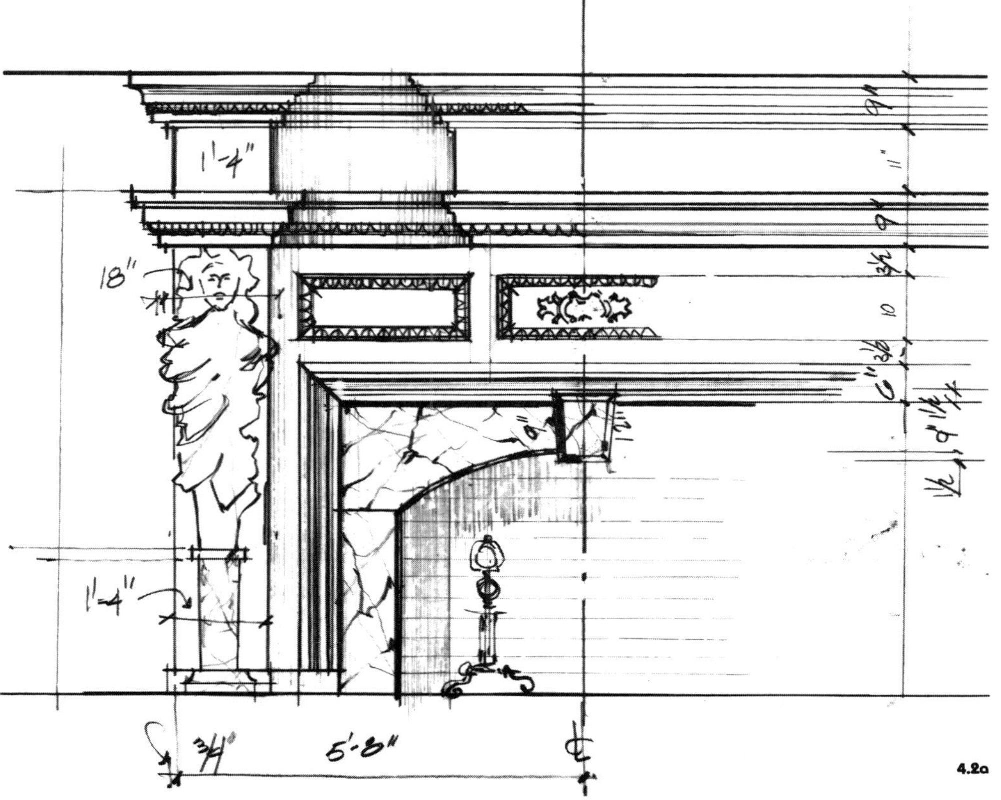

4.2a

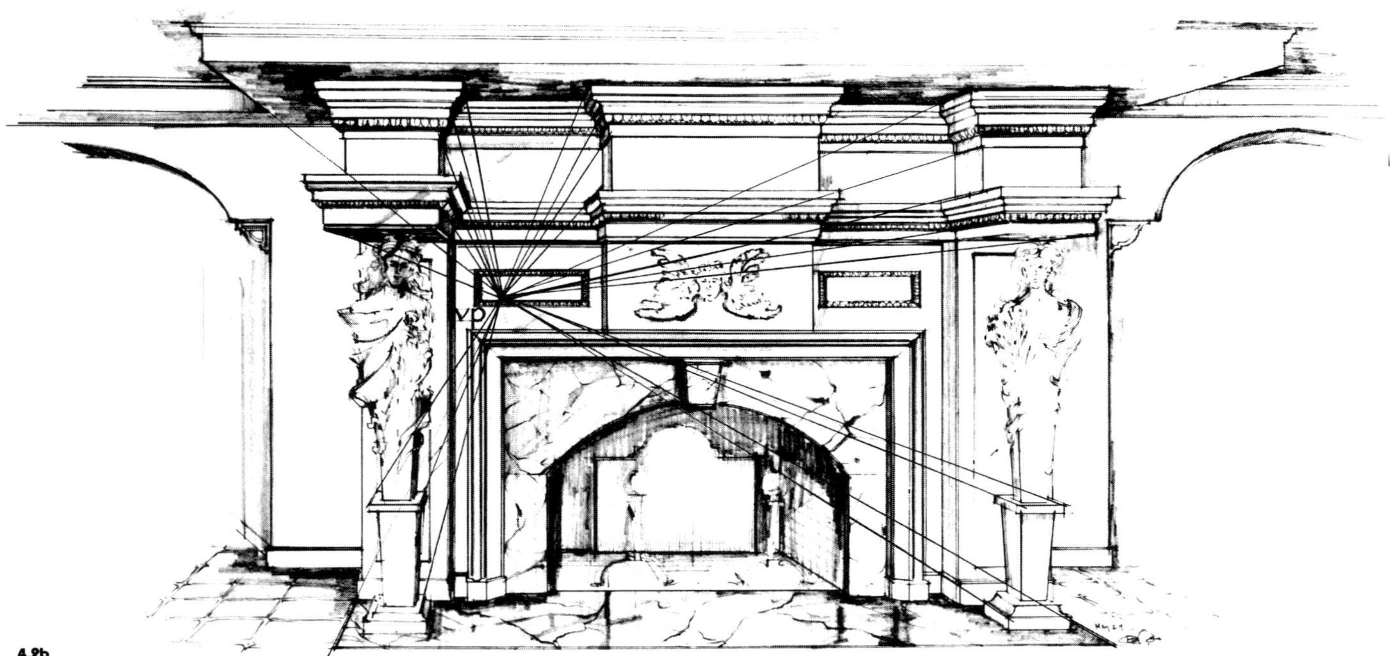

4.2b

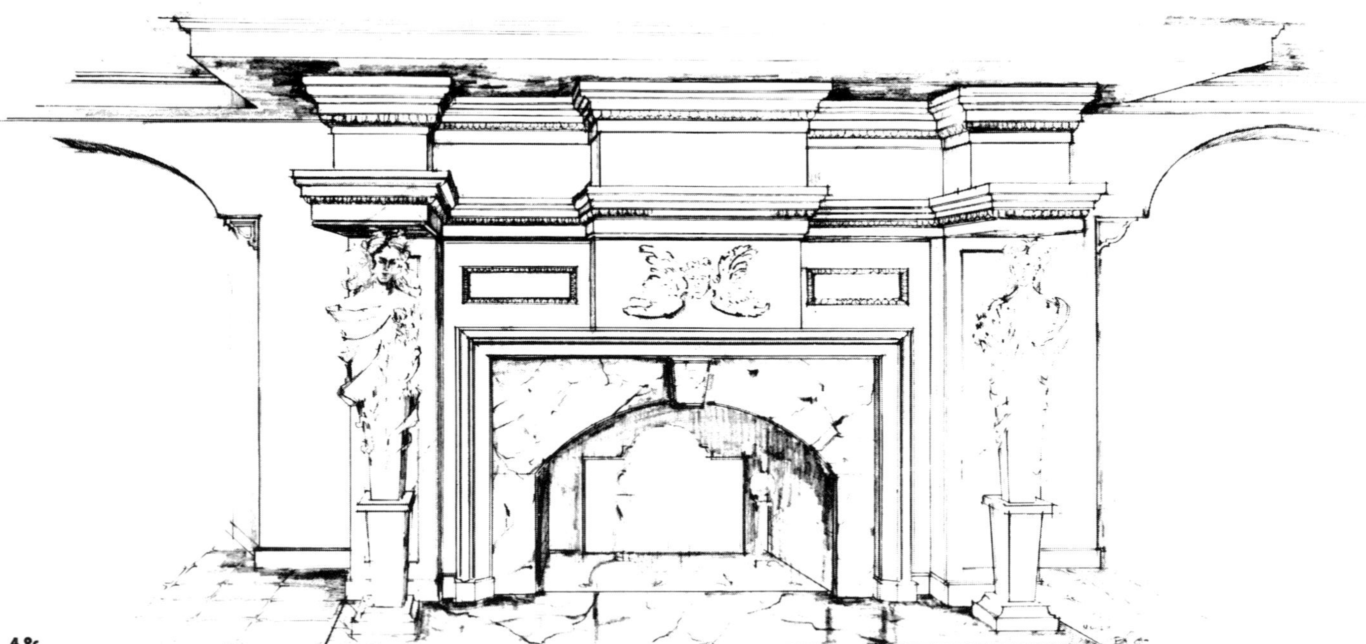

4.2c

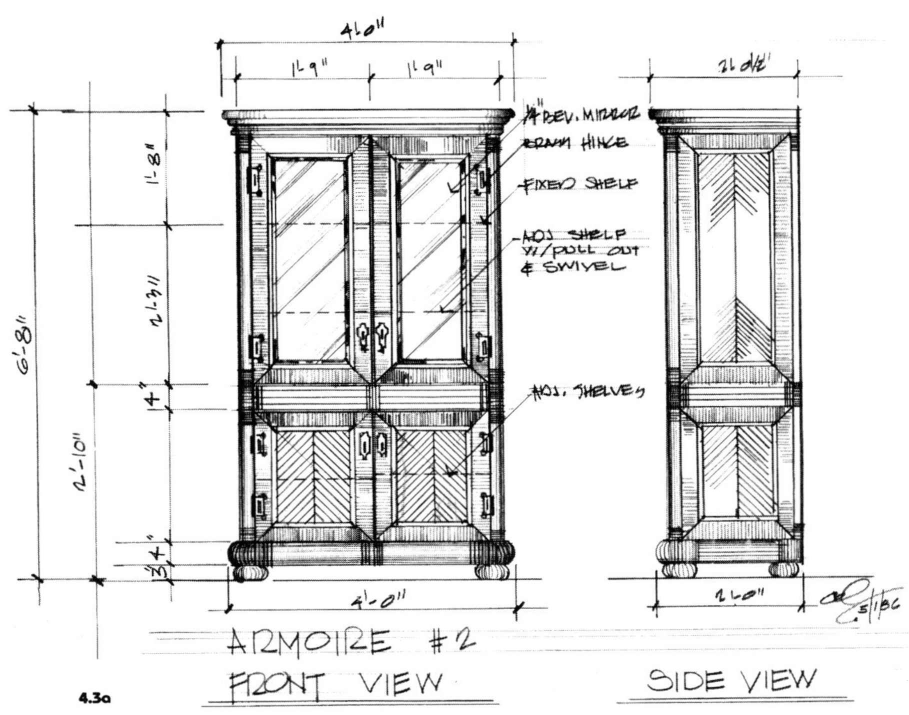

4.3a

FIGURE 4.3 The Projected Elevation: Furniture The armoire shown in the rendered pencil illustration in (c) was designed by the author and drawn at ½″ = 1′0″ scale in front and side elevation. Figure 4.3a shows all primary and secondary dimensions for the piece. The shade and shadow principles of Chapter 5 are used in the sketch to create dimension and the feeling of rounded shapes found on this rattan armoire. The cylindrical shape of even the smallest pieces of rattan to the large bun feet is suggested merely by lines that get closer together as they reach the outer perimeter of the rounded surfaces. This principle is shown in Figure 5.13a through c.

Figure 4.3b shows the elevation being used as a proportional vertical measuring device in creating a finished drawing from a cubic solid. The basic cubic solid that will become the armoire is shown in (b). Dimensions taken from the elevation are easily transferred directly from the right-hand vertical edge of the piece shown in elevation. This edge is designated the TMC for this drawing.

A flat, chisel-shaped 2H lead and conical, pointed H and F leads were used on frosted Mylar to create all areas of the pencil drawing in (c). The sharp points of the lead formed the fine lines of the paneling and rattan divisions. The wide portions of mirror bevels, diagonal strokes, and shadow suggestions were formed by a chisel-shaped H lead. Each palm leaf was formed by one H-lead pencil stroke. You start at its intersection with an imaginary stem and branch out to each side, while bearing down and twisting the lead simultaneously and finally lifting off the drawing surface at the tip of each frond.

Deep-valued shadows made with a chisel-shaped 4B lead were indicated on the wall and under the piece, to tie it down to the floor. The planes of the piece receiving more light are silhouetted against the deep shadows on the floor, to create a crisp dimensional outline of the needed profiles.

Flat tiles on the floor were indicated by leaving the linear definitions open and vague and by sometimes allowing them to disappear altogether.

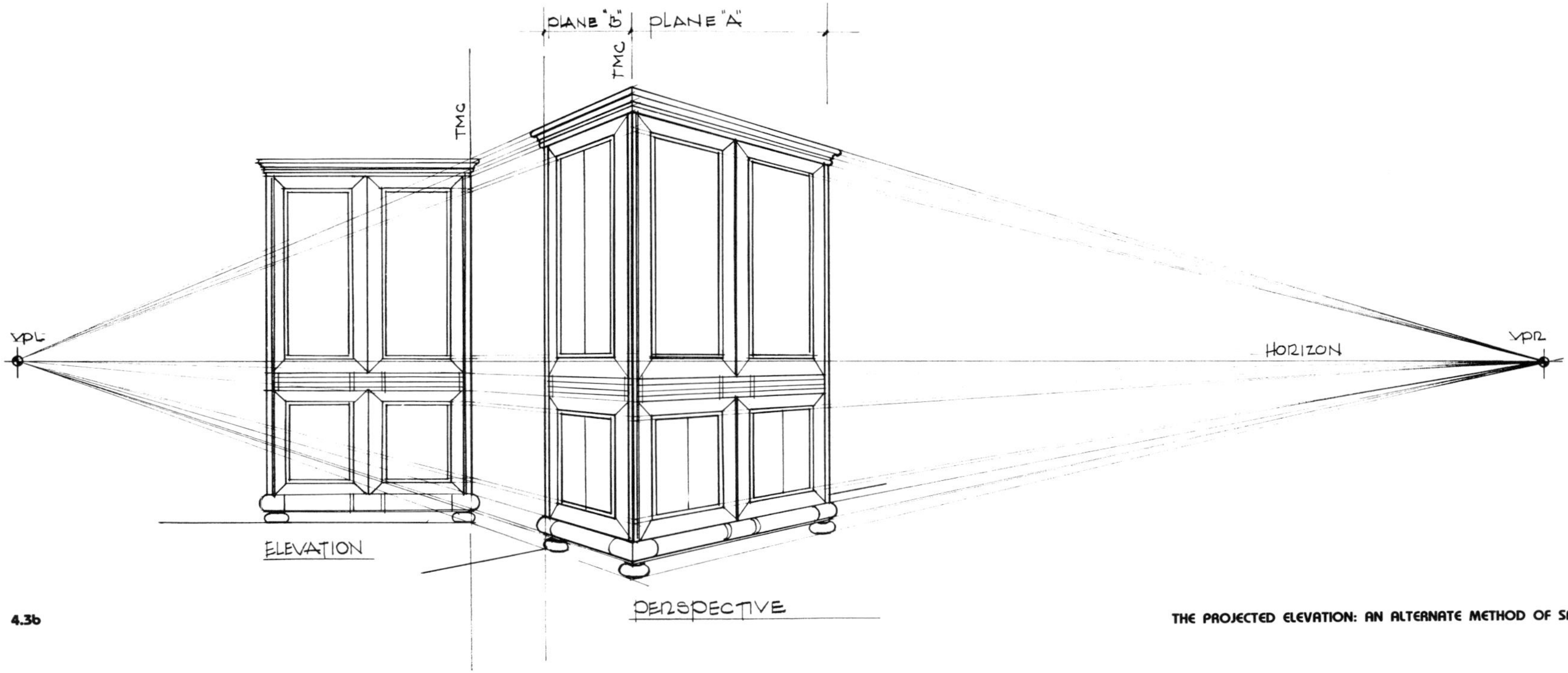

PLANE "B" PLANE "A"
TMC
TMC
VPL
HORIZON
VPR
ELEVATION
PERSPECTIVE

4.3b

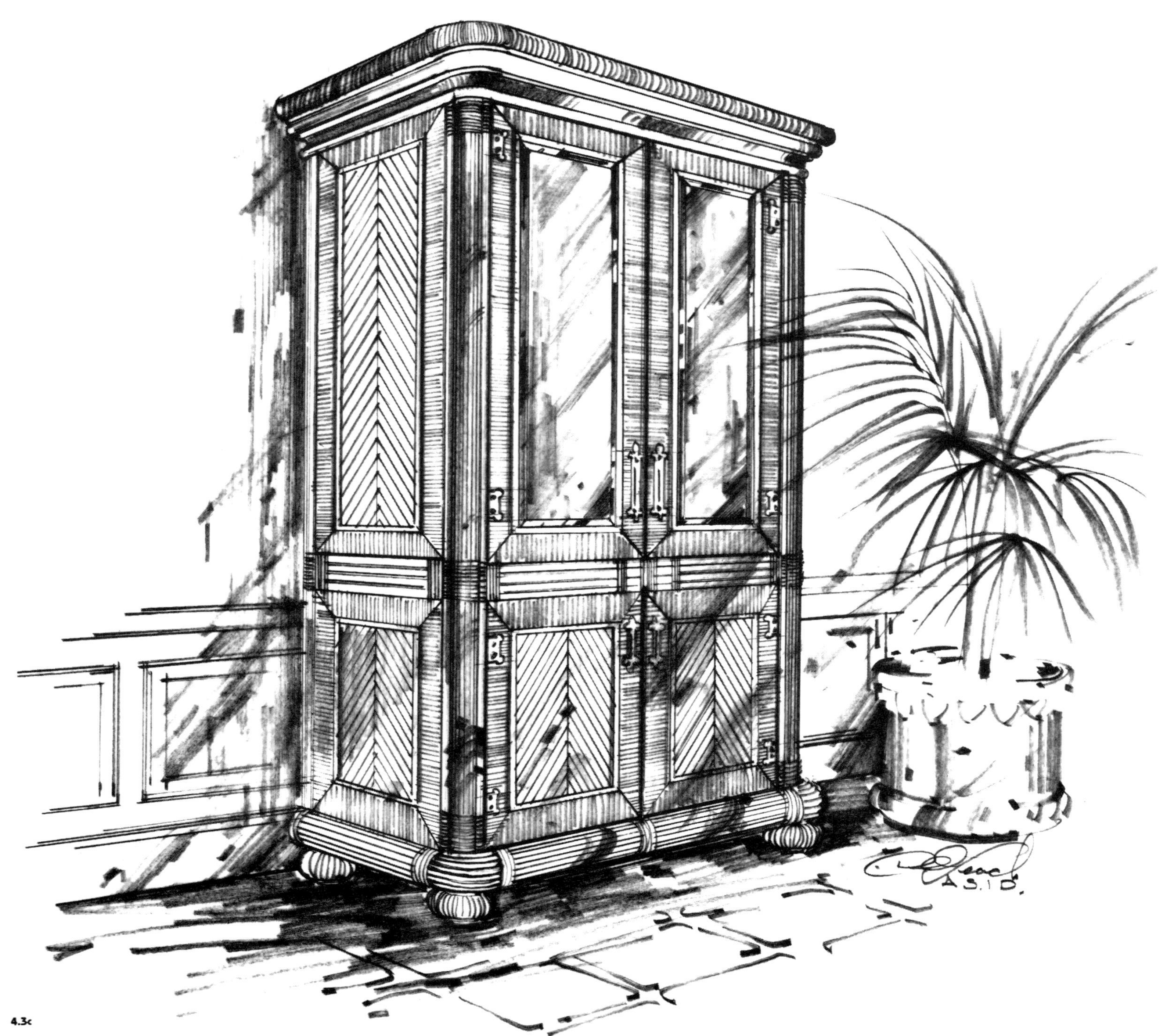

4.3c

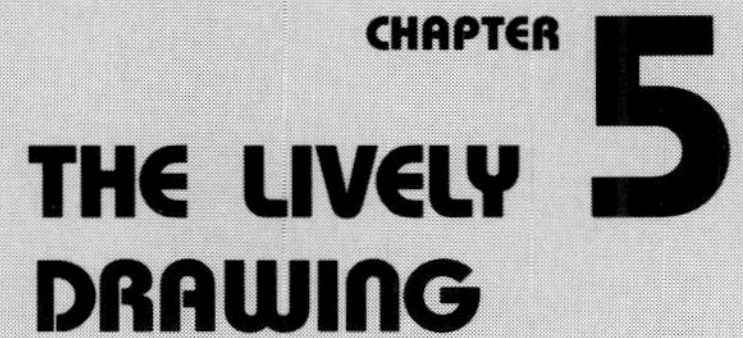

CHAPTER 5
THE LIVELY DRAWING

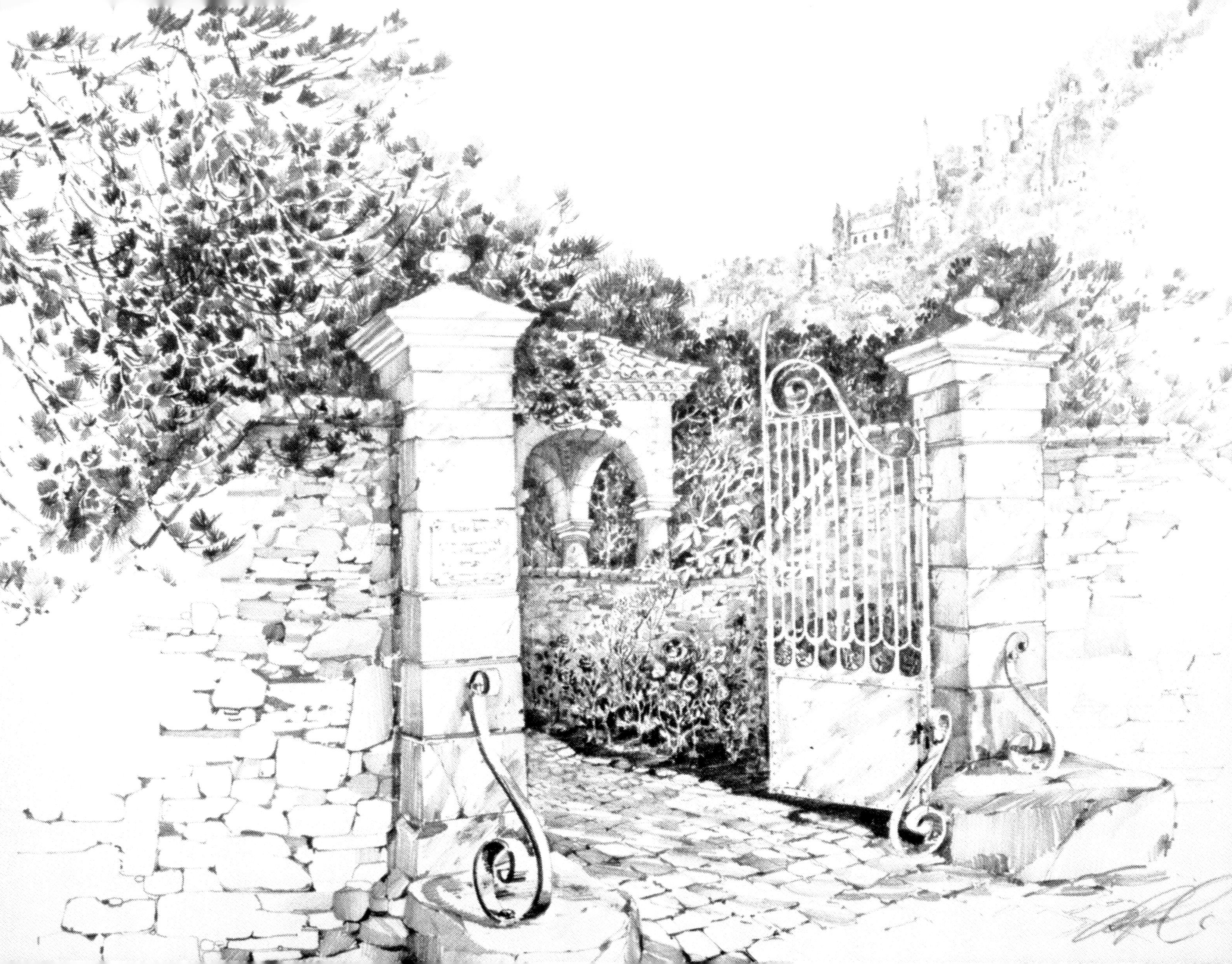

A Drawing Must Invite the Viewer In

It is important to infuse drama and life into a simple line drawing to create something that is striking and memorable for the client. Both the angle chosen and techniques, such as the addition of light and shade, are key factors in creating a dramatic drawing (see Figure 5.1) regardless of the medium chosen.

Dark shadows against light areas are always dramatic — a litany one cannot repeat too often during the drawing process.

In this chapter, we look at the basis of three-dimensional drawing techniques, i.e., how to accurately plot shadows by using some theories of mechanical projection. You will see how the pencil and pen can be used to give a line drawing shape and dimension with proper strokes. But first you must get the right materials that will aid you in these exercises.

Drawing implements: Pencils and pens The same pencil or pen can create a dramatically different effect, depending on the kind of paper on which you draw. The rougher the surface or *tooth* of the paper, the more graphite it will scrape from the pencil or the more ink it will absorb from a pen, and the darker the drawing will be. A soft lead such as 6B produces a darker line than a harder lead such as 2H. If you use a pen with a wide chisel point, you will be able to "paint" with ink instead of having to depend on a larger number of strokes to cover the same surface.

Know your drawing surface It is important to get the right combination of drawing implements and paper. For this reason, you should experiment with lots of different types of drawing implements and papers. As you do this, you will start to develop a style of your own. You will discover which tools you feel most comfortable with.

A pencil allows you a freedom that a pen does not: namely, you can erase lines and change your drawing. In the beginning, however, it is good to be spontaneous in your drawing and not to worry about correcting things.

Materials You will need a stock of materials, including the following:

1. Drawing surfaces: Clearprint 1000H tracing paper; typing bond paper for rough sketches; Mylar, 0.400 = mil thickness drafting medium, frosted on two sides

CHAPTER 5

THE LIVELY DRAWING

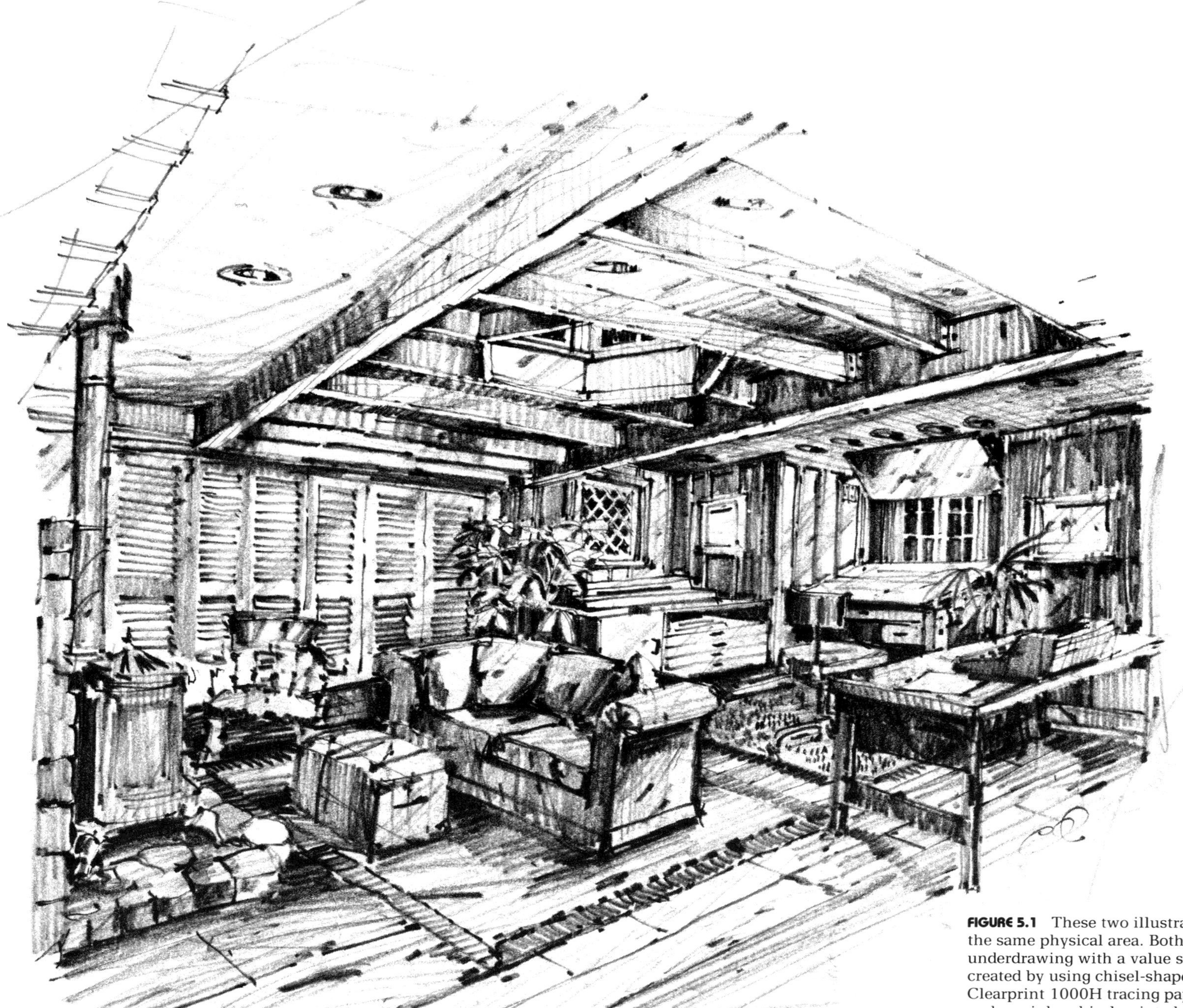

5.1a

FIGURE 5.1 These two illustrations of a studio office depict the same physical area. Both were drawn from a common underdrawing with a value study as a guide. Figure 5.1a was created by using chisel-shaped F and 2B pencils on Clearprint 1000H tracing paper. Figure 5.1b employed new and semi-dry chisel-pointed, felt-tip pens on the same type of tracing paper.

The light and dark areas that create the feeling of light, shade, and shadow in a drawing are those elements that give the drawing life, by making it seem three-dimensional.

PROJECT: Office
DESIGNER: The author
ILLUSTRATOR: The author

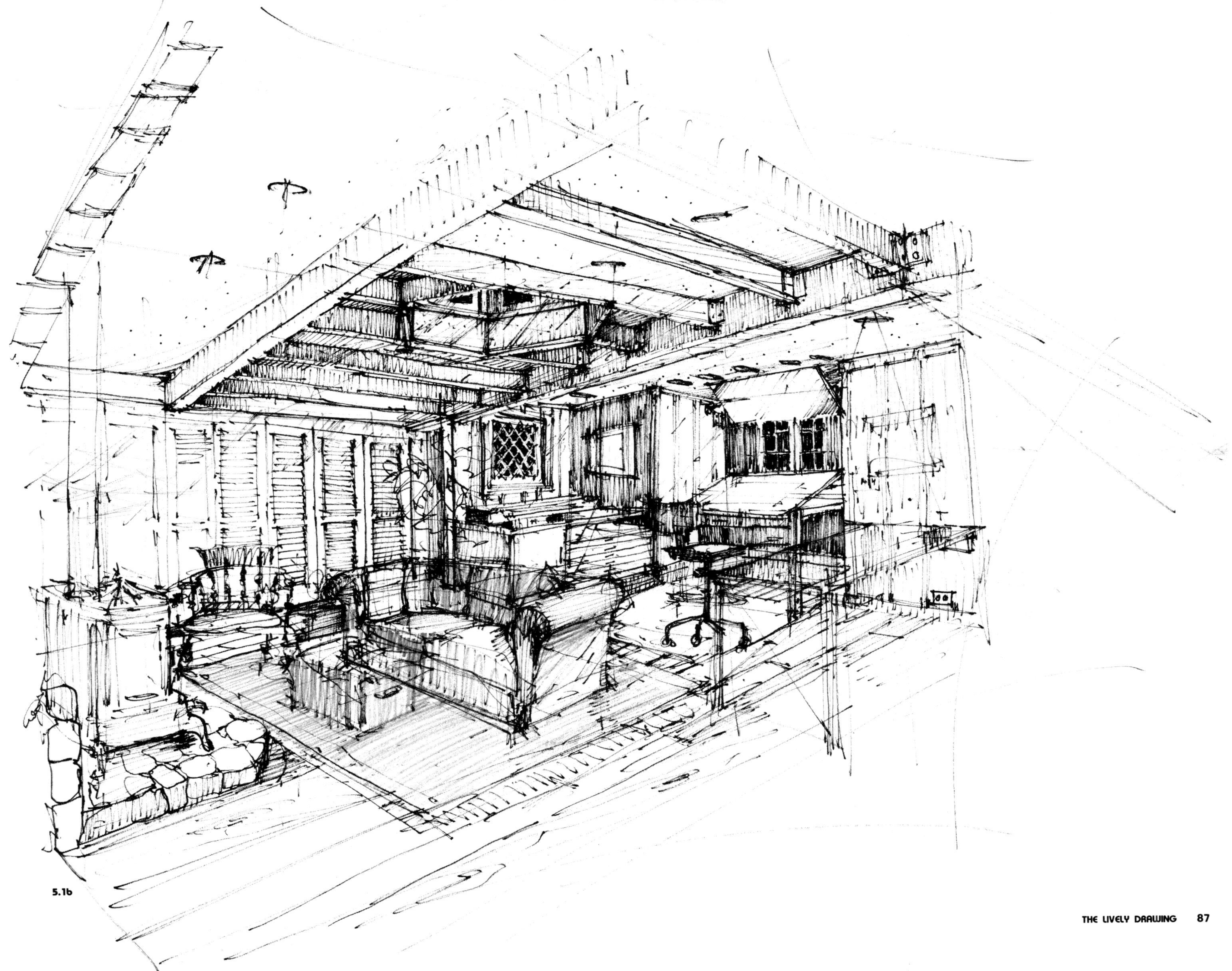

5.1b

2. Graphite pencils: grades 2H, HB, F, 2B, 4B, 6B (from hardest to softest)
3. Hard and soft flat-lead carpenter's pencils (these approximate the hardness of 3H and F)
4. Felt-tip pens: conical points in several colors; flat-tip (chisel-point) pens; used pens (semidry) for shading (chisel-point)
5. Sharpeners: very sharp utility knife or X-acto knife; sanding block for obtaining the proper pencil point for drawing
6. Erasers: hard white or Pink Pearl, soft kneaded, and a bag of dry eraser powder commonly sold in art stores as a "dry cleaning bag"
7. A 3″ carpet square for cleaning excess graphite from pencil leads
8. Graphite sticks: ¼″ × ¼″ × 3″ or ¼″ × ½″ × 3″, soft

When you are using a pencil, sharpen it with a mat knife and then sand it to a chisel point that will lie flat against the drawing surface. Don't expose too much of the graphite in sharpening because the lead may break, especially in the softer-lead pencils. See Figure 5.2.

Matching Pen or Pencil to Paper

- On heavy vellum or Clearprint 1000H tracing paper, a hard lead such as 2H produces a light gray stroke, and a soft lead such as 6B gives an almost black stroke. (See Figure 5.3a.)
- On frosted drafting Mylar (Figure 5.3b), a hard lead produces a medium to dark gray stroke, and a soft lead comes out nearly black.
- On porous typing paper, a felt-tip or quill pen produces a dark, fuzzy line. The darkness of the stroke depends on how much ink is being deposited on the paper with each stroke (Figure 5.3c).
- On less porous architectural sketching paper, a felt-tip or quill pen produces a lighter, crisper line, again depending on the ink-to-paper deposit.

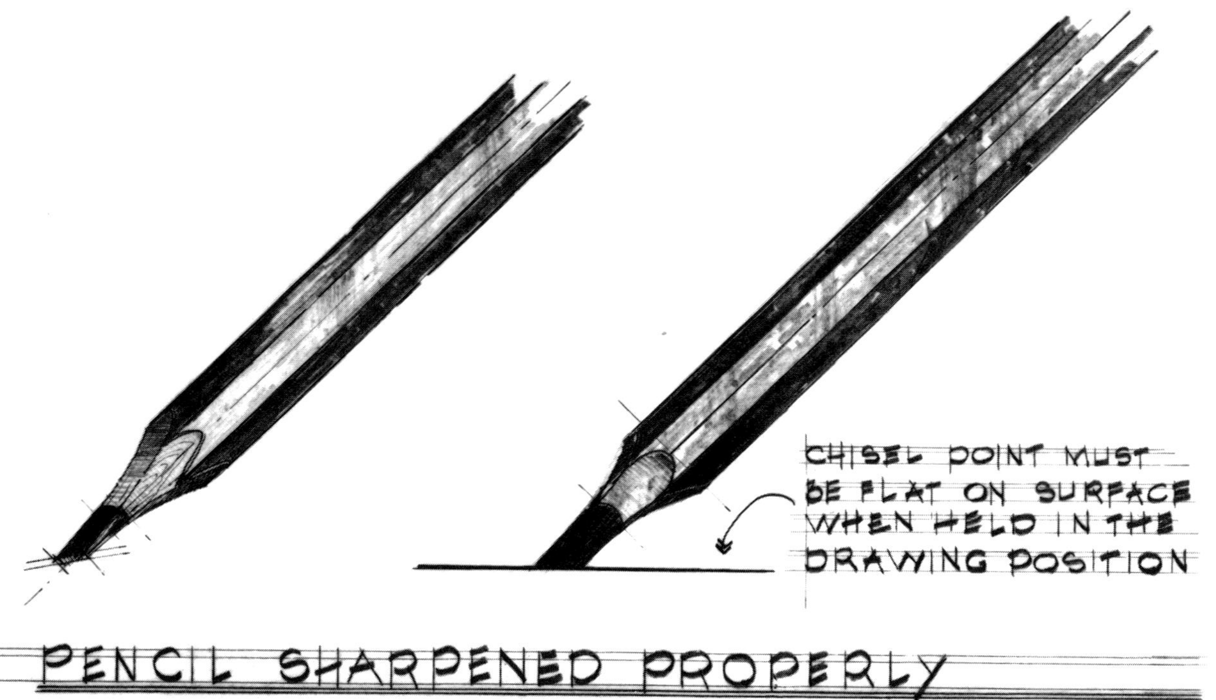

FIGURE 5.2 Sharpen Pencil Properly The pencil, in order to be most effective for applying shade and shadow areas to a drawing, must be sharpened properly into a chisel shape.

Trim enough wood away from the lead to allow it to be sharpened like the pencil in this drawing. A sanding block can aid in forming the correct angle of the lead while the pencil is held in the normal drawing position.

Soft leads such as 4B and 6B require more wood support than H, 2H, and HB leads. Expose only enough graphite to form the proper drawing surface.

This drawing was made with H and 2H leads on frosted drafting Mylar.

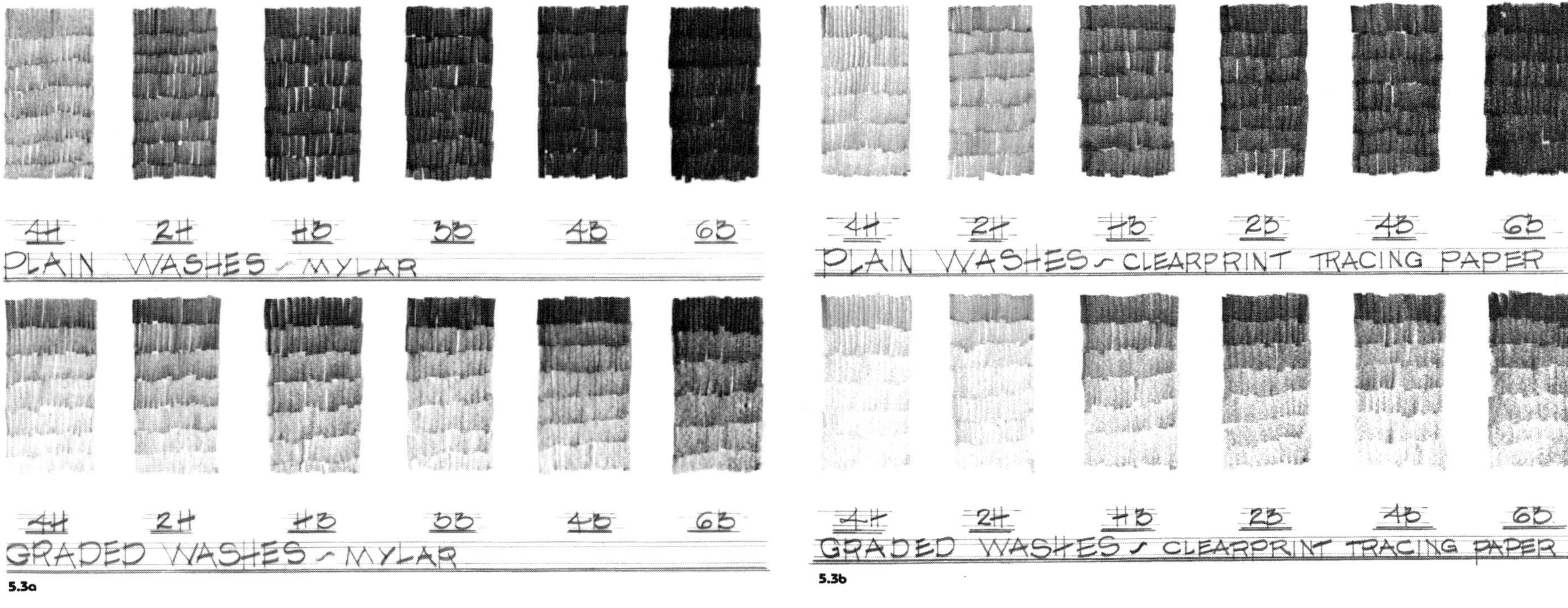

5.3a

5.3b

A B C D E F

G H I J K L M

VARIOUS QUILL PEN STROKES

5.3c

FIGURE 5.3 Matching Pencil to Paper and Pen Both Mylar (frosted, drafting medium) and Clearprint 1000H tracing paper have been compared in these exercises by their acceptance of six leads of various hardness and of quill pen strokes as well. The hardest lead is 4H, and 6B is the softest. The softer the lead and the rougher the tooth of the paper, the more graphite will be scraped off with each pencil stroke and the darker the stroke will be.

Many combinations of drawing effects can be achieved by proper matching of lead hardness to the drawing surface. For instance, a hard lead such as 3H will produce a medium, dark gray stroke on frosted Mylar drafting medium which has a tooth like fine sandpaper and a light gray stroke on heavy tracing paper, which has a much more subtle tooth. Soft lead such as 4B or 6B will produce a very dark to almost black stroke on both frosted Mylar and heavy tracing paper such as Clearprint 1000H. Similarly, a new felt-tip pen with either a conical or chisel point will give heavy, dark, continuous tones to most tracing papers as long as the ink supply does not run out. A quill pen filled with India ink will produce strokes of a consistent intensity depending on only the width and closeness of the strokes for darkness of value. See lower left. However, a semidry felt-tip pen can be used to lay medium to light ink strokes on almost any surface. A more porous surface, of course, such as typing paper, will produce a darker line than a smoother, nonporous architectural sketching paper will, when you are using the same pen.

Examples of pencil and pen strokes Now, with materials in hand, you are ready to begin. For examples of various line and shading techniques, see Figure 5.4a through f. These illustrations show various combinations of pen, pencil, and paper. Note the line quality in each drawing as well as the types and density of strokes used to create the various values.

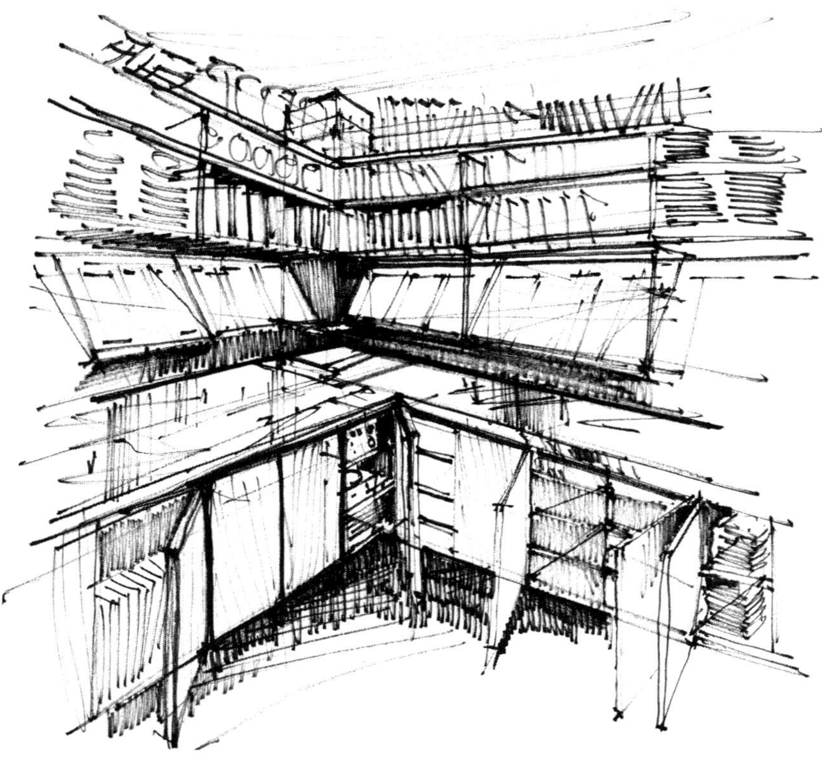

FIGURE 5.4a The book shelves and lower storage cabinets were drawn as a quick sketch on bond typing paper with a chisel-point semidry felt-tip pen (fuzzy line quality).

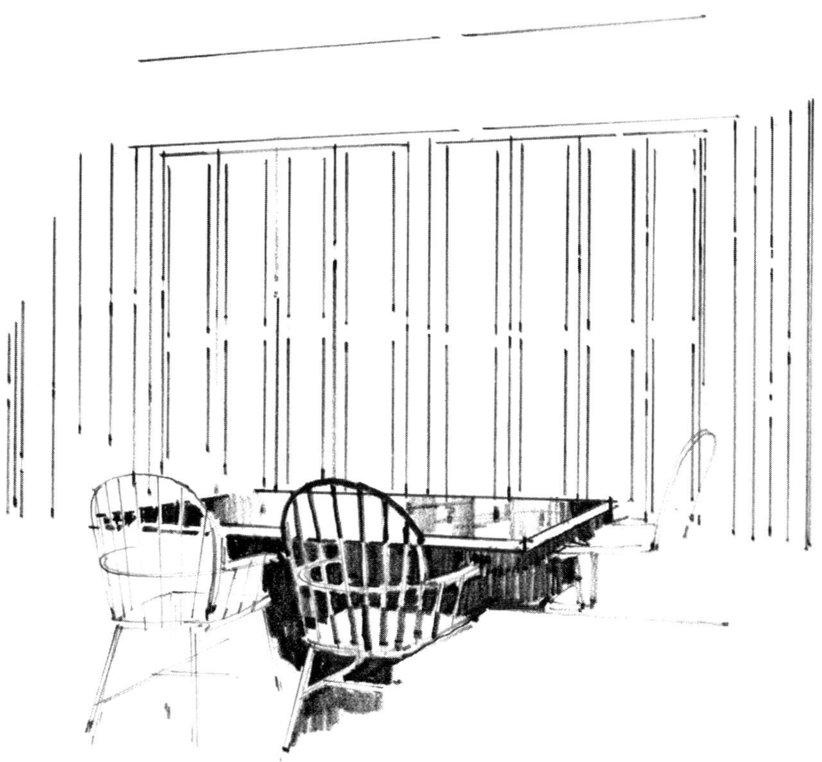

FIGURE 5.4b These chairs with their defining shadow areas were drawn on Clearprint 1000H tracing paper with H lead for line work and 2B and 4B leads for the deeper shadows.

Note how the continuous lines that denote the chair back spindles change from dark, where they are seen against the tabletop, to light, where they are seen against the deep shadows. It is this continuous play of dark against light and light against dark that gives a drawing its drama.

There is a fuzzy line quality but good depth of darkness in shadows.

FIGURE 5.4c This table was drawn on Kidd finish Bristol Board with H, 2B, and 4B leads. The reflections have been accentuated by lifting graphite from the surface with a Pink Pearl eraser.

Note how the carpet is suggested by individual pencil strokes in the shadow area. There is a crisp, dark line character and good shadow quality under the table.

DESIGNED BY: The author
ILLUSTRATED BY: The author

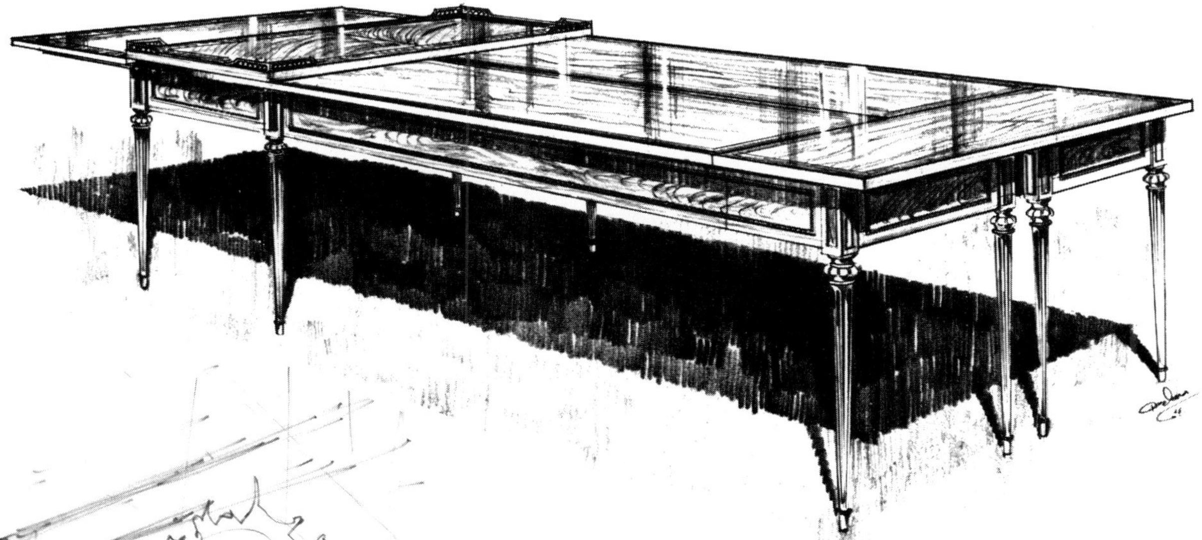

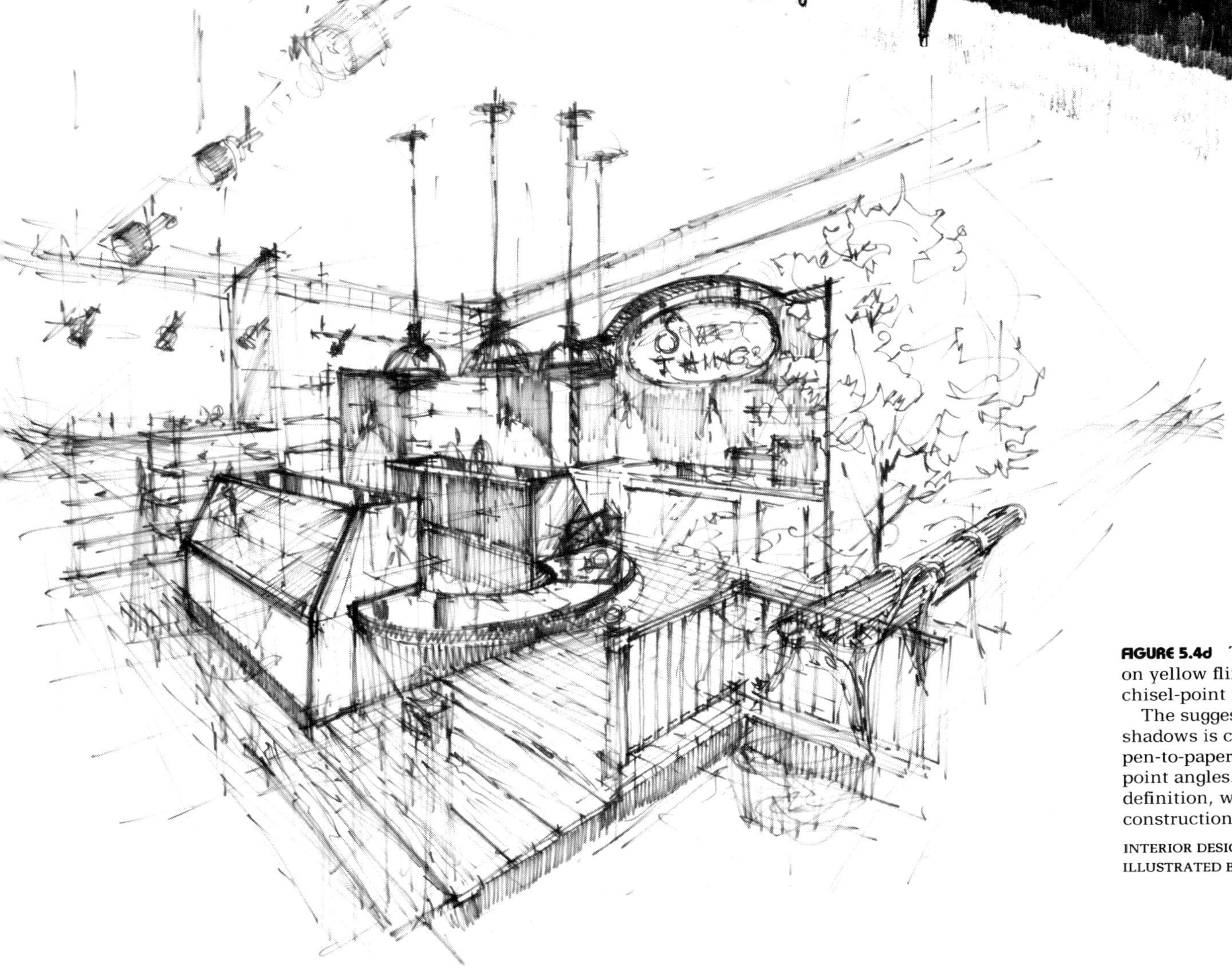

FIGURE 5.4d The bakery in this sketch was first drawn on yellow flimsy architectural sketch paper with chisel-point medium-dry felt-tip pens.

The suggestion of wood grain as well as heavy shadows is created by using various degrees of pen-to-paper contact pressure as well as several pen point angles. The quality is crisp to fuzzy line definition, with a good mood created by the construction lines left in the sketch.

INTERIOR DESIGN BY: The author
ILLUSTRATED BY: The author

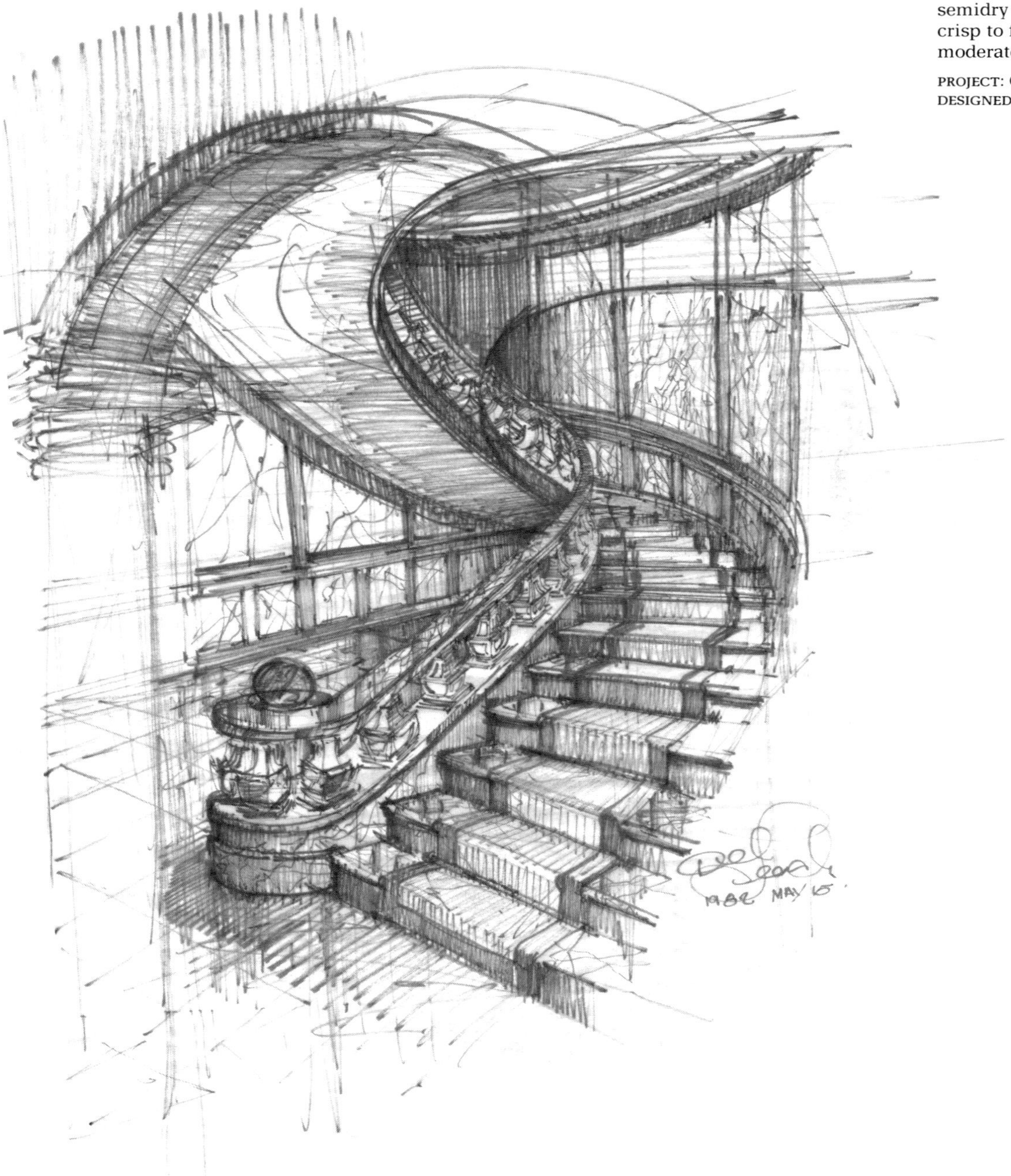

FIGURE 5.4e This grand staircase was sketched on white flimsy architectural sketch paper with both new and semidry felt-tip pens. The quality is crisp to fuzzy line definition, with moderate shadow depth and definition.

PROJECT: Grand Residence, South America
DESIGNED BY: The author

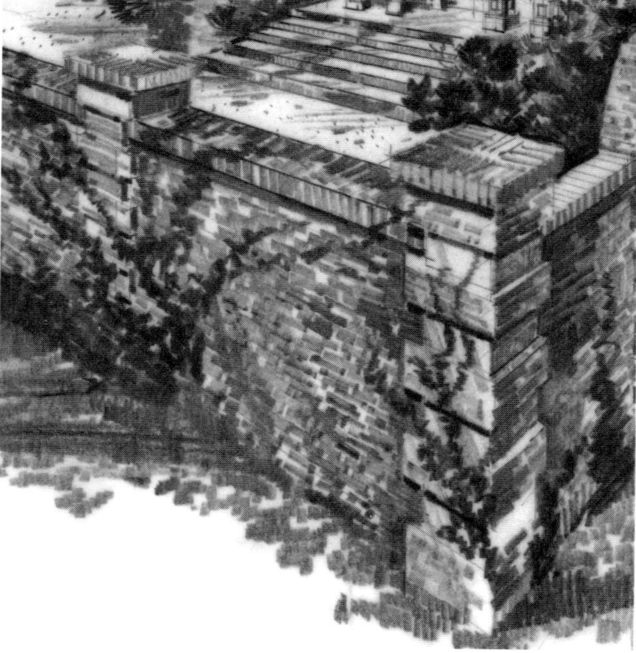

FIGURE 5.4f This brick wall was drawn on frosted Mylar with H, 2H, and HB leads. The harder leads are required with Mylar because its tooth acts as sandpaper in the removal of graphite, thus creating dense, dark strokes. The quality is crisp to fuzzy line definition, with intensely dark strokes possible.

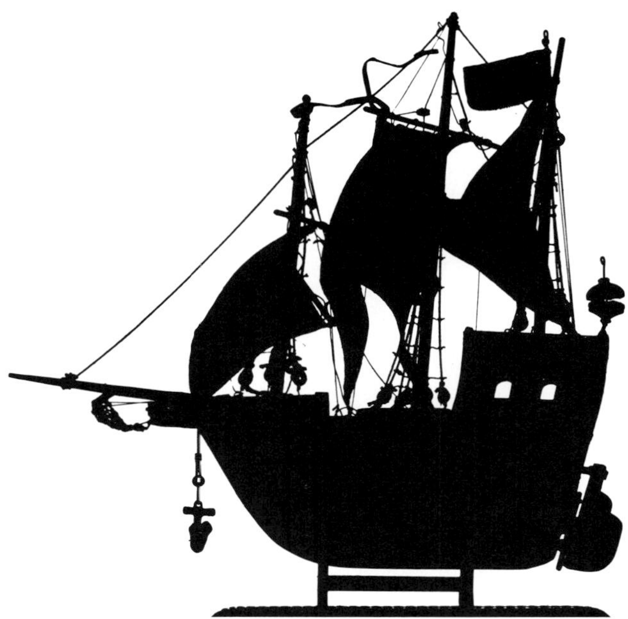

5.5a

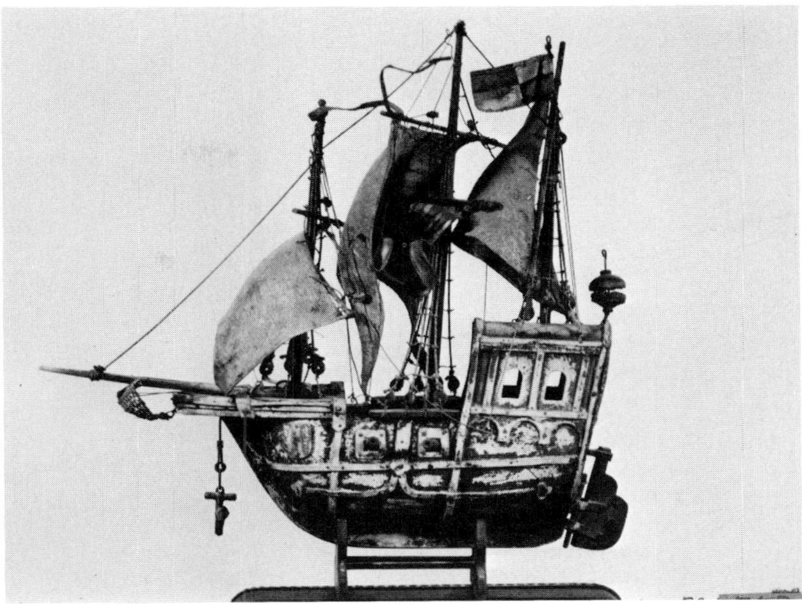

5.5b

FIGURE 5.5 When no light falls on an object but its background is illuminated (a), the object appears as a silhouette. Figure 5.5b shows the object illuminated. When some element comes between the source of light and a surface upon which the light rays are falling, three things take place: (1) The element blocks light rays, causing a definite *shadow* on the surface; (2) that part of the object not receiving direct light rays will be in *shade;* and (3) light will be reflected back onto the object from the surface to form *reflected light.* (Figure 5.5c)

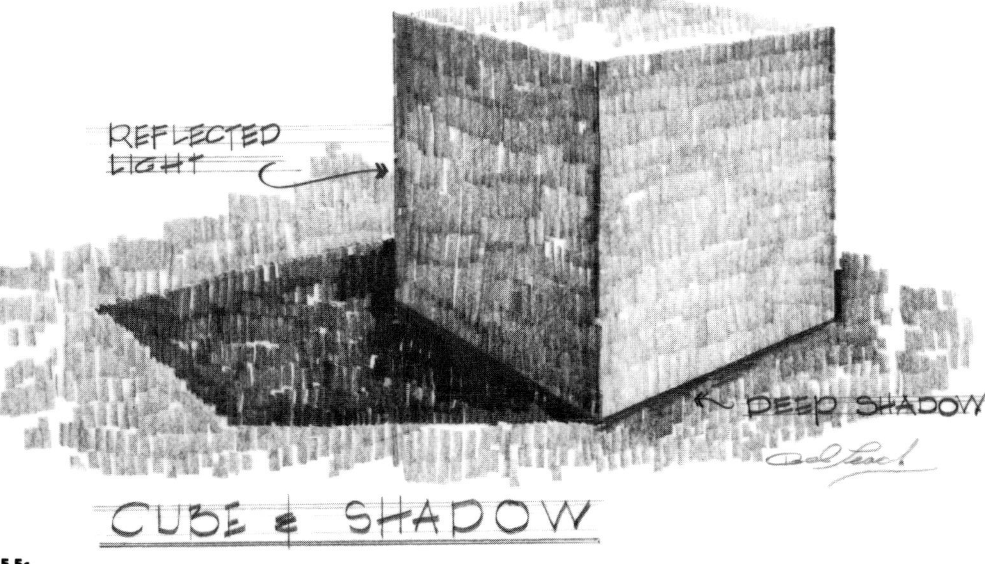

5.5c

Mechanical Projection of Shadows

How to accurately figure out where an object casts its shadow It is light that defines objects (Figure 5.5b). When no light falls on an object, that object appears in silhouette (Figure 5.5a). If a light source is blocked by an object, a *shadow* will fall on the surface on which the object is resting and the surface of the object not receiving light will be in *shade.* Some light will reflect back onto the surface of the object in the form of *reflected light.* (See Figure 5.5c.)

To accurately depict the way the light falls on an object and the shadows cast by that object, mechanical projection is indispensable. (See Figure 5.6.)

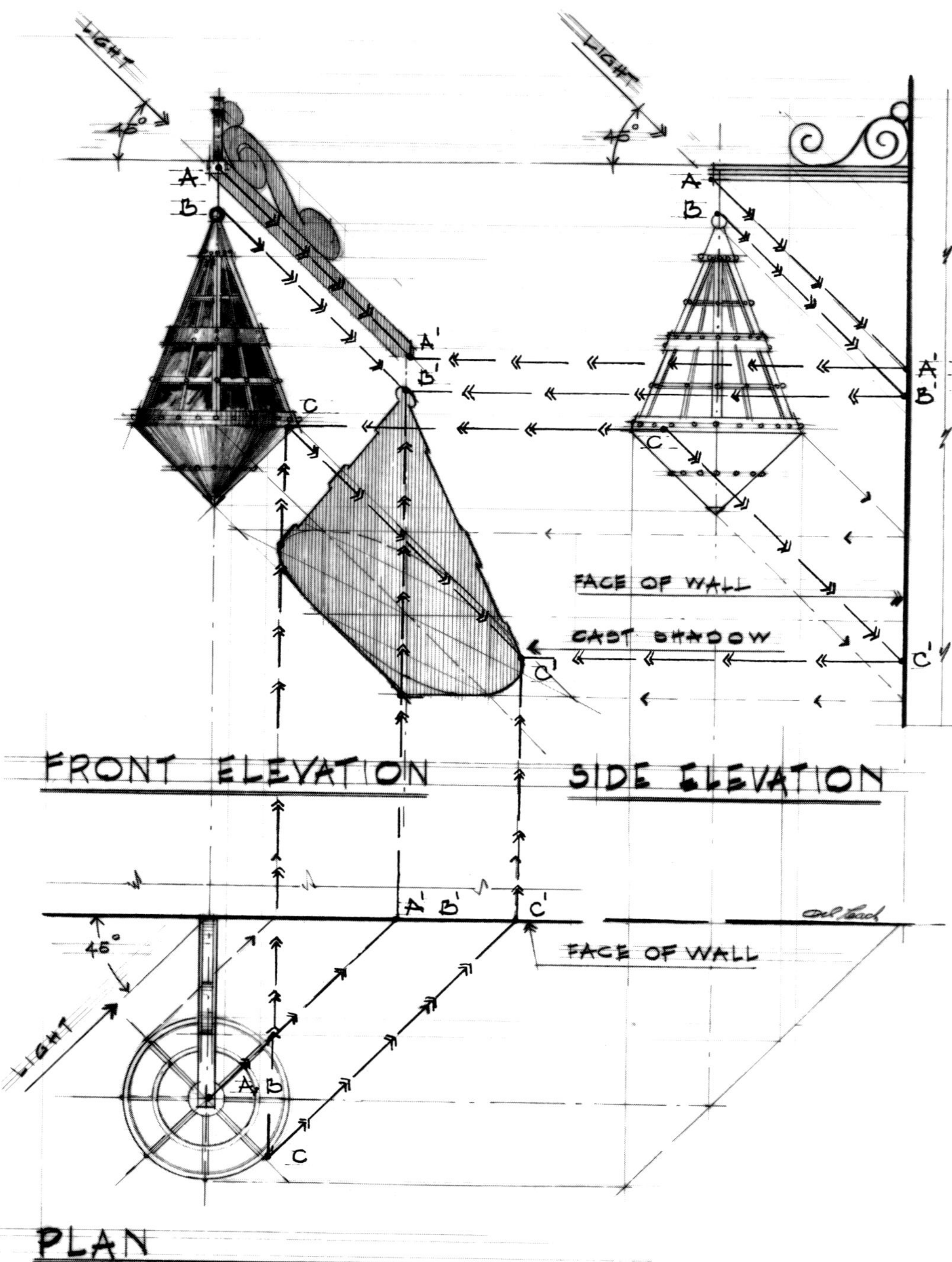

FIGURE 5.6 Shadows by Mechanical Projection The hanging lantern shown here is seen in elevation, both front and side, and in plan.

In this case, parallel light rays fall from the left top area to the lower right area of the hanging lantern, as seen in front elevation. Parallel light rays, if blocked, cast the shadow shown. Any point on the wall-mounted bracket can be projected orthographically and plotted on both elevations and in plan. Similarly, any point on either elevation can, through projection, be similarly noted.

FIGURE 5.7a The Cube and Its Shadow The theory of conventional light is a method used by illustrators to plot simple but convincing shadows. Simply put, parallel light rays fall at a 45° angle from the upper right to the lower left. This is illustrated with the cube shown here. Light falls from point *B* to *F*. Points *A, E,* and *G* block out the light and cast a shadow on A^1, E^1, and G^1.

To plot the shadow seen here in perspective:

1. First draw 45° angle lines from the *upper right* to the *lower left* a short distance from points on the upper cube perimeter *A, E,* and *G*. These line extensions represent parallel light rays.
2. To find points A^1, E^1, and G^1, draw the cube as transparent, showing hidden lines *dotted.*
3. Now draw base diagonal *CF* and extend it to the *left* until it intersects *light ray E* at E^1. Then extend lines parallel to base diagonal *FC,* that is, from points *D* and *H,* left until they intersect light rays *A* at A^1 and *G* at G^1.
4. Connect and darken base shadow perimeter lines $D\ A^1\ E^1\ G^1$ not hidden by cube on a tracing-paper overlay. Darken all exposed cube perimeter lines and shadow definition.

See Figure 5.7b for value designation of the cube by this theory.

The shadow perimeter lines, as you see, are extensions from the VPL and the VPR, just as the primary upper and lower cube perimeter lines are.

Objects and Their Shadows

For purposes of drafting and sketching, a universal light designation, conventional light, is often employed. *Conventional light* is defined as that light which falls on an object at a 45° angle from the upper right to the lower left. (See Figures 5.7a through 5.14.)

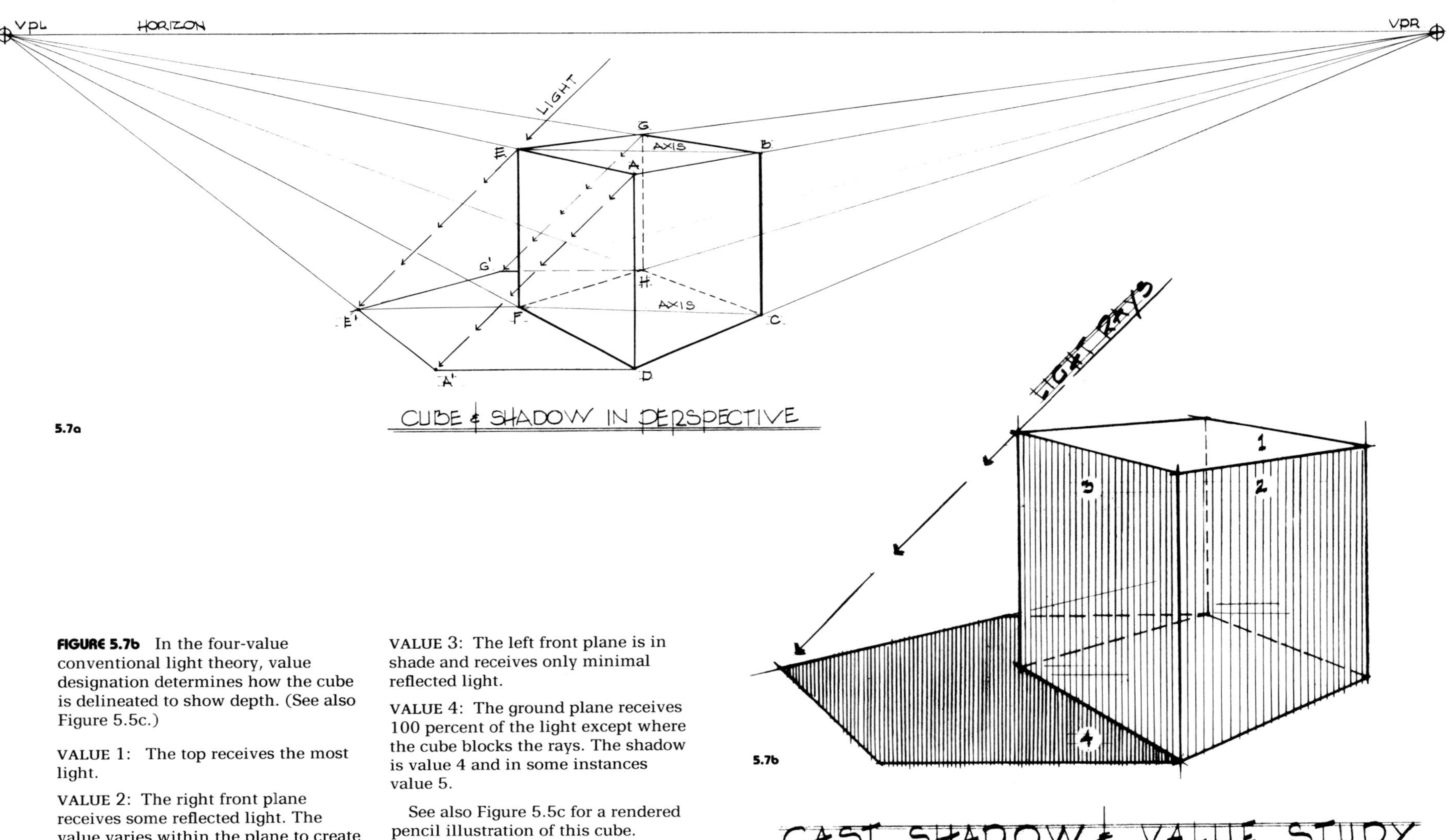

FIGURE 5.7b In the four-value conventional light theory, value designation determines how the cube is delineated to show depth. (See also Figure 5.5c.)

VALUE 1: The top receives the most light.

VALUE 2: The right front plane receives some reflected light. The value varies within the plane to create contrast, where it meets 1 and 3 values.

VALUE 3: The left front plane is in shade and receives only minimal reflected light.

VALUE 4: The ground plane receives 100 percent of the light except where the cube blocks the rays. The shadow is value 4 and in some instances value 5.

See also Figure 5.5c for a rendered pencil illustration of this cube.

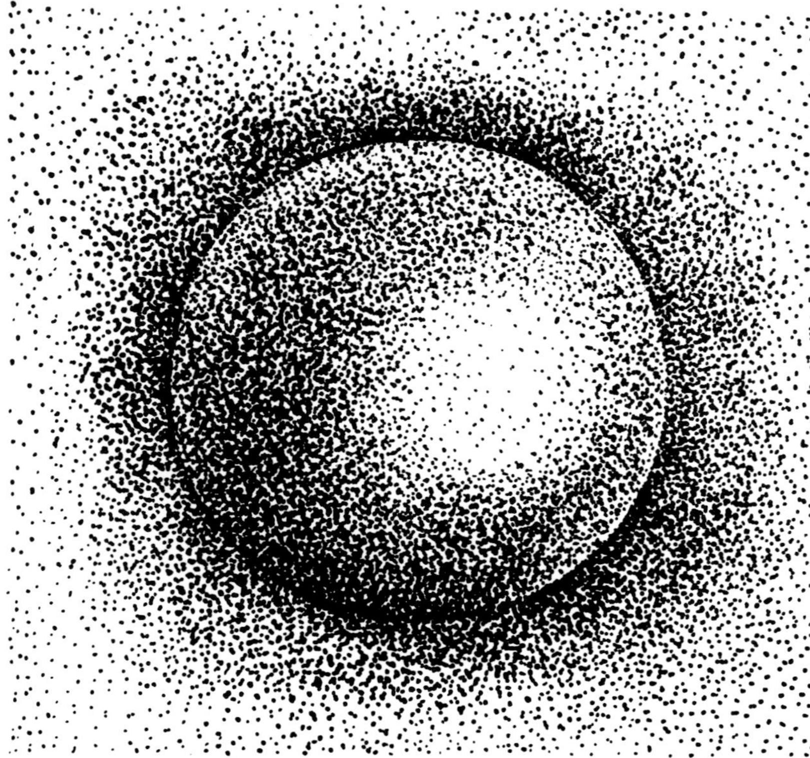

5.8

FIGURE 5.8 45° Light Falling on a Sphere This ink illustration shows conventional light values as they relate to a sphere. In conventional 45° light, parallel light rays tend to wrap around a curved surface slightly, causing a gradual blending of light to dark.

FIGURE 5.9a The Cone and Its Shadow A conical solid will cast a shadow when it blocks parallel 45° light rays (except this time it is from the right rear to the lower left front of the drawing).

1. Project a 45° line from the vertical axis at the cone's apex at *A* to the lower left a short distance.
2. Draw the horizontal axis line *TOS*.
3. Now draw another line parallel to the horizontal axis *TOS* and tangent to the ellipse at T^1 left until it intersects the 45° projected line AA^1 at A^1.
4. Connect tangent points T^1 and T^2 with intersection point A^1, at the horizontal baseline extension, and darken these lines.

FIGURE 5.9b A five-value system variation of conventional light is shown here. Note that the reflected light is approximating a 2 value while a 1 value denotes the surface receiving the most light. The shadow is a 4 to 5 value and defines the elliptical base.

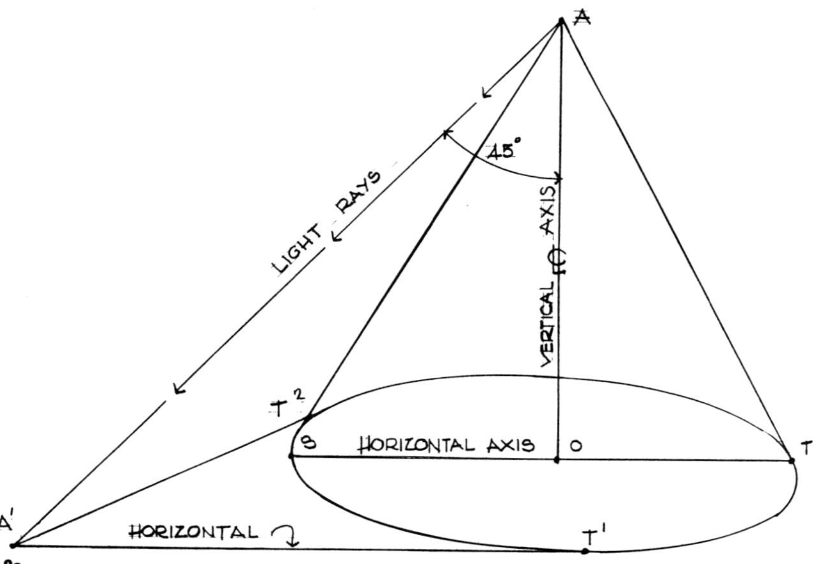

5.9a

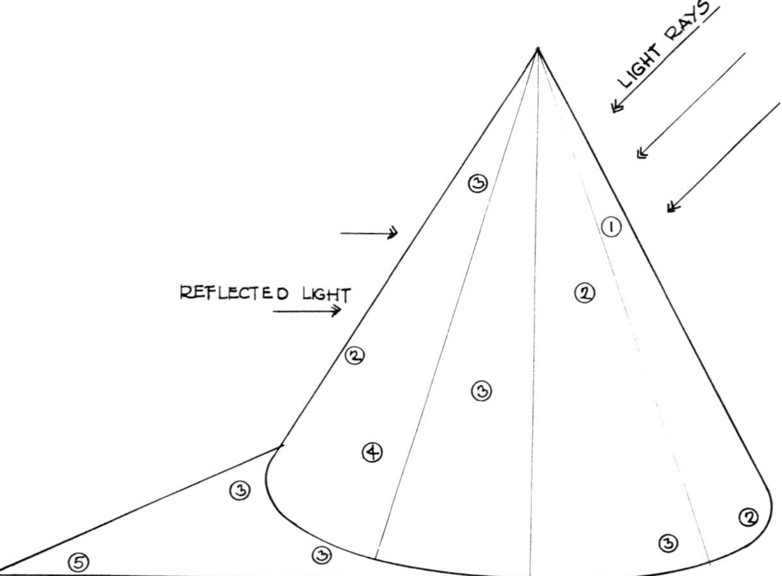

5.9b

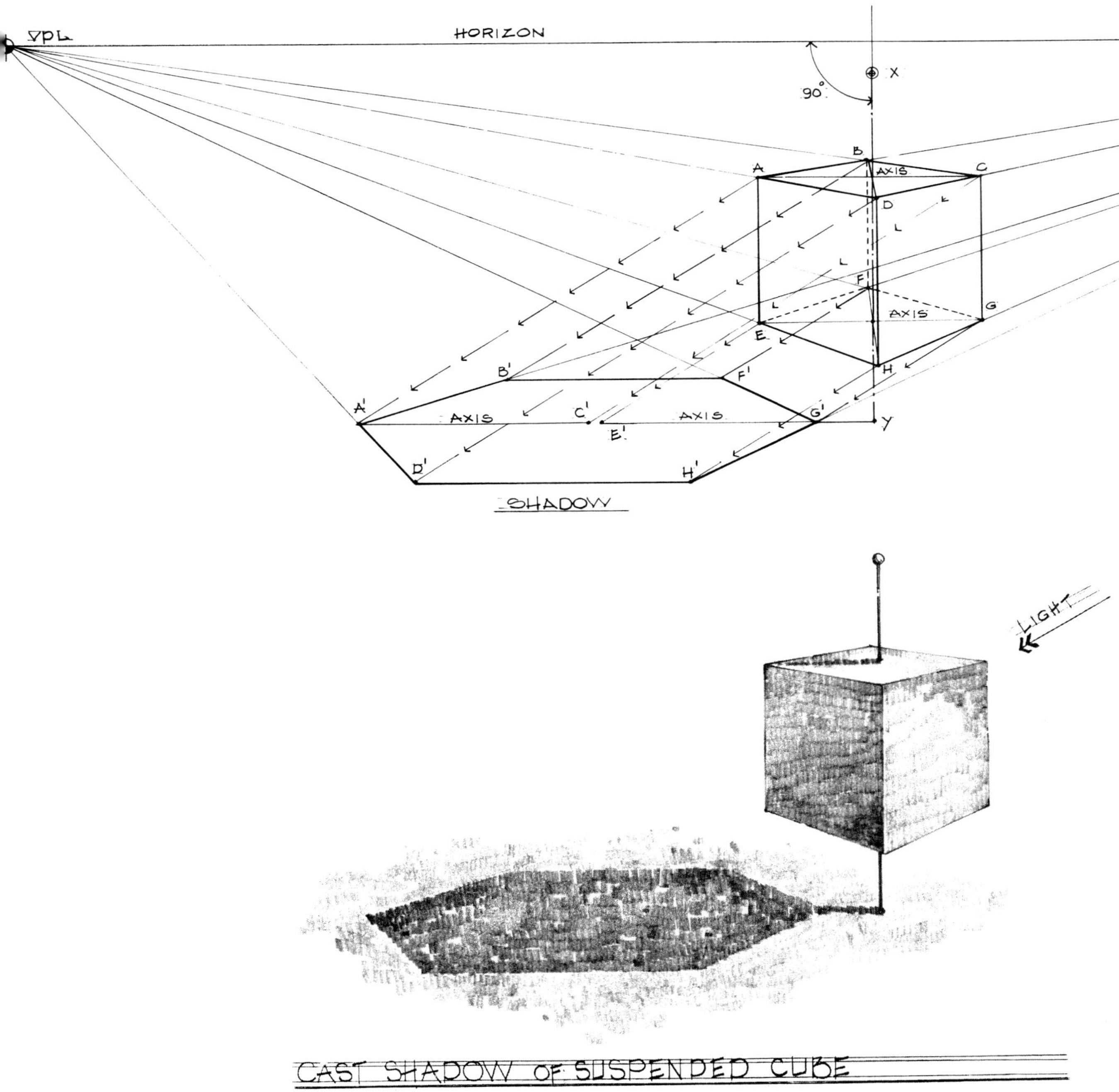

FIGURE 5.10 Suspended Cube When light is blocked by an object suspended above a horizontal surface, the following mechanical projection method can be used:

Project a horizontal line to the left a short distance from the resting point *Y* or vertical centerline axis *XY*. Starting from each of the four base corners of the cube, project a 45° line down and to the left. Note the hidden lines of the cube, shown dotted.

The projected line from *G* intersects the horizontal line that was drawn through *Y* at G^1. From G^1, connect a line to the same two vanishing points that were used to form the original cube, the VPR and VPL. The projected line from G^1 to the VPL will intersect the 45° line from *F* at F^1. A forward extension of the projected line from the VPR through G^1 will intersect the 45° line drawn from *H* at H^1.

Now continue the base axis line *YG* to the *left* until it intersects a 45° line from *A* at A^1. This is the far left extension of the shadow.

Project a line from A^1 to the VPR, which will cross the 45° line brought down from *B* at B^1.

A forward extension from the VPL through A^1 intersects the 45° line brought down from *D* at D^1. Now connect the perimeter lines of the shadow at A^1, B^1, F^1, G^1, H^1, D^1, and A^1 of this suspended cube and darken these lines.

Next, using the four-value system and referring to Figure 5.6c and Figure 5.7a and b, lay in shading strokes that give the volume and its shadow dimension and definition.

Note that each plane of the cube becomes a graded wash, formed by the pencil strokes with values that vary within each plane in order to create contrast at each plane intersection.

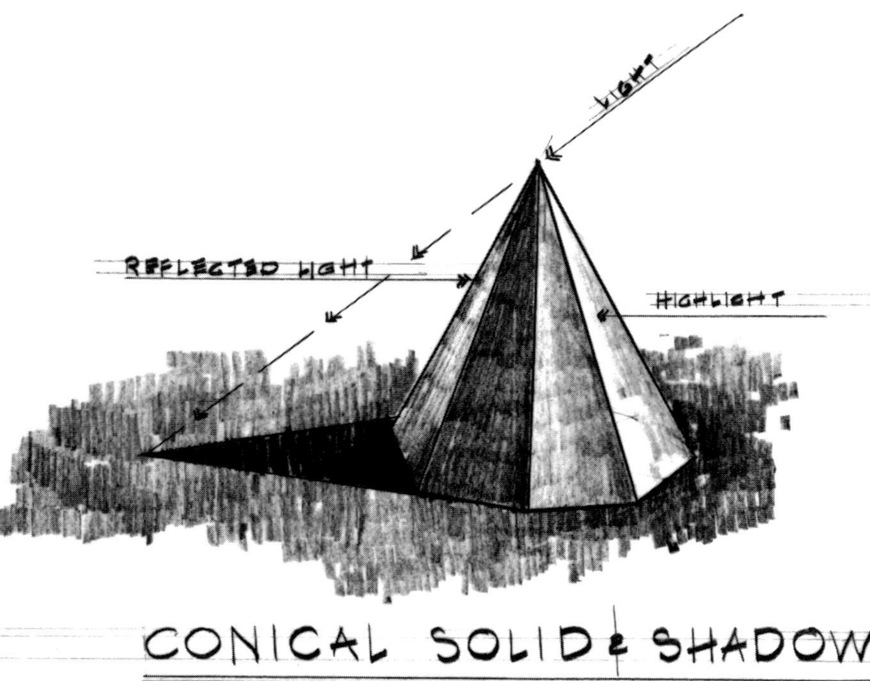

FIGURE 5.11 A Conical Solid and Its Shadow The shadows of this cone are similar to Figure 5.9a and b, except this time the shadow in Figure 5.11c is plotted by projecting a horizontal line from the center of the base to the left, to intersect with a line projected down and to the left 38° from the apex, as in Figure 5.9a. Again the four-value system of conventional light in Figure 5.11a and b is employed to give the geometric solid dimension.

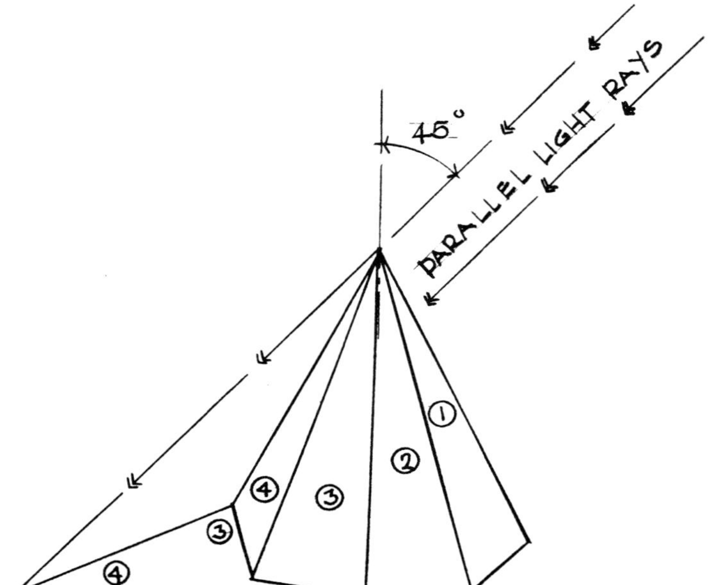

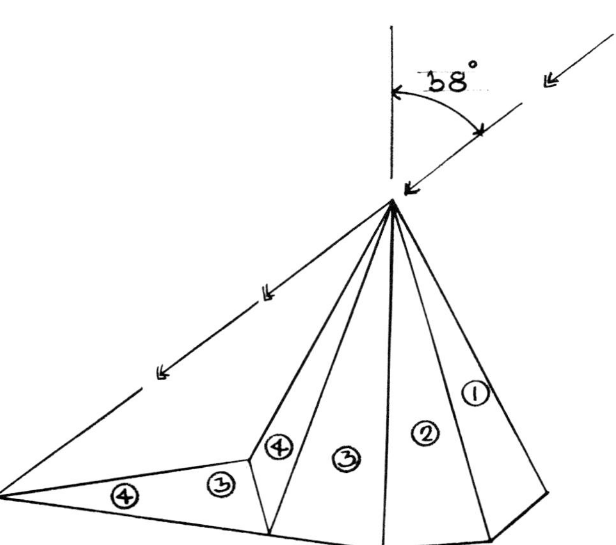

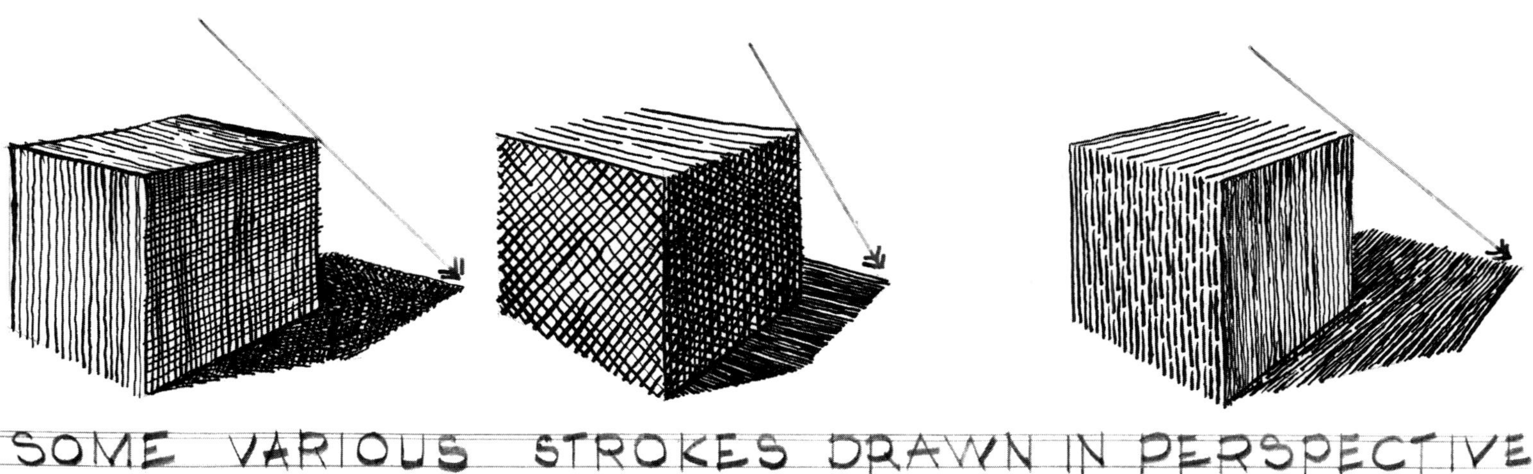

FIGURE 5.12 Cubes and Their Shadows These three illustrations show parallel light rays falling at various angles and the shadows cast by each cube on the ground plane. Here the four-value system is used to delineate dimension and form. Each cube is made up of individual pen strokes laid down with various degrees of pressure, which causes the thickness of the ink lines to vary. This variation in ink line weight can be created by using either a quill pen with India ink or a chisel-point felt-tip pen with variations in direction and pressure.

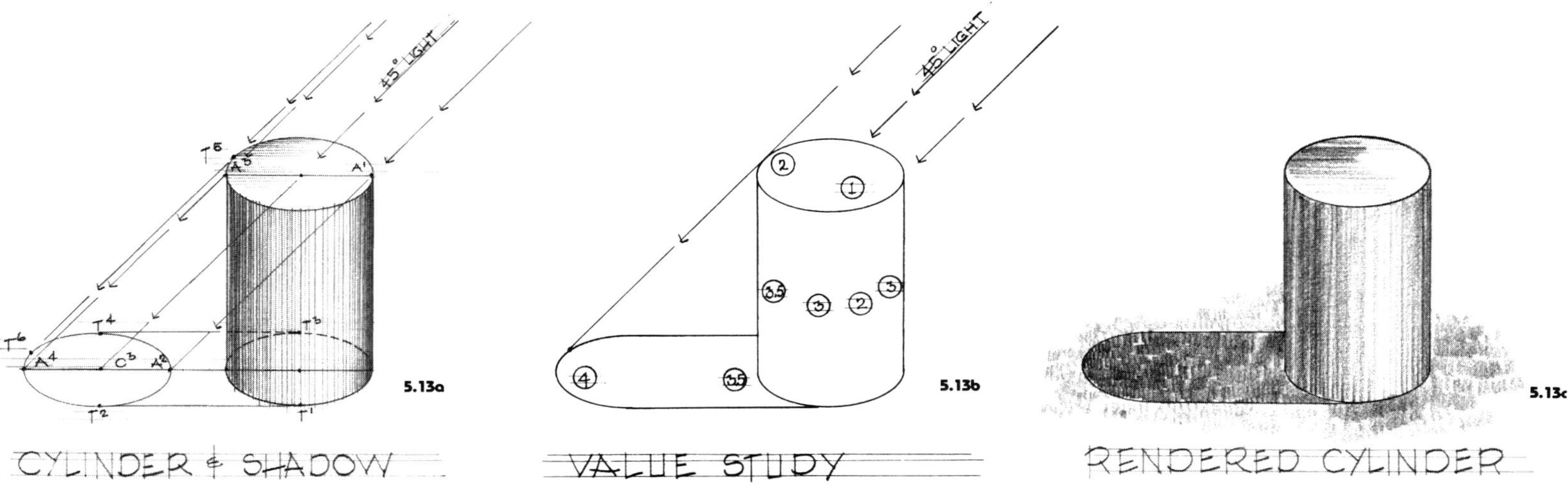

FIGURE 5.13 The Cylinder and Its Shadow Circles shown in perspective become ellipses. These, in turn, cast elliptical shadows on surfaces parallel to them. Tangents T^1 and T^3 on the cylinder shown here, when projected to the left, will intersect corresponding tangents T^2 and T^4.

The elliptical shadow has an axis parallel to the upper ellipse and is a continuation of the base elliptical axis when this line is projected to the left. The shadow cast by the surface of the upper ellipse will conform to the shape of the ellipse casting the shadow.

To find the elliptical shadow, connect corresponding points on each ellipse of the cylinder with their projections, as in A^1 A^2, A^3 A^4, T^5 T^6, and so on.

Figure 5.13b and c shows the four-value system and the pencil-rendered cylinder with its shadow, each following a variation of the principle of conventional light.

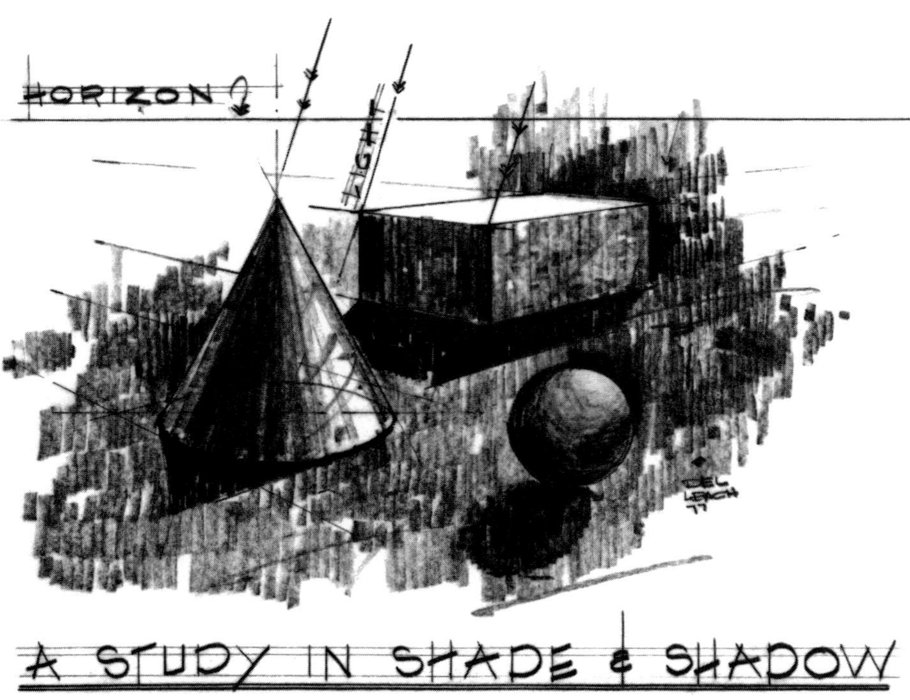

FIGURE 5.14 A Value Study of Geometric Solids The shadow placement and the value designation of these geometric solids rendered in pencil are all based on the previous examples and a variation of conventional light. Note the pencil strokes that make up the planes and how a light area is defined by the darkness around it. *Light defines dark* and *dark defines light.* These are two principles used to create a value study in any drawing.

Shadows Cast by Familiar Objects

Now that you are familiar with basic shadows created by a single light source, let us examine the four-value shade and shadow system using more complicated subjects. The light for the examples shown here comes from the right or left at a 45° angle. Although the theory of conventional light uses light falling on the object at a 45° angle from the front and right, it is common in design illustrations to vary the angle of light as well as the direction, depending on the subject matter being illustrated. See Figures 5.15 through 5.17.

Proper pen-and-pencil techniques, when combined with the shade and shadow techniques seen in the preceding illustrations, can give any line drawing dimension and form. All the illustrations on the following pages incorporate the techniques of shade and shadow, proper pencil sharpening, and proper pencil application. Paper or drafting medium has been used in combination with various hardnesses of pencil lead to obtain variation of value within each drawing.

FIGURE 5.15 Window and Its Shadows The double casement window has been rendered to show the shadows cast by projecting head, jamb, and sill members upon both the window and the wall.

This orthographic drawing is similar to Figure 5.6 in its use of 45° light rays from the *upper left.* As the light is blocked, shadows are cast in a manner that can be plotted accurately in plan, elevation, and section simultaneously.

FIGURE 5.16 Three-Dimensional Wall Paneling Three-dimensional wall paneling and surface-mounted wall-hung items such as picture frames cast shadows on the wall as well as on themselves.

Parallel conventional light rays falling from 45° will be blocked and will cast shadows below and to the right, as seen in this elevation and section. The large molding detail shows how light is blocked by curvilinear shapes.

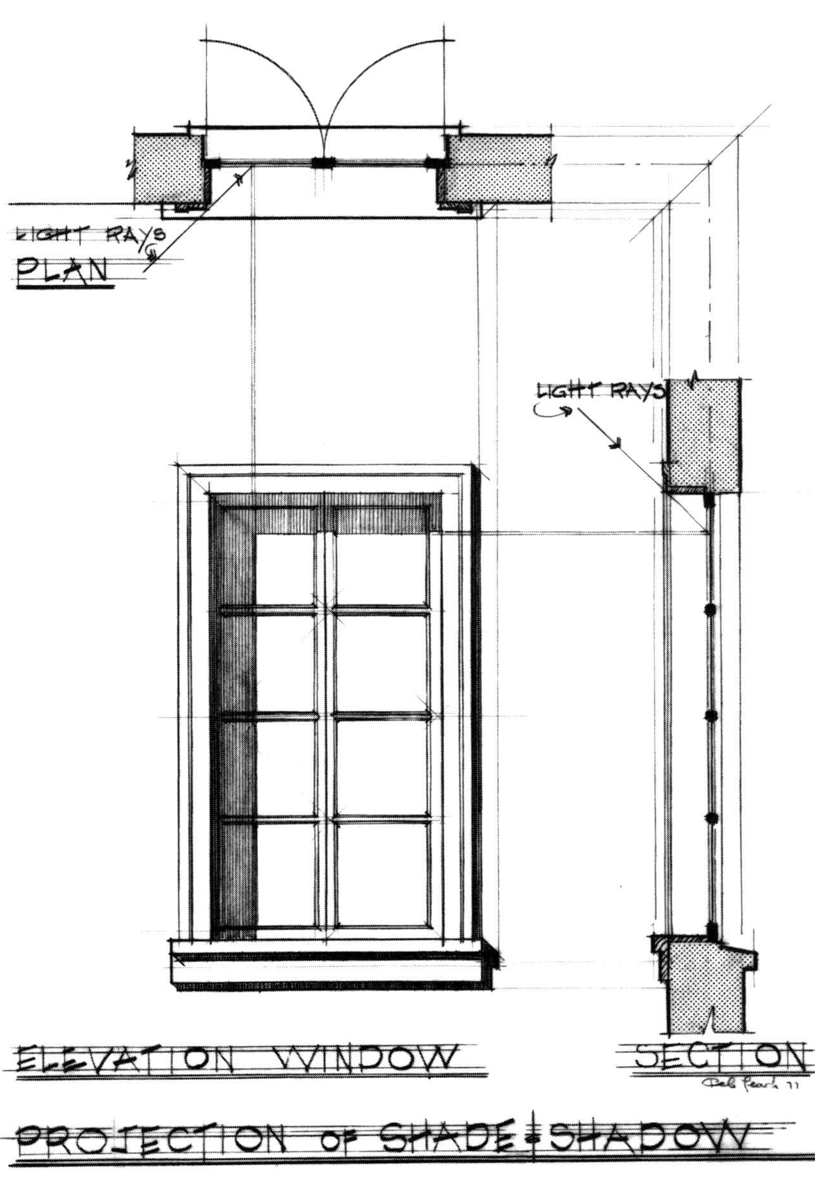

5.15

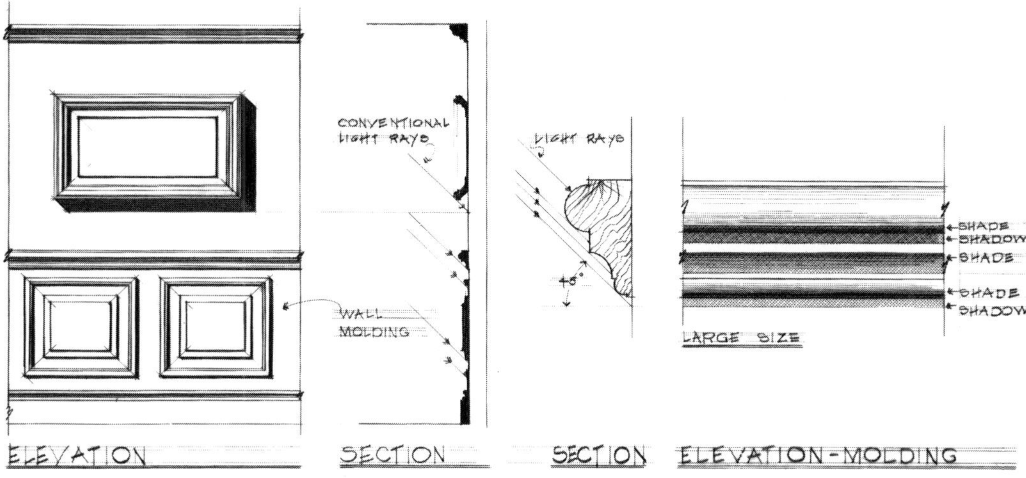

5.16

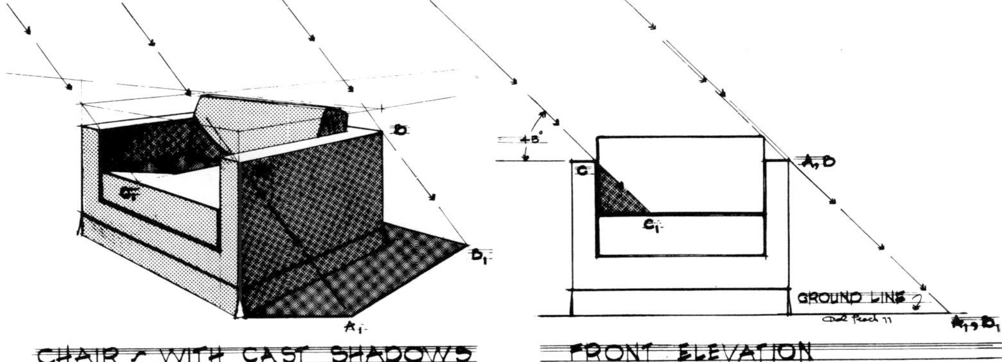

5.17

FIGURE 5.17 Chair and Its Shadows To plot the shadows of the chair shown in this illustration:

1. Trace the lines of the chair to their VPR and VPL. (This step is not illustrated.)

2. Project 45° lines from each corner of the volume that will block out the parallel light rays, but this time reverse the direction of light to extend from the upper left to the lower right, a variation on the conventional light theory.

3. Project a horizontal line from the front apron of the chair to the right until the line intersects the 45° line brought down from *A* at A^1.

4. Now connect A^1 to the VPR, which will intersect the 45° line brought down from *B* at B^1.

5. Connect B^1 to the VPL (part of which will not be seen because of the chair).

6. Darken the shadow perimeter.

7. The shadows for the seat and back cushions are formed in a similar manner. Refer to the front elevation while plotting the shadow areas.

8. Here Zipatone has been used to introduce the value system that gives the chair dimension.

"Light against dark and dark against light" is the motto that should govern all areas of any illustration. Examine Figures 5.18 through 5.28 carefully, and inspect each in detail before going onto the cottage bath addition project that begins with Figure 5.29a.

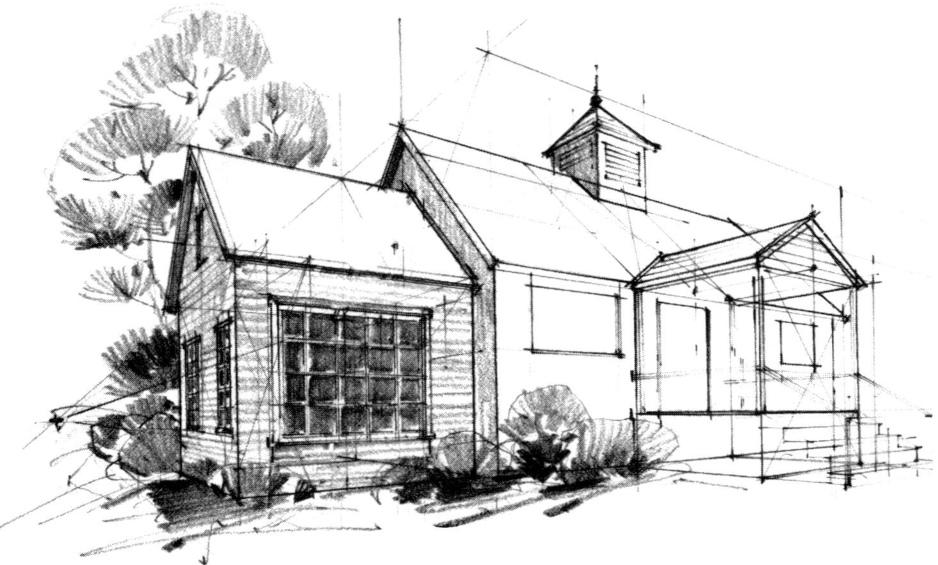

5.18a

FIGURE 5.18a A Practical Application of the Use of Conventional Light The house shown here has a small addition added to the left side. Note how the lack of sufficient contrast can result in a drawing that is "flat," with no apparent dimension.

FIGURE 5.18b This figure shows how, with the addition of the value system of shade and shadow, and careful pencil work, the drawing can become much more lifelike. Each implied *A* plane has, as in previous examples, been separated from the adjacent A^1 plane with a darker *B* plane with each receiving the appropriate value (according to the theory of conventional light). Finally, note how the finished illustration of the new addition incorporates the appropriate contrast between implied planes *A* and *B*. Note also how the use of chisel-pointed 2B and F pencils on frosted Mylar creates the required dark values within the window areas and in the plants and trees that silhouette the subject.

5.18b

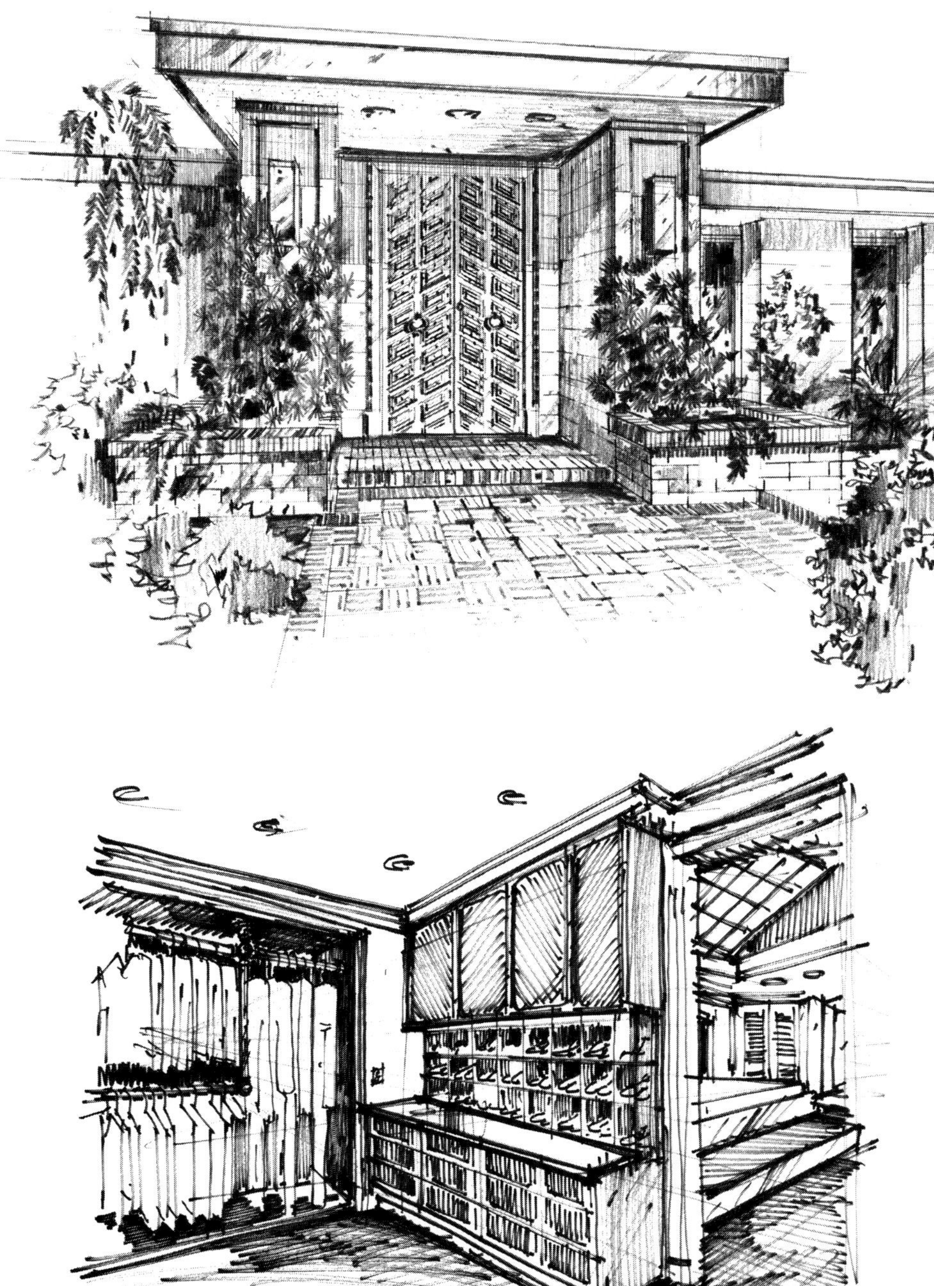

FIGURE 5.19 This entrance was drawn on Clearprint 1000H tracing paper with three lead hardnesses. A 2H lead was used for lines created with a conical point; B lead was used to apply value from a chisel point. The pressure of the lead on the paper's surface was varied to create the gradual value changes on the vertical surfaces.

Also B lead was used to fill in the shadow area that was darkened by using lines spaced very close together. The value was applied to the lines with a chisel point by "painting in" the individual strokes of equal intensity.

A 4B lead was used to emphasize shadow and for the window glass areas, planting, and intense brick-and-mortar shadows.

Note how the underside of the overhang becomes lighter as it reaches the vertical wall area. This would happen normally because of light bouncing off the sidewalk. But if the bricks were too dark in value, most light would be absorbed and little would be reflected. Regardless of the actual brick color, it is good to keep such areas light, to permit detail to be shown.

PROJECT: Residential entry
DESIGNER: The author
ILLUSTRATOR: The author

FIGURE 5.20 "Light against dark and dark against light" is a phrase that typifies this illustration. The clothes and shoes read against their dark background because of the crisp value change achieved by using a new felt-tip pen for most line work and deep shadows. A used chisel-point pen was selected for the lighter areas. The drawing was done on lightweight tracing paper from a tracing pad.

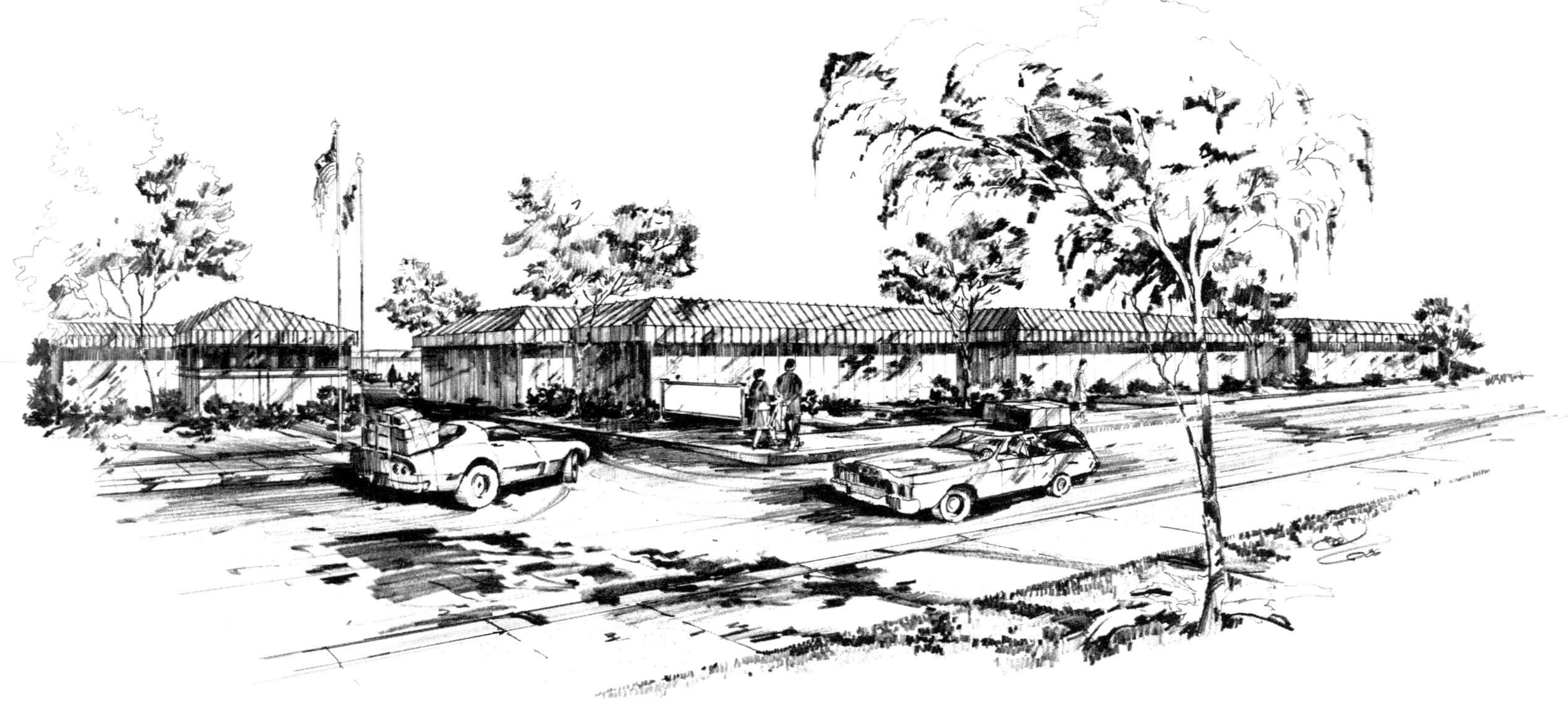

FIGURE 5.21 For the simplicity of plane designation in this pencil illustration, we depend on value to define breaks in this long storage facility building. Clouds are suggested and shadows are created with an H chisel-shaped lead and a 2B graphite stick. These add interest to an otherwise plain landscape.

Notice the strong overhang and raised-rib definition of the roof, created by using strokes from a 2B chisel-shaped lead. The rib shadows are interrupted with small patches of light to lend interest to the staccato repetition of the ribs.

The 8″ × 18″ illustration was done on Clearprint 1000H tracing paper.

PROJECT: Storage facility, Vallejo, California
ARCHITECT: William Kirsch
ILLUSTRATOR: The author

FIGURE 5.22 This addition to a long, low California house is an example of how the dark values of roof, shingles, shake siding, stonework, glass, and entourage all blend into a readable design with the use of shade and shadow and varying light patterns. The roof was drawn with no value designation so it would be highlighted against the dark foliage. The dark tree mass hiding the front corner of the building (that was the TMC of the illustration) provides depth perception by pushing the house into the middle ground of the assumed front-to-rear distance in the drawing.

A strong roof overhang is shown by the pronounced shadows, which were made with 2B and 4B pencils on Clearprint 1000H tracing paper. Shadows of trees and plantings on the lawn were made with B and 4B pencils.

PROJECT: Residence addition, Kentfield, California
DESIGNER: The author
ILLUSTRATOR: The author

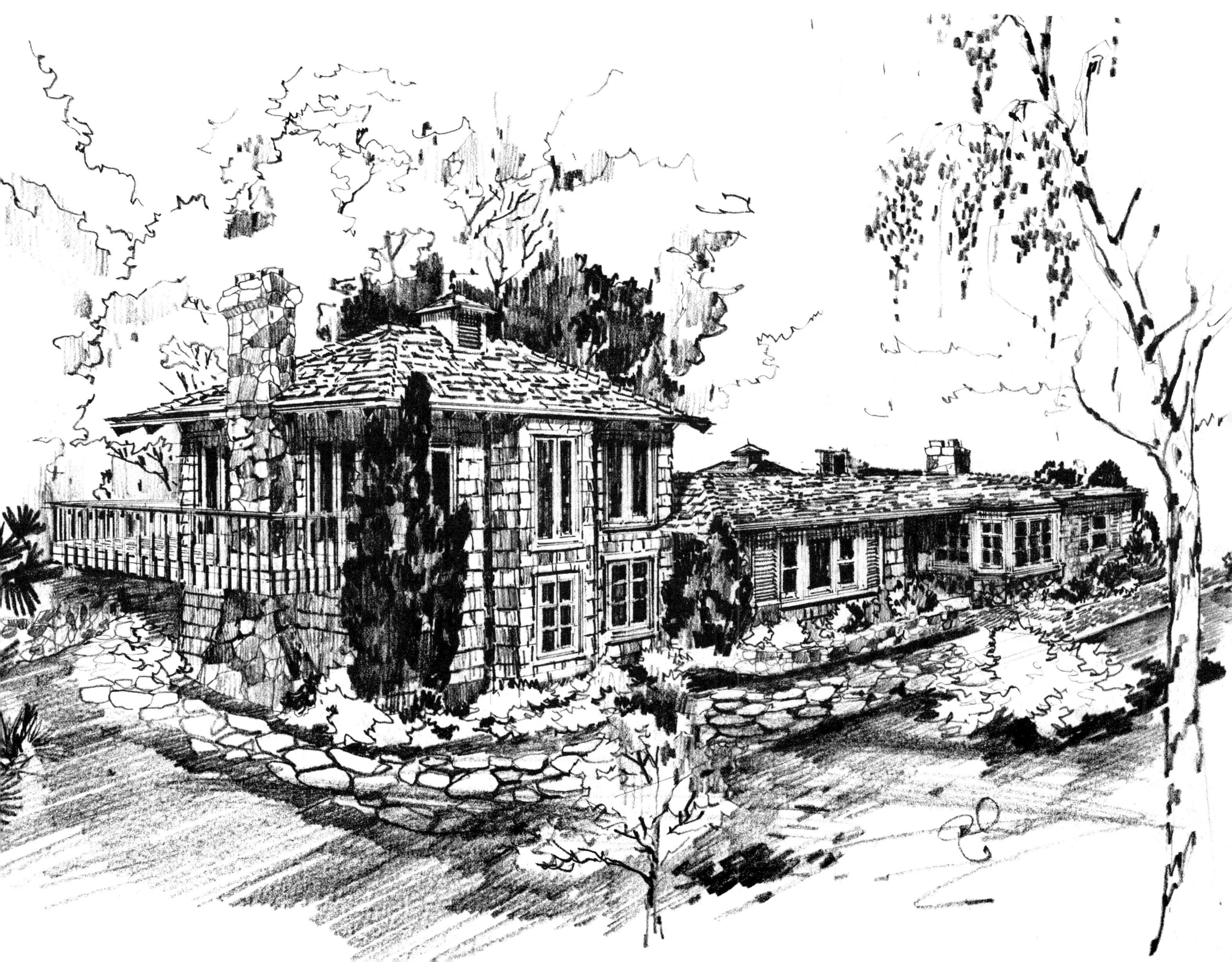

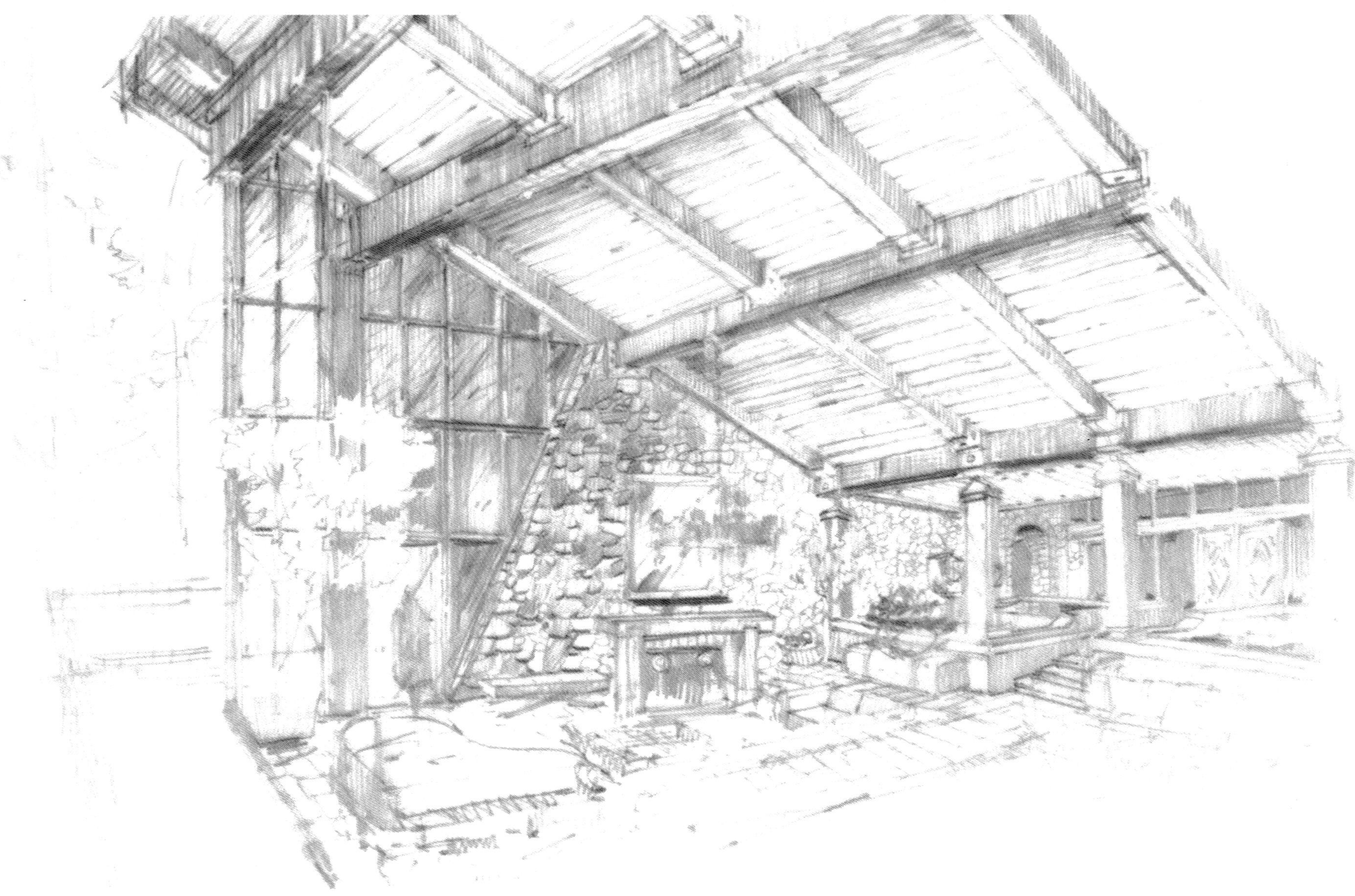

FIGURE 5.23 First this pencil illustration was traced from a close-up photograph of a cardboard model. Then all line work and shading strokes were applied to an overlay of plastic drafting medium (frosted on two sides).

Note that the window areas have been shown in detail at the fireplace wall, but the primary fenestration has been almost entirely eliminated in the foreground, in order to create an inside-outside feeling and to show the entire room without the interference of window mullions.

H and 2H pencils were used for all line work, and B and F for all shade and shadow work. The window area to the rear was darkened with a 2B lead.

PROJECT: Residence, Lake Arrowhead, California
DESIGNER: The author
ILLUSTRATOR: The author

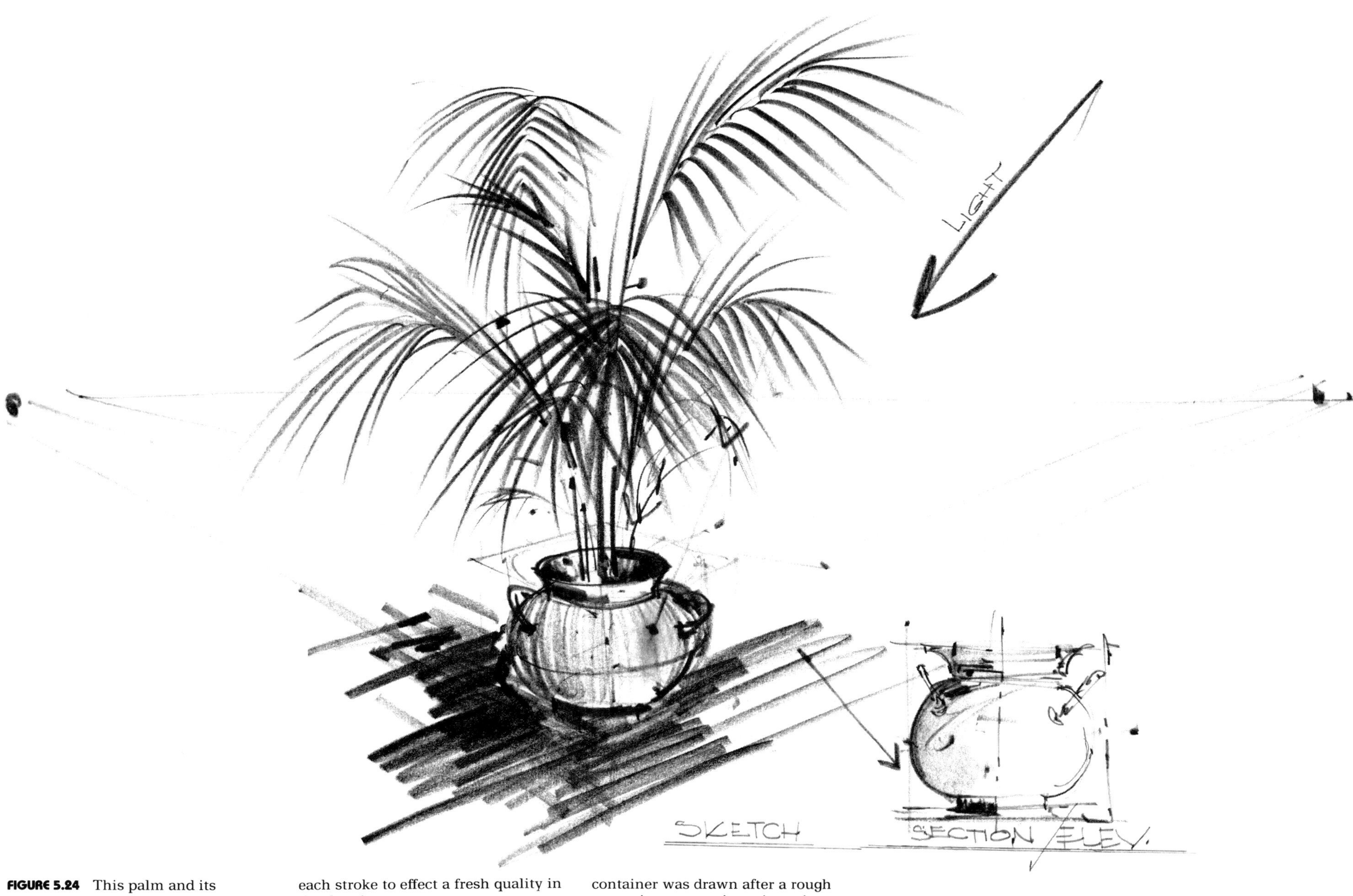

FIGURE 5.24 This palm and its container were drawn entirely with a 2B chisel-point pencil. Each palm frond is created by a single stroke from the center of each stalk to its termination at the tip.

The pressure of the pencil on the drawing surface must be varied during each stroke to effect a fresh quality in the drawing.

The container and its shadow were drawn in decisive strokes by varying the contact of the chisel-point lead to the paper in order to vary the width of each stroke.

Notice the box into which the container was drawn after a rough two-point perspective orientation was made. Light is assumed to come from the upper right in the direction of the arrow.

ILLUSTRATOR: The author

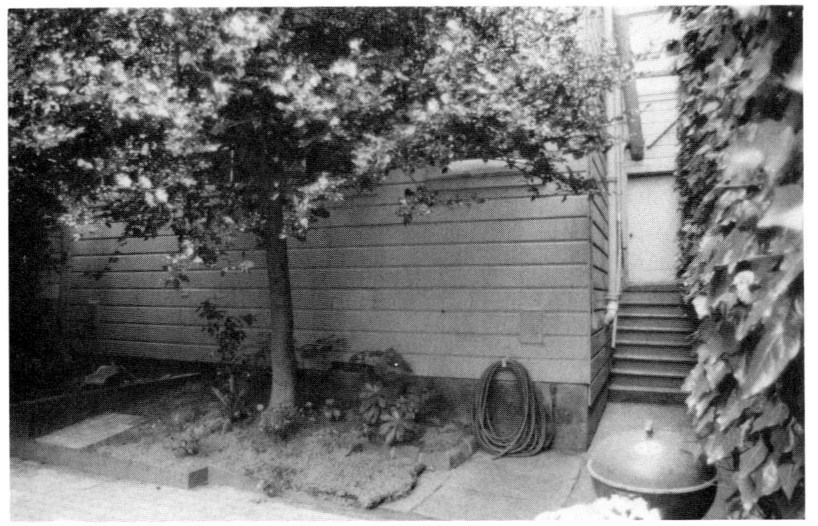

5.25a

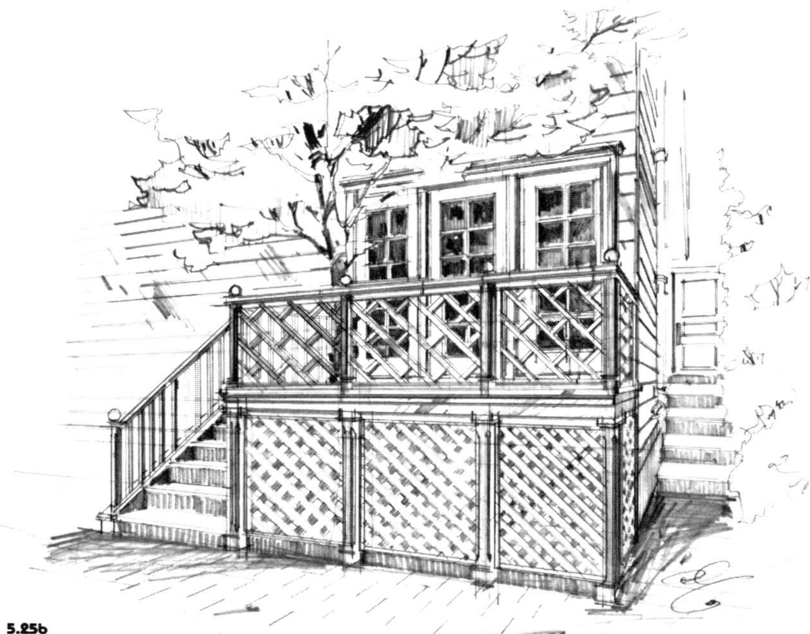

5.25b

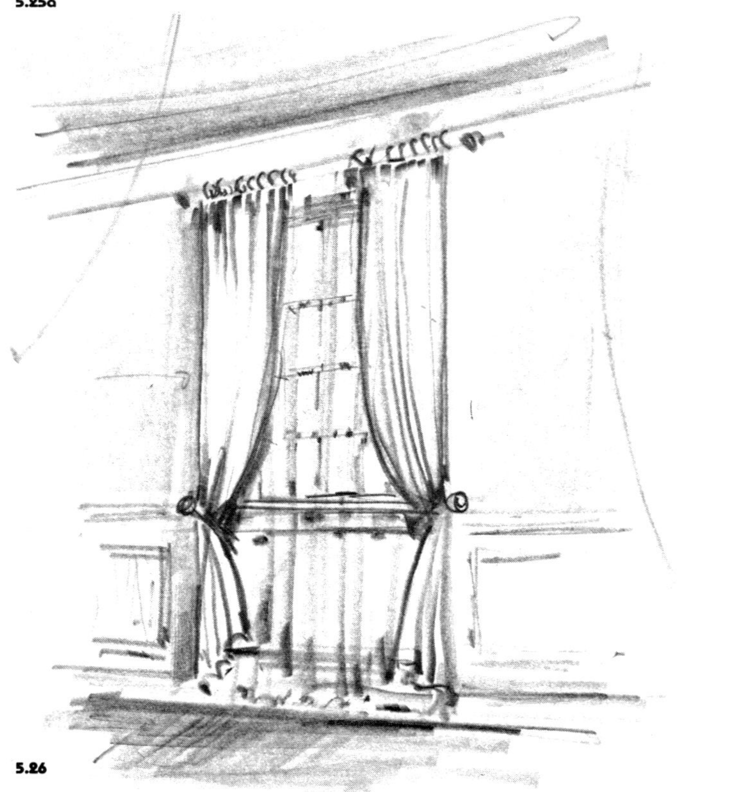

5.26

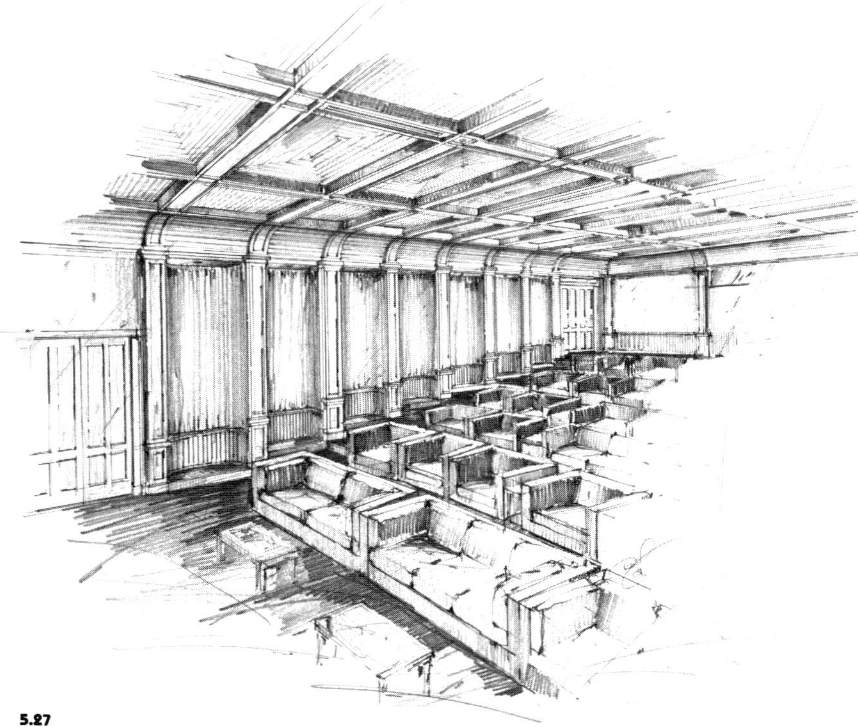

5.27

FIGURE 5.25 This simple deck addition is another example where the siding of a building creates extremely strong directional lines which divide the height of the building in even multiples. This pencil study, done on a Clearprint 1000H overlay after first tracing the photograph to find the two vanishing points, shows strong contrast between the railing and its background. Where there is no dark background, the diagonal members of the railing have been given an approximate 2 value, while the glass areas of the French door lights have been given a 4 value, to contrast with the 1 value of the railing in front of them. Note the shadows cast by each overlapping lattice member and the dark background used to give shade to the square openings between.

PROJECT: Deck addition
DESIGNER: The author
ILLUSTRATOR: The author

FIGURE 5.26 This drapery was created with a 2B graphite stick on thin architectural sketch paper. Again, as with the freehand palm illustration in Figure 5.24, each stroke was varied in pressure, direction, and the angle with which the graphite stick was applied to the paper. Note the light-to-dark gray value that gives the fabric a softness. Often this softness needs to be created in a drawing that has as its basis a traced photograph. A graphite stick allows the user to create feathered edging in each stroke, thus conveying the impression of soft fabric.

FIGURE 5.27 The pencil illustration of this movie theater is, in reality, a study in values. The depth and dimension of the seating and the architectural woodwork are achieved with broad 2B and 4B pencil strokes on Clearprint 1000H tracing paper.

PROJECT: Movie theater, preliminary design, Marin County, California
DESIGNER: The author
ILLUSTRATOR: The author

FIGURE 5.28 One-stroke pencil work traced directly over the line tracing of a 4″ × 6″ color print adds dimension to this simple value study. One dark 4B pencil stroke was used for each pane of glass. This overlay was sketched on Mylar frosted paper (one side).

PROJECT: Hotel suite, Preliminary design, Laplaya Hotel, Carmel by the Sea, California
DESIGNER: The author
ILLUSTRATOR: The author

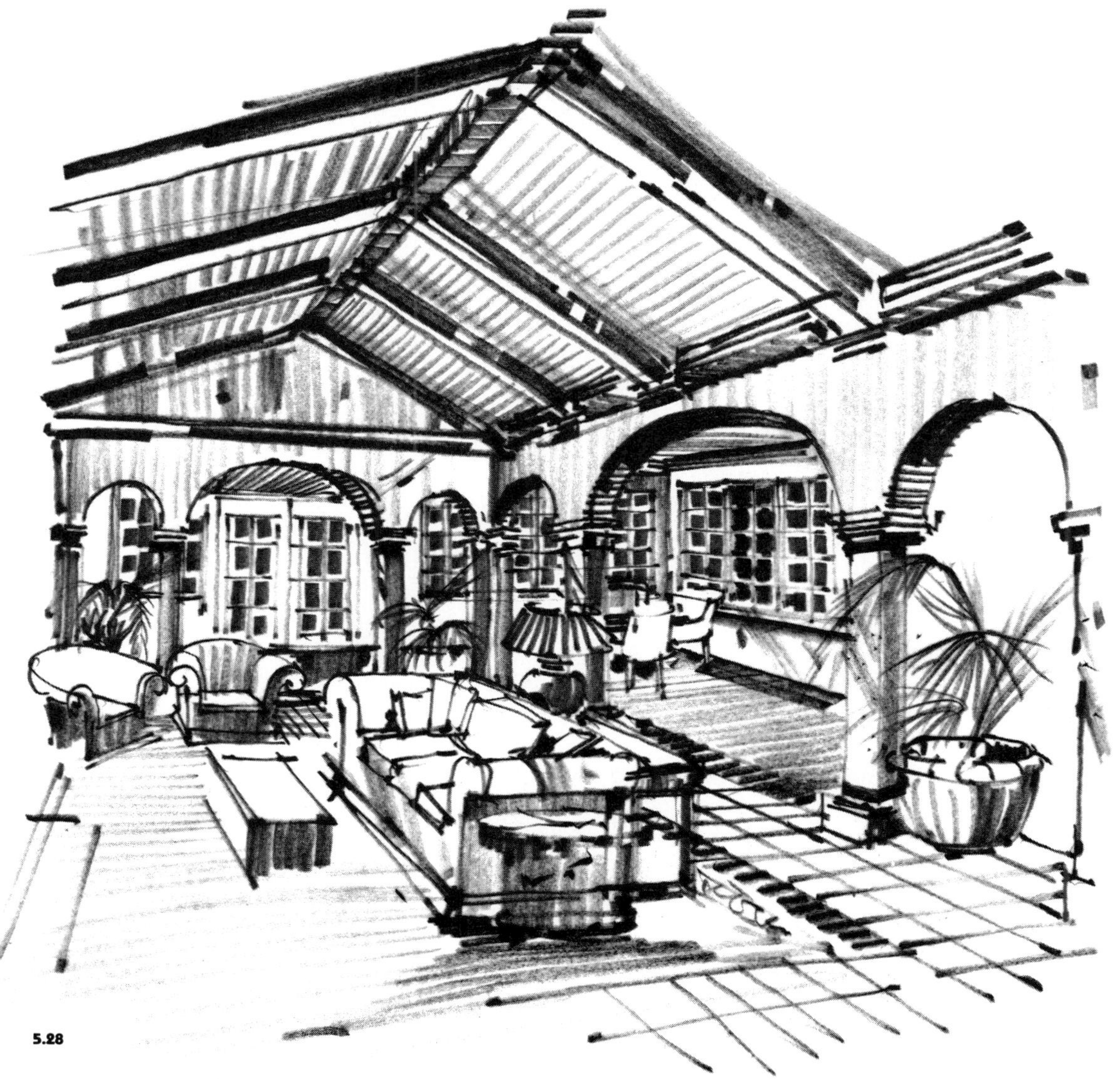

5.28

Practical Application: Bath Addition

Choose the Proper Photograph

The first step when you are building a drawing utilizing the photolinear perspective method is to choose a photograph that offers an interesting and characteristic view of the interior or exterior that you want to draw — or a good close-up shot if it is a detail. As we noted earlier, shots into angles and onto outer corners can be more interesting than shots straight onto the surfaces of walls.

The cottage bath addition, which has been chosen for this exercise, is examined from its plan (Figure 5.29a), elevation (Figure 5.29b), and photographs and tracings (Figure 5.29c through f) through all steps necessary to create a presentation-quality drawing. This is a very practical application of the photolinear perspective method.

Review the Previous Steps

First, review the procedure; then examine the step-by-step procedure for this illustration.

After choosing the initial photograph for this exercise (Figure 5.29e), trace the image, using Clearprint tracing paper or frosted plastic drafting film and a mechanical pencil or, if you are confident, a felt-tip pen. Refer to the cottage pictures in Figure 5.29c and Figure 5.29e for this exercise as well as all overlay drawings required to create a line drawing of the proposed addition and its surrounding environment. Refer to all step-by-step processes used to create the final line drawing, and study these very carefully before you go on to the final pencil drawing (Figure 5.29g through v).

The Value Study

In the drawing process, after completing an initial line drawing, you need to create a drawing that shows just the shades and shadows. This designation of light and dark or shade and shadow, which is known as a *value study,* will give your drawing depth and bring it to life, as we have seen in the previous examples of shadows created by geometric solids and other familiar objects. Without value designation, a drawing does not have any object division. Without the suggestion of light and shade and shadow, objects appear flat and uninteresting.

For clarity, the value study for a completed line drawing (underdrawing) should be done on a separate sheet of white architectural tracing paper, so that the sheet may be placed conveniently for constant referral during the final drawing process. The information from both the line tracing and the value study will help you create the final presentation drawing.

Procedure To create your value study (Figure 5.29q), you will need a soft-lead carpenter's pencil, lightweight architectural sketch tracing paper, and a graphite stick, which will be used to cover large areas quickly and easily.

Tape a big piece of lightweight architectural tracing paper directly over the preliminary line drawing, so that the underdrawing shows through. White architectural sketch paper is preferred to the yellow-buff variety, because subtle tones of gray left by the graphite seem to read better on this surface. Although the buff color is easier on the eyes, it seems to tear more easily than its white counterpart.

Build up the areas of light and shade by using a soft graphite stick. You can plot the shadows roughly based on the theory of conventional light, but feel free to deviate from the rules if you think it will lend character to the drawing.

The Final Presentation Drawing

For the final pencil drawing you will need to refer constantly to the cottage photograph (Figure 5.29e), line tracings, elevations, and overlay sheets that make up the line underdrawing to be used for this exercise (Figure 5.29g through p). For this presentation-quality drawing, it is best to work on Clearprint 1000H tracing paper or frosted drafting Mylar. Both reproduce easily through either photocopy or Ozalid (blueprint) processes. The large-format Xerox delivers a true, crisp, black-and-white reproduction of almost any size of original pen or pencil drawing up to 42″ wide and almost any length, and the image is erasable. The Ozalid or traditional blueprinting methods do not offer a print that can be erased, but the image can be any of several selections of blue, black, or sepia.

Procedure for creating the final presentation drawing It is necessary to place Clearprint or Mylar drafting film over the line underdrawing in order to trace all pertinent linear definition for this drawing (Figure 5.29p). Always register the sheets with a visible register mark or a pinhole through the vanishing points, in case later you need to go back with your overlay sheet to the underdrawing.

FIGURE 5.29a through f These photographs and tracings, along with the floor plan and elevations, were original material used for the final illustration shown in Figure 5.29v. Note the *siding lines* that occur at 7″ heights. These will be used as the *vertical measuring scale* for this subject. Figure 5.29e was chosen as the selected view for the illustration to follow.

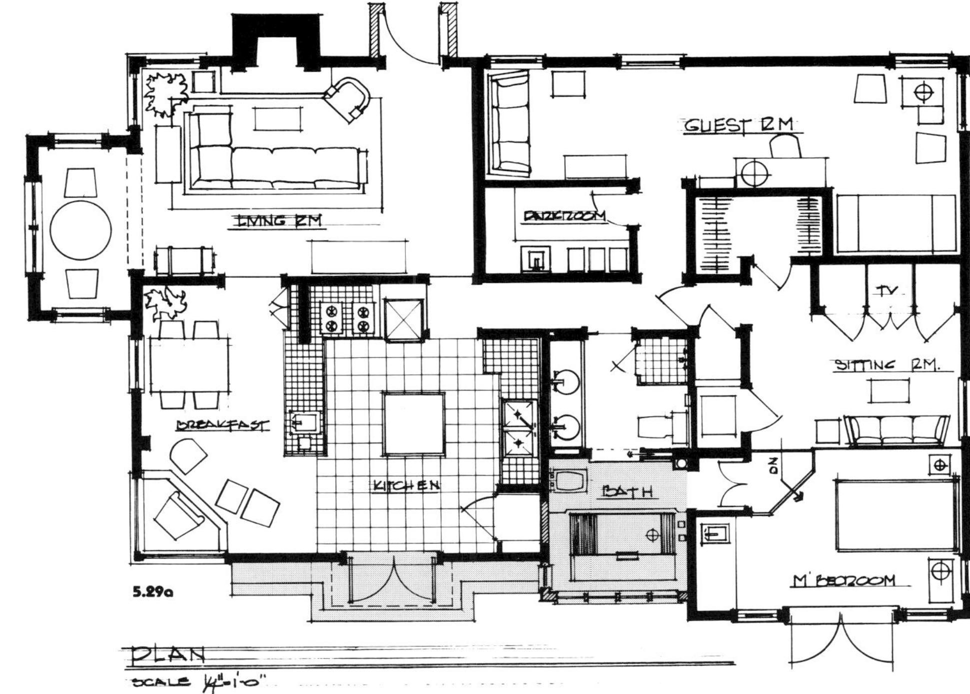

5.29a

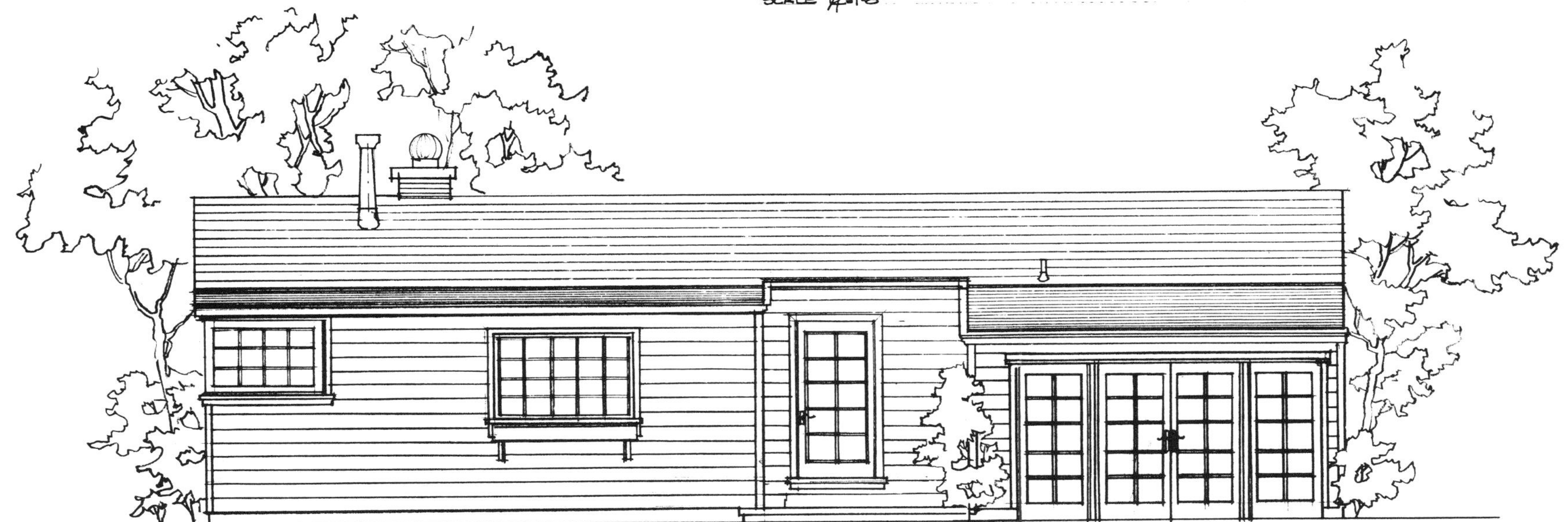

5.29b

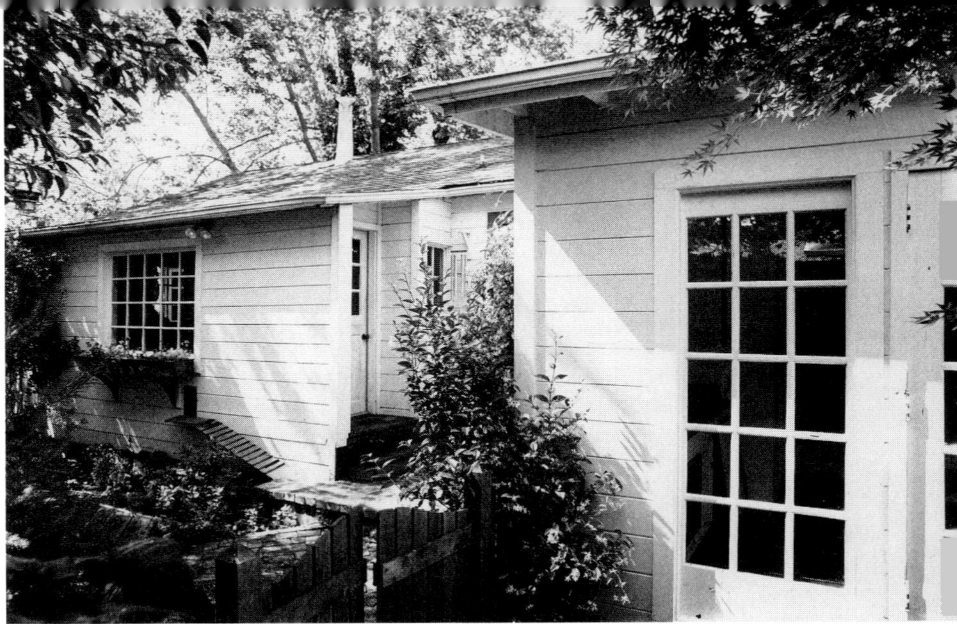

5.29c

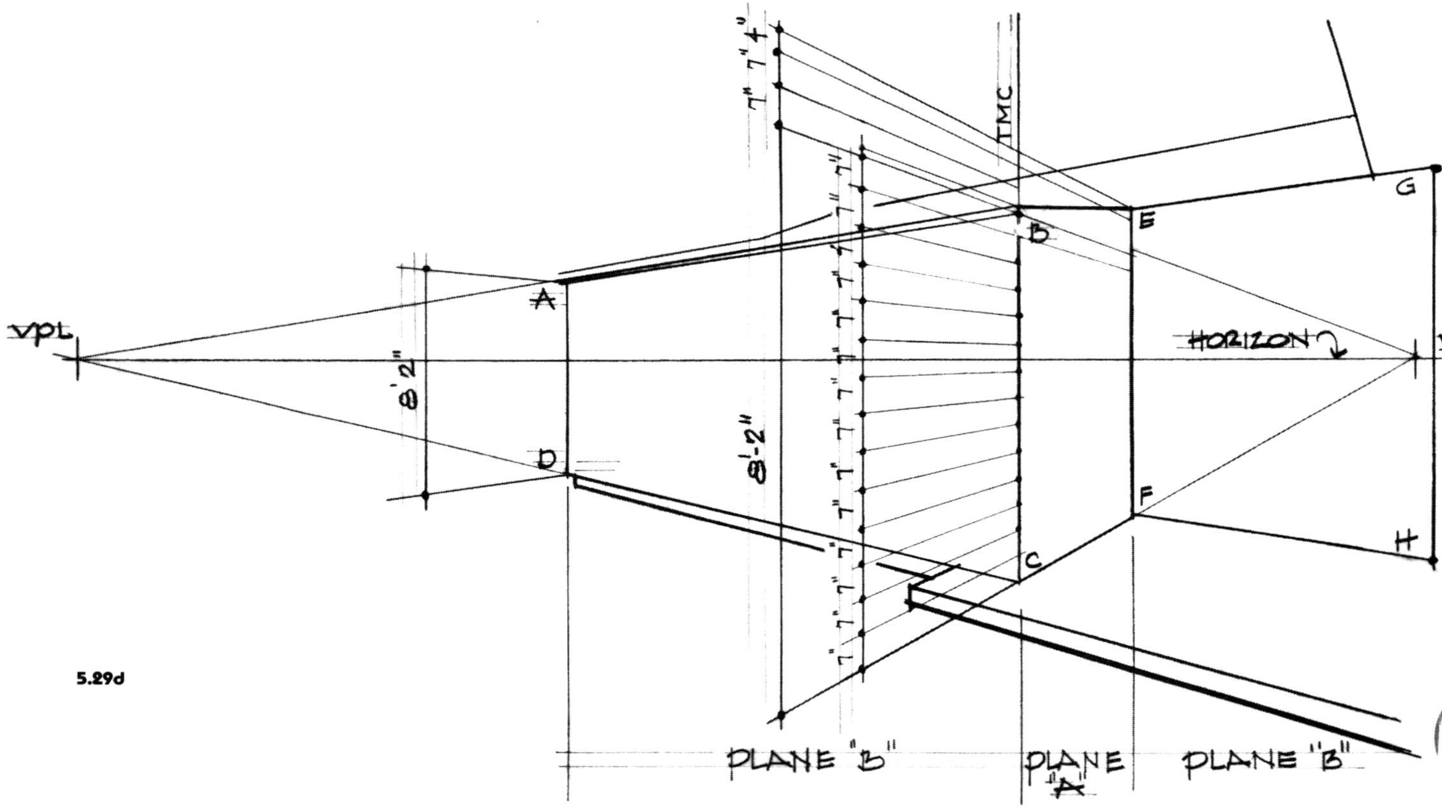

5.29d

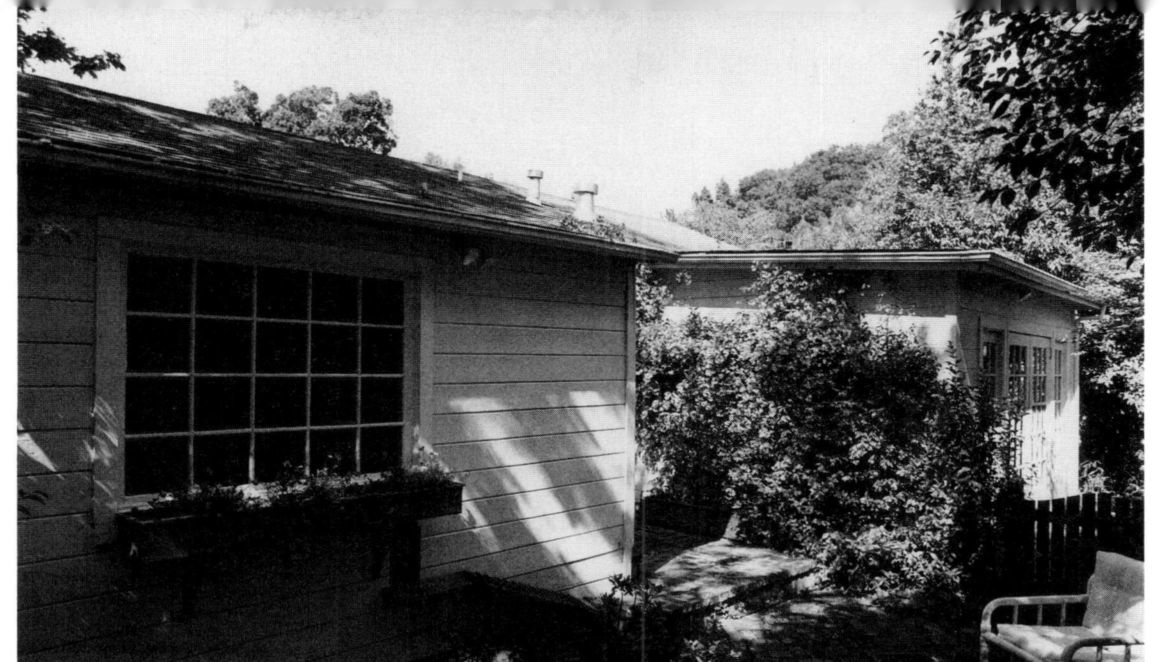

5.29e

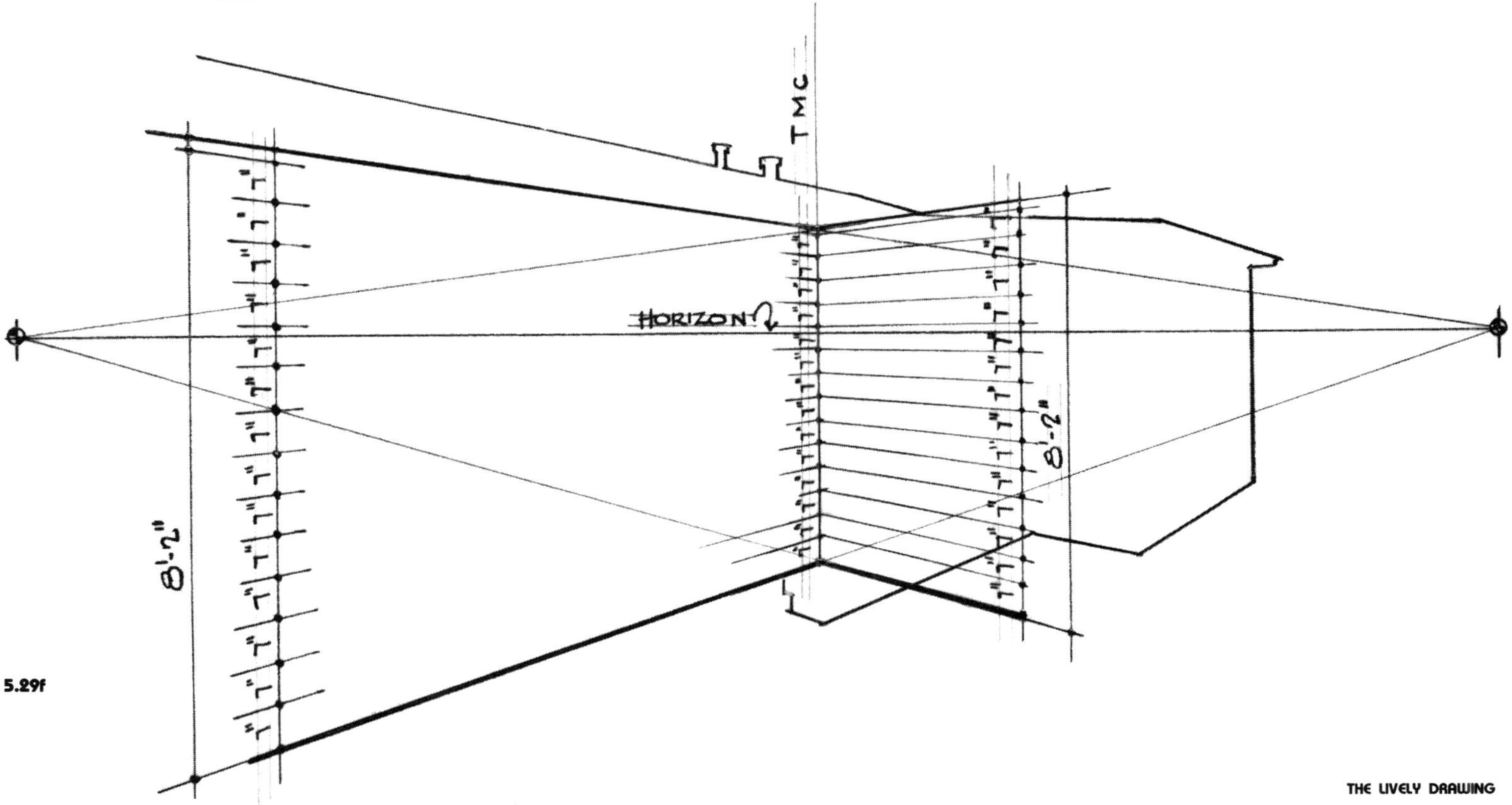

TMC

HORIZON

8'-2"

8'-2"

5.29f

FIGURE 5.29g This partial, in-progress working elevation had been traced in part from the original building elevation (Figure 5.29b). The new construction has been noted as well as the 7″-high siding lines indicating primary visual divisions that will be drawn in the perspective tracing of the photograph (Figure 5.29e).

Note the upper line of siding that is 8′2″ (14″ × 7″) from the bottom of the building's siding line. Next observe the additional 7″-high siding divisions that have been carried vertically to indicate the height of the new window opening, upper window trim, new roof line, new roof apex, lower brick sill, and height of the new brick steps.

Diagonal lines have been used to bisect major window and door openings. This procedure was explained in Chapter 2.

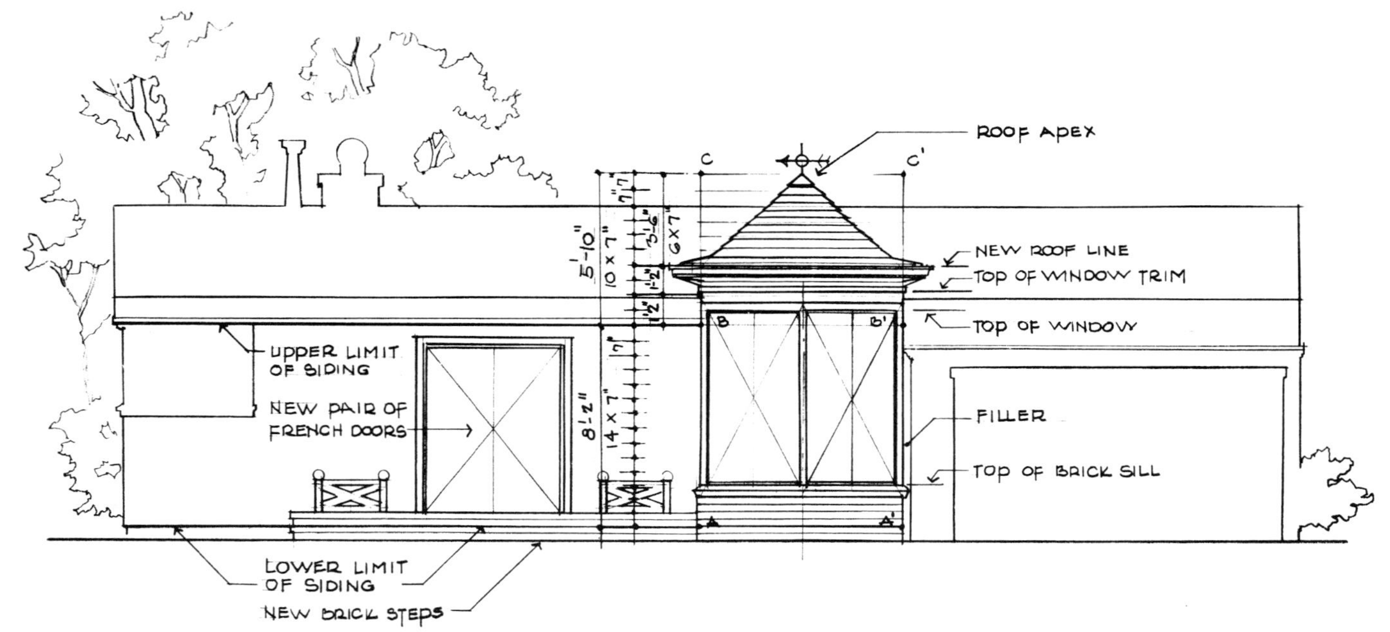

FIGURE 5.29h The completed revised elevation of this cottage shows the proposed bath addition, brick steps, and a new pair of French doors to the kitchen.

The indication of landscaping and planting is used to soften the outlines at each end of the structure. Glass, brick, siding, and shingle indications make this elevation a satisfactory selling tool when combined with the perspective drawing seen later in Figure 5.29v.

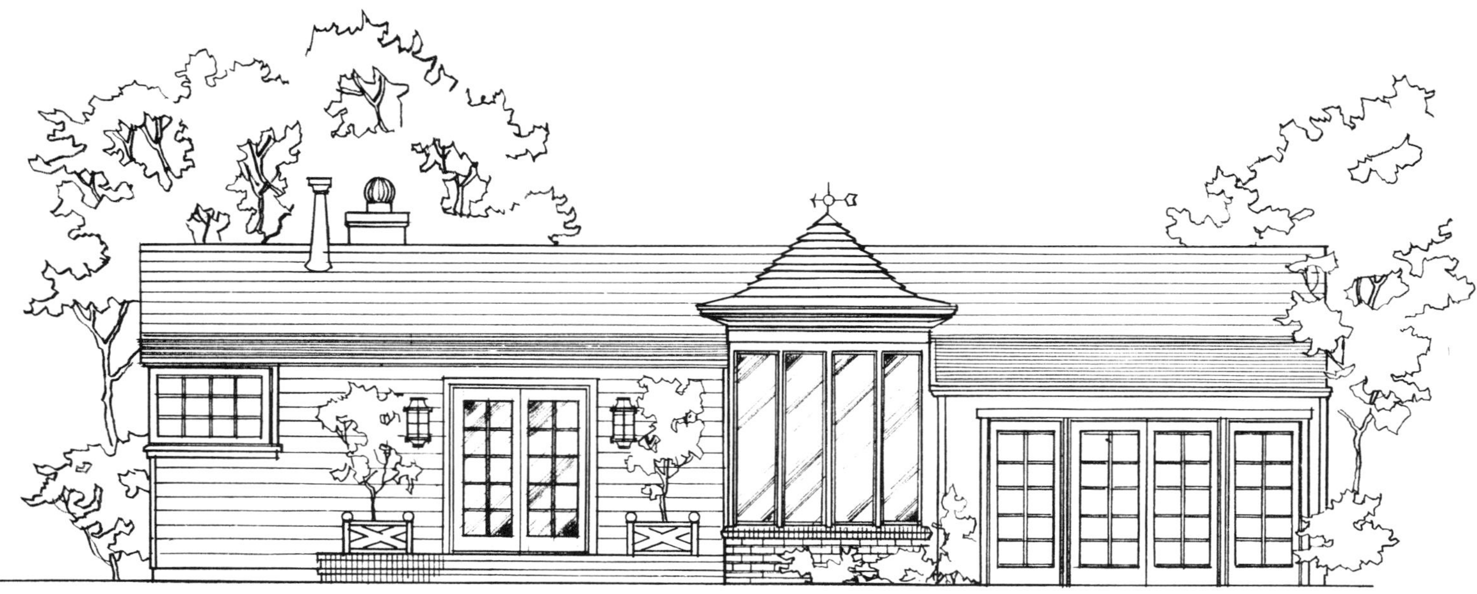

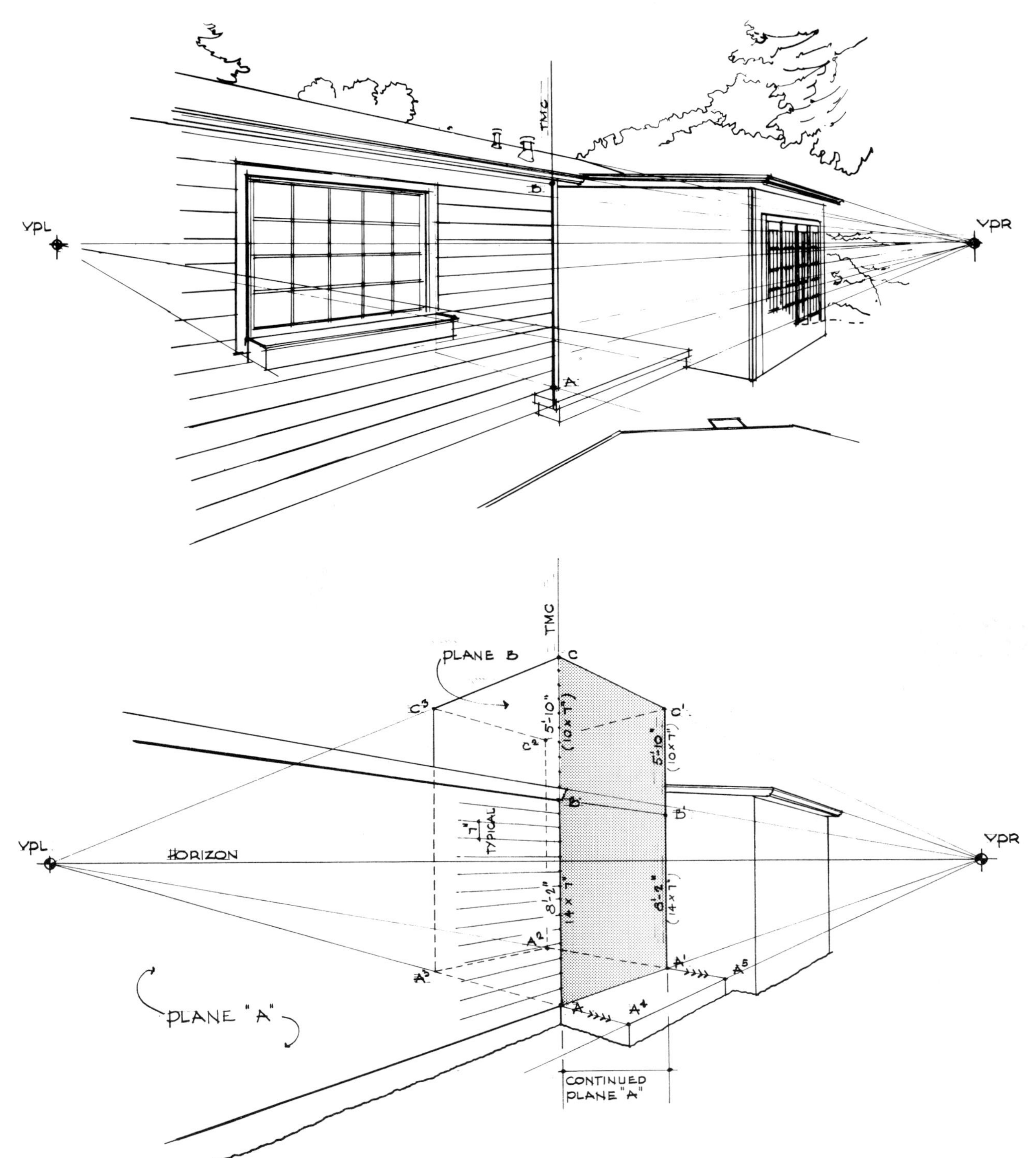

FIGURE 5.29i This tracing of Figure 5.29e will be used as the underdrawing for all subsequent overlay sheets of architectural sketch paper. The VPR and VPL are used in this instance to register these tracings. Each tracing will be carried one or two steps further than the preceding one. Do not try to combine too many steps on each overlay sheet—it will only create confusion.

Note the TMC that has been indicated as vertical line *AB*.

FIGURE 5.29j In this illustration the major plane *A* is continued across the opening between the two buildings. The partial bath floor area has been labeled as $AA^1 A^2A^3$, and the latter two base corners are hidden. The front extended portions of the *proposed* plan have been labeled A^4 and A^5. These two lower corners will form the base of the *extended* plane A^1 shown (shaded) in Figure 5.29k. Note the height extension of this new *continued* plane *A*. Each typical 7″-high increment has been marked on the original TMC and extended to the roof apex boundaries at C, C^1, C^2, and C^3.

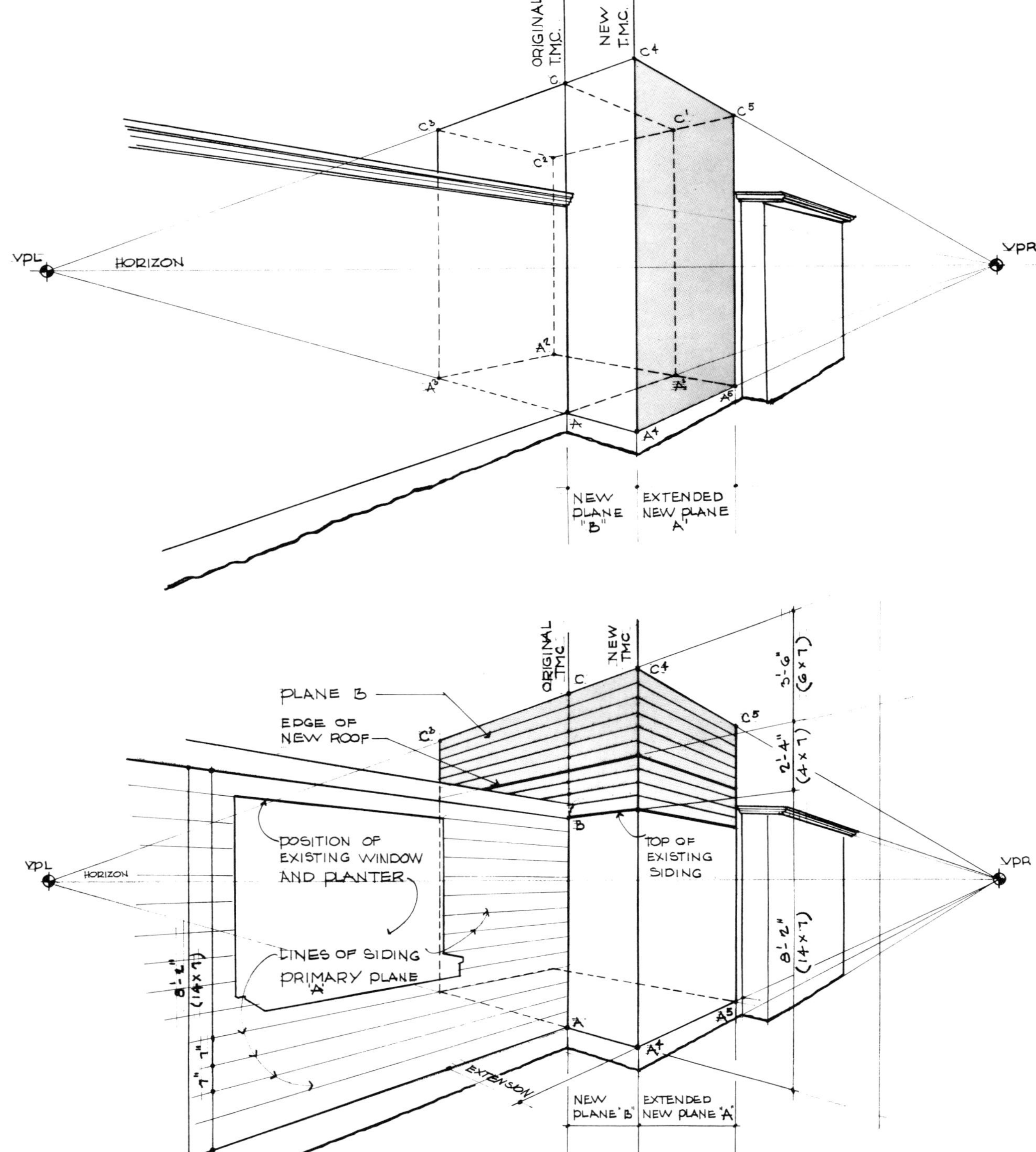

FIGURE 5.29k The extended plane *A* (shaded) has been brought forward to correspond visually to the floor plan (Figure 5.29a) and to provide a new plane of windows. This plane is labeled $A^4A^5C^5C^4$. The new plane *B* extension will form the left-side window plane of the new structure and is labeled AA^4C^4C. Note also the new TMC brought forward from the original location, forming a new plane *B*.

FIGURE 5.29l On this overlay the vertical 7″-high siding divisions have been drawn on both *A* and *B* planes. The existing window and planter box are outlined, and the lines of siding are shown on primary plane *A*. Note the darkened division lines on the new planes A^1 and *B*, indicating the upper lines of siding and the new roof line.

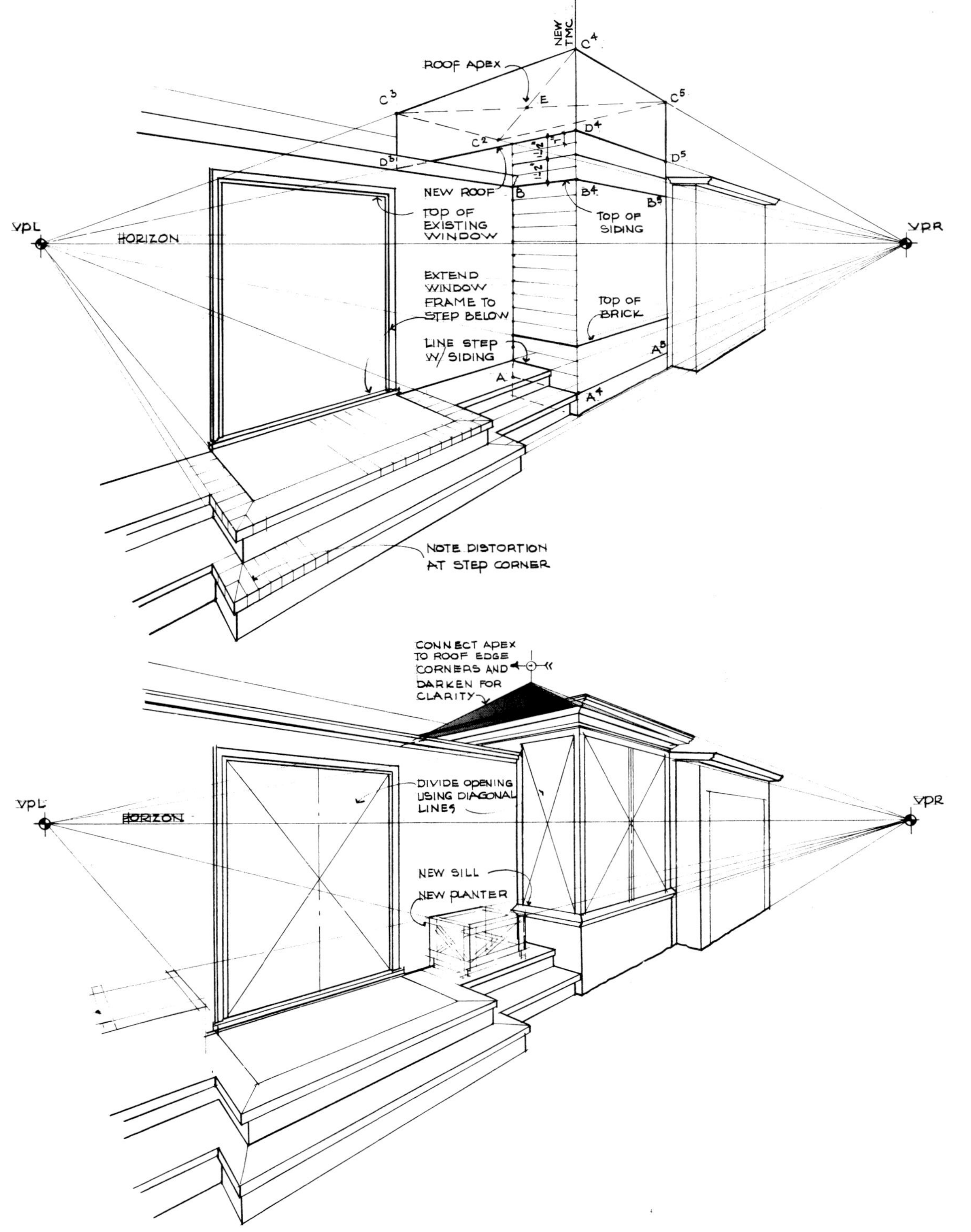

FIGURE 5.29m On this overlay, the center of the roof apex for the addition is at *E*, which is the intersection of diagonals of the upper plane bounded by $C^4C^5C^2C^3$.

The roof is formed by drawing lines from this center point *E* down to each of three corners of the roof line drawn around planes *A* and *B* at visual points D^3 (hidden), D^4, and D^5.

Note again that the new roof line, $D^3D^4D^5$ is $2 \times 1'2''$ or $4 \times 7''$ or four siding units above the line formed as an extension to the top line of the existing siding. The brick steps have each been drawn at a height of 7″ by using the siding as a guide and referring again to the plan (Figure 5.29a).

The distortion noted in the steps at the left front corner will be adjusted in Figure 5.29o.

The brick sill line for the proposed windows is drawn three 7″ siding divisions high above points A^4 and A^5.

The existing window jamb and frame lines on primary plane *A* have been carried down to the top of the brick step, where a new threshold is indicated. This will form the outline of a new pair of French doors.

FIGURE 5.29n Here the new roof apex has been connected to the roof edge corners, and the rain gutter suggestion has been drawn. Note the values designating the two roof planes. Intersecting diagonals bisect each window area, and the sill profile and planter box locations have been noted.

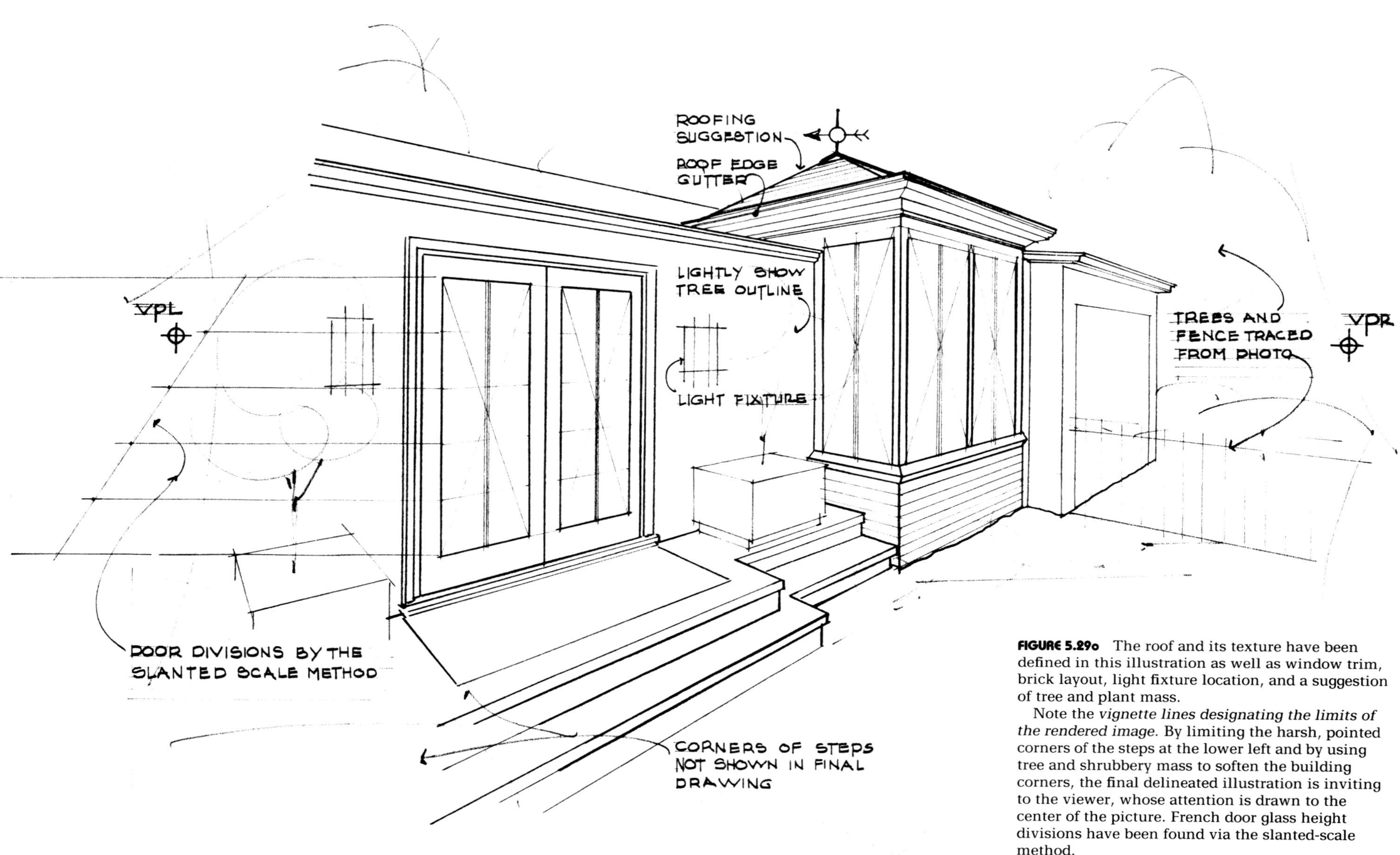

FIGURE 5.29o The roof and its texture have been defined in this illustration as well as window trim, brick layout, light fixture location, and a suggestion of tree and plant mass.

Note the *vignette lines designating the limits of the rendered image.* By limiting the harsh, pointed corners of the steps at the lower left and by using tree and shrubbery mass to soften the building corners, the final delineated illustration is inviting to the viewer, whose attention is drawn to the center of the picture. French door glass height divisions have been found via the slanted-scale method.

The fence and tree outlines are traced from the original photograph (Figure 5.29e), from which the basic outline of this illustration was derived.

This completed underdrawing is now ready to be covered with either Clearprint 1000H tracing paper or frosted Mylar drafting medium, to create the final illustration.

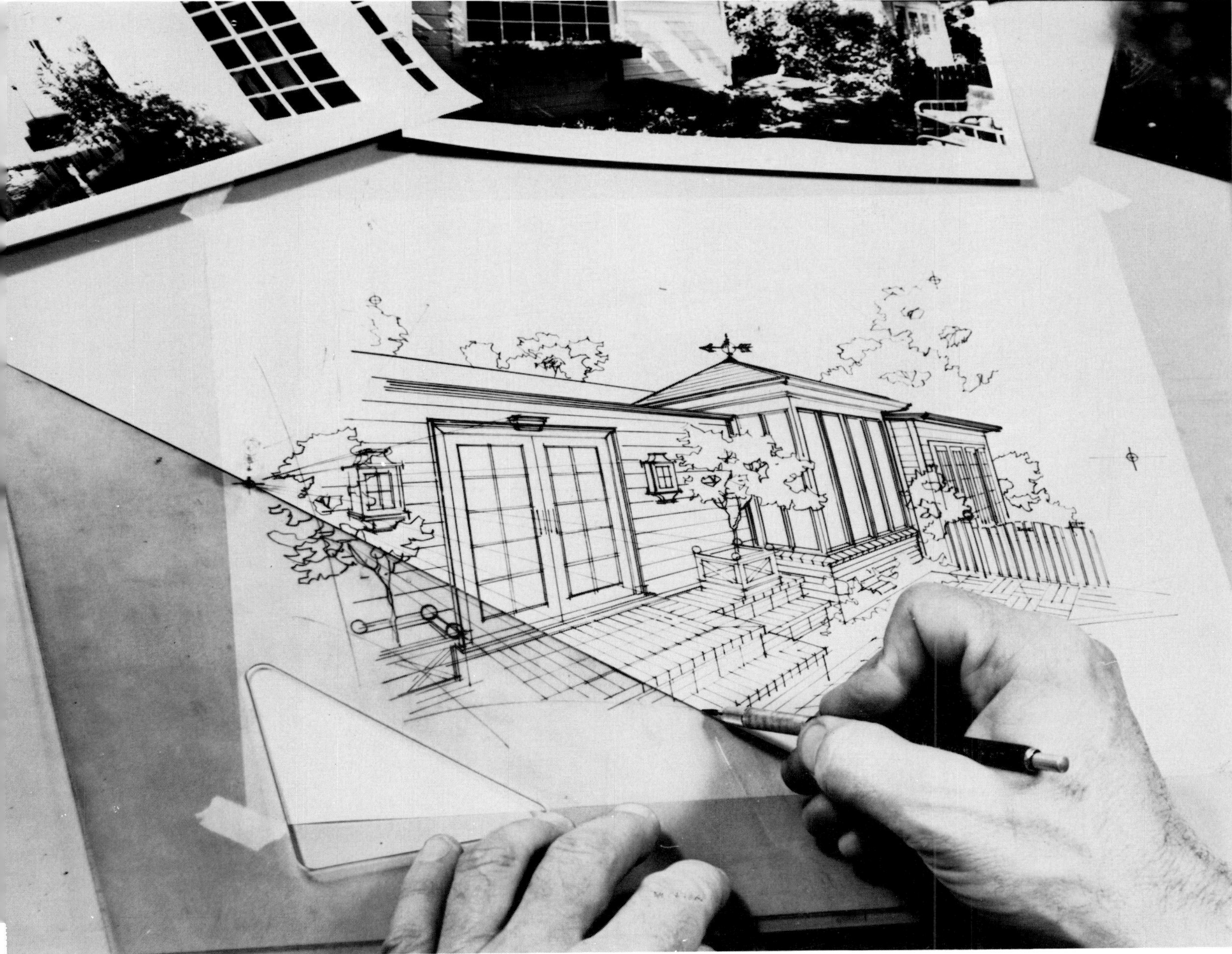

FIGURE 5.29p The main elements of the building and its additions can be lightly traced from the completed underdrawing with a mechanical pencil or a felt-tip pen. Then by working from one side of the drawing to the other with a chisel-point pencil, some of the main shapes and volumes that create the shade and shadow can be laid in. Before that is done, however, a value study must be made. This will be referred to at all times in doing the final drawing.

FIGURE 5.29q and r Tape a sheet of white architectural sketch paper to the table, directly over the completed underdrawing and the beginning of the final pencil work. The underdrawing should be clearly visible beneath. Use a soft 4B graphite stick to build up value, following both the drawing and the conventional light theory. Remember: light against dark and dark against light. Sometimes you must break the rules to give the drawing both definition and character.

Apply areas of graphite to the overlay sheet of tracing paper in varying tones of gray until, by squinting at this value study, you can determine where added tonal buildup may be needed for the drawing to read. Refer often to the geometric shade and shadow exercises in this chapter. Work very carefully from light to dark trying not to erase if possible. Remember, lines are not necessary for this study — only areas of light and dark.

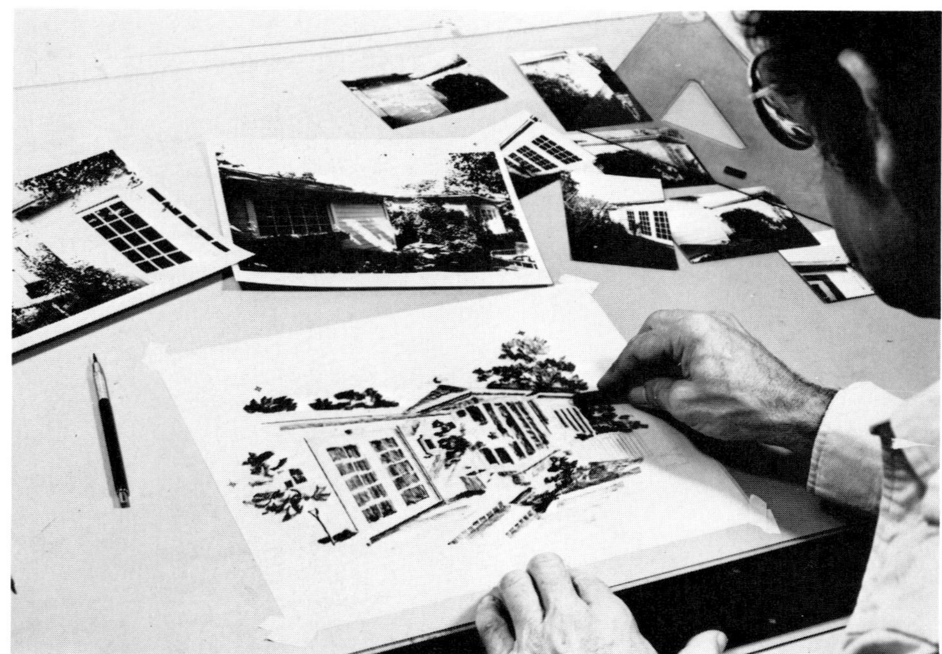

5.29q

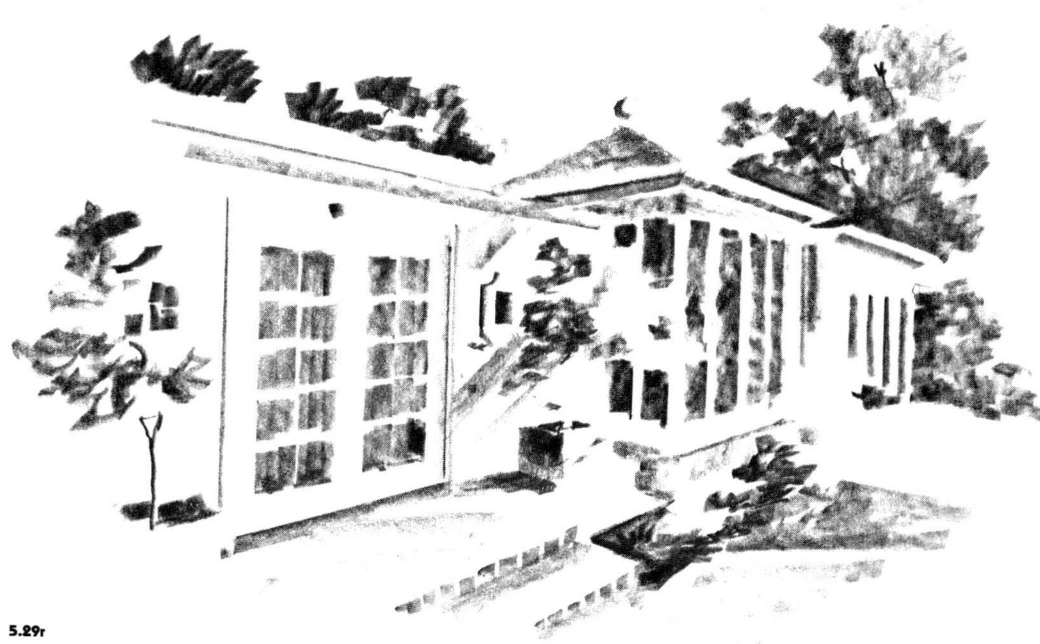

5.29r

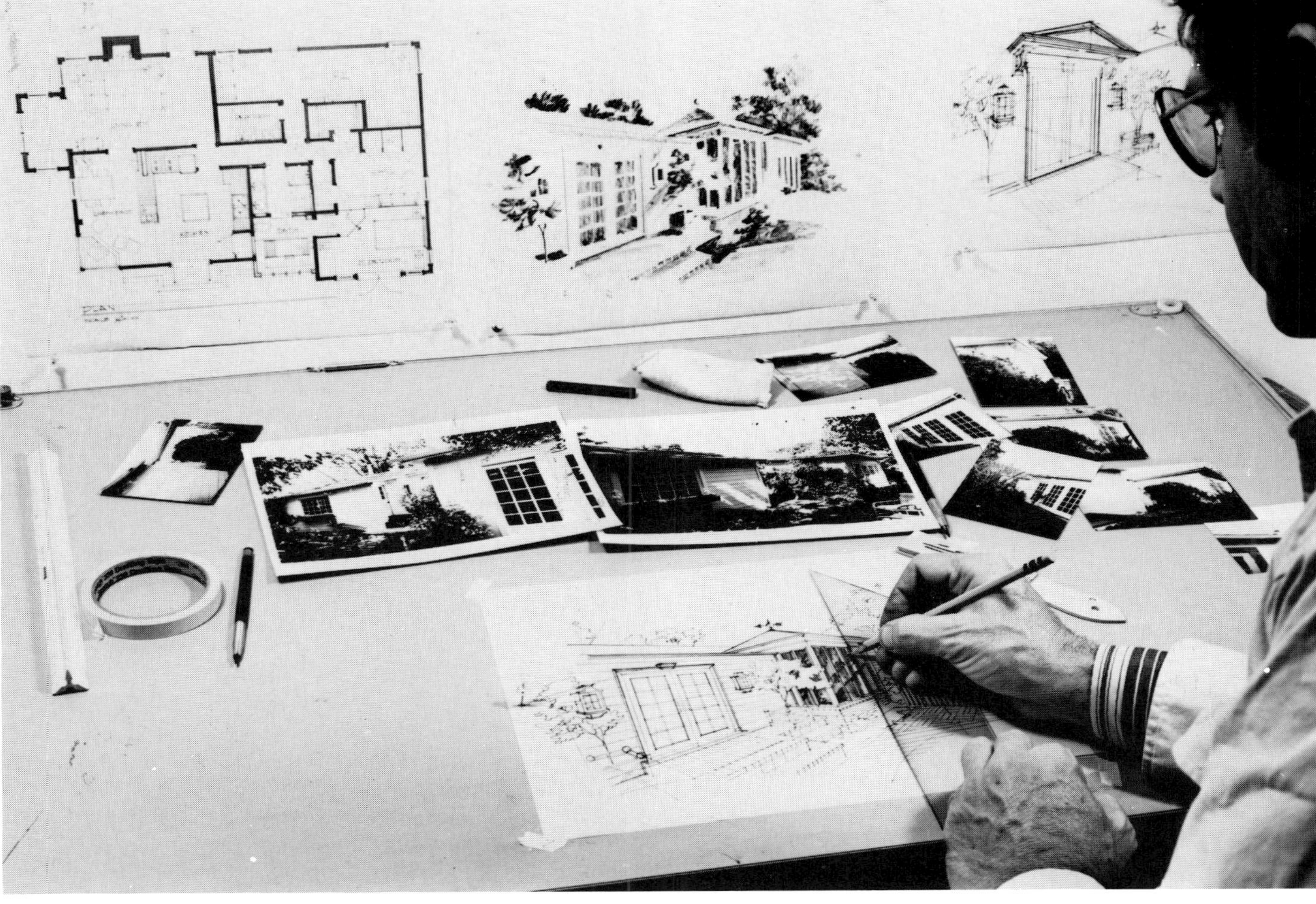

FIGURE 5.29s Once the value study has been completed, the finished illustration may be continued in either pencil or pen. The drawing in our illustration process is done on Clearprint 1000H tracing paper for ease of reproduction with F, 2B, 4B, H, and HB lead pencils. We also used a common household yellow no. 2 wood pencil sharpened to a chisel point.

Working from one side of the illustration to the other, complete as much as possible in one area before you go on to the next. Use a combination of pencil lead weights to create the necessary value designations.

Be certain that you have placed registration marks in at least two corners and far from any area that might be part of the actual drawing, or else use the original vanishing points to register the tracing. Stick a pen through each registration mark through the illustration sheet. Circle these pinholes on the illustration and on the underdrawing for later ease of location after the registration marks have been erased.

The value study, the additional building-condition photographs, and the floor plan should be tacked up in front of you for ready reference while you are working on the final illustration.

Paint full-height strokes on each pane of glass, using properly sharpened 2B and 4B pencils. Refer again to Figure 5.2. Use a straightedge to keep continuous, flat pencil strokes parallel in the dark glass area. And don't forget to leave some areas white to create interest.

The 8″ × 10″ photographs and the 4″ × 6″ snapshots on the drafting table in Figure 5.29s show the glass areas of the French doors and window as dark gray to black, interrupted only by the thin, white window mullions and reflections of shrubbery and sky. It is this clear, dark area of shadow that you are duplicating with these pencil strokes.

Use the pencil to apply individual strokes of varying intensities and to create as closely as possible the value shown on your value study. If you prefer, you may use a chisel-point felt-tip pen on Clearprint 1000H.

If you are drawing with felt-tip pens on Clearprint 1000H tracing paper you should keep three or four chisel-point felt-tip pens that have *partially dried out* in addition to new felt-tip pens to be used for outlining, heavy shadows, and for creating the lighter values in the drawing.

The direction of the individual strokes, whether produced by pencil or felt-tip pen, should help to define the shape of objects, just as value helps to imply depth within the sketch. Use a triangle resting on a parallel bar as a guide for your chisel-point pencil to aid you in making crisp divisions between dark and light. The pencil chosen for most medium values shown in this sketch was a medium no. 2 household-variety yellow pencil complete with an eraser. Chisel-point 2B and 4B leads were used for the darker values. For the line work an HB lead and an H mechanical pencil lead, conically sharpened, were employed.

FIGURE 5.29t and u Diagonal light and shadow suggestions are placed very lightly across siding, doors, and window areas to give the feeling of trees casting shadows. Use a graphite stick for this purpose.

A ¼″ × ¼″ × 2½″ piece of 4B or 6B graphite will cover more area than a chisel-point pencil lead and will yield a smooth, soft-edged shadow.

Work from right to left, from one side of the illustration to the other, leaving foliage in the foreground light against its architectural background.

PROJECT: Residential addition
DESIGNER: The author
ILLUSTRATOR: The author

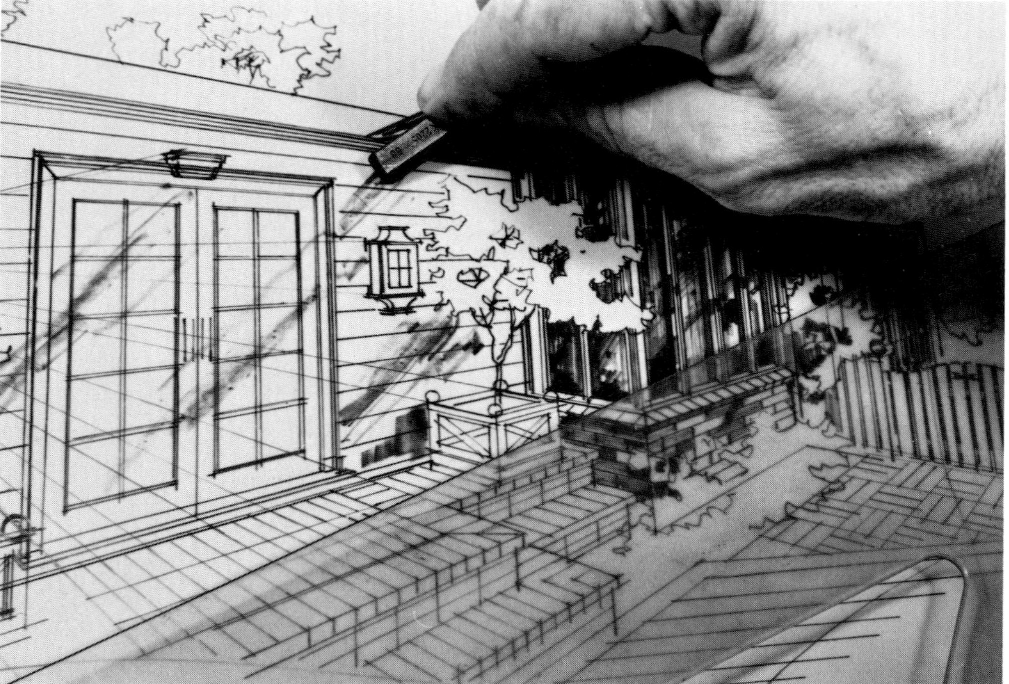

5.29t

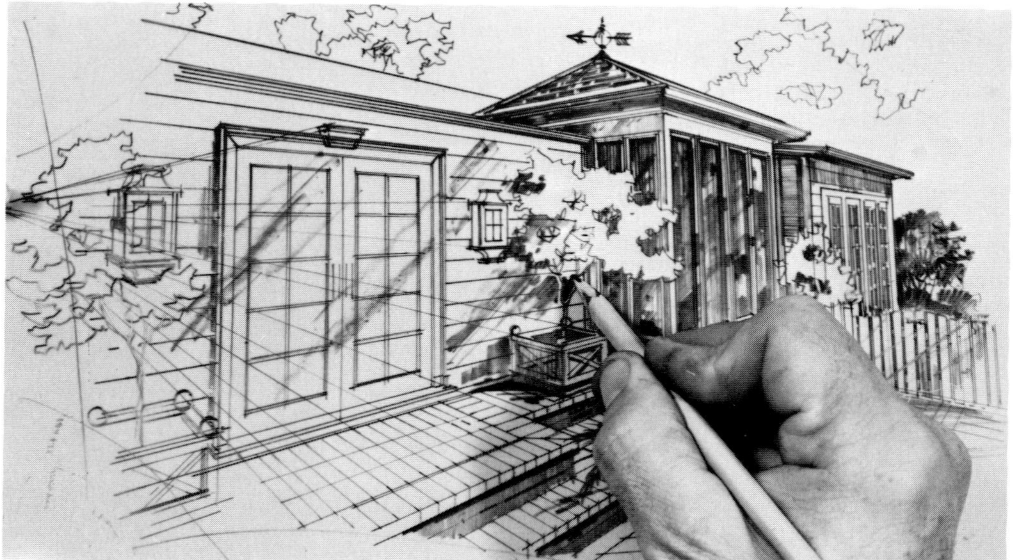

5.29u

As you build your final pencil drawing on its overlay sheet, you should work methodically from right to left (or left to right if you are left-handed), laying in the value shapes with a chisel-point pencil or, if your confidence prevails, a chisel-point felt-tip pen guided by a T square and triangle. Don't forget to protect the pencil strokes from smudge marks by using a sheet of clean paper to rest your hands on.

Match Pencil to Paper

Your drawing implement and the texture of the paper on which you draw will determine the impact of the final drawing.

Quality of Strokes

If you are using pencil, you can employ bold, parallel strokes to denote the shade and shadows, pressing hardest to create a bold black stroke where the shadow is deepest, as in the glass, and relaxing the pressure for the lighter, shaded areas. The value study should be referred to constantly. You will be placing the pencil strokes close together, but be sure to leave some space showing between the strokes. This keeps interest within the pencil work.

Varying intensities of shadow in pen-and-ink drawings can be created by spacing strokes close together or farther apart, or by using felt-tip pens that have partially dried out. Rather than throw these pens out, it is a good idea to start collecting them for this purpose, if you choose to do your final drawing in ink.

Note: The size, intensity, placement, and direction of individual strokes should help define the shape of all objects and surfaces. Do not overlook contrast, for it is one of the most important tools for creating definition of an object from its adjacent surroundings.

Different Strokes for Different Effects: Line, Shade, and Shadow Wash

Lines It is important to give lines character, so that they are not static and boring. You can do this by varying the pressure on the pen or pencil, creating lines that "pulsate" and vary in thickness and darkness. This is the rule: *Don't let a line go very far without changing something about it, be it the width or the tone.*

Lessen confusion within the drawing Don't clutter the drawing with too many lines. Sometimes the lines you leave out can be as important as those you put in. And don't overestimate the power of shadows to create form. Remember to use the value system of shade and shadow to define objects and to give them importance as they relate to the background.

Shade and shadow Parallel strokes within pencil drawings are much more effective in creating shading than crosshatched ones. Avoid making the strokes too dark or of the same value, for this can be boring. A good rule is to start the shadow with a lighter stroke and ease into the darker area. You can also create light spots in the shadows by decreasing the pressure on your pencil or felt-tip pen. Sometimes, though, you will want a continuous tone, which requires a very steady hand.

Graded washes Firm, uniform strokes that vary from light to dark will create a "graded-wash" effect. Let your arm, between your wrist and elbow, do the work here, not your fingers. The movement should be easy and loose.

It is a good idea to practice these techniques before you embark on an elaborate sketch. See Figure 5.3a and b for examples of graded washes in pencil.

A Final Examination of Procedure: The Bath Addition Drawing

This drawing (Figure 5.29v) was built up from the initial line drawing (Figure 5.29o) and completed value study (Figure 5.29r). The examples were done on double-coated Mylar drafting film with a medium 2B lead pencil for the shadows, a mechanical drafting pencil with a pointed F lead for the line work, and 4B and 6B-¼″ square graphic sticks (see Figure 5.29t) for the creation of the soft, diagonal strokes that fall across the building.

The intensity of the shadows is created by varying the pressure on the drawing instrument from heavy to light. Although some construction lines used to create the perspective drawing as well as the vanishing points have been left in the final sketch overlay shown here (see Figure 5.29v), they should not be included on the final presentation drawing.

Let us examine the techniques used in various areas of the drawing (Figure 5.29v, details A through E).

Examples: Windows and glass doors To enliven a window area, it is important to indicate the darkness of the interior behind it and the reflection of exterior elements, such as plants and trees, in the glass (see details B and C in Figure 5.29v).

It is always difficult to convey reflection in glass panes. To do this,

FIGURE 5.29v The completed illustration is the sum of its parts. The details that follow should be studied and compared with the illustration in its entirety.

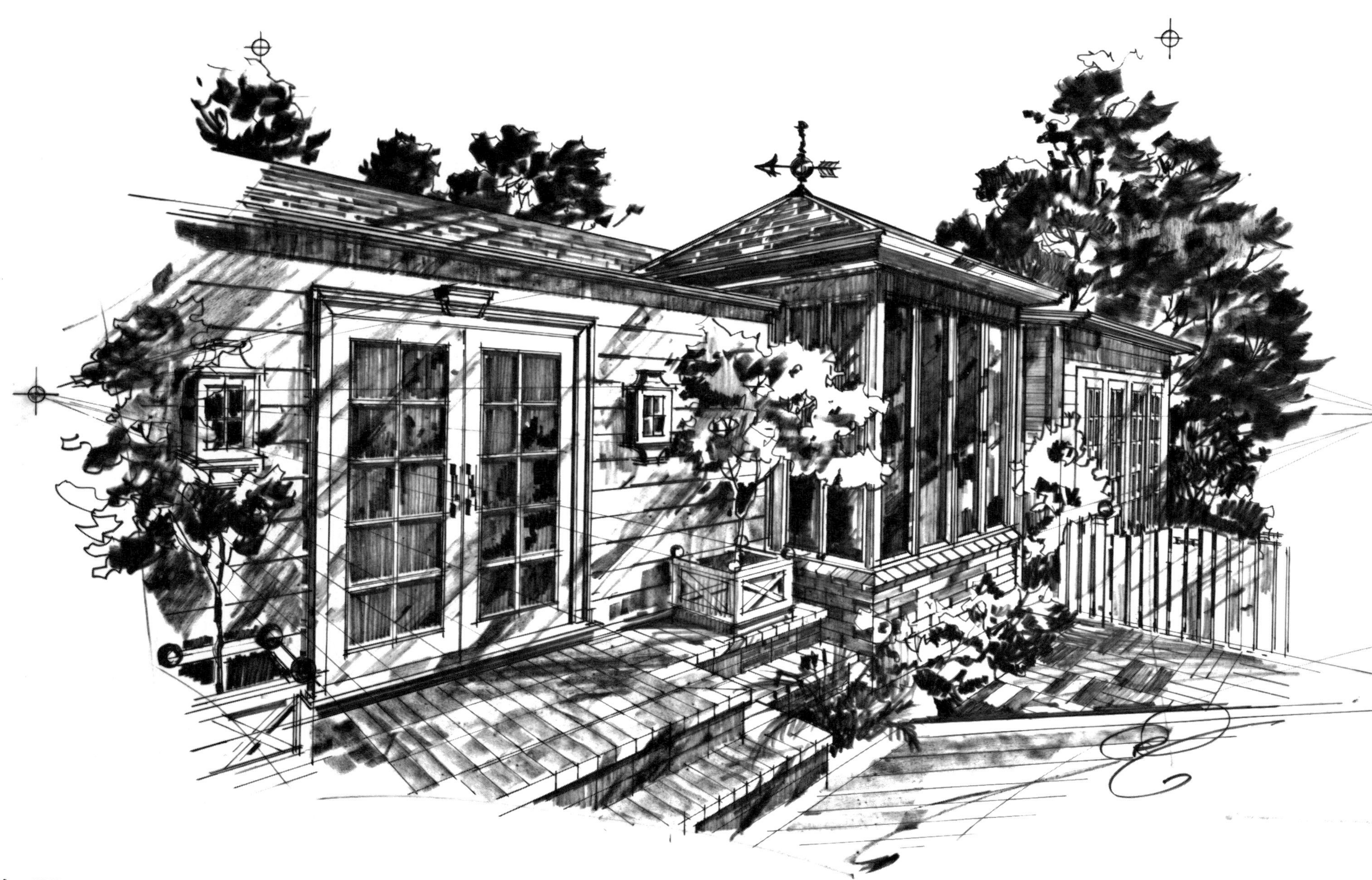

FIGURE 5.29v Detail A Deep, dark shadows are needed to visually complement the more defining edges of the structure, and shadows are used to silhouette the structure to pique interest. With the exception of diagonal shadow strokes, pencil strokes should follow the surface being shown; for example, each brick is made with one pencil stroke. Contrast and stroke direction, along with proper placement of shadows, can be used to define objects.

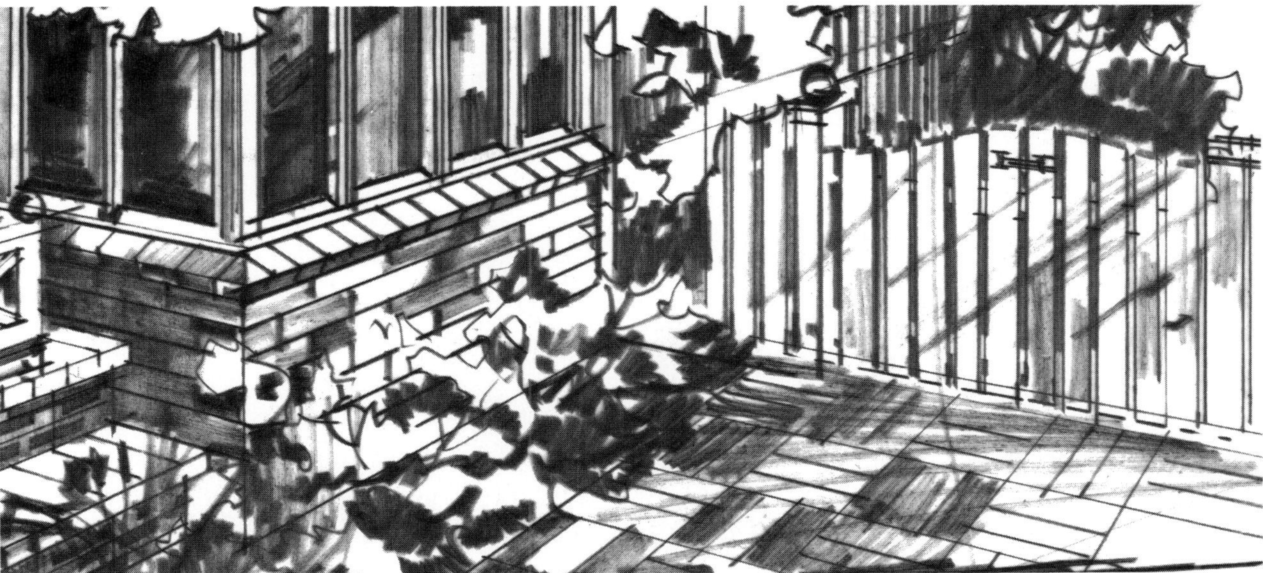

Detail A

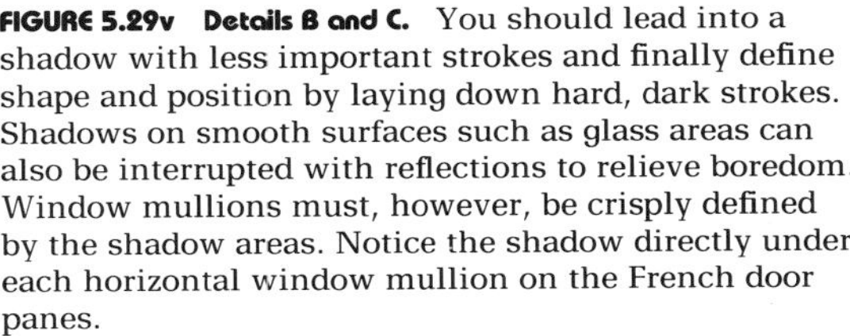

FIGURE 5.29v Details B and C. You should lead into a shadow with less important strokes and finally define shape and position by laying down hard, dark strokes. Shadows on smooth surfaces such as glass areas can also be interrupted with reflections to relieve boredom. Window mullions must, however, be crisply defined by the shadow areas. Notice the shadow directly under each horizontal window mullion on the French door panes.

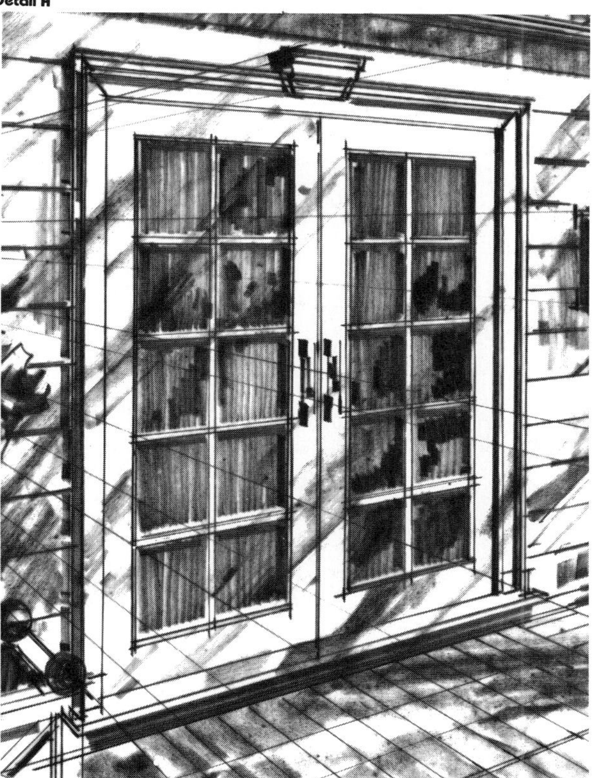

Detail B

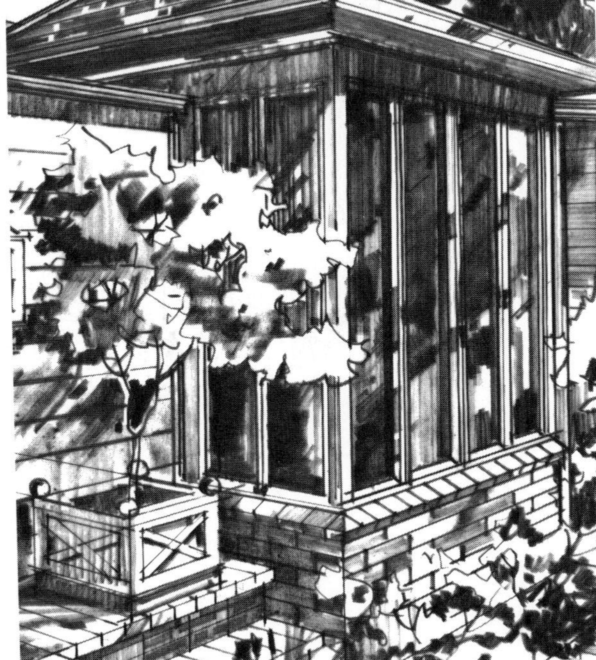

Detail C

FIGURE 5.29v Details D and E Use a soft 2B pencil to create foliage and dark tree branches. The foliage is an important part of the whole illustration. The structure must look as if it were in a natural setting, and its surrounding trees and shrubbery should soften the angular lines. Limbs should read through holes left between the leaf masses. The dark tree mass should be used to silhouette the sharp angular building corners while the mass of the small shrubbery trees should read as light against their dark backgrounds.

Notice the definition of each brick in the steps shown in detail E as well as shadows under the brick overhangs. Dark areas of earth silhouette the angular step corners.

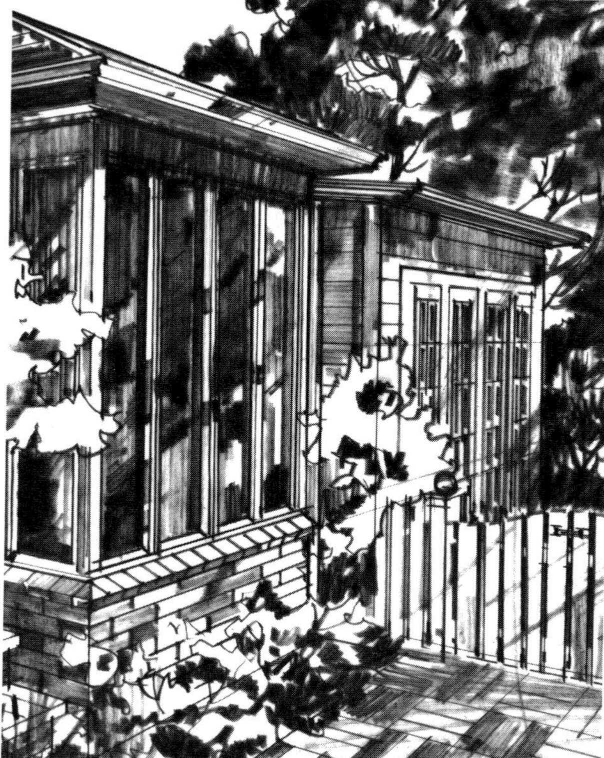

Detail D

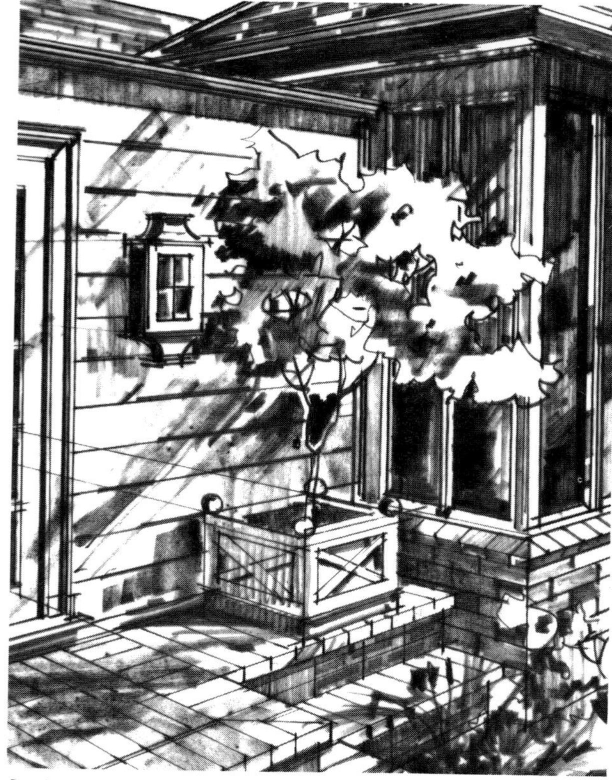

Detail E

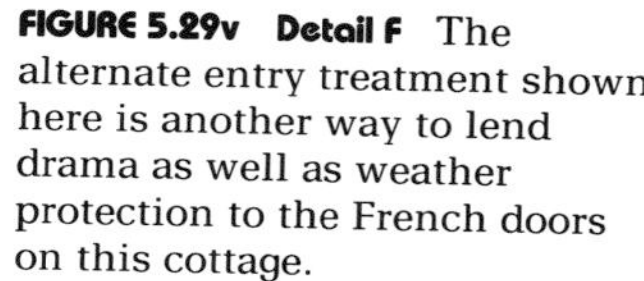

FIGURE 5.29v Detail F The alternate entry treatment shown here is another way to lend drama as well as weather protection to the French doors on this cottage.

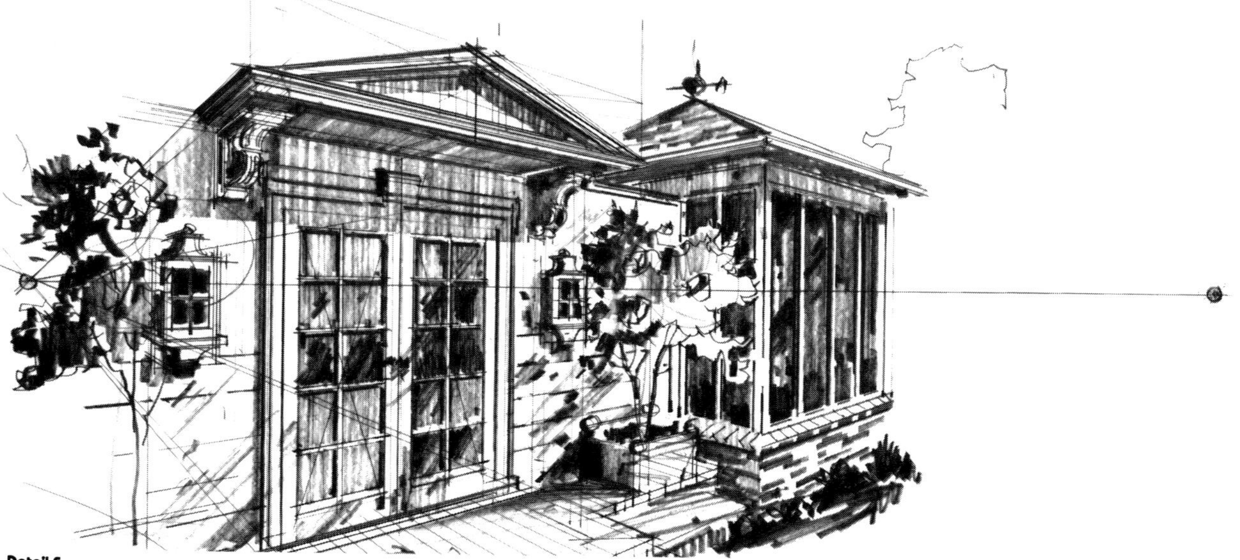

Detail F

hold the chiseled lead flat and firmly against the paper surface. Verticality is conveyed through grades of vertical uniform upright strokes of medium intensity to create a "wash" effect.

Objects behind the glass Then, to convey the suggestion of objects behind the panes of glass, almost black, closely grouped 4B or 6B strokes and broken diagonal lines of darker intensity are used. To indicate the shadows cast by the mullions on the glass, a 4B pencil has been used.

If you do not put bold shadows around the mullions, the edges of the windows will appear jagged and undefined. To create a sleek line, use a triangle to guide your pencil. Remember, numerous small, consistent strokes are required to create the even tone that marks a professional drawing (detail B).

To indicate reflected light, use less pressure on the pencil or lift it entirely, such as at the bottom of each pane of glass on the doors.

Large trees Using a graphite stick, draw the foliage, leaving enough space between the masses of leaves to indicate the growth of tree limbs and branches, with dark to medium strokes of the graphite (detail D).

Small trees Unlike for larger trees, the foliage here is rendered sketchily. The main purpose of these trees in the picture is to provide a round, soft contrast to the angular architecture (details C, D, and E). The tree shape is only suggested by an outline that is not continuous. The dark window glass silhouettes the tree foliage, creating a softness in the angular glassed-in area. Vignetting lines such as in Figure 5.29o are used to frame the drawing; they let you know where to stop the pencil strokes. The eye of the viewer can be led into the drawing in this manner.

Developing the Interior Drawing

A drawing is the assembled sum of its elements Overlay sheets of tracing paper are the basis for both interior and exterior drawings. *Do not try to create a drawing on one sheet of paper.* The many steps involved in putting down all overlapping pieces of graphite information can only be followed if you use translucent sheets of tracing paper.

In Figure 5.30a, the floor plan was used as a reference, along with the original photograph (not shown) of the bare concrete walls to create the initial underdrawing in Figure 5.30b. Each successive overlay incorporates specific complicated portions of this design, and then they are all combined into one final illustration.

The ceiling and floor designs (Figure 5.30c), because of their complicated nature, were laid out first on a separate overlay sheet registered with the underdrawing. Next the furniture (Figure 5.30d) was sketched onto an additional registered overlay sheet. When these sheets were combined (Figure 5.30e), only those portions of each overlay were traced onto the final Mylar drawing. Then a value study was created to show all the light and dark areas.

The final pencil illustration was made on frosted drafting Mylar, and 2H, 2B, H, and F pencils were used.

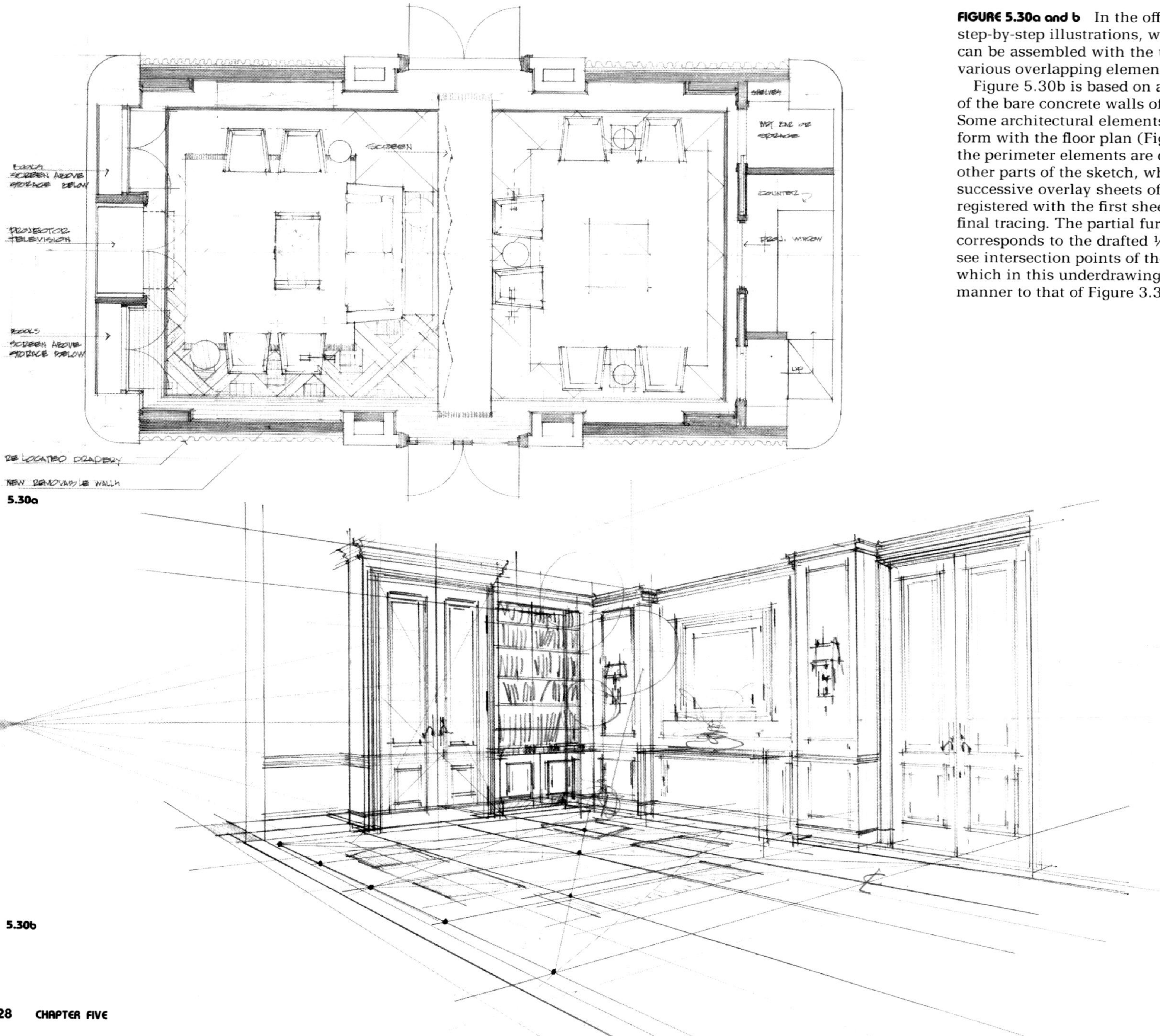

5.30a

5.30b

FIGURE 5.30a and b In the office depicted in this group of step-by-step illustrations, we see how an interior sketch can be assembled with the use of overlay sheets showing various overlapping elements.

Figure 5.30b is based on a line tracing of a photograph of the bare concrete walls of an *inside corner* of the space. Some architectural elements have been sketched in linear form with the floor plan (Figure 5.30a) as a guide. Only the perimeter elements are drawn on this first sheet; all other parts of the sketch, which will be drawn on successive overlay sheets of tracing paper, must be registered with the first sheet to enable assembly of the final tracing. The partial furniture layout in perspective corresponds to the drafted ½″ = 1′0″ scale plan. You can see intersection points of the grid layout on the floor, which in this underdrawing was formed in a similar manner to that of Figure 3.3e.

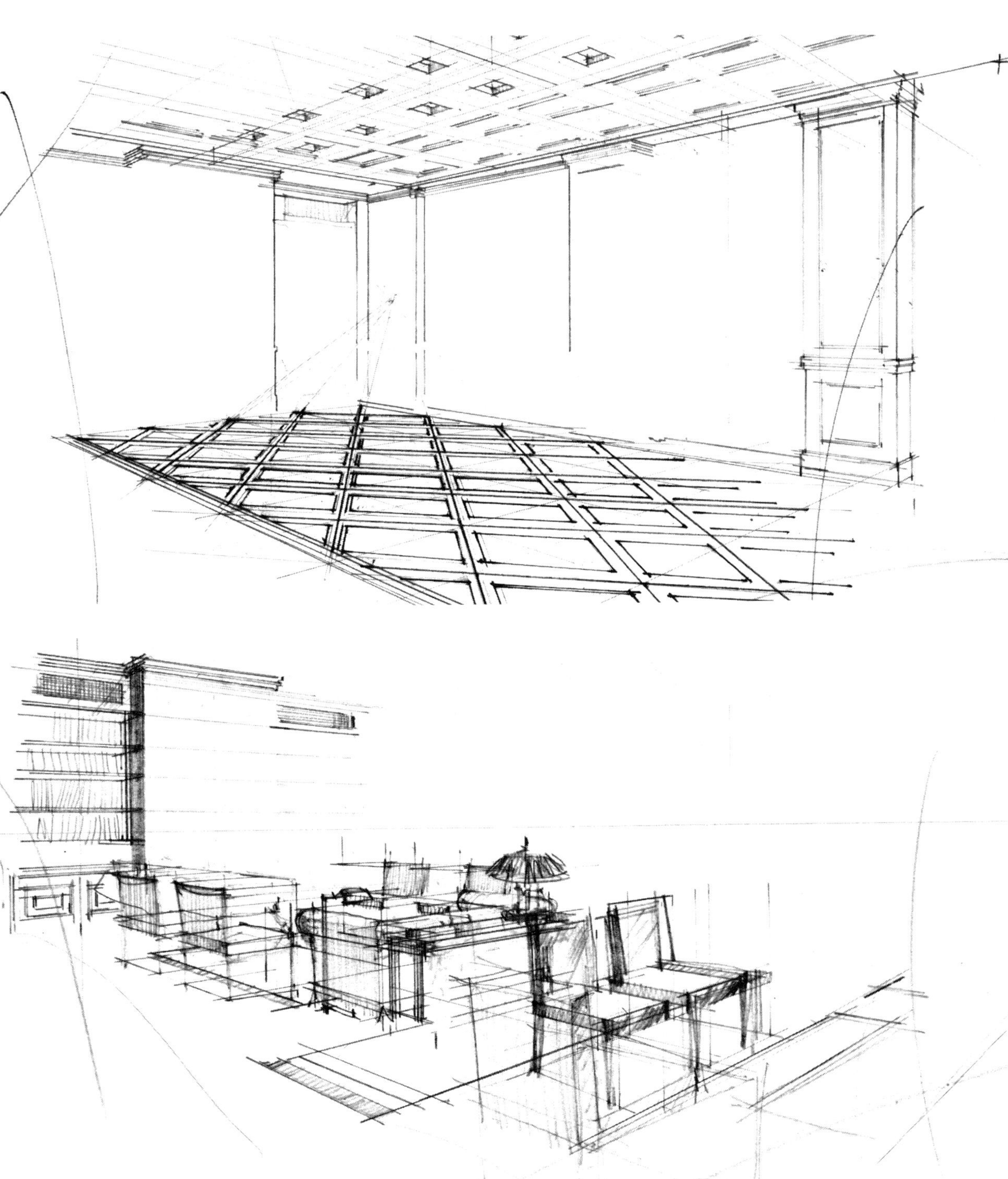

FIGURE 5.30c Complex floor and ceiling designs are drawn on this overlay sheet in their entirety. The VPR and VPL as well as a *third vanishing point* also located on the horizon line in the drawing are used to create the diagonal wood floor pattern. For ease in this procedure, all floor line designations that do not radiate from this vanishing point will be parallel to the base of the completed drawing. Note the values that indicate depth in the coffered ceilings.

FIGURE 5.30d The boxes into which furniture is placed comprise this overlay sheet. The bookcase designation acts as a register mark for this tracing.

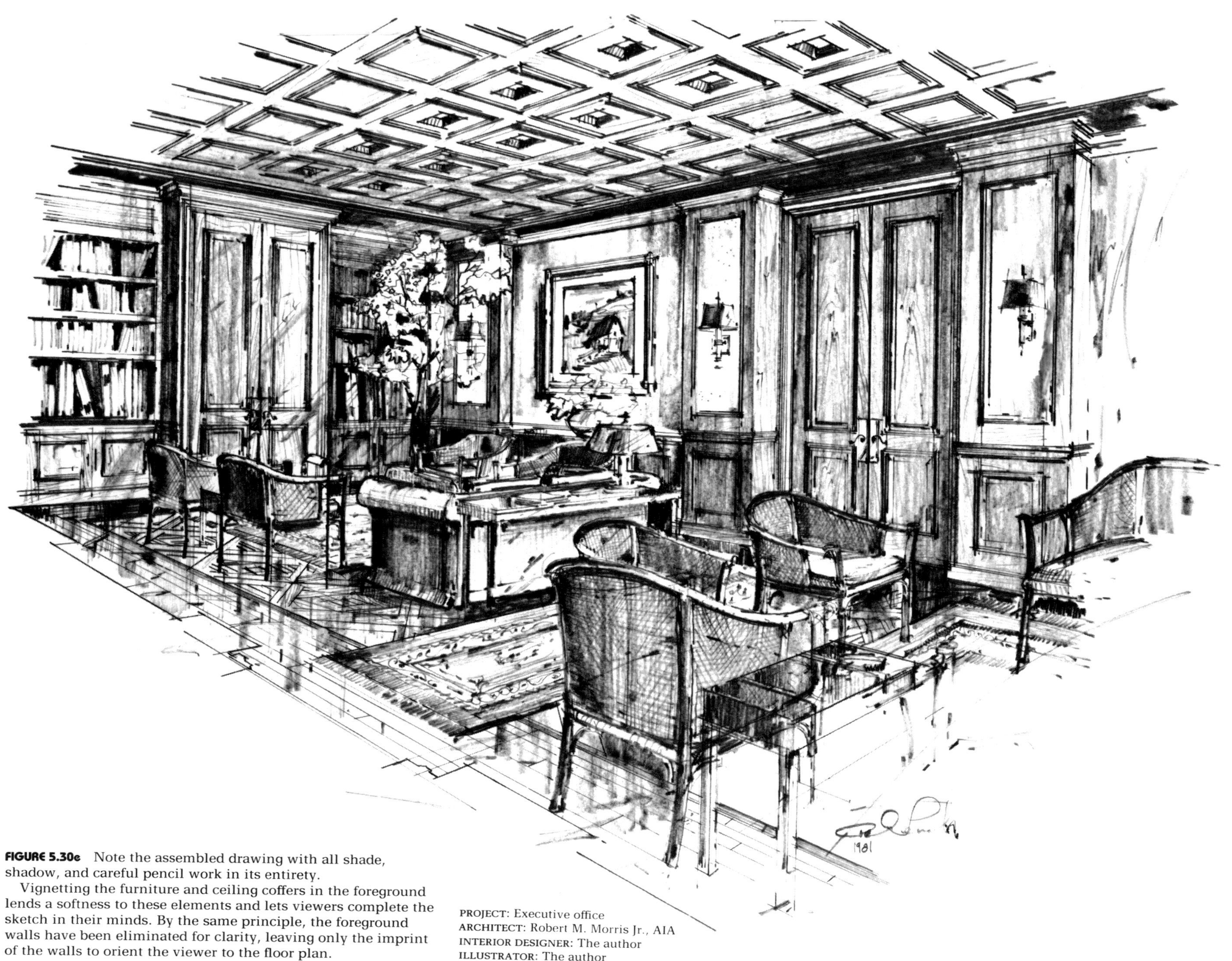

FIGURE 5.30e Note the assembled drawing with all shade, shadow, and careful pencil work in its entirety.

Vignetting the furniture and ceiling coffers in the foreground lends a softness to these elements and lets viewers complete the sketch in their minds. By the same principle, the foreground walls have been eliminated for clarity, leaving only the imprint of the walls to orient the viewer to the floor plan.

PROJECT: Executive office
ARCHITECT: Robert M. Morris Jr., AIA
INTERIOR DESIGNER: The author
ILLUSTRATOR: The author

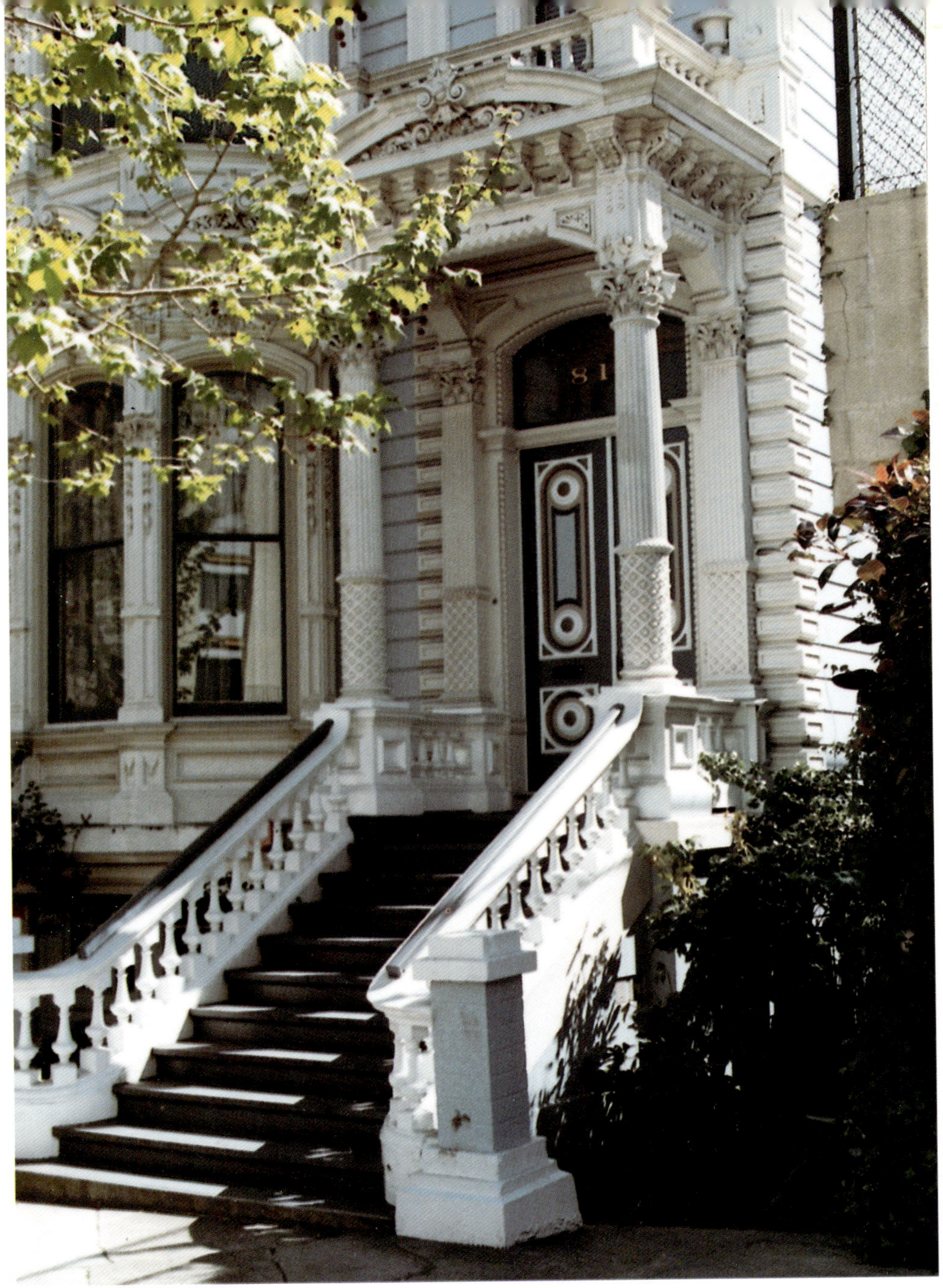

PLATES 1 and 2 Entry and details of a San Francisco Victorian. (See page 9.)

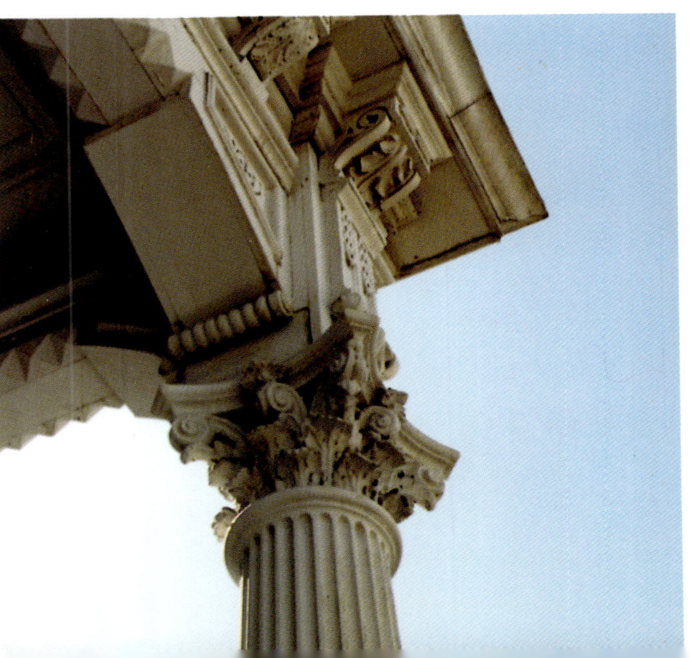

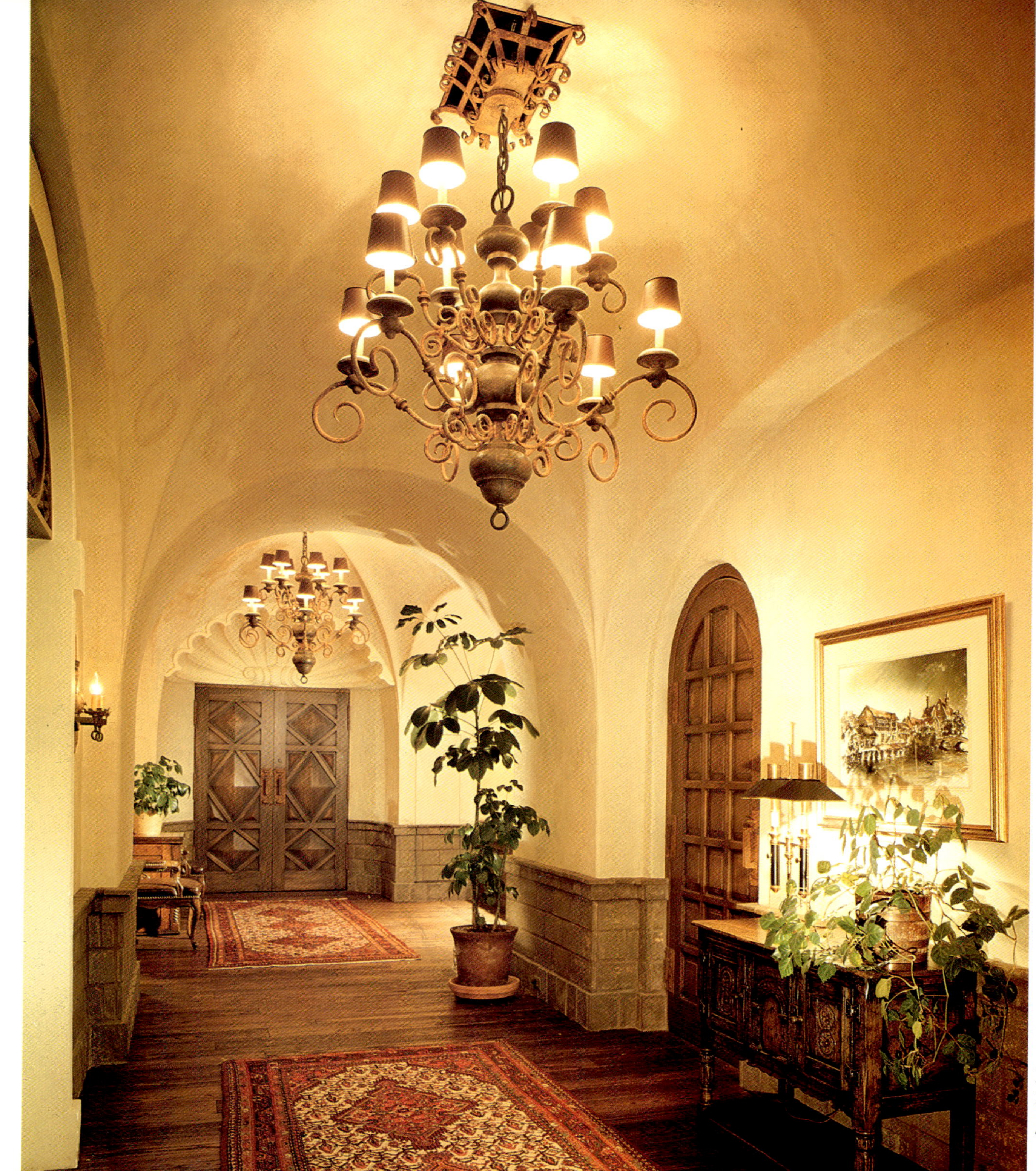

Jeremiah O. Bragstad

PLATE 3 Completed installation of a corporate reception area. (See page 168.)

PLATE 4 Original color photograph used to create the proposed entry and living room drawings of a San Franciscan Victorian. (See pages 2 and 29.)

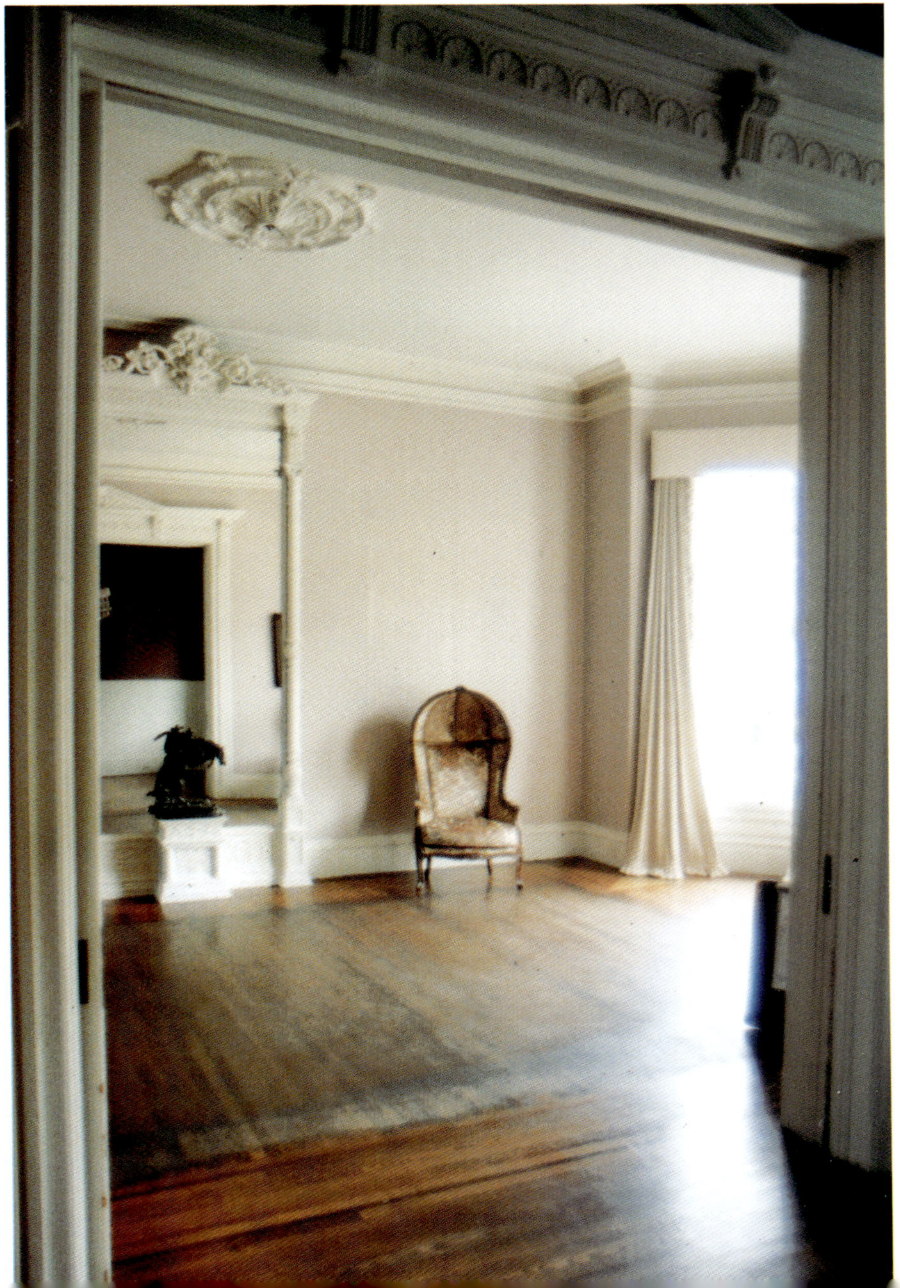

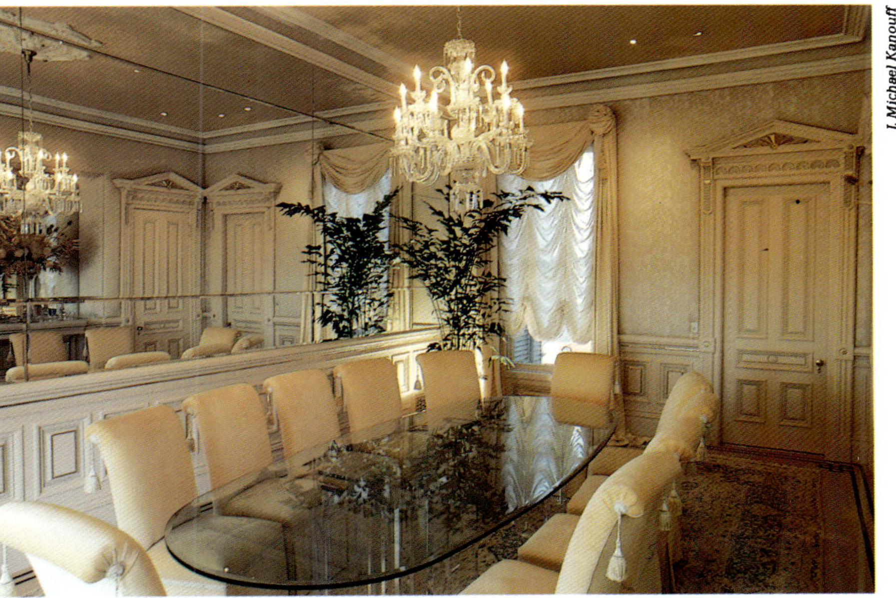

J. Michael Kanouff

PLATE 5 Completed installation of the dining room in a San Francisco Victorian. (See page 54.)

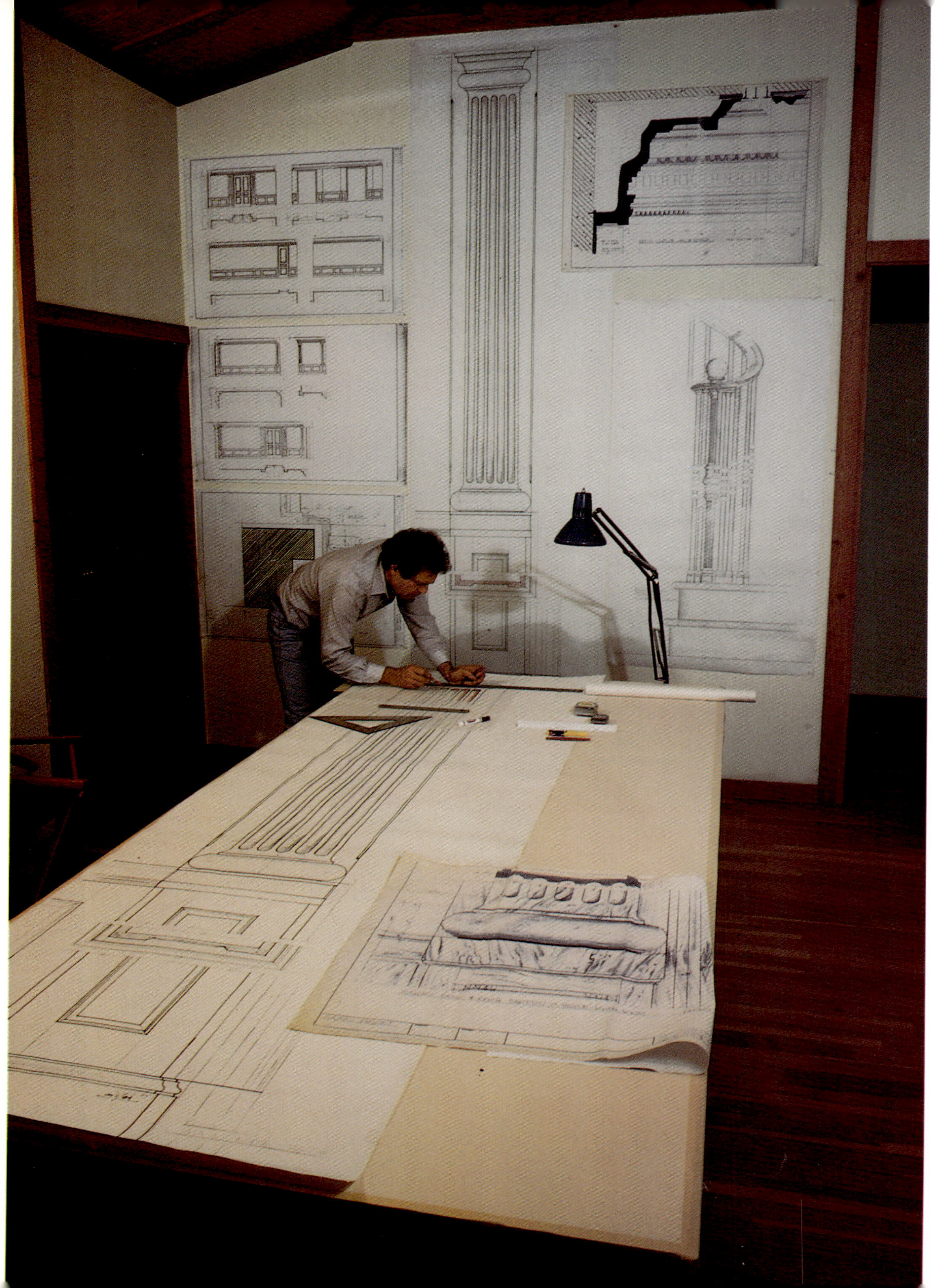

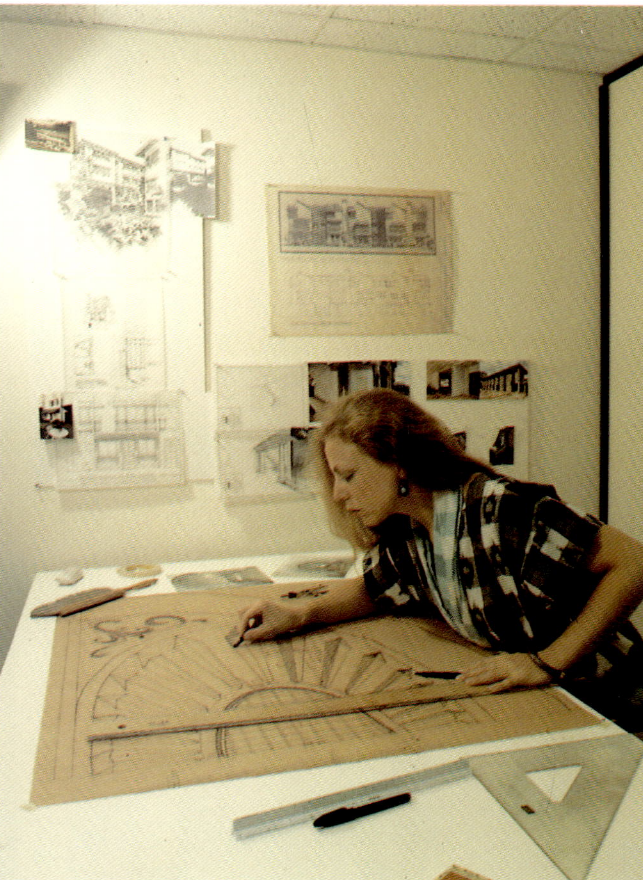

PLATE 7 Use of a graphite stick in rendering full-size cabinet work details. (See page 164.)

PLATE 6 Author working on full-size elevations and sections, along with various classical details, for a South American residence. (See page 144.)

J. Michael Kanouff

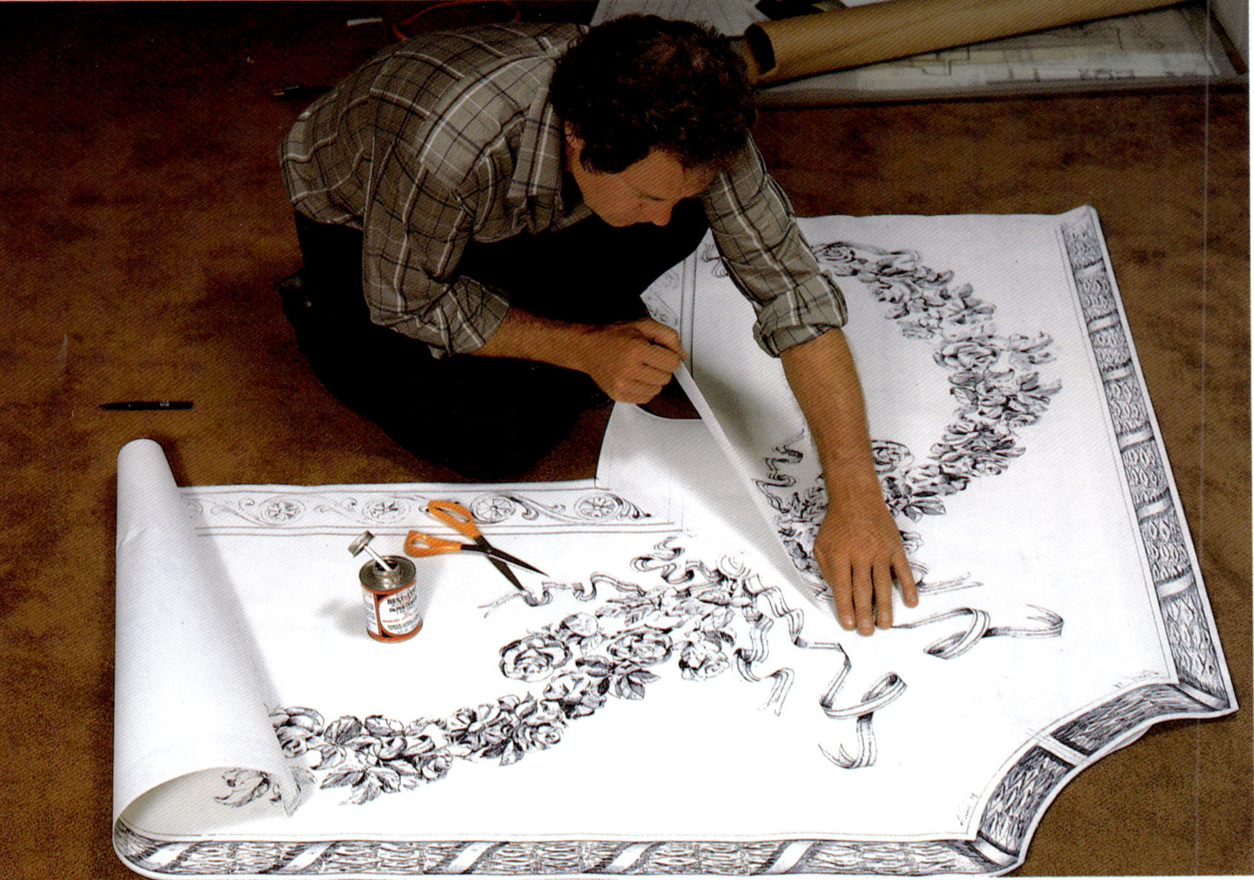

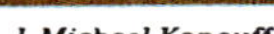
J. Michael Kanouff

PLATE 8 Reverse printing of a full-size rug corner detail allows one to reproduce a mirror image of the original design. (See page 162.)

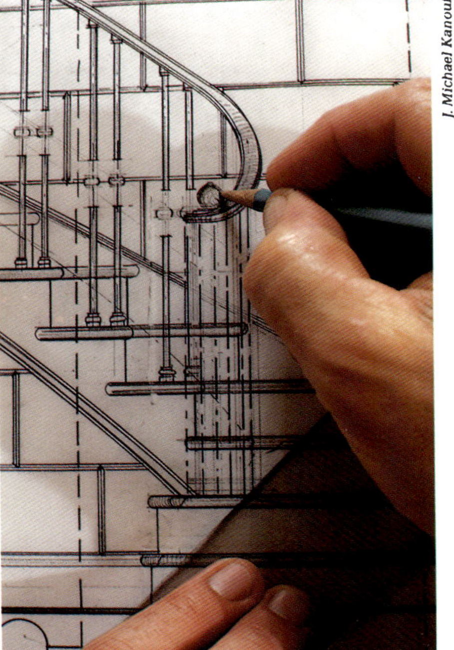
J. Michael Kanouff

PLATE 9 Rendering a volute and handrail termination for a grand staircase. (See page 161.)

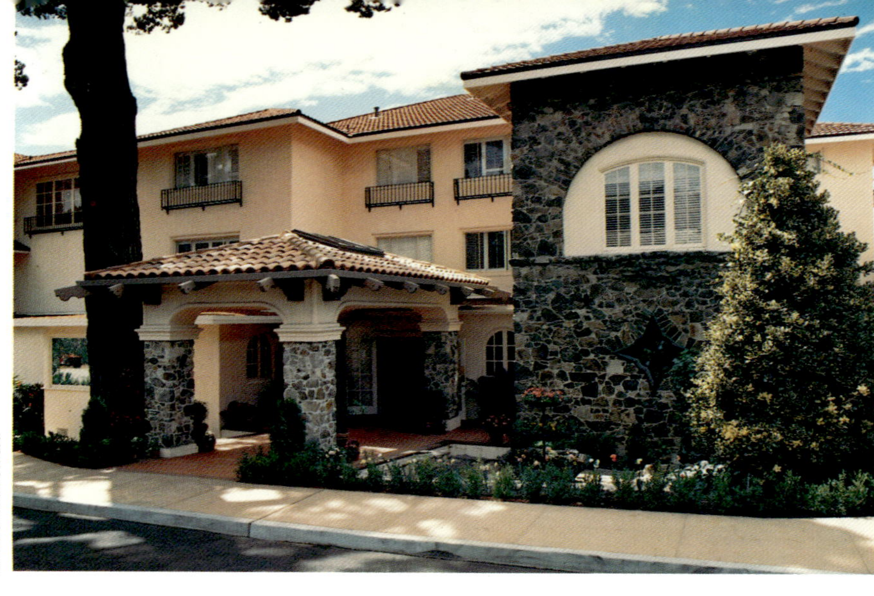

Batista Moon Studio

PLATE 10 Entrance to La Playa Hotel in Carmel by the Sea, California. (See page 172.)

PLATE 11 Exterior garden room of La Playa Hotel. (See page 187.)

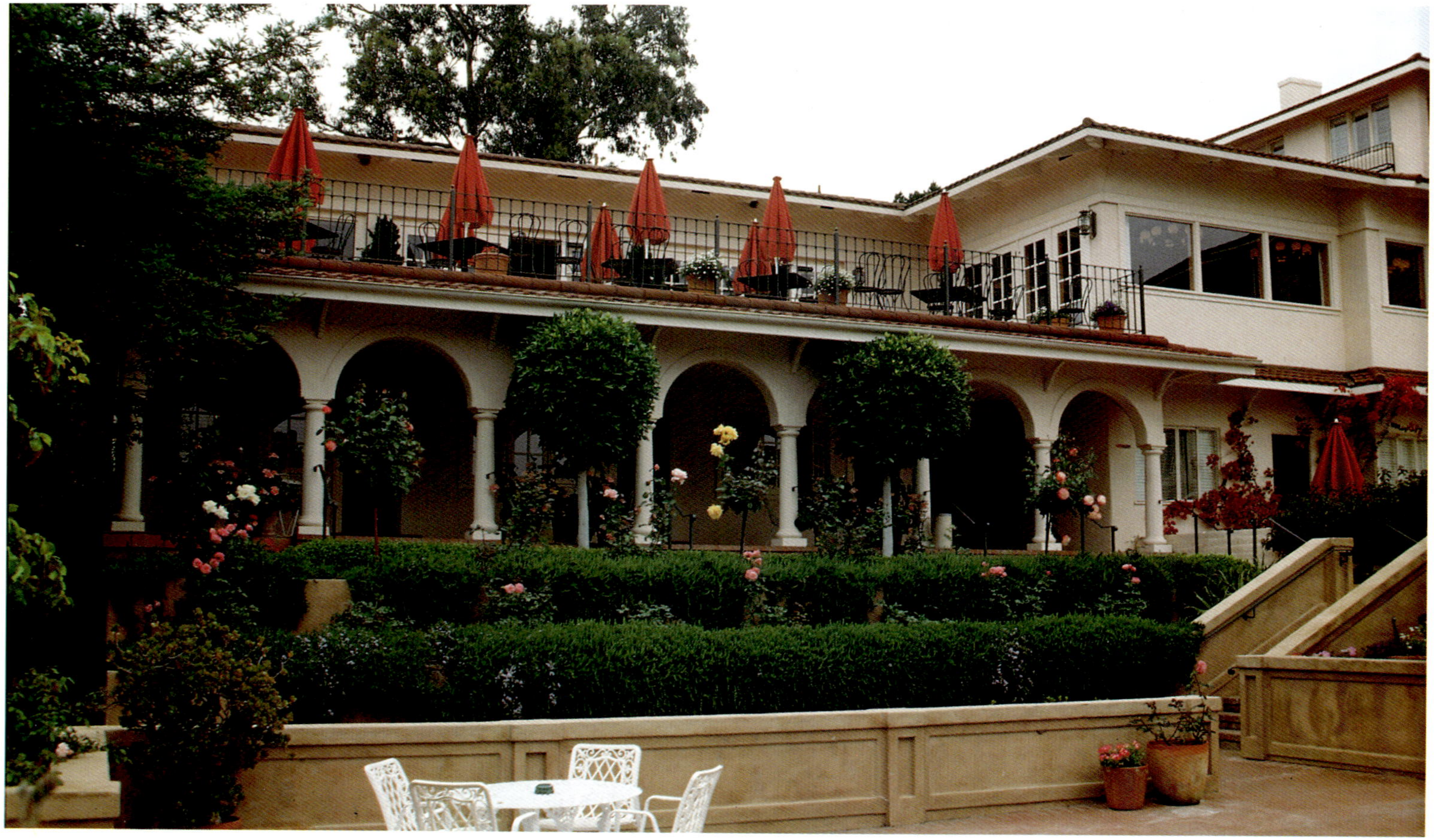

Richard Shelby

PLATE 12 Interior lobby of the La Playa Hotel, which was refurbished within an existing space using the photograph on page 178 as the basis for a concept sketch.

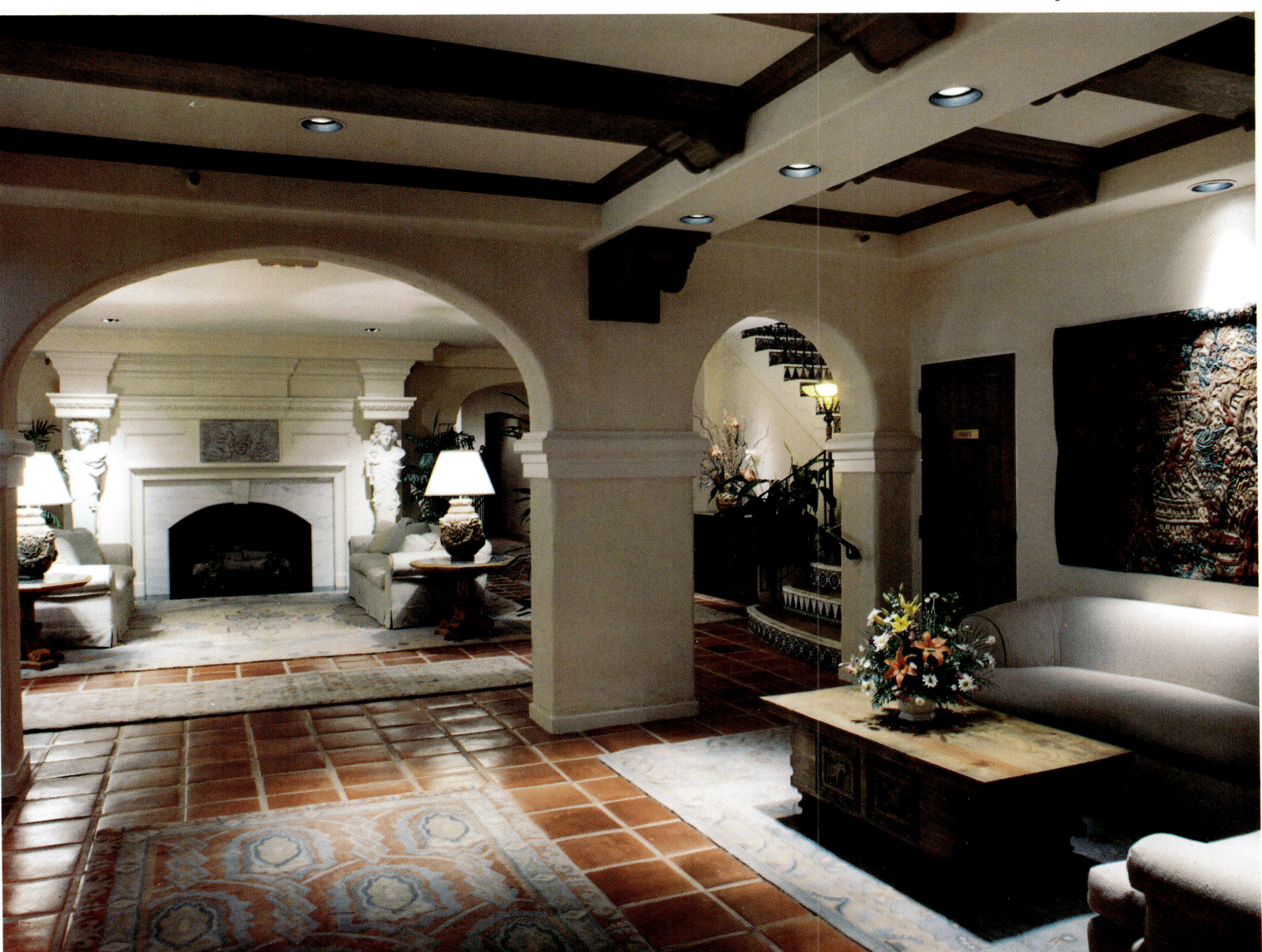

Batista Moon Studio

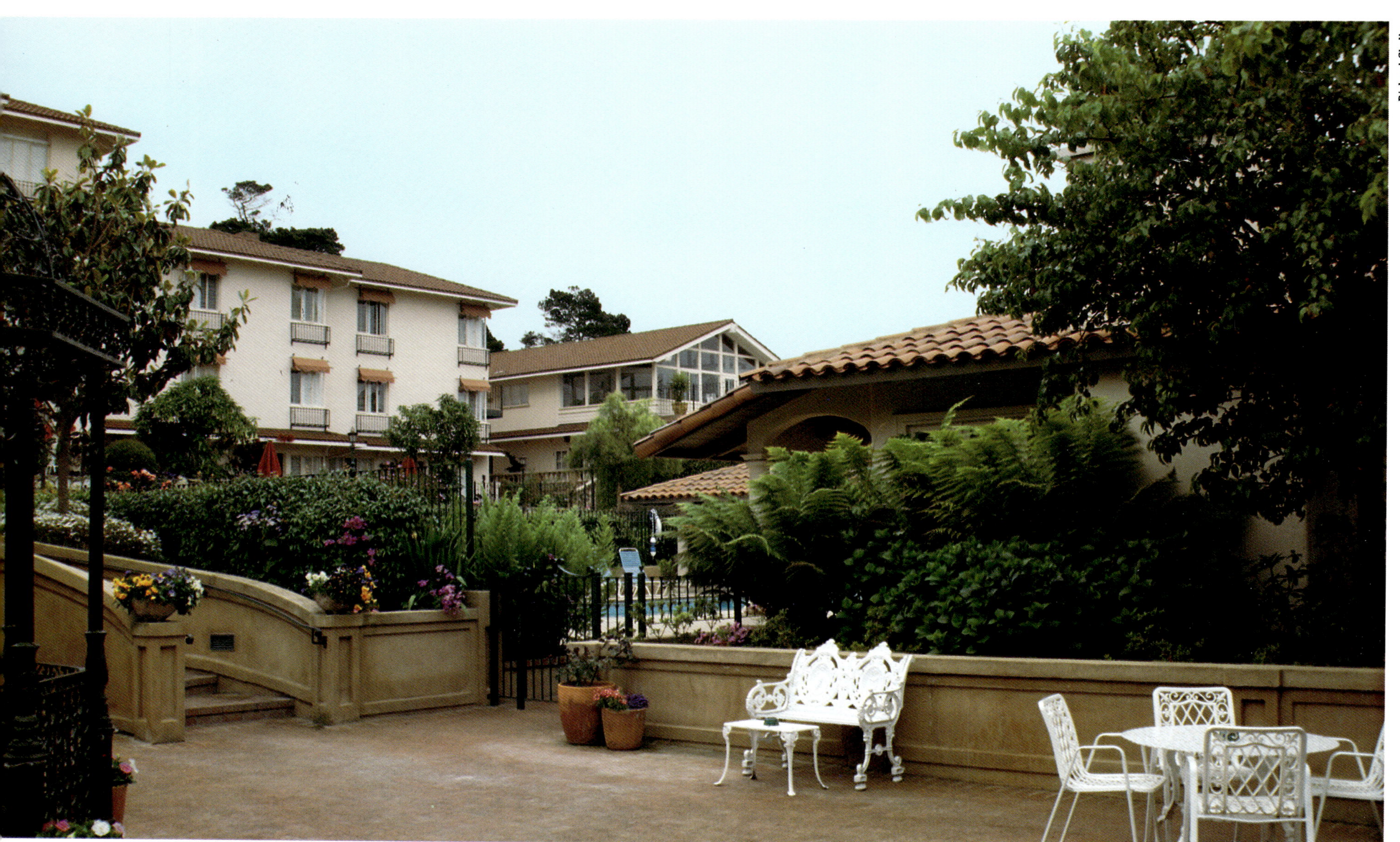

Richard Shelby

PLATE 13 Lower pool courtyard of La Playa hotel. (See page 20.)

CHAPTER 6

PROBLEM SOLVING IN PHOTOLINEAR PERSPECTIVE

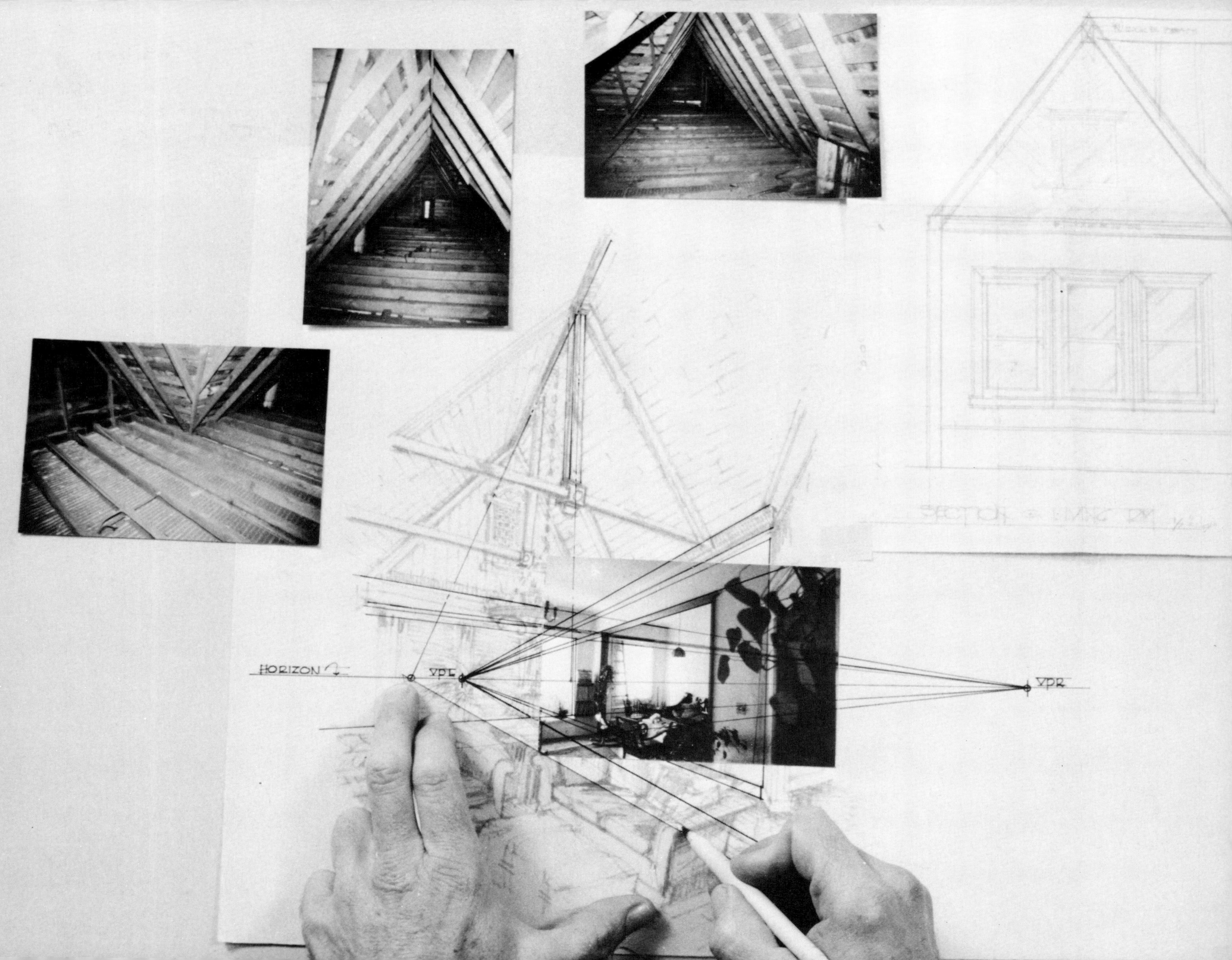
HORIZON
VPL
VPR
SECTION @ LIVING RM

Overcoming Distortion in Drawings Through the Use of Multiple Vanishing Points

The remodeling required shown in the plan (Figure 6.1a) for the addition to the existing Spanish-style house (Figure 6.1b) is much more extensive than can be drawn without having at least one vanishing point in the picture area. This creates a condition that is not acceptable. The addition of a third vanishing point becomes necessary to alleviate distortion caused when the VPL falls in the picture viewing area.

The right-hand major vertical building mass units shown in this photograph were first traced in perspective, and the original two vanishing points located. The photograph was taken so that all vertical lines remain vertical and so that the leading corner of the major building could be designated as the TMC. All heights of architectural elements on all building wall surfaces shown in the following drawings were projected from measurements located on this corner.

Adding Another Vanishing Point

By adding a third vanishing point to the left of the VPL, so that the point lies outside the primary image and to the left of the primary traced photograph, the resulting drawing will become more expansive. You must examine the addition of a third vanishing point in either direction in sketch form (see Figure 6.1c) before you attempt a final drawing. *Note:* In this case only the VPL is affected.

Often the perspective will become more, rather than less, distorted with the addition of a vanishing point, but the principles explained here should be applied in problem cases like this example and the house and garage sketch shown in Figure 6.2a and 6.2.d.

The Freehand Sketch as a Study

In the true freehand sketch (Figure 6.1c) of this Spanish-style estate house, the original mass of the structure is true to its two vanishing points, which are found from tracing the photograph. But in other planes, the additional mass blocks of the proposed building were projected partly from the additional vanishing point to the left of the original VPL and partly from the original vanishing point to the right, the VPR. The transition between these two vanishing-point projection systems (in this case the center building mass) requires the introduction of trees or other planting in front, to hide the discrepancy in line

CHAPTER 6

PROBLEM SOLVING IN PHOTOLINEAR PERSPECTIVE

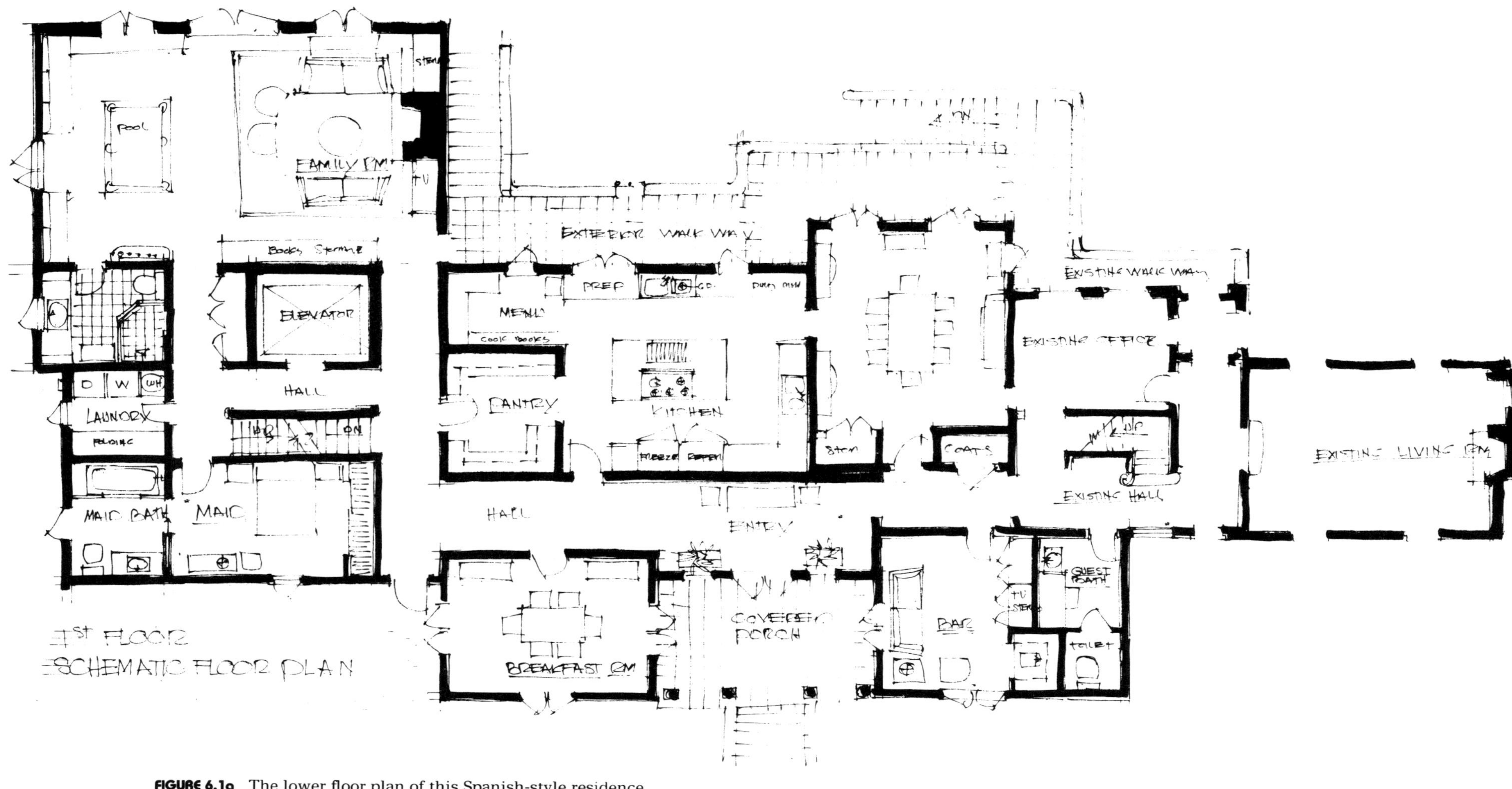

FIGURE 6.1a The lower floor plan of this Spanish-style residence shows the building mass that has been translated into the trial ink sketch in Figure 6.1c.

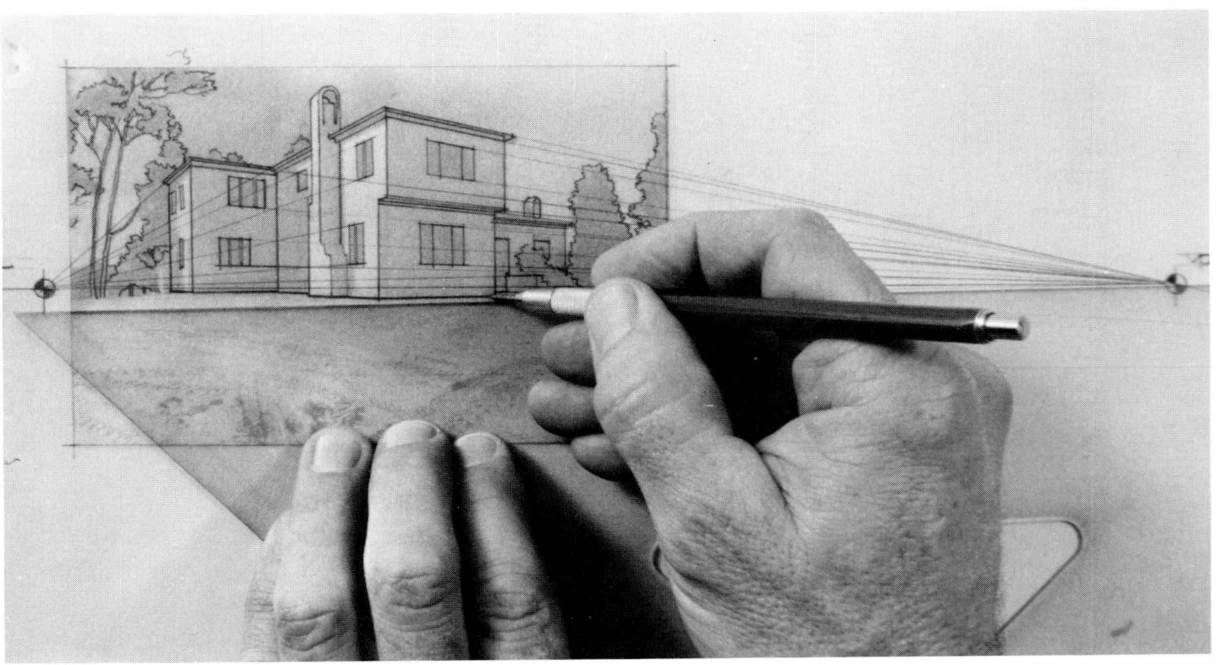

6.1b

FIGURE 6.1b This 4″ × 6″ glossy photograph, taken with a 35-mm camera equipped with a 50-mm lens, is being traced onto semitransparent frosted acetate with an F lead in a drafting pencil.

Note that building mass and trees are traced accurately. The tree masses can be photographically enlarged for future use when the final illustration or rendered elevations are drawn, as seen in Chapter 7.

Note the *two* major vanishing points.

The tracing of the building portion that is to remain and act as the basis for this large house extension shows two vanishing points and a linear representation of the house structure. Trees and shrubbery are traced directly and are part of the final drawing. The leading corner of this building has been chosen as the TMC. All eave, building, and division lines will originate from this tracing.

FIGURE 6.1c A trial ink or pencil sketch of the building traced in part from the original two-point photograph shows a covered porch and a somewhat different building mass structure than the final illustration of this series.

This freehand sketch was made on architectural sketch paper. At this stage of the drawing a *third* vanishing point was needed to eliminate the distortion that can occur when the original two vanishing points are too close together.

PROJECT: Southern California Residence
ARCHITECT: Roger Bush, AIA
BUILDING DESIGNER: the author

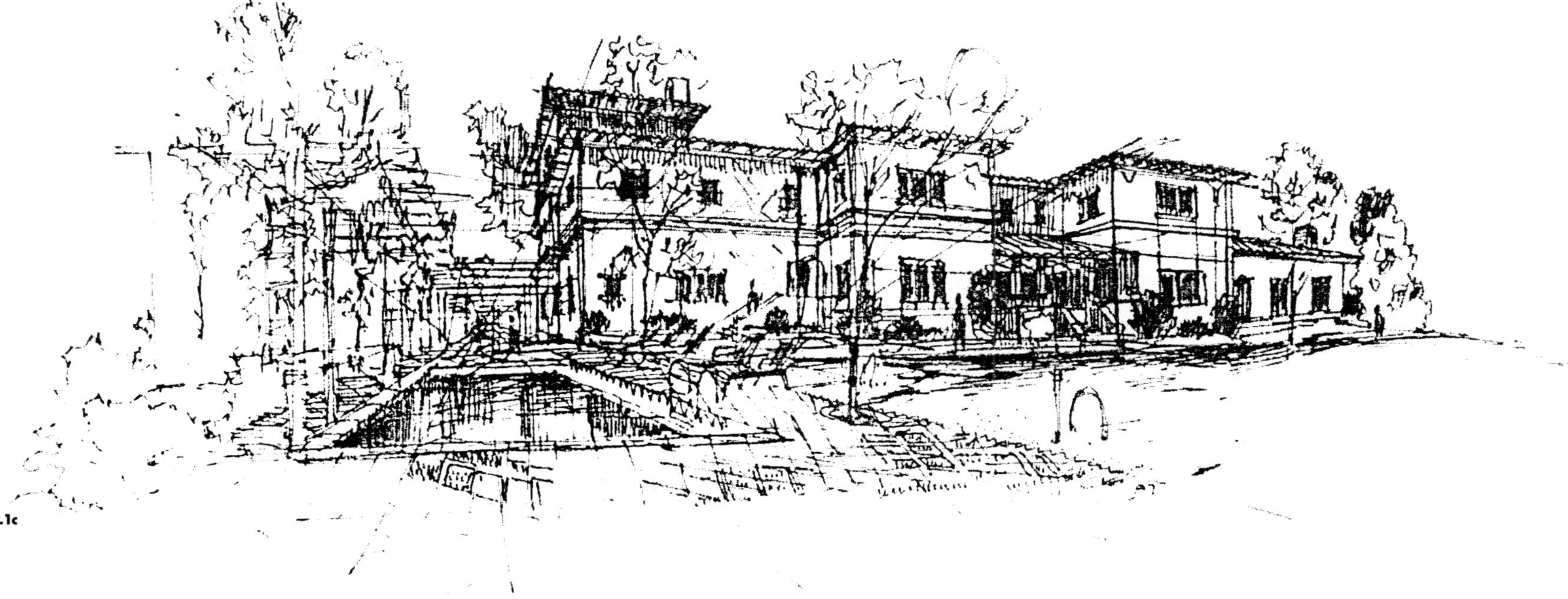

6.1c

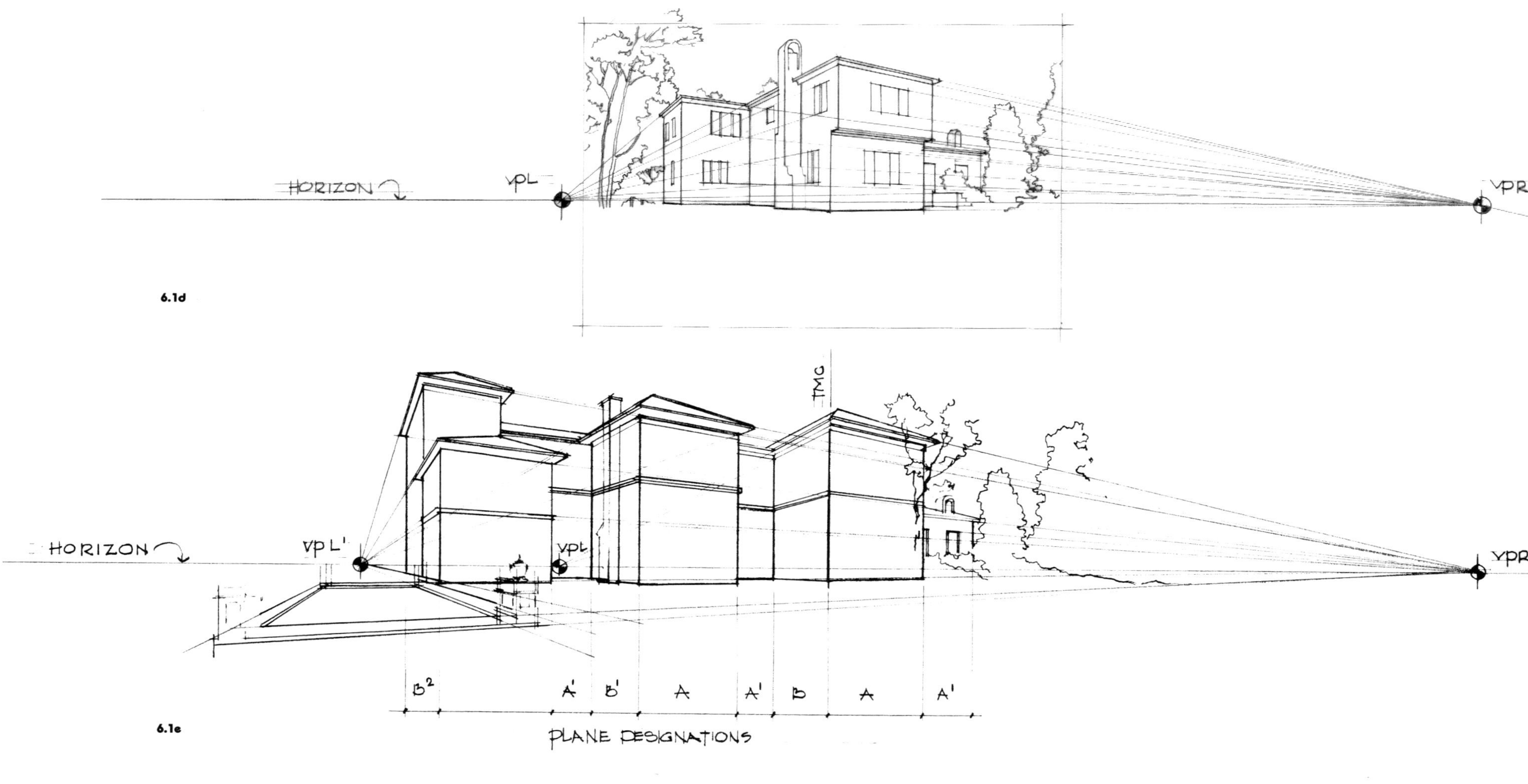

FIGURE 6.1d The third vanishing point has been added to keep the main building masses as distortion-free as possible. If the far left vanishing point is placed too far to the left, the transition between the two portions of the perspective drawings will not be successful.

Distortion in the center building mass is not apparent, although its major *B* planes as well as those of the far left building mass employ the new VPL instead of the original one found by tracing the two-point photograph.

The original VPR is used for all building masses.

FIGURE 6.1e The architectural features and landscaping developed in this line drawing will act as the basis for the final pencil rendering, seen in Figure 6.1h.

A redesign of mass placement was decided after examination of the original ink sketch in Figure 6.1c. The covered porch has been removed, and the left building mass has been decreased to create a second recess in the building facade.

direction where the two systems join. The building mass of the center tower is positioned so that only the roof overhang is affected by the change in vanishing-point projection. A rethinking of the building design based on elements discovered while drawing the ink sketch (Figure 6.1c) is shown in Figure 6.1d. Note that the VPR remains constant in the illustration.

Refinement in the Building Mass

Once the major planes and building mass have been firmly established and the cubic solids defined, roof elements can be added by projecting heights taken from the TMC (the leading edge of the building mass shown in the original photograph). Vertical measures such as window head and windowsill heights, plaster molding position, and eave and roof peak heights are all transferred measurements established first on the TMC and then "walked around" the building, with each of these lines on each plane being true to its respective vanishing point. (See Figure 6.1e.) Remember that the building or portions of it must be drawn transparent when additions such as a peaked roof atop a cubic solid are desired. See Figure 5.29m to review the placement of a peaked roof atop a cubic solid.

Light and Shadows on the Building

Eave extensions will cast shadows on the walls of the building below. These shadows along with their related values, which give the building dimension, are shown in Figure 6.1f and g. The value study in Figure 6.1g incorporates the four-value system based on conventional

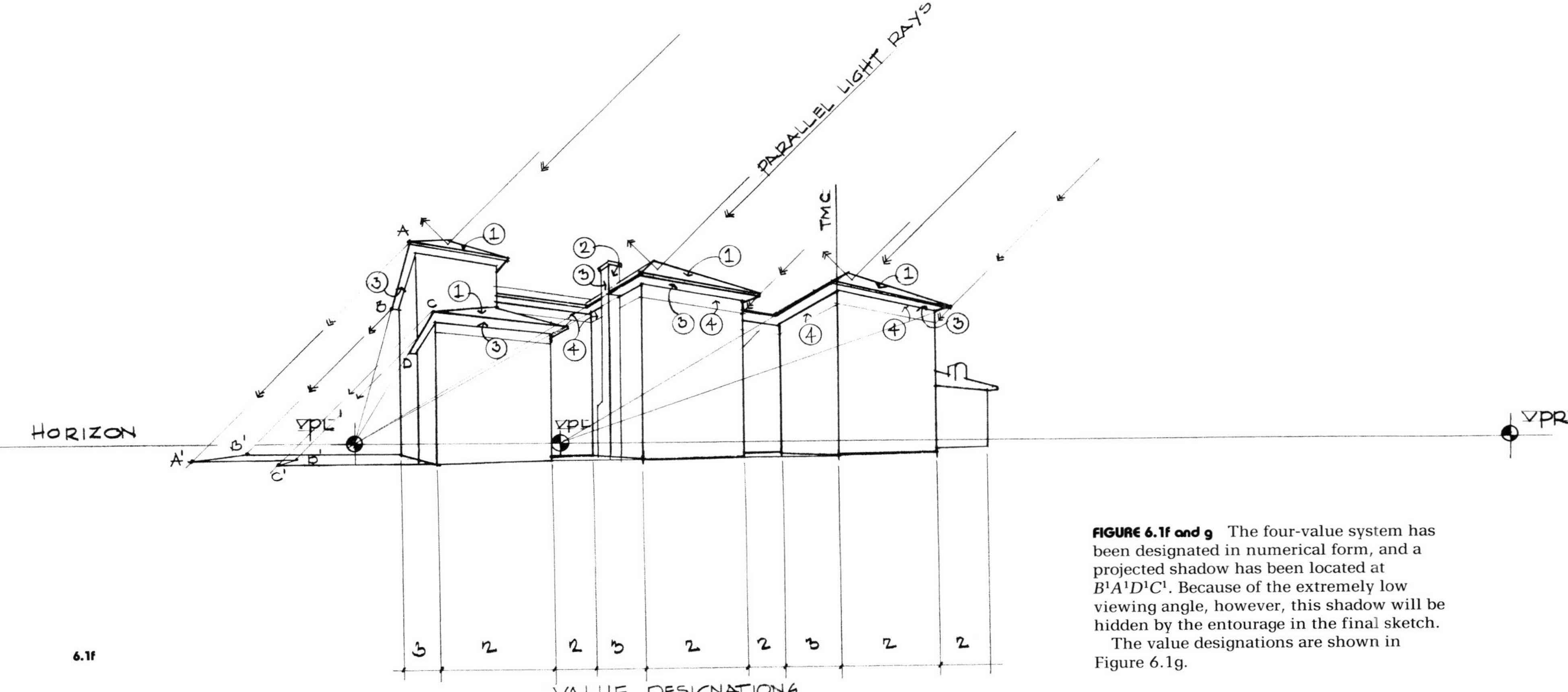

6.1f

FIGURE 6.1f and g The four-value system has been designated in numerical form, and a projected shadow has been located at $B^1A^1D^1C^1$. Because of the extremely low viewing angle, however, this shadow will be hidden by the entourage in the final sketch.
The value designations are shown in Figure 6.1g.

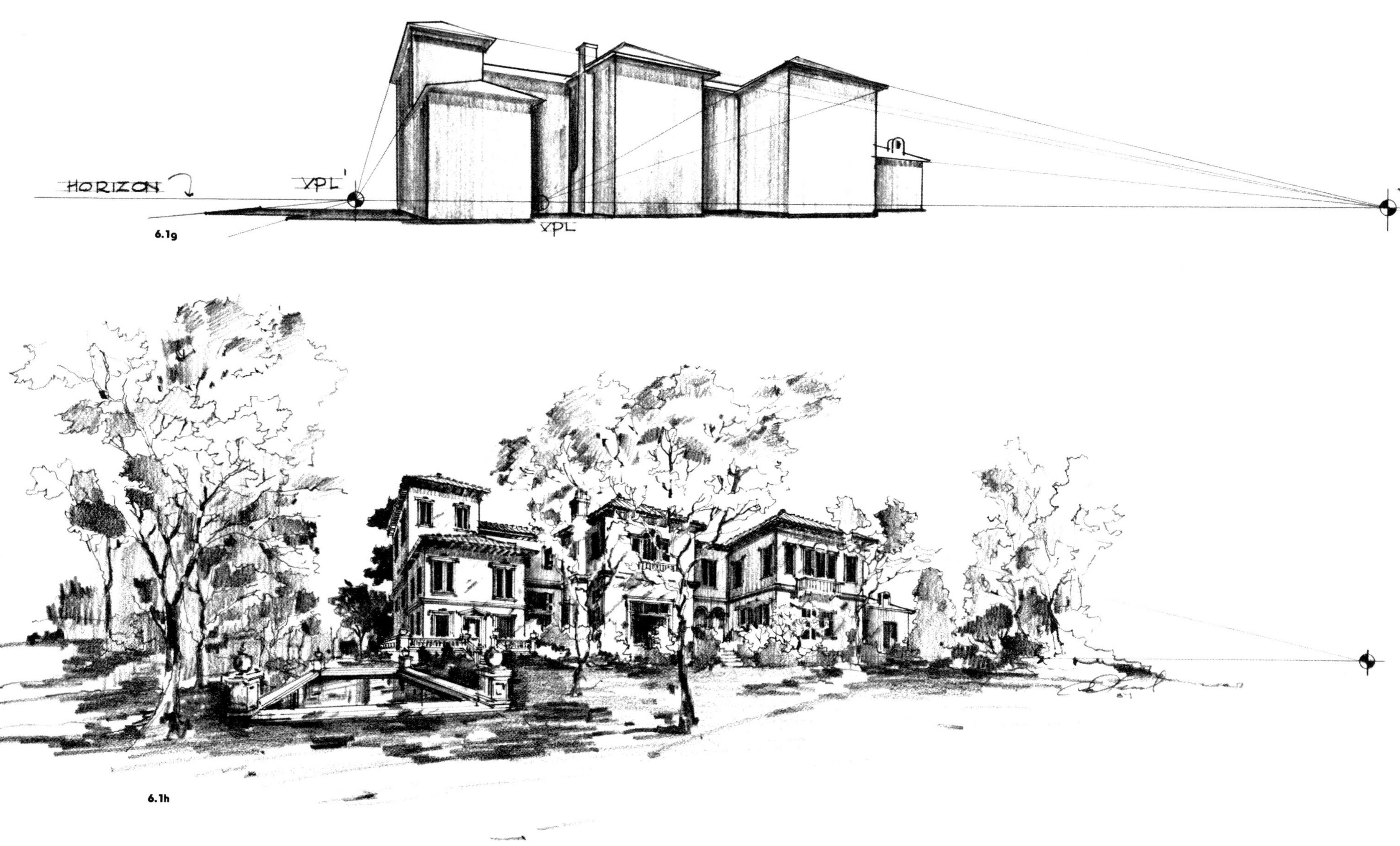

FIGURE 6.1h Shade and shadow suggestions on the building, rendering of the entourage, pool reflections, shadows across the lawn, and the intense dark value of the window areas all contribute to the illustration as a whole.

Vignetting of the drawing by using shade, shadow, and tree suggestions tends to soften the otherwise harsh, cubic form of this large Spanish-style estate.

PROJECT: Southern California Residence
ARCHITECT: Roger Bush, AIA
ARCHITECTURAL DESIGNER: the author
ILLUSTRATOR: the author

light. Note the cast shadow on the ground to the left of the building. Although this shadow will be hidden by trees, trellis, and shrubbery in the final drawing, it is a good practice to include all cast shadows on an overlay for your own information. *Note:* Shadow line perimeters also conform to the vanishing-point projections just as architectural features that create them. Refer to the discussion of shadows of simple cubes in Chapter 5.

The Final Pencil Drawing

Pencil work and the four-value system are shown on the final overlay of Clearprint 1000H tracing paper. The values used, shown in Figure 6.1g, clearly define the major planes of the building. The window areas will be drawn almost black, in contrast to the large, plain wall surfaces which surround them. These window designations, as seen in the value study, have a 4 value whether they lie on plane *A* or plane *B*. Notice the shadow areas caused by the eave projections and "run" plaster moldings that carry around the building masses. They appear as a 4 value while the underside of the eaves that receives some reflected light would read as a 3 value; the division between the horizontal and vertical surfaces becomes apparent with the slight change in value designation.

The pool shown in Figure 6.1e and h is drawn in perspective by employing not only the VPR (a constant in this drawing) but the new VPL[1] to the left of the VPL. After shade and shadow in the form of carefully rendered pencil work were added to the foreground at the pool area (Figure 6.1h), the left front corner of the pool appeared to visually drop slightly to the lower left, even though the building site incorporates a slight slope. (This is because the third vanishing point is in the picture area.) When the vanishing point was added to the left of the VPL, this vanishing point was moved just far enough to not affect the building in a negative way. If it were to move farther to the left, the transition between the two systems would not have been successful. However, the pool can be put back into the correct visual position merely by making the front and back horizontal edges parallel to each other rather than relying on extensions from the VPR to create them.

Multiple Vanishing Points Result from Combining Two Photographs

When a subject is photographed for photolinear perspective drawings, it is often advantageous to overlap photographs taken from the same height to increase the viewing angle of the intended drawing. This exercise is best performed with a tripod with a pivot head that allows for 360° camera movement in a completely level and circular direction or with the photographer pivoting on a foot and snapping successive photographs, each including some recognizable element from the previous shot. In this manner the shots can be spliced together later. This process enables the creation of an underdrawing of the existing structure and its environment that includes a wider viewing angle than in either of the 24-mm wide-angle photographs seen individually.

Two Sets of Vanishing Points

Examine the Spanish colonial redesign of the tract house based on the two combined photographs shown in Figure 6.2b and the underdrawing of the combined photographs shown in Figure 6.2a. The two sets of vanishing points that have been successfully combined have allowed the illustrator to increase the viewing angle to a great extent. The area of overlap in this case happens to work to the advantage of the illustration, a condition which does not always hold when this type of photographic illusion is attempted.

Elevations and sections should be drawn simultaneously with sketches when remodeling drawings are delineated. The combination of photographic scale and scaled drawings serve as cross references (see Figure 6.2c). The final pencil illustration can be seen in Figure 6.2d.

The sky area was purposely left white to allow the roof tile edges to silhouette sharply against a plain, white surface. Tree and shrub forms have been suggested but not truly delineated. This increases the emphasis on the structure.

PROJECT: Residence remodeling, Foster City, California
DESIGNER: the author
ILLUSTRATOR: the author

TMC
CHECK VERTICAL
VERTICAL
PRIMARY VPR
HORIZON
SECONDARY VPR

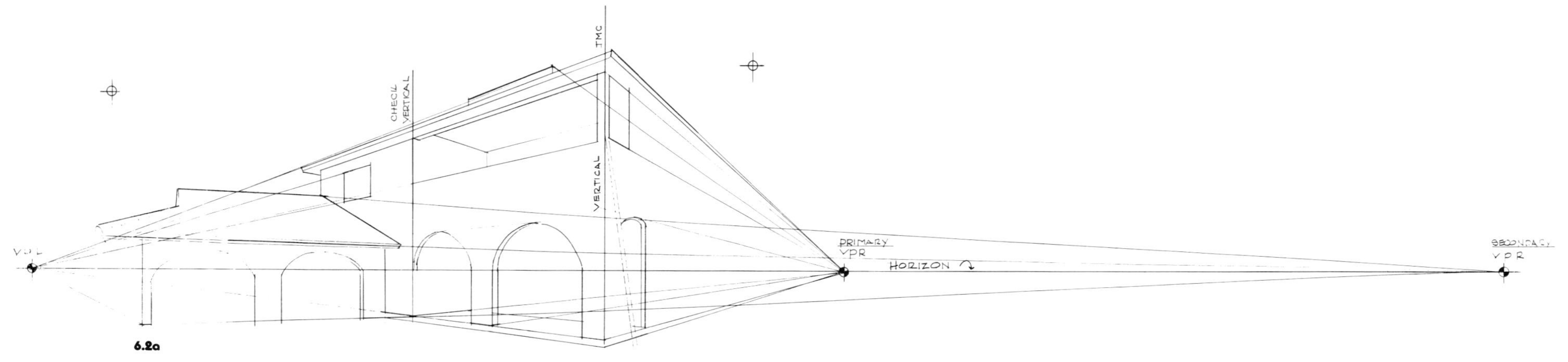

6.2a

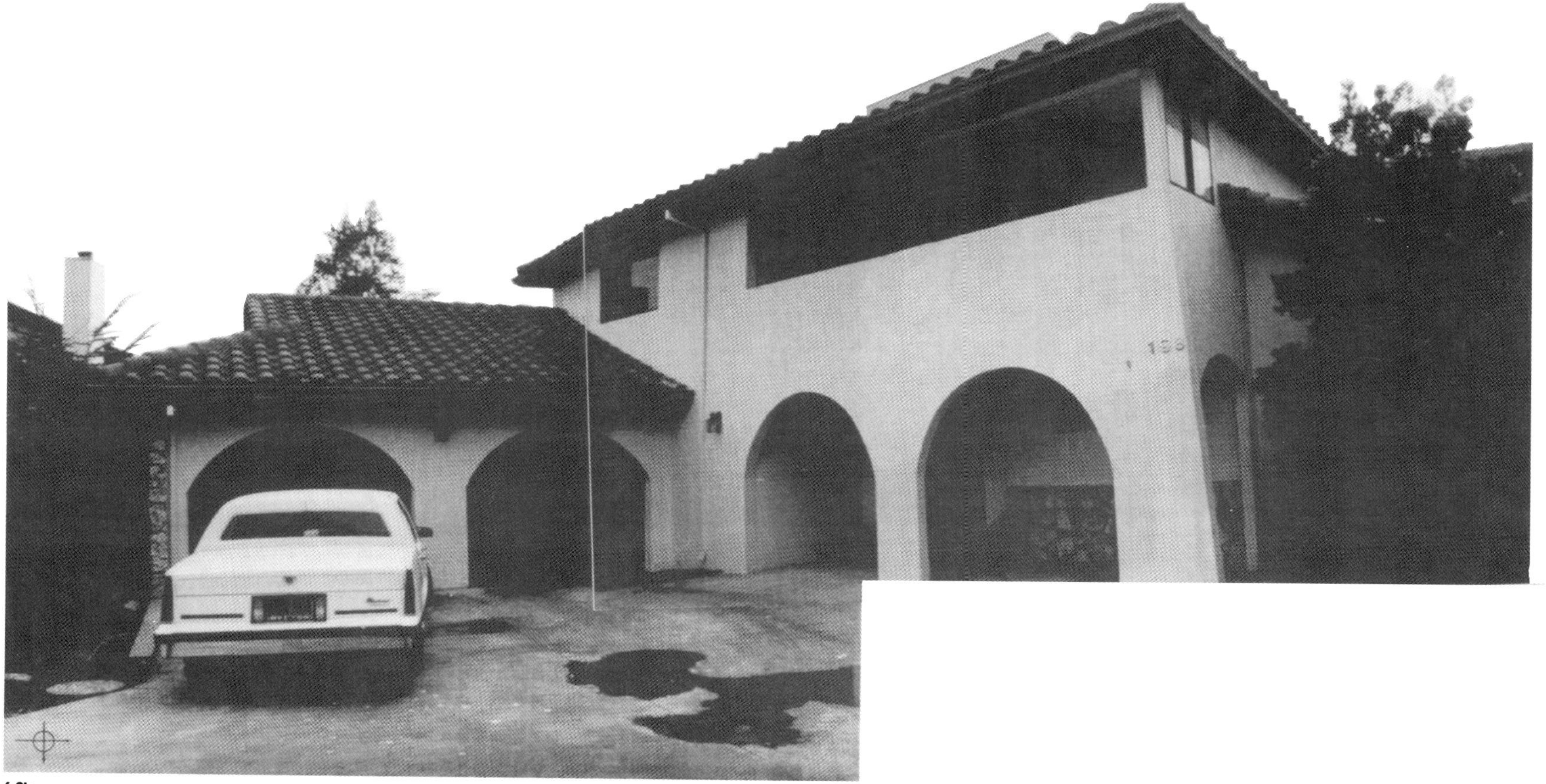

6.2b

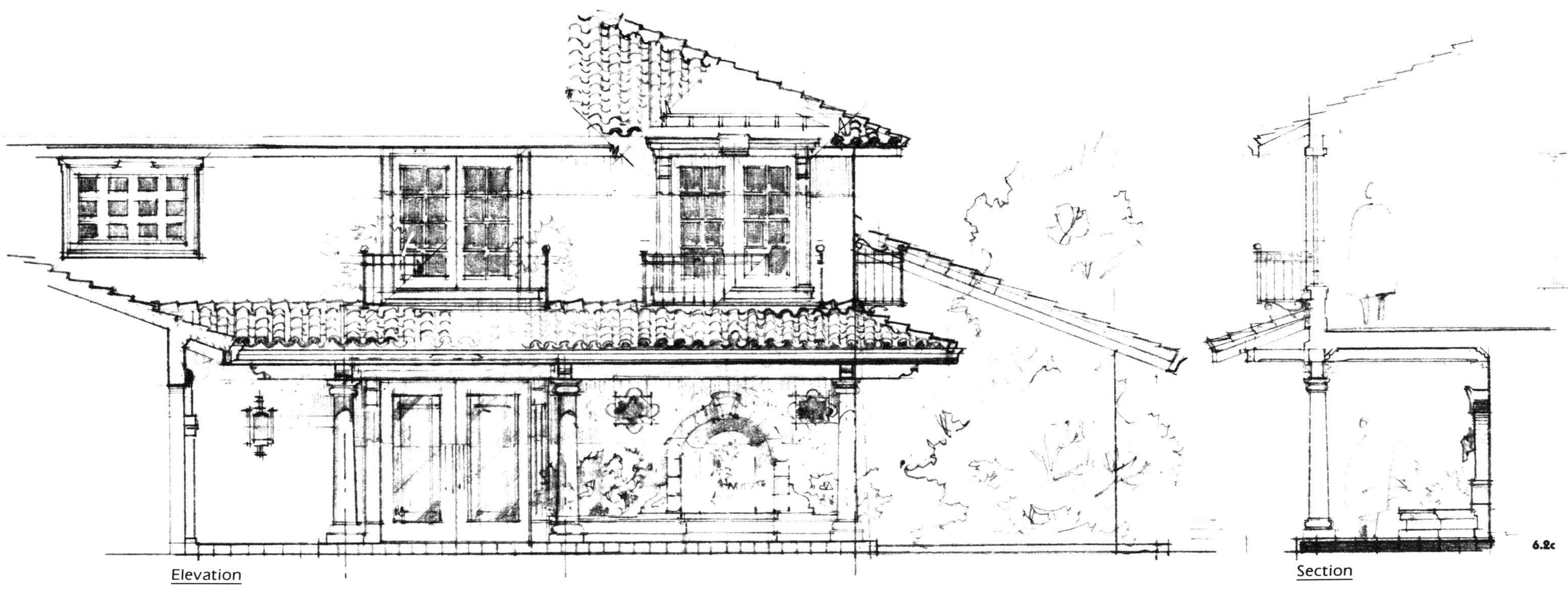

FIGURE 6.2a Although the corner of this house slants to the left somewhat, as seen in the photograph of this subject, the angle appears to be greater in the photograph than it is in reality. This is a direct result of the use of a 24-mm wide-angle lens and is caused by lens distortion. This effect was corrected on this overlay tracing by creating a truly vertical TMC along that prominent building corner and extending this vertical line from the roof-wall intersections to the ground.

FIGURE 6.2b The two photographs combined here into one image were each taken from the same vantage point, and the same lens, lens opening, and light setting were used for both. When the two photographs are combined, clearly each has its own complete set of vanishing points (a VPR and VPL in each photograph).

Note on the overlay tracing (Figure 6.2a) that when the vanishing points are found by tracing the two photographs, each lies on a horizontal line (the horizontal line).

When photos are traced for the purpose of combining images, either a tripod must be used or the photographer must pivot on one foot while snapping successive, vertically aligned overlapping shots. This allows the same horizon line to appear in all photographs.

These two photographs were combined by first enlarging them to 8″ × 10″ via a screened photocopy process. The fine photographic screen reduces the images to a series of dots, much as a newspaper photograph does. By using this system the photographic 4″ × 6″ prints can be enlarged successfully while controlling contrast and value so that fine, definitive lines and building breaks are visible during the tracing process.

FIGURE 6.2c The elevation and section shown employ the *corrected* right vertical perimeter of the main building as the TMC for the sketch shown in Figure 6.2d.

Note the dimensionality of the elevation drafting technique. The greater depth you can show in the elevation drawing process, the easier the drawing will be to understand.

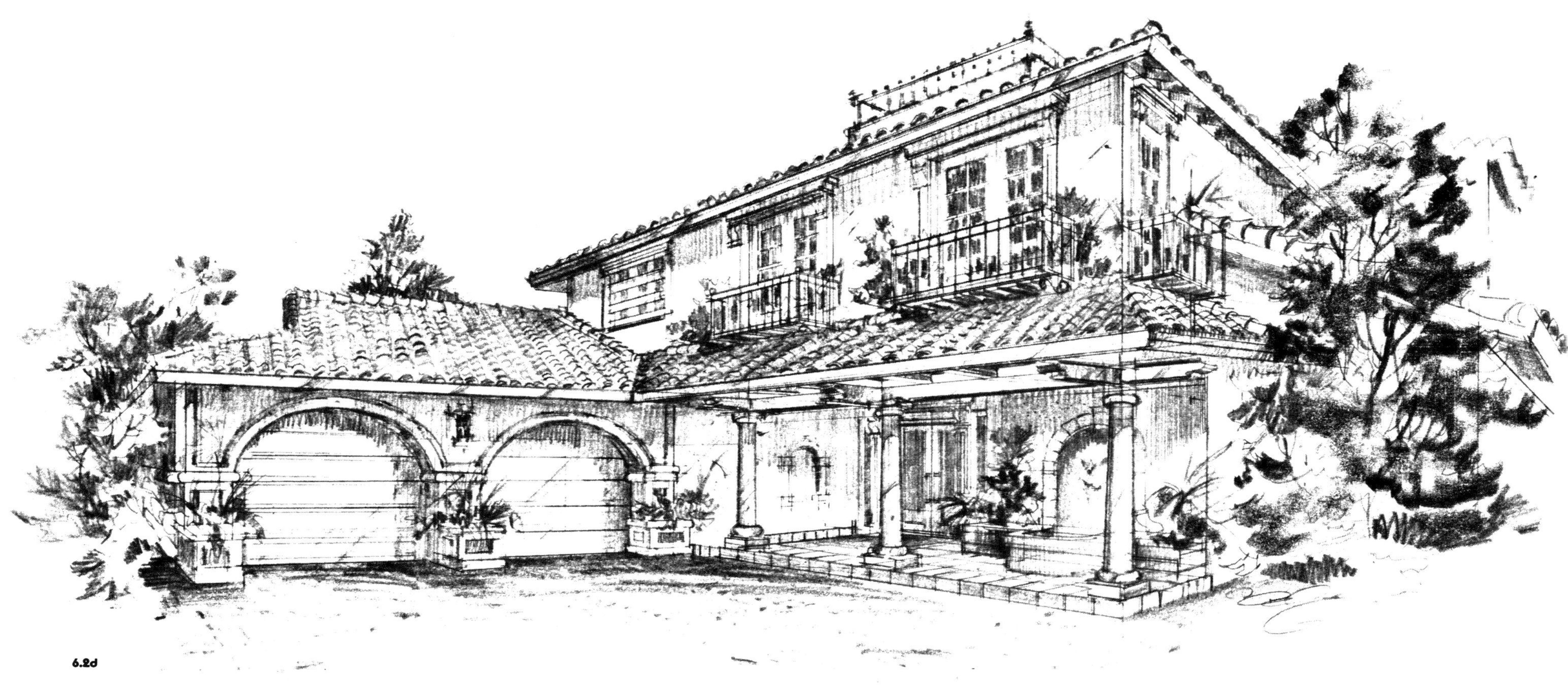

6.2d

FIGURE 6.2d The newly designed Spanish colonial house addition shown here is drawn over the tracing overlay while the illustrator refers at all times to the elevations and sections in Figure 6.2c. It is through direct proportional measurements plotted onto the TMC that positions of column height, roof height, and balcony height and width were approximated. The resulting sketch is surprisingly accurate for this project.

PROJECT: Residential remodeling, Foster City, California
DESIGNER: the author
ILLUSTRATOR: the author

CHAPTER 7
SPECIALTY TECHNIQUES

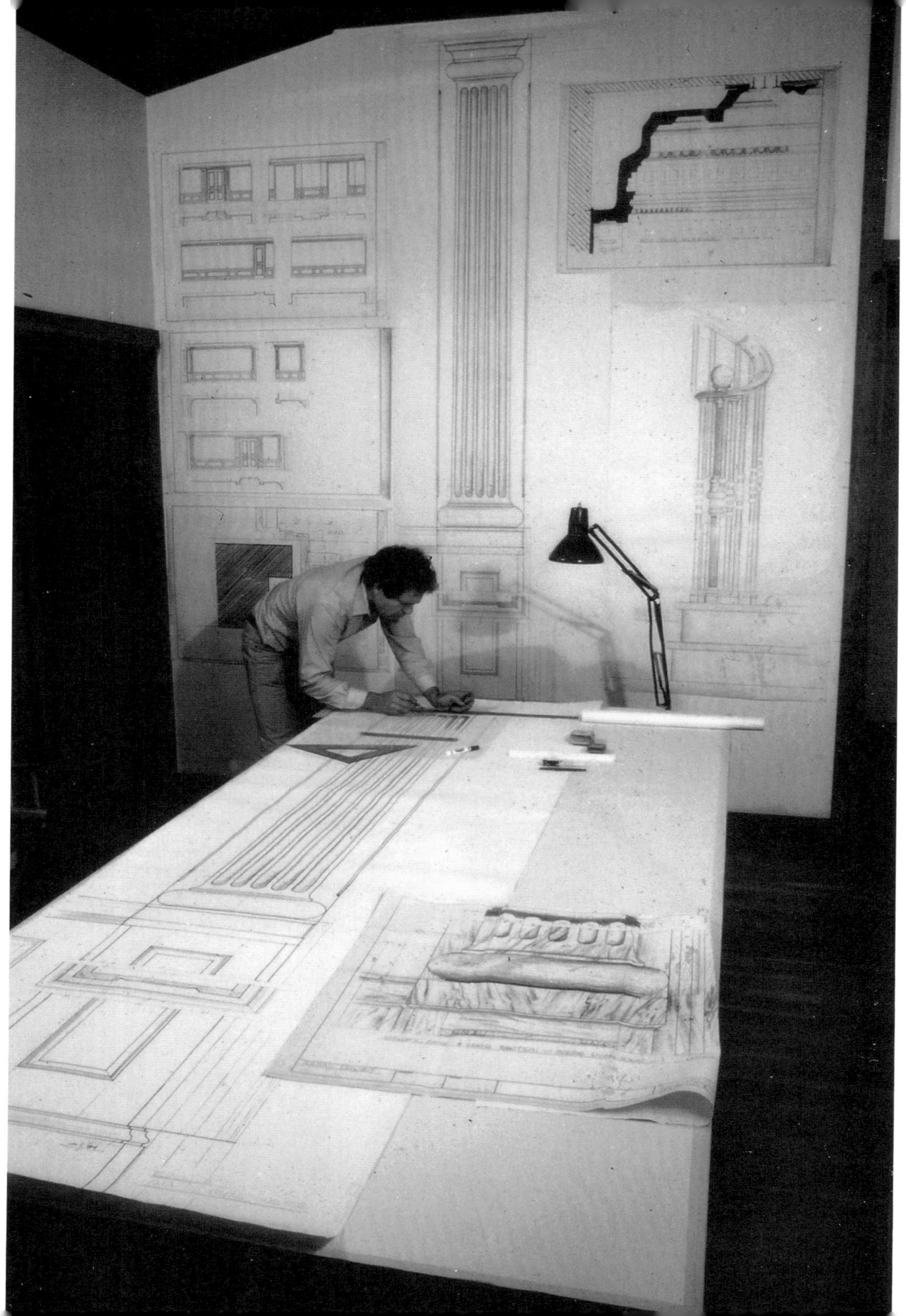

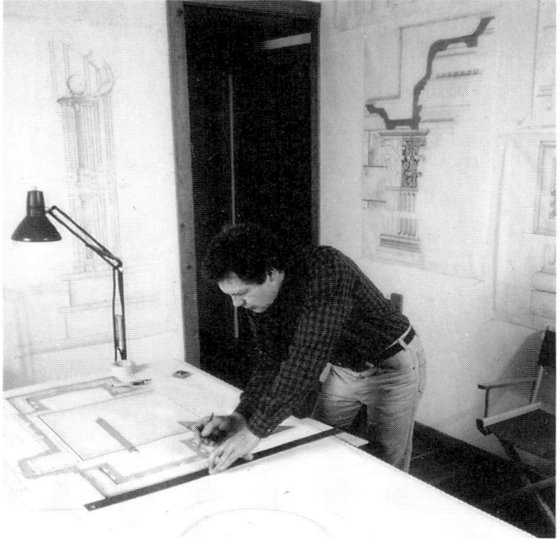

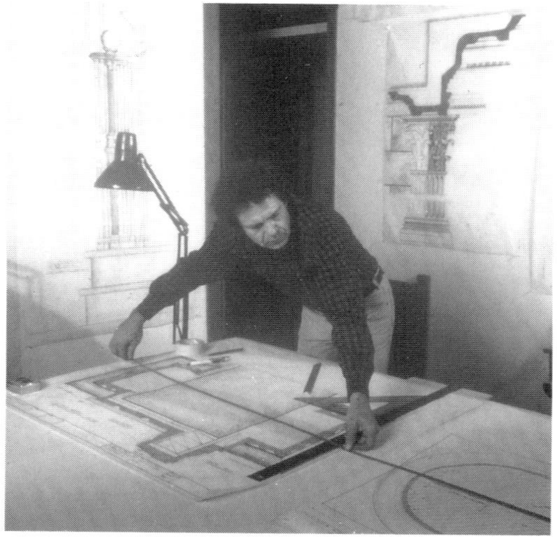

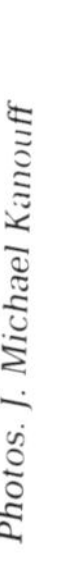

Photos. J. Michael Kanouff

CHAPTER 7

SPECIALTY TECHNIQUES

SPECIALTY TECHNIQUE 1: Three-Dimensional Rendered Elevations

The laborious process of perspective construction can be bypassed in many instances where dramatic and representational drawings are needed to sell or communicate design ideas by adding the illusion of a third dimension to standard two-dimensional architectural elevations and details. The professional designer, architect, or builder can benefit greatly from using this technique.

A variation of the four-value system of conventional light can be either approximated in elevation or mechanically projected, as seen in Figures 5.15 and 5.16.

Shade and Shadow on an Elevation

By using the rules of light, shade, and shadow, a three-dimensional effect can be transferred to an elevation by following a few simple steps:

Light Source

1. Parallel light rays on the elevation should originate from the upper right or left at 45°.
2. Projections of 45° shadows can be located by plotting simultaneously on the plan and elevation as in Figure 5.6.

Window Areas

3. Windows must read as dark gray to black (4 to 5 value), with all mullions having a 1 value, silhouetted sharply against the dark (4 to 5) interior.

Recessed Areas

4. Recessed areas on the elevation must read as a slightly darker 2 value than the 1 value of the primary face of the elevation. (See Figure 7.1c.)

Examples of Three-Dimensional Elevations

The elevation of the line drawing before alteration in Figure 7.1 shows a lifeless linear building; nothing helps the viewer to establish visual depth in the drawing. The addition of texture, shade, and shadow and

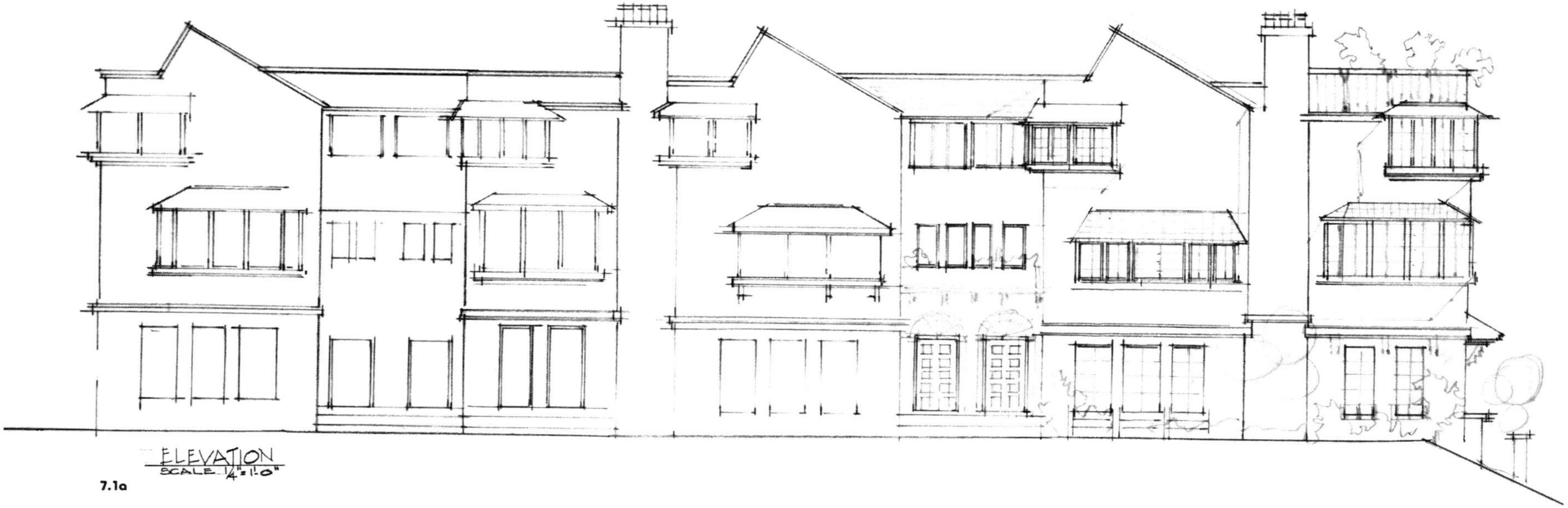

ELEVATION
SCALE 1/4"=1'-0"

7.1a

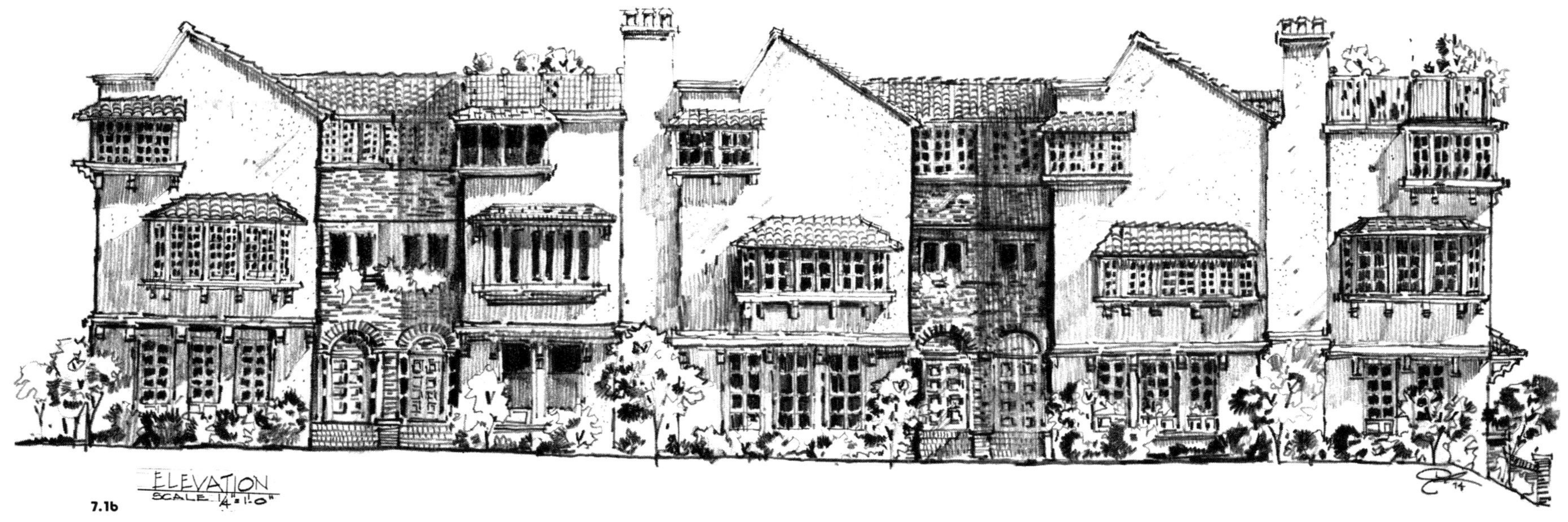

7.1b

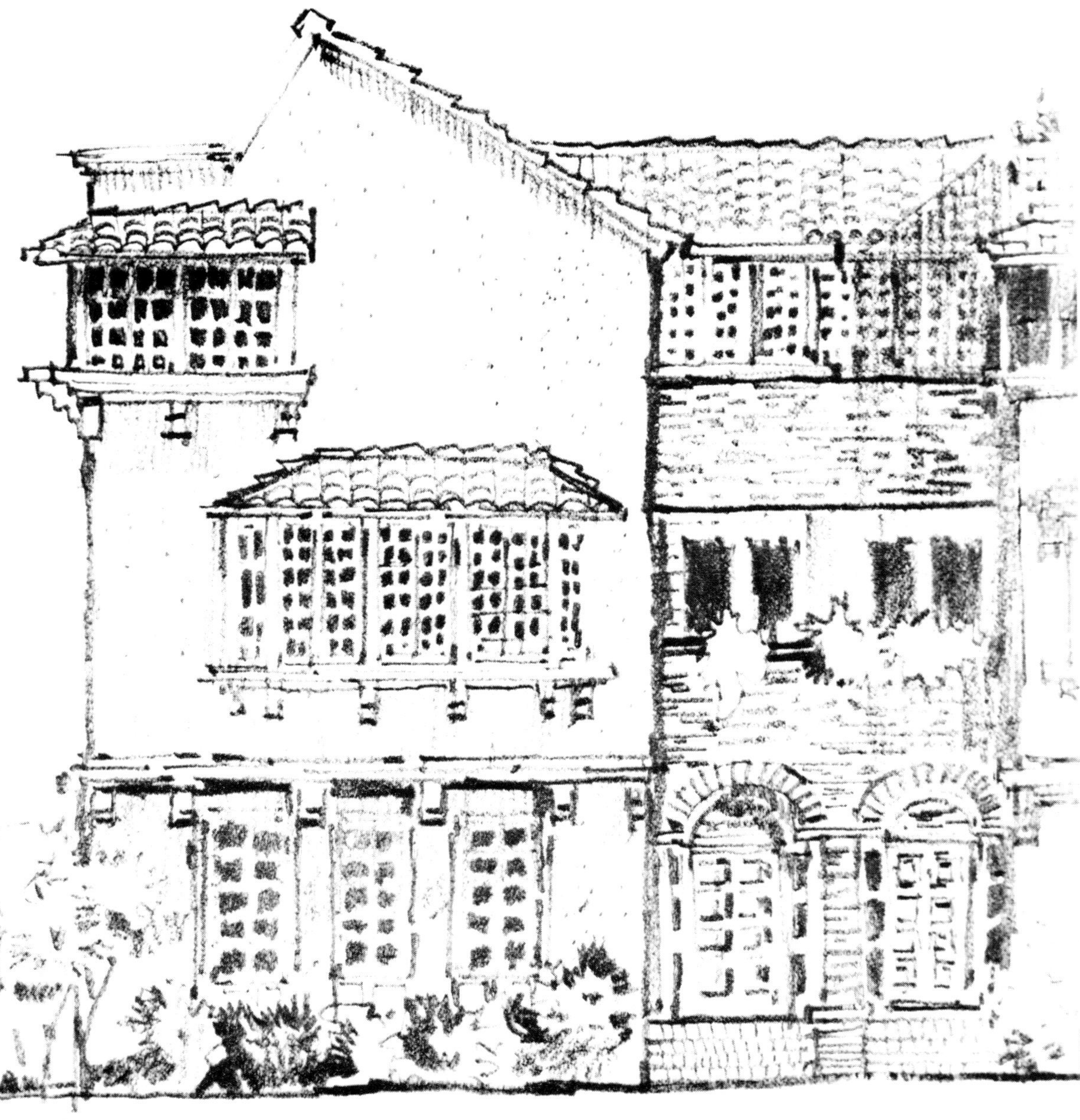

7.1c

FIGURE 7.1 This elevation of adjoining townhouses (a) shows a typical construction elevation drawn at ¼″ = 1′0″. The drawing shows no depth or surface texture.

When you compare this to the rendered elevation in Figure 7.1b, you can see how proper pencil technique can be combined with an implied four-value conventional light system to create a drawing that requires little explanation.

Figure 7.1c shows an enlarged portion of the drawing. Note how each pencil stroke is laid down to accomplish a specific task. There are no wishy-washy strokes.

The proper pencil point, combined with a good tracing paper, can help achieve this type of three-dimensional result over a common two-dimensional underdrawing.

PROJECT: Townhouses
ARCHITECT: Ted Moulton
ILLUSTRATOR: the author

the materials representation seen in Figure 7.1b shows how even freehand textural representations based on conventional light theory can liven up the drawing and give it instant appeal (see also Figure 7.1c, detail).

5. Each item of dimension should cast its own shadow on the elevation, which should read as a 3 to 4 value. Ground shadows are not usually seen in elevation, although a suggestion of ground cover can approximate that used for a perspective drawing and can range from a 2 to a 4 value. See Figure 7.2b and c.

Texture

6. The texture of materials such as roof tile, brick wall, and stucco should be approximated and emphasized with shadows.

Entourage

7. Entourage should be drawn as three-dimensionally and realistically as possible and should show limbs, leaf and foliage masses, and their approximate shadows on the walls of the building (Figure 7.2b and c).

Proportional Entourage

The elevation of the remodeled Spanish-style house shown in Figure 7.2a to d employs proportional entourage; i.e., existing trees were first photographed from the approximate location as seen in the elevations, and then the resulting print photograph was enlarged to correspond visually to the building height drafted at ¼″ = 1′0″ scale, with the related height of the existing structure as a guide. The major trees were traced from these enlarged photographs and carefully rendered to show dimension and to create a reason for a suggestion of shadow on the building, a technique that adds an enormous amount of realism to a drawing. Figure 7.2c shows the end elevation of the house shown in perspective in Figure 7.2a and d. After the large trees were traced and rendered to show their position on the rear elevation, they were reverse-printed by the Ozalid method, enlarged, and superimposed on this elevation. The fact that the tree will look different from all angles is not apparent in the right- and left-hand measured two-dimensional images shown in these elevations.

FIGURE 7.2 This series of illustrations depicts another design of the house illustrated in Figure 6.1h. Rendered elevations such as those in (b) and (c) were combined with the proportional entourage that was photographically enlarged from 4″ × 6″ glossy prints. The illustrations were instrumental in obtaining design review acceptance from local city officials as well as client approval of this private residence.

PROJECT: Southern California residence
ARCHITECT: Roger Bush, AIA
ILLUSTRATOR: the author

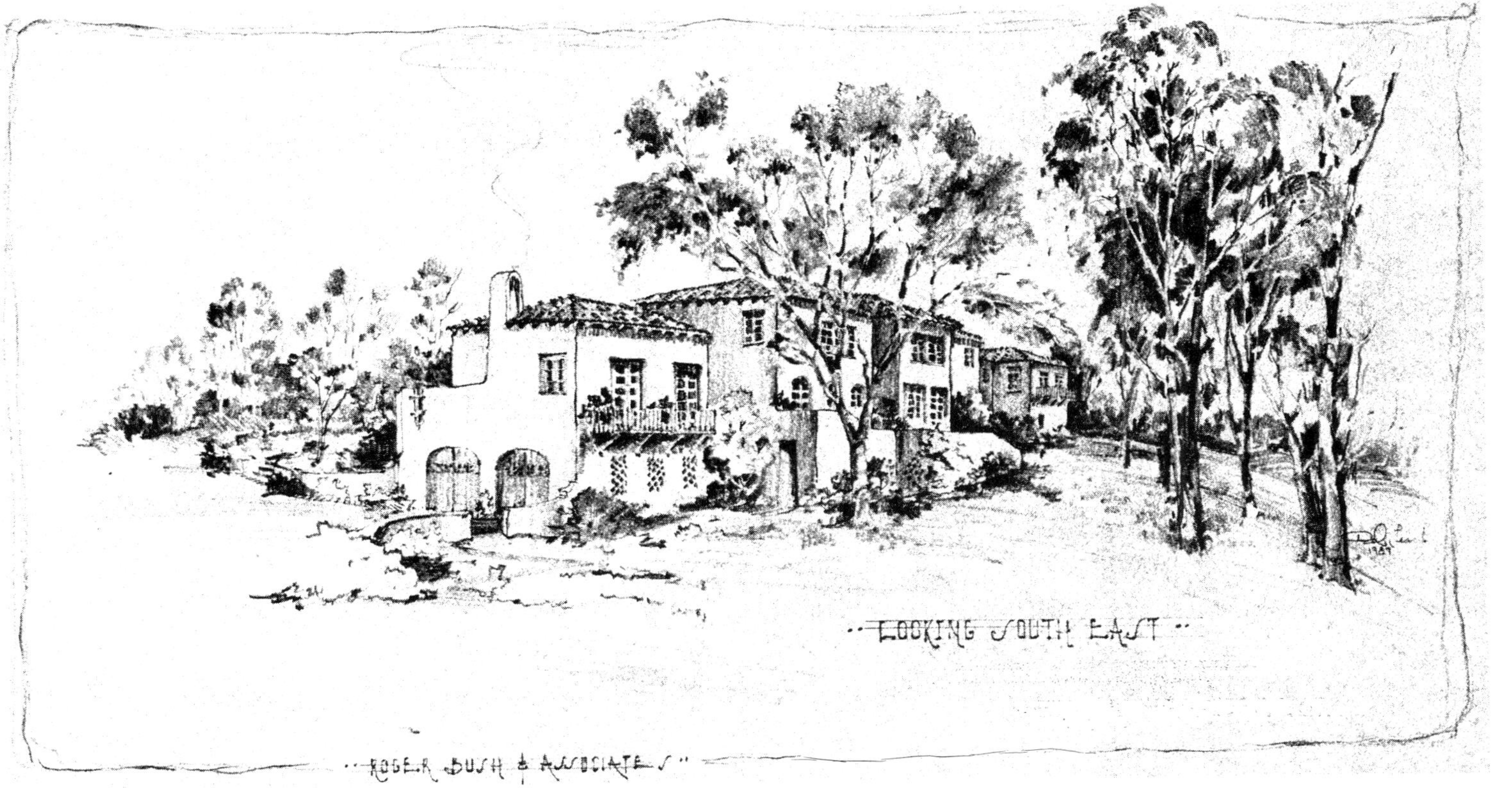

LOOKING SOUTH EAST

ROGER BUSH & ASSOCIATES

7.2a

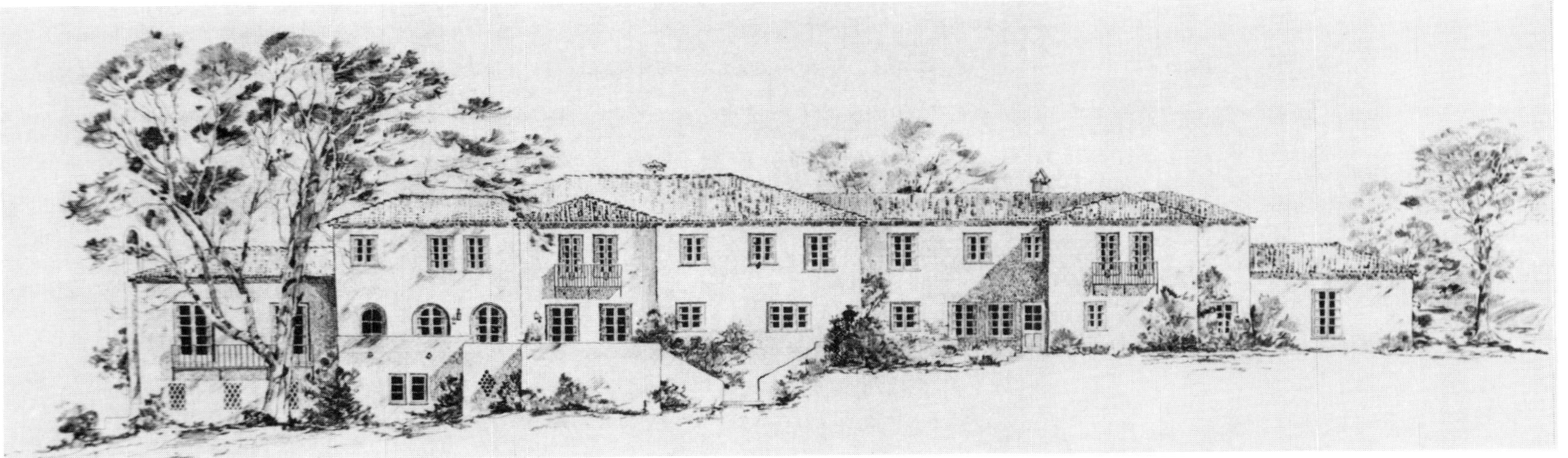

7.2b

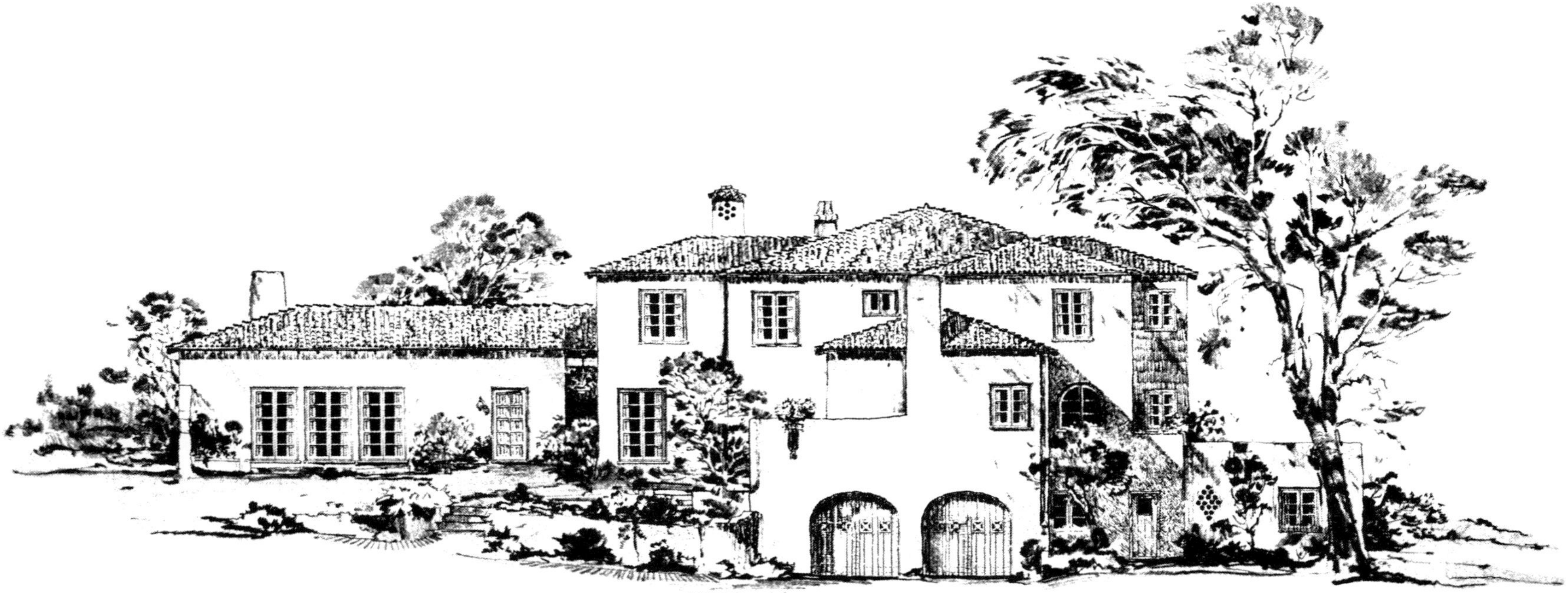

7.2c

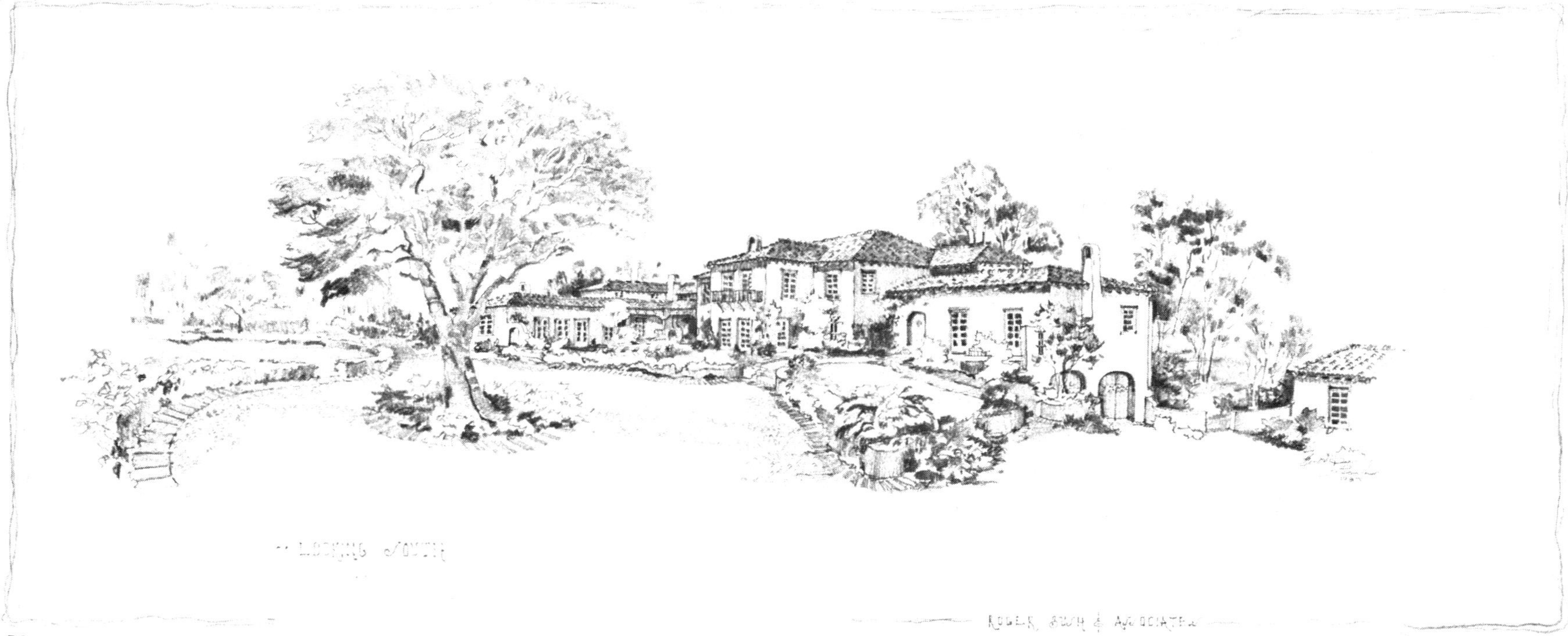

ELEVATION
SCALE 1/4"=1'-0"

7.2d

Give Dimension to Your Drawings

The elevations shown in Figures 7.3, 7.4, and 7.5 use shade and shadow to illustrate dimensional wood, stonework, and glass. In these illustrations, light rays are assumed to be projected from above either right or left at 45° to the page.

A three- to four-value system is used along with proper pencil techniques to create an illusion of wood, stone, glass, and mirror.

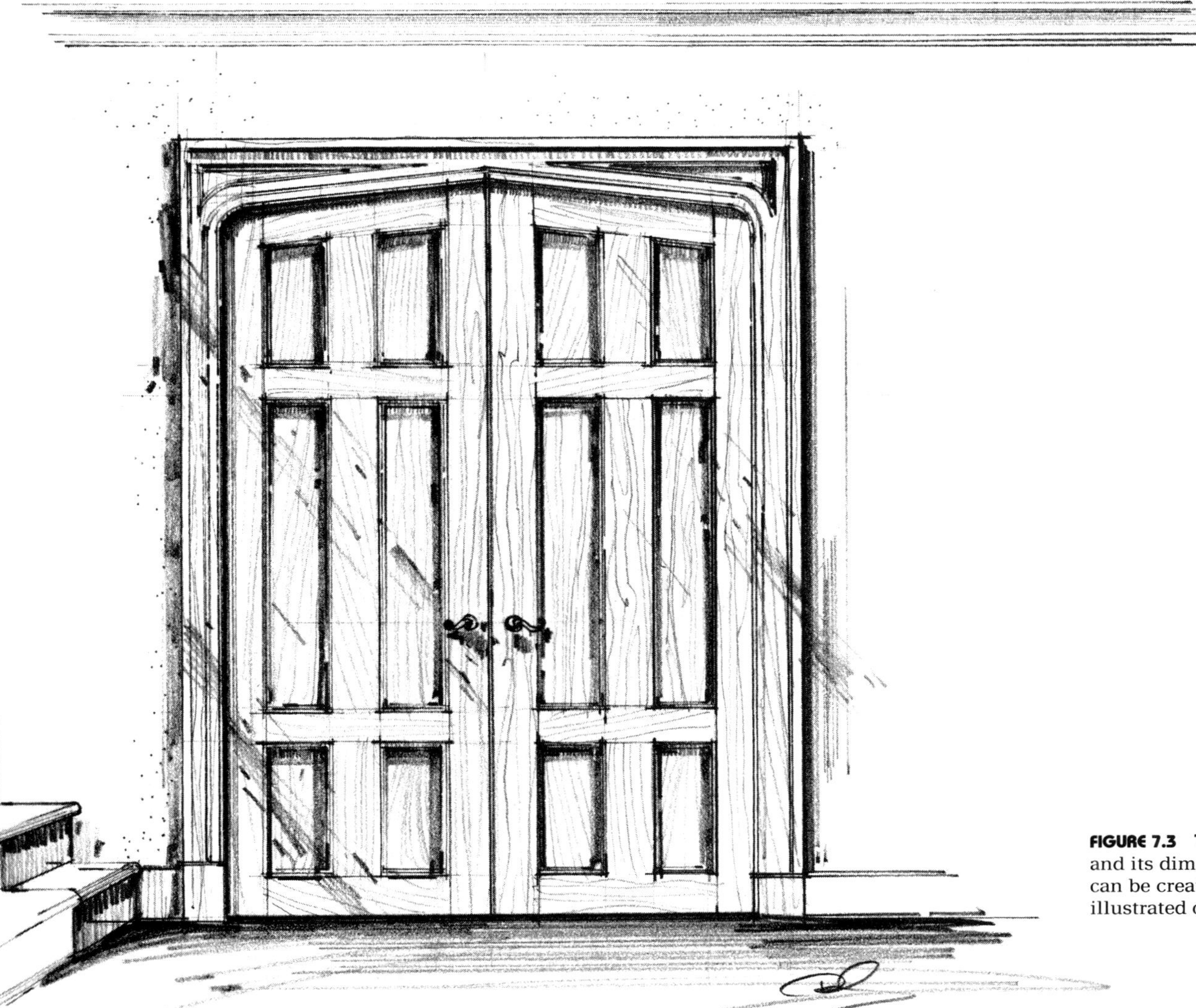

FIGURE 7.3 The drawing of this Tudor paneled door and its dimensional casing illustrates how illusions can be created on molded surfaces that must be illustrated on a two-dimensional drawing.

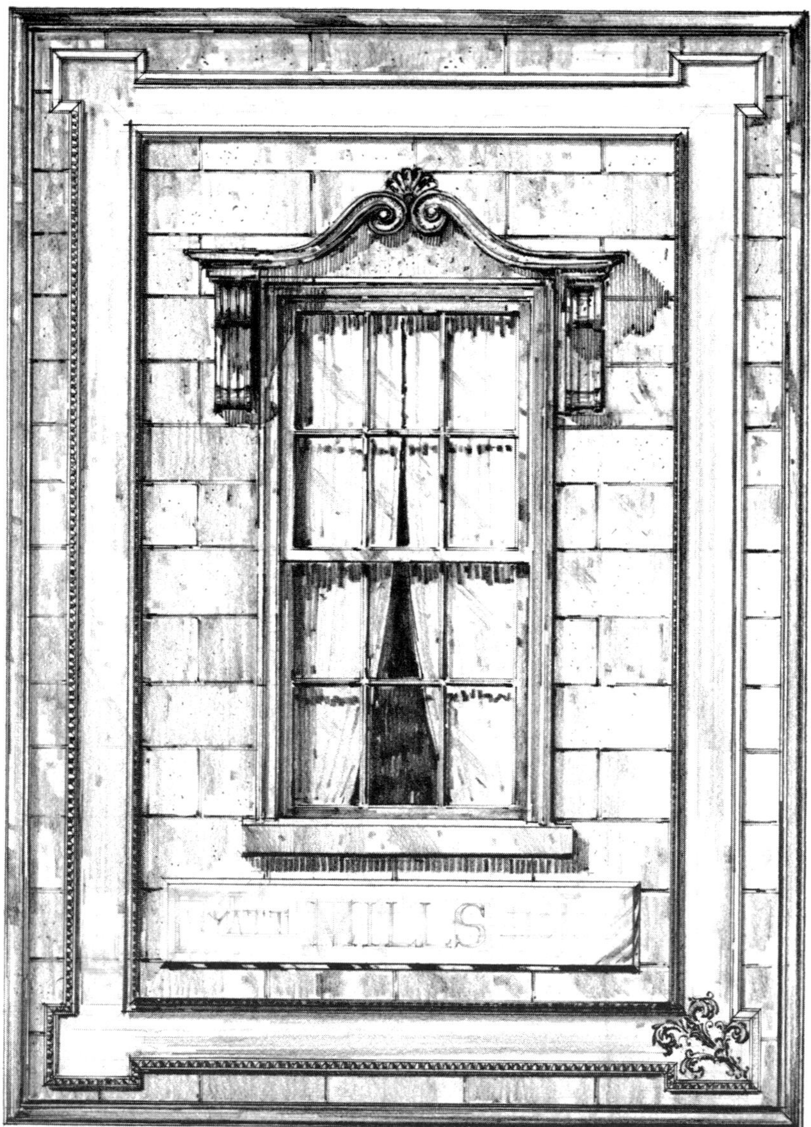

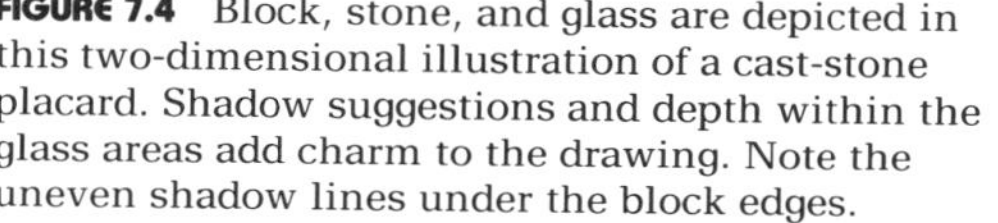

FIGURE 7.4 Block, stone, and glass are depicted in this two-dimensional illustration of a cast-stone placard. Shadow suggestions and depth within the glass areas add charm to the drawing. Note the uneven shadow lines under the block edges.

PROJECT: Mills Hyatt House, Charleston, South Carolina
INTERIOR DESIGNER: Anthony Hail
ILLUSTRATOR: the author
PLACARD DESIGN: the author

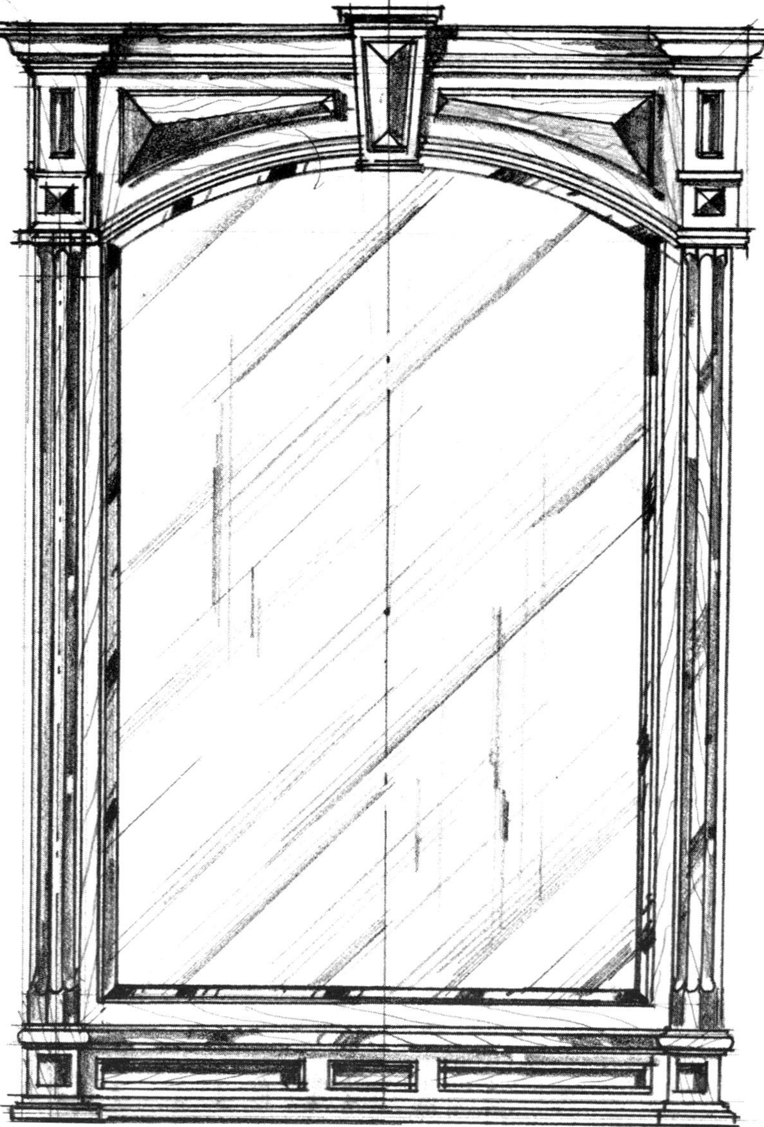

FIGURE 7.5 This two-dimensional illustration of a molded wood-framed beveled mirror shows how pencil can be used to create the illusion of a reflective surface with beveled edges. The value designations were carefully thought out before the final dimensional elevation was attempted.

DESIGNER AND ILLUSTRATOR: the author

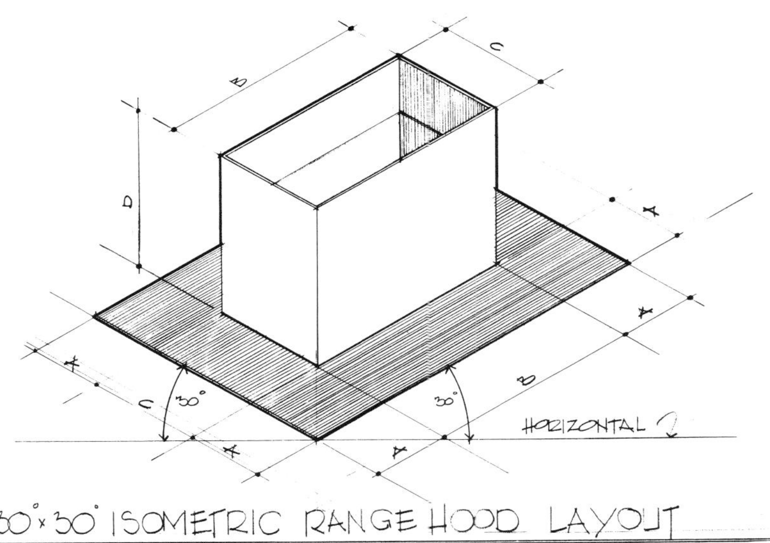

7.6a

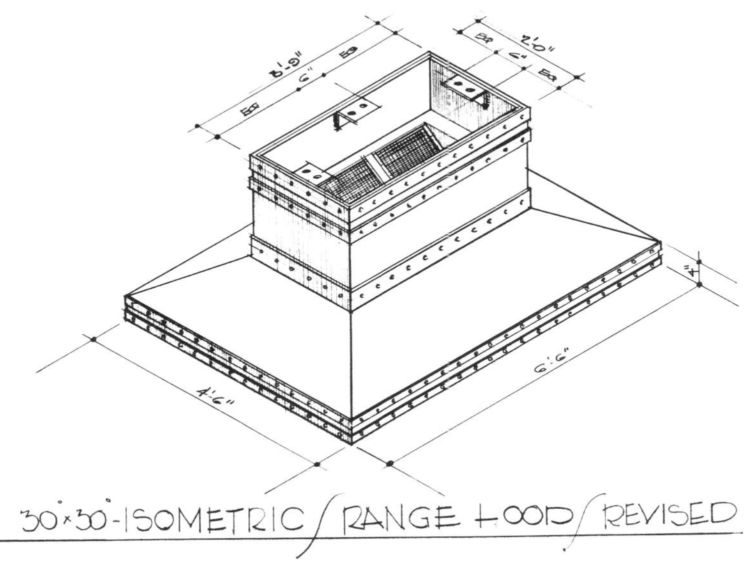

7.6b

SPECIALTY TECHNIQUE 2: The Handy Isometric Drawing

To draw a quick thumbnail sketch of a detail such as a piece of molding, a pipe connection, sheet-metal duct work, a stair railing, or a connection of construction elements, one alternative to the photolinear perspective method is the *isometric drawing.*

The baselines of the traditional isometric drawing are created by projecting one line to the left of the TMC on a 30° axis and one to the right on a 60° axis. This method can also be reversed, or each leg can lie on a 30° axis to the horizontal if desired (see Figure 7.6a). In the case of an isometric section, one leg can be horizontal, i.e., parallel to the bottom of the page. See the molding section in Figure 7.7a.

FIGURE 7.6 In this 30° by 30° isometric drawing, all lines on every implied plane are parallel to others on the same plane.

The rendered isometric drawing in (b) looks very much like a perspective drawing. This is because the two baselines are *each* close to 30° from horizontal instead of the traditionally accepted 30° by 60° method.

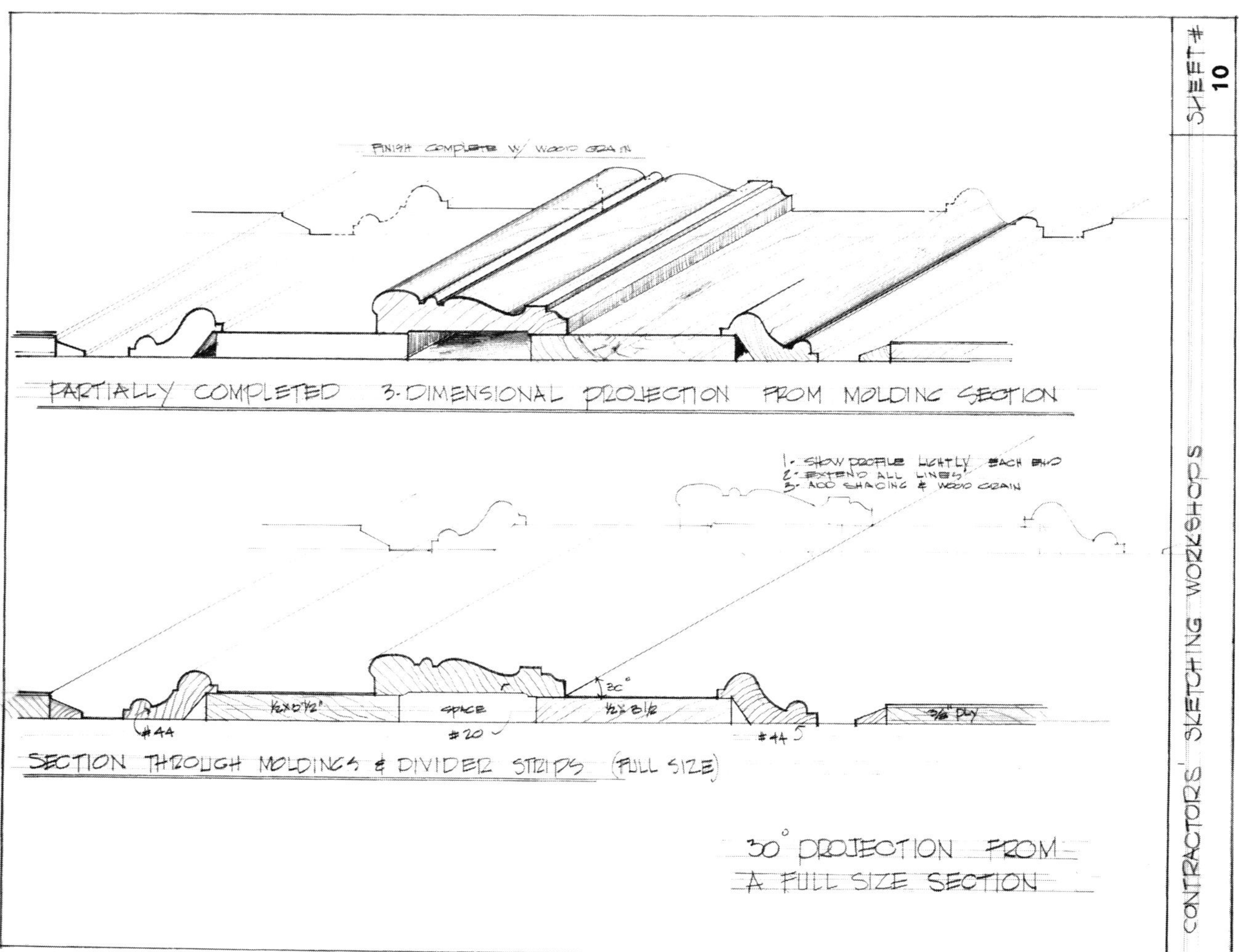

7.7a

FIGURE 7.7 The elevation and section drawing shown in (b) was one of the construction documents used to show the client what the dimensional paneling would look like. The isometric section method shown in (a) provides an acceptable substitute for the perspective drawing when rendered carefully.

PROCEDURE To give this flat, normally undelineated type of informational drawing a three-dimensional shape, begin by taping two photocopies of the section to your board, one at the top right and one at the bottom left, about 10″ apart. Each drawing must have horizontal lines parallel to each other and horizontal in relation to the bottom of the board. Corresponding points on each section should line up on a 30° axis from the horizontal.

Cover the board with tracing paper, and trace the lower section in its entirety. Next connect points on the two sections with parallel lines along the 30° axis. Some lines in the finished dimensional drawing will, of course, not be visible because of their position relative to the viewer, so only after carefully analyzing the drawing should you darken the defining lines. Once the three-dimensional line drawing has been made, the four-value system of shade and shadow can be added to give the drawing volume and dimension. Add values as if it were a perspective drawing, and don't forget to delineate the lower section with the proper traditional architectural symbols for materials. You can copy these directly from the section on the architectural drawings, for most drawings of this type are completely rendered with material notations in 3″ = 1′0″ scale and are part of construction documents.

Using this method one is able to quickly sketch construction assembly details, such as the molding shown here, with lines that are parallel to each other instead of diminishing to a vanishing point. It is much easier to line up corresponding parts when each is of a like size and when diminishing lines are not a negative factor. An item that is 2′0″ high on one side of the drawing will be 2′0″ on the opposite side and can be measured as such. The connecting lines will be parallel to each other.

PLAN
LIVING ROOM
ELEVATION A
ELEVATION B
ELEVATION C
ELEVATION D
SECTION A
FULL SIZE
SECTION B
TRIM SURROUND
#44
#20
TOP
OPEN
RE-LOCATE SWITCH TO CENTER ON TRIM
1- CHAIR RAIL #20 3½" x ¾"
2- NOTE! REMOVE CORNICE & REPLACE AFTER APPLICATION OF ½"
3- TRIM SURROUND / COPE CORNER INTERSECTIONS AS REQ.
4- RE USE EXISTING BASE IF POSSIBLE
RE USE CASINGS OF WINDOWS & DOOR

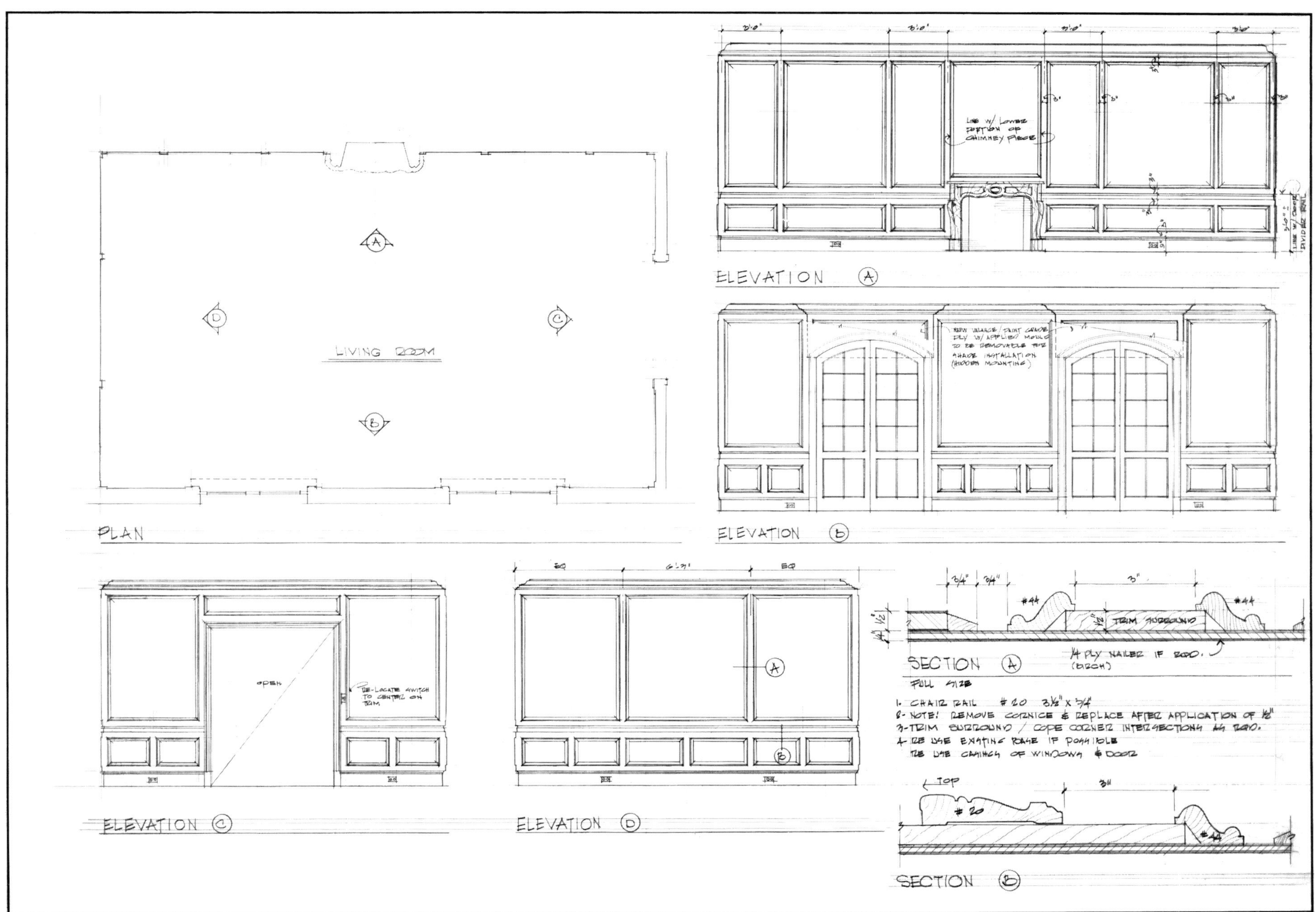

7.7b

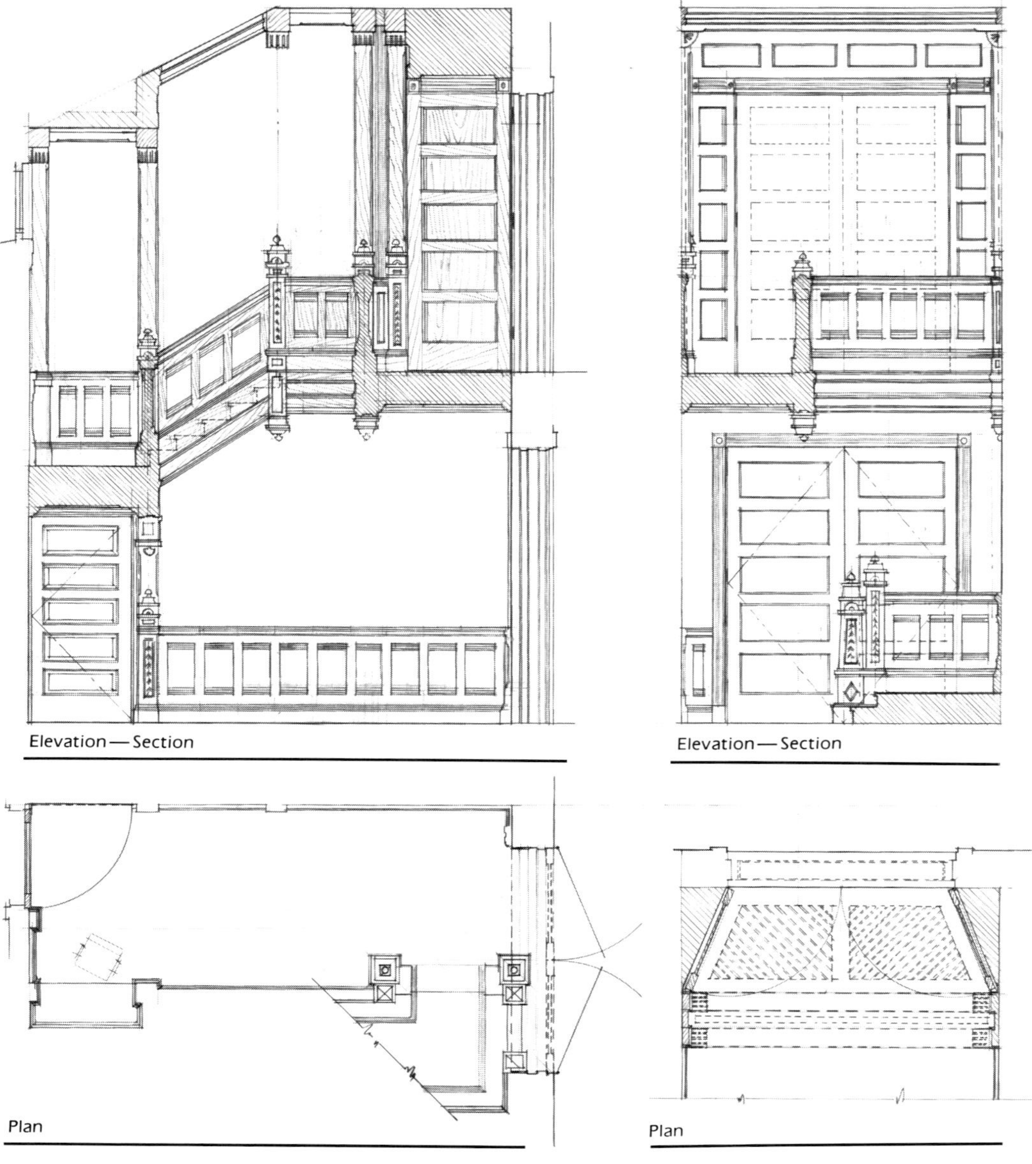

The Isometric Drawing as a Substitute for the Perspective Drawing

An isometric drawing has no vanishing points, and all lines are parallel to each of the two baselines, with vertical lines always being vertical.

There is, however, no need to follow the traditionally accepted 30° by 60° formula, which often yields a somewhat stilted and unrealistic-looking drawing. To make the drawing more lifelike, feel free to vary the axes anywhere from 20° to 40° from the horizontal on either leg. You can make an isometric drawing look much like a perspective drawing in this manner, even though lines are parallel and do not converge at one or two vanishing points.

Isometric Mill Work Drawings

Isometric descriptive sections (Figure 7.7a) that explain complicated mill work (Figure 7.7b) are often an important factor in gaining client acceptance for a project. They also aid in the fabrication of critically assembled woodwork.

The isometric design and installation sketches (Figure 7.8b to e) showing landing area variations for the stairwell elevation drawing (Figure 7.8a) are visual three-dimensional representations of the detailed measured elevations and sections. The third dimension plays an important part in concept, construction, and assembly of complicated cabinet work such as this.

Don't forget to add some shade and shadow in approximating the four-value conventional light system. To make your isometric sketches look as realistic as possible, use the wood grain, floor reflection, carpet texture, and other surface indications to help the viewer to quickly recognize and identify the drawing as a true-to-life representation of a real three-dimensional object.

FIGURE 7.8 The elevation section drawings of this Victorian mill work are augmented by isometric sketches that were created as design and construction studies. The 30° by 60° rigid traditional format was not followed in the drawings, but the sketches are believable and informative and show little apparent distortion.

PROJECT: Men's club, San Francisco, California
ARCHITECT: Ted Moulton
ILLUSTRATOR: the author

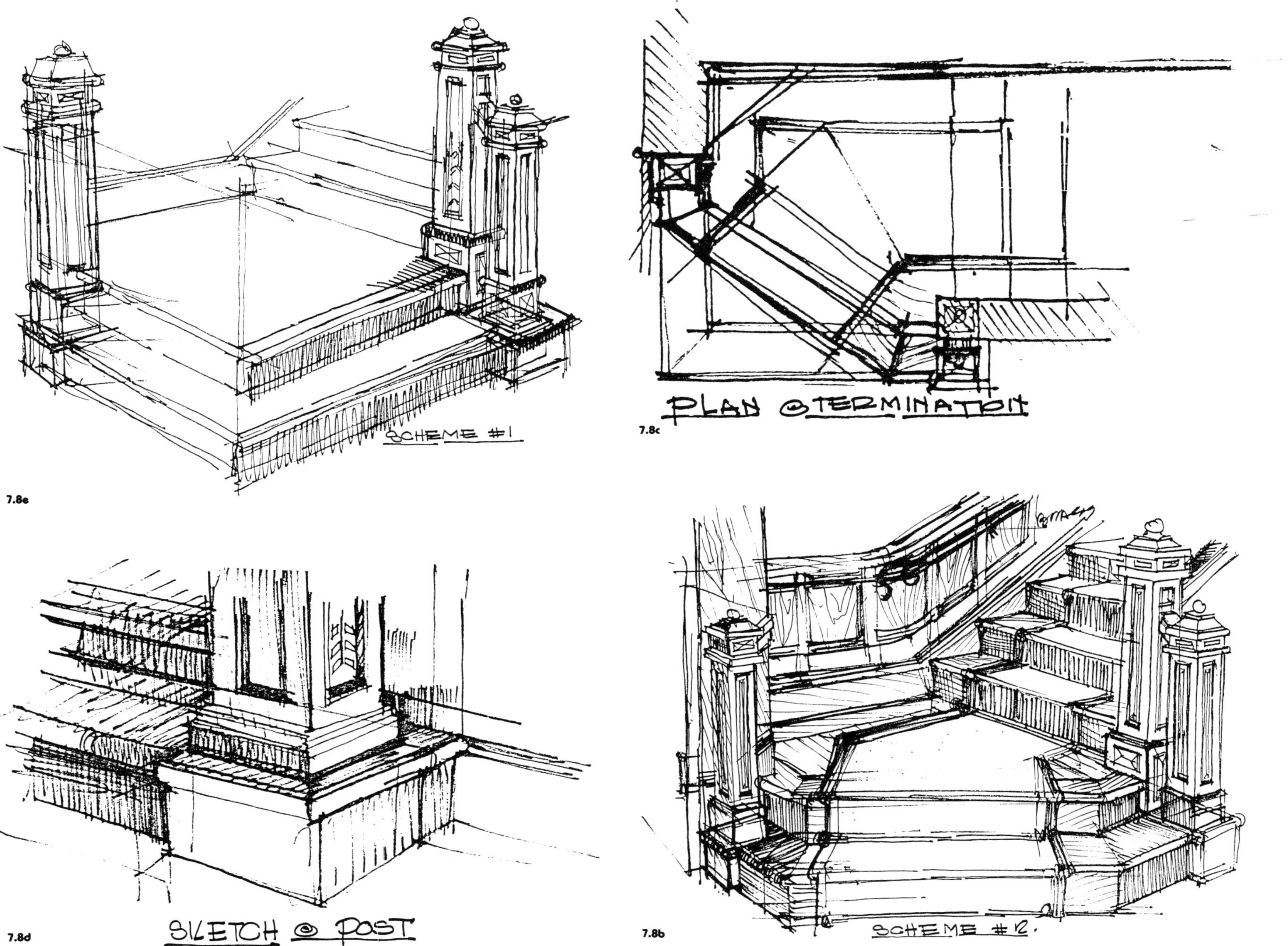

7.8e

7.8c

7.8d

7.8b

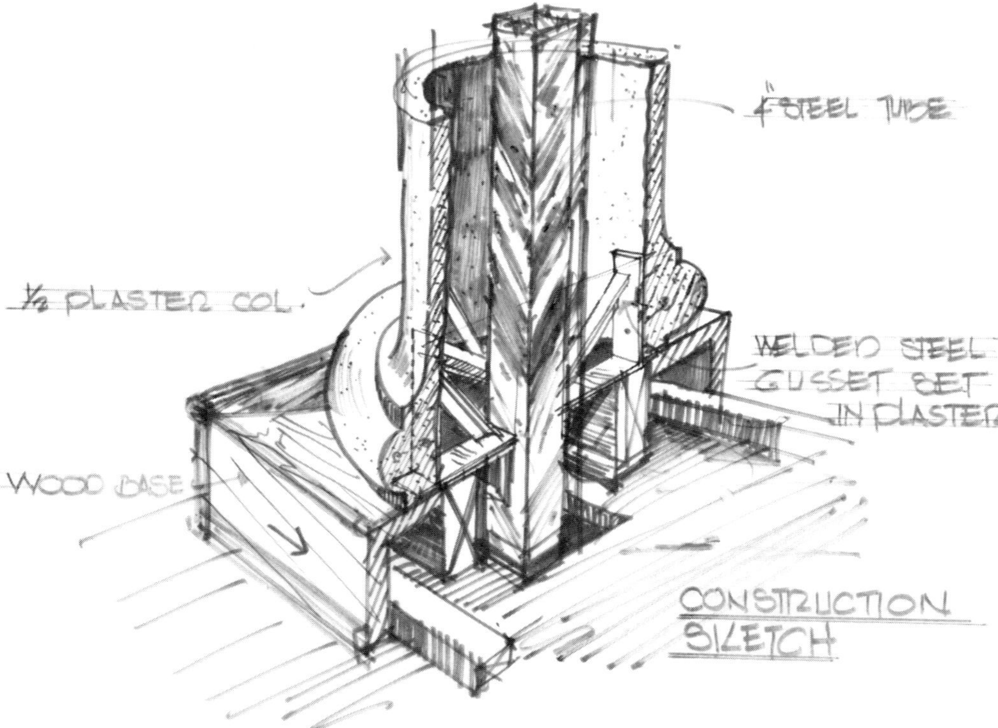

FIGURE 7.9 This column section shows how a cutaway section that is based on an isometric format can act as an informative construction or design document. Note how the cylinder is rendered to show the roundness that makes it look real.

Figure 7.9 shows how an isometric construction sketch and line drawing can indicate underlying construction methods not normally shown on an elevation of two-dimensional detail.

The Axonometric Drawing

The isometric format that is used for a multilevel interior architectural section or other large-format application is called an *axonometric drawing.* It is used in pictorial architecture layouts where both interior and exterior space must be shown in the same drawing, and so it is only mentioned here.

Food service and other architectural "action" sketches also employ the axonometric format, with the addition of the human-scale element to show work station layout and traffic flow.

The advantage of the axonometric drawing is that it offers an alternative to the laboriously constructed perspective drawing where photolinear perspective is not possible (i.e., where the subject does not already exist to photograph for the photolinear perspective sketching process).

SPECIALTY TECHNIQUE 3: Full-Size, Three-Dimensional Details

Creating a dramatic statement through the use of full-size, pictorial details
Full-size, three-dimensional details are a dramatic and clear way to communicate construction information and design ideas to clients, artisans, and workers on the job. The importance of details should not be overlooked when you are compiling contract documents or are involved in on-site construction supervision, especially if the job is of an extremely complicated nature, or located in another country where language is a problem and the site cannot be visited regularly. See Figures 7.11 through 7.15.

Rendered Full-Size Details

Full-size details and elevations that are rendered with the addition of shade and shadow (similar to the four-value system) are indispensable when it comes to creating universally understood construction details and patterns that are often required for complicated and curvilinear traditional architectural motifs.

A three-dimensional freehand sketch and even scaled elevations

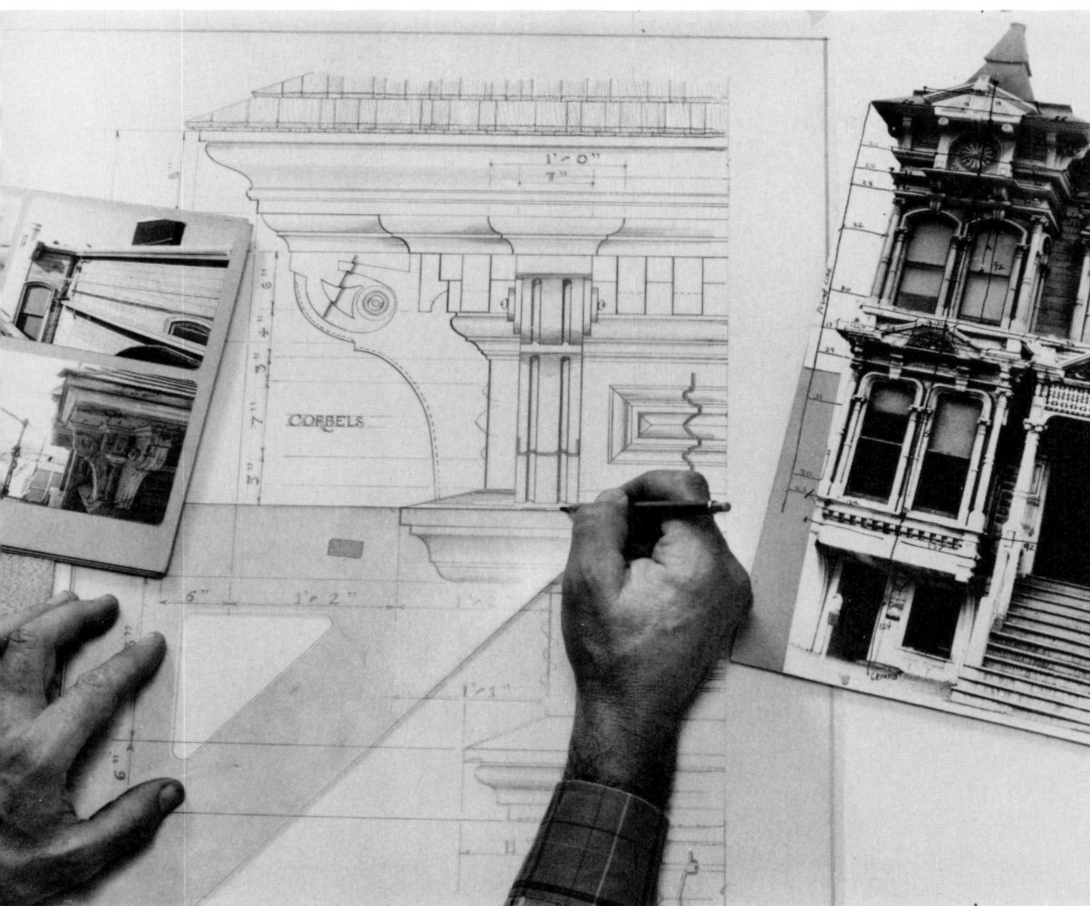

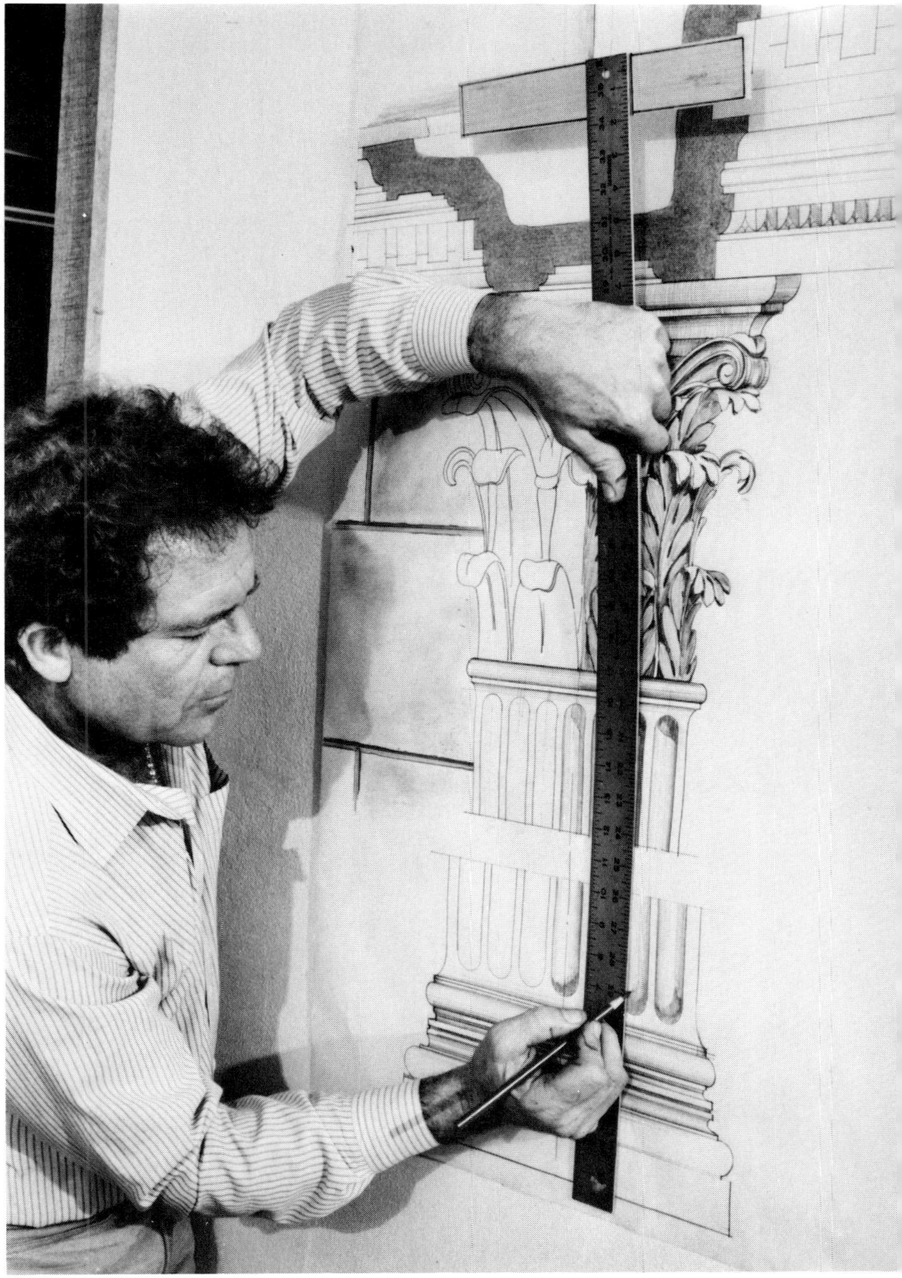

J. Michael Kanouff

FIGURE 7.10 Line work as well as flat pencil strokes can be used to delineate dimensional form on these full-size corbel and molding details. To create rounded forms by using line work instead of flat, pencil strokes, the lines should be very close together at the tangent of a cylindrical shape, grow wider apart toward the center, and get closer together as the form is rounded on the opposite side of the centerline. See also Figure 5.13a.

Note the section designations superimposed over portions of the drawing. Time is saved in this manner by allowing full-size sections to be determined without additional drawings.

FIGURE 7.11 Full-Size Rendered Elevations Shade and shadow techniques give life and dimension to this full-size elevation of a highly ornamented pilaster, its capital, base, and plaster cornice above. The plaster block indications on the wall, also to be tooled in plaster, are shown full size with joints that are rendered to show the dimension of the V to be cut into the plaster surface. Here the four-value system is used to lend dimension to the drawing.

The capital, which is to be cast in plaster after the initial full-size carving and mold are made, is fully rendered on the right side. The left half is shown in its two-dimensional outline form before delineation of the more clearly defined details.

J. Michael Kanouff

and details can be deceptive. A full-size, three-dimensional drawing, however, is particularly vital when it comes to showing intricate details in the surface design and true-size representations of connections, joints, and materials used in the construction. It is very important for the successful outcome of a job to accurately show how these extremely complicated architectural components fit together. This can save money and time, especially if the job is being done over a long distance and frequent visits to the job are impossible.

Full-Size Details for Three-Dimensional Construction

Full-size details are extremely important for renovation projects, where historic moldings and other complicated architectural motifs and details must be copied exactly (Figure 7.10). With the mastery of some simple techniques and the four-value system of shade and shadow, you can create these life-size, three-dimensional drawings, which are cost-effective in terms of time saved in the overall construction process.

Three-dimensional details drawn to full size are an excellent way to indicate architectural elements such as mill work, wall paneling, columns, cornices, door panels, mantelpieces, or a handrail volute. Custom-made items benefit greatly from the use of full-size rendered details, especially if their size, form, and construction methods are of an era unfamiliar to the workers who will be building them. Whether English or metric or a combination of the two measuring systems is used on a job, the full-size factor bridges all gaps in communications among architect, designer, client, contractor, and worker.

Full-Size Patterns for Two-Dimensional Work

The full-size format also allows you to convey more accurately the impact of a particular tapestry, rug pattern, or other design in a room. If, for example, you are ordering a foreign-manufactured custom-woven carpet for the client, you can communicate the design more effectively if it is in full scale (see Figure 7.13). Once the design has been approved, the fabrication is greatly aided by the continued reference to a full-size version, a copy of which is given to all concerned parties. (See Figure 7.14.)

FIGURE 7.12a and b The volute and handrail termination for a grand staircase is shown here in its fully rendered form. Although this drawing is a two-dimensional representation of a three-dimensional object, the proper use of limited shade and shadow gives this construction drawing both dimension and three-dimensional form.

Materials such as brass and crystal are given highlights to fill in their identity. Here the brass turnings are being checked for dimension by the author.

PROJECT: Residence, South America
SPECIALTY INTERIOR ARCHITECTURAL DESIGN: the author
ILLUSTRATOR: the author

J. Michael Kanouff

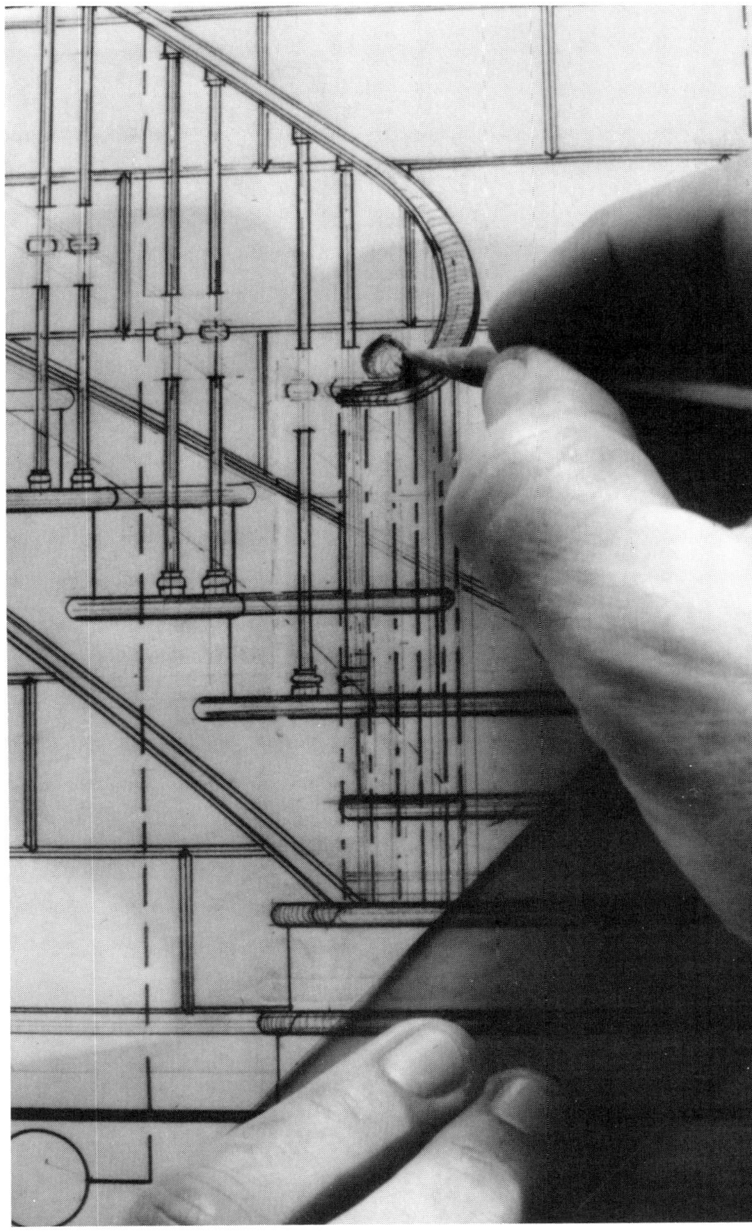

7.12a

J. Michael Kanouff

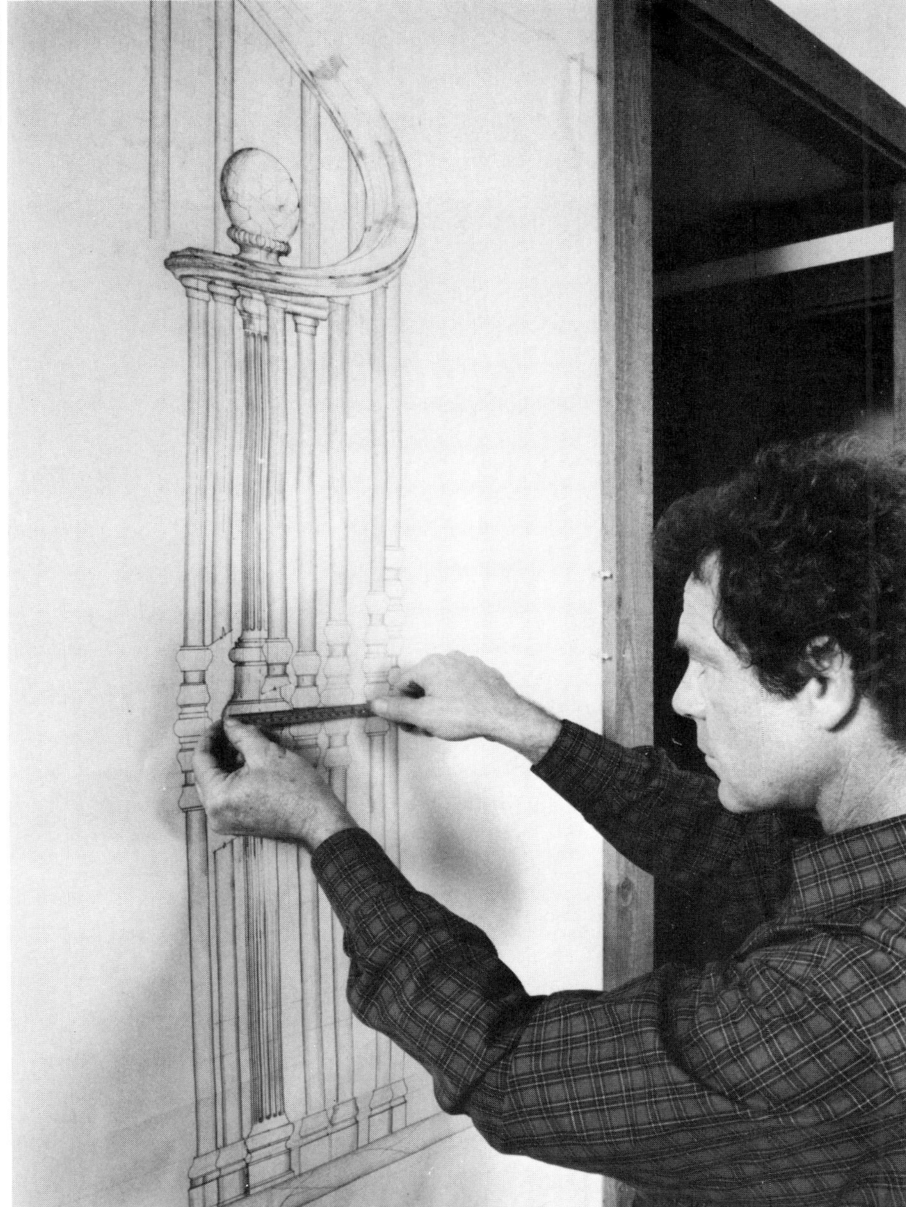

7.12b

Photos, J. Michael Kanouff

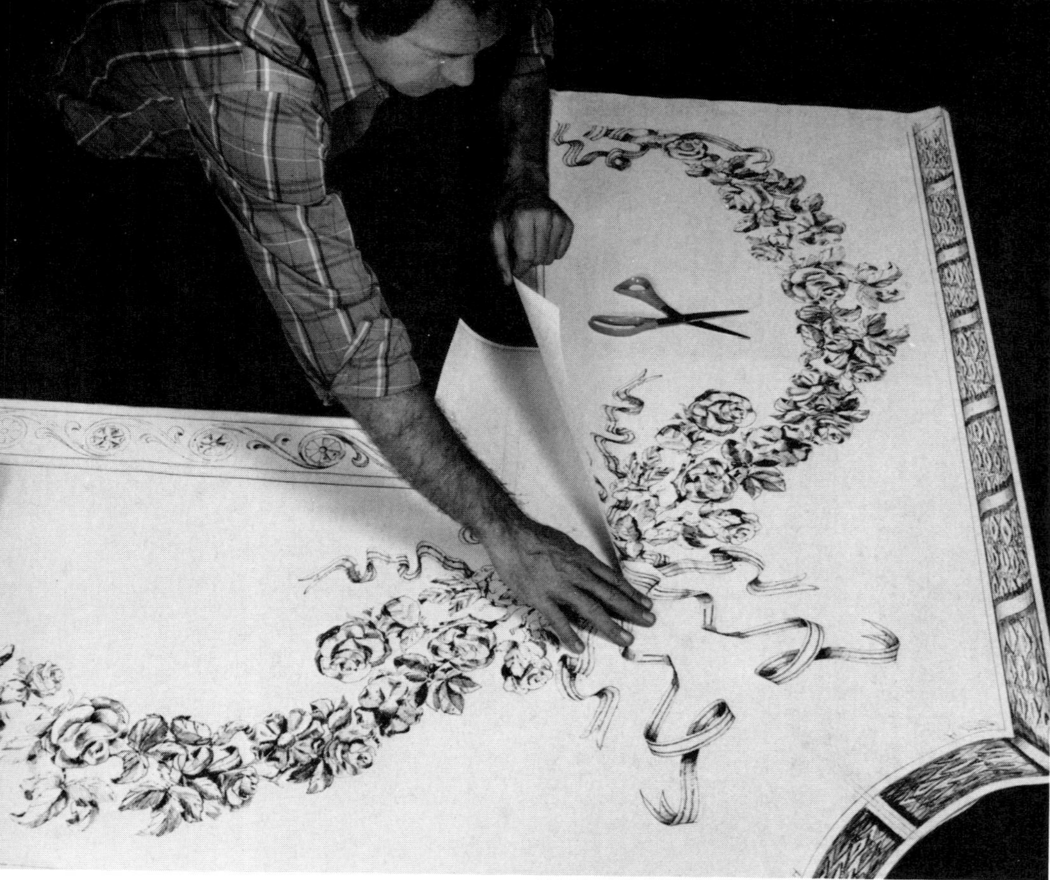

FIGURE 7.13 The technique of reverse printing on roll-size vellum allows you to reproduce a mirror image of almost any size design.

The rug corner shown here was first drawn in line form with a nonreproducible blue pencil. Then with 2B, 4B, and 6B pencils the value designations were rendered with care and precision. In this way, soft outline suggestions are visible on those areas that should read dimensionally without the aid of lines. Line work, of course, is important for the border areas where it defines the otherwise curvilinear pattern.

RUG DESIGN: the author
ILLUSTRATOR: the author

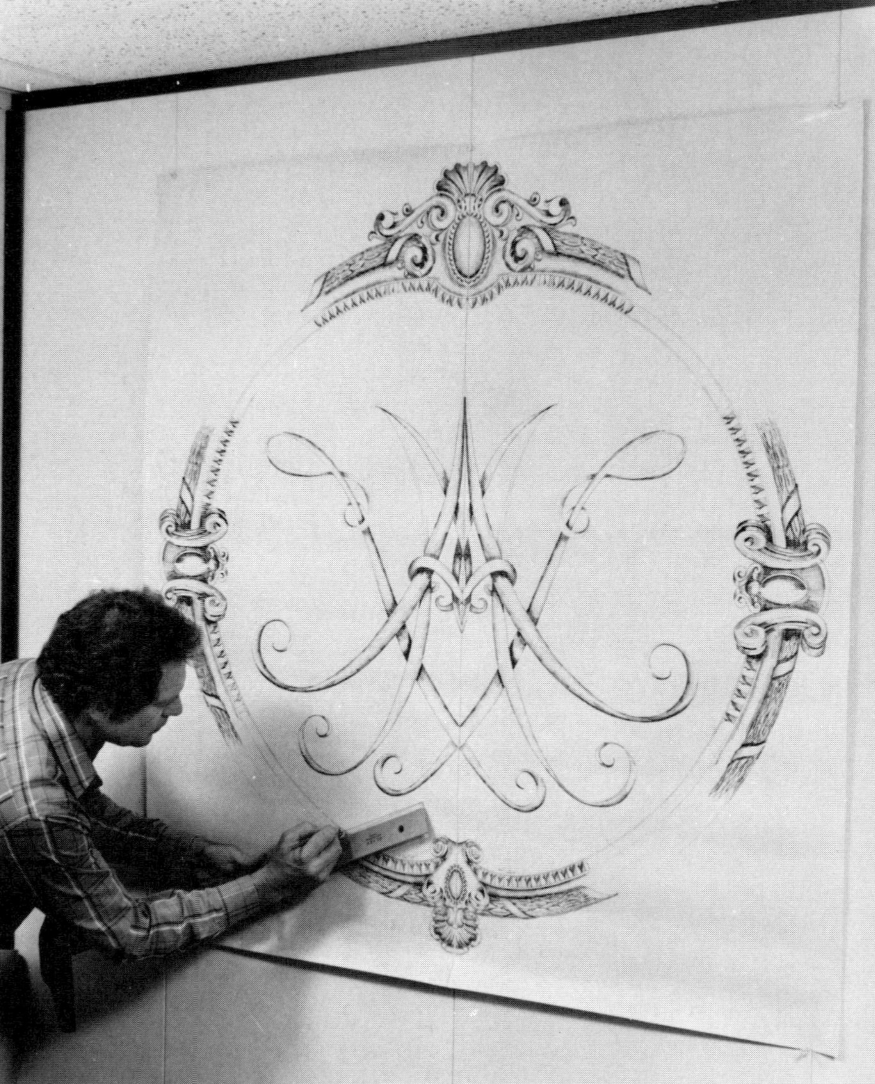

FIGURE 7.14 This highly ornate, full-size medallion is to be woven into a tapestry. In order that a "cartoon" can be made to accurately depict the design and its value designations, a three-dimensional value study is required. The classical detail of this drawing is revealed with a chisel-point carpenter's pencil (soft) and a T square that acts as a hand rest.

To save time, a full-size linear drawing is done of half of the design. From this, right- and left-hand prints are made on vellum on a large-format Xerox copy machine. Then the two halves are taped together, and the values and color added to the line drawing.

Next an artist will place a minute grid over this illustration and program the loom to correspond to the rendered colors and values.

TAPESTRY DESIGN: the author
ILLUSTRATOR: the author

Shop drawings and full-size patterns Since many items arrive prefabricated at the job site, it is essential that full-size patterns be made prior to prefabrication. *Shop drawings,* as they are called in the construction industry, are duplicated and sent to all parties involved in fabrication of the item. Thus there is little margin for human error in the interpretation of dimensions. See Figure 7.15.

Creating the full-size drawing: What to use The tools needed to create a full-size drawing are a large, flat drawing surface; a large-scale compass and a set of French curves; flexible-curve guides, straightedges, T squares, and triangles; and, of course, both English and metric scales and tape measures. For the line and shading work, you will need soft and hard lead mechanical drawing and carpentry pencils, a 2B or 4B graphite stick, and large-format tracing paper.

A scale drawing complete with overall and secondary dimensions is needed for constant reference while you are plotting the full-size drawing. First, draw the overall dimensions. Next, lightly plot all secondary divisions, using the T square and triangle just as you would for a scale drawing.

Time-saving steps Repetitions in the drawing such as those of molding profiles can be traced from photocopy prints. If a reverse-reading detail is needed for either a right- or left-hand drawing, just run a reverse-reading Ozalid print to read reverse and trace this onto the drawing.

Curves can be plotted freehand, by using a compass if geometrically perfect curves are required, with the aid of proportional grid squares, by using a combination of French curves, or by using any combination of these.

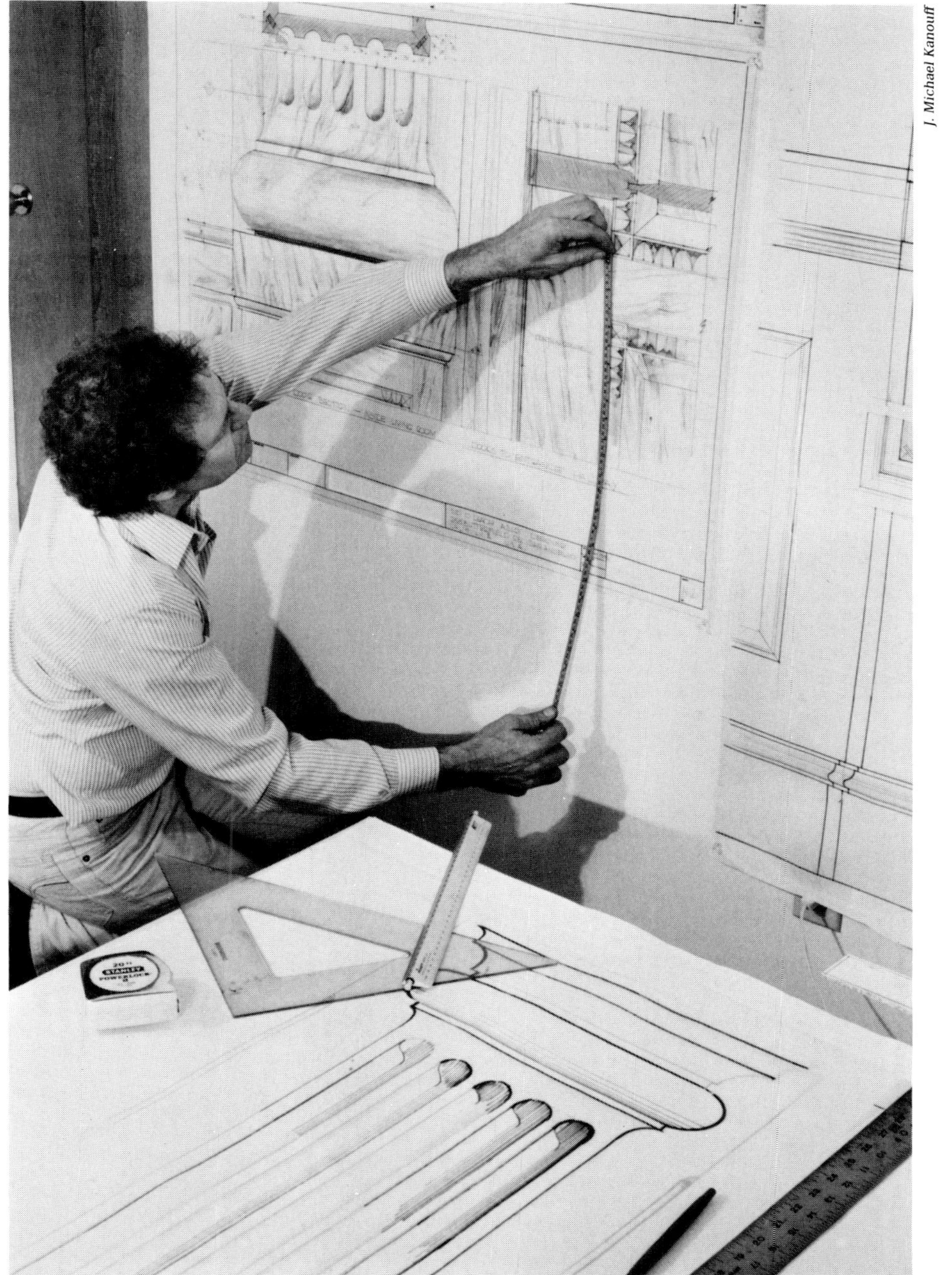

J. Michael Kanouff

FIGURE 7.15 When custom mill work of a very high order is drawn full size, all carving, shaping, and joinery can be visually approximated. Also the wood grain direction, structure, and intensity can be suggested. Full size also reflects the true reality of architectural motifs that do not manifest themselves in a small drawing.

A graphite stick is employed to create the dimensional shading that gives the drawing form. By rotating the square edge and using uneven pressure, thin wavy lines as well as wide shading strokes are possible. Wood grain can be applied in this manner very rapidly, to create very realistic, full-size mill work drawings.

PROJECT: Residence, Brazil
SPECIALTY INTERIOR DESIGN AND ARCHITECTURAL MILL WORK: the author

Shade and shadow Once the outline is complete, shade and shadow can be introduced through varyingly spaced line work or by using a graphite stick for varying tonal effects. See Figures 7.16 and 7.17.

FIGURES 7.16 and 7.17 Full-Size Cabinet Work Details The over-door air conditioning grill and its traditional wood trim are delineated with a ¼″ square stick of 2B pressed graphite. By using this medium on sepia reproducible paper, you can create a dimensional drawing that allows all concerned parties to visualize and prepare on-site conditions prior to ordering and fabricating expensive mill work.

PROJECT: Winery corporate offices
PROJECT DESIGNER: the author
PROJECT ARCHITECT: Robert M. Morris Jr., AIA
ASSISTANT DESIGNER: April Kinsburg

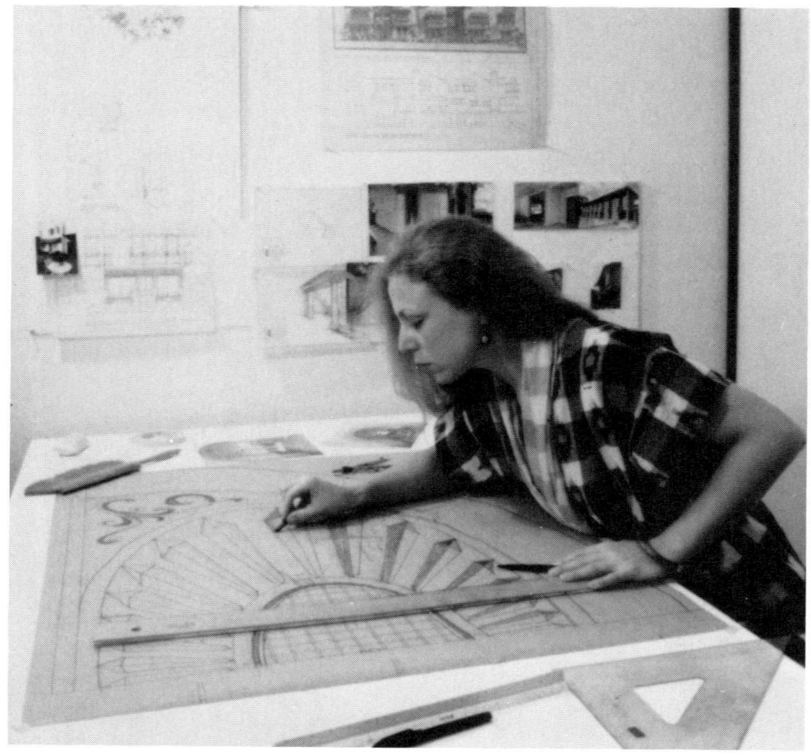

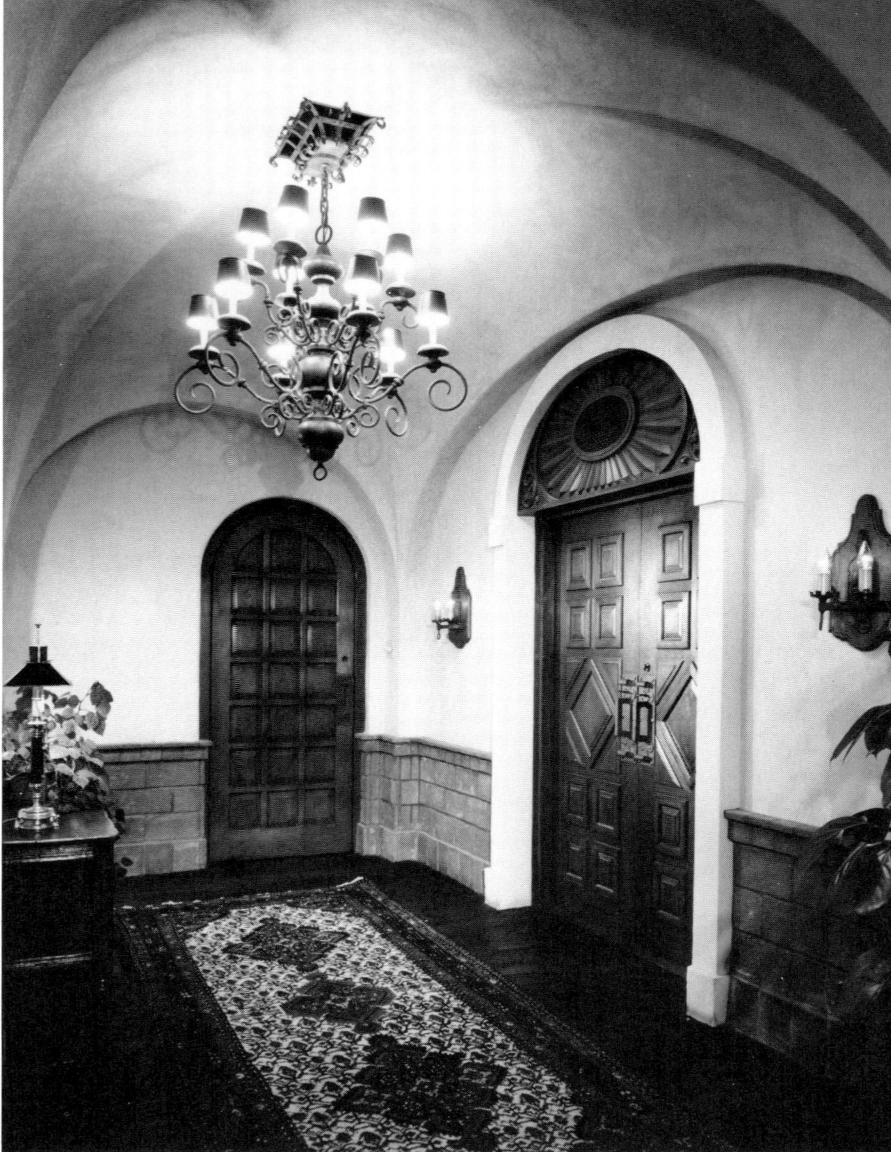

SPECIALTY TECHNIQUE 4: Models Aid in Design Illustrations

Curvilinear volumes of space are difficult to illustrate in three dimensions. Vanishing points must be formed based on known elements in order to make a remodeling sketch as accurate and as true to the existing space as possible.

The drawings of the vaulted ceiling environment shown in Figure 7.18a (concept sketch) and b (the plan) do not accurately represent the curves of vaults and arches required for this type of architectural design. A more accurate approach to the creation of design drawings begins with a three-dimensional model (Figure 7.18c and d) that can be photographed from various positions. The resulting photographs are traced to create sketches according to the photolinear perspective theory.

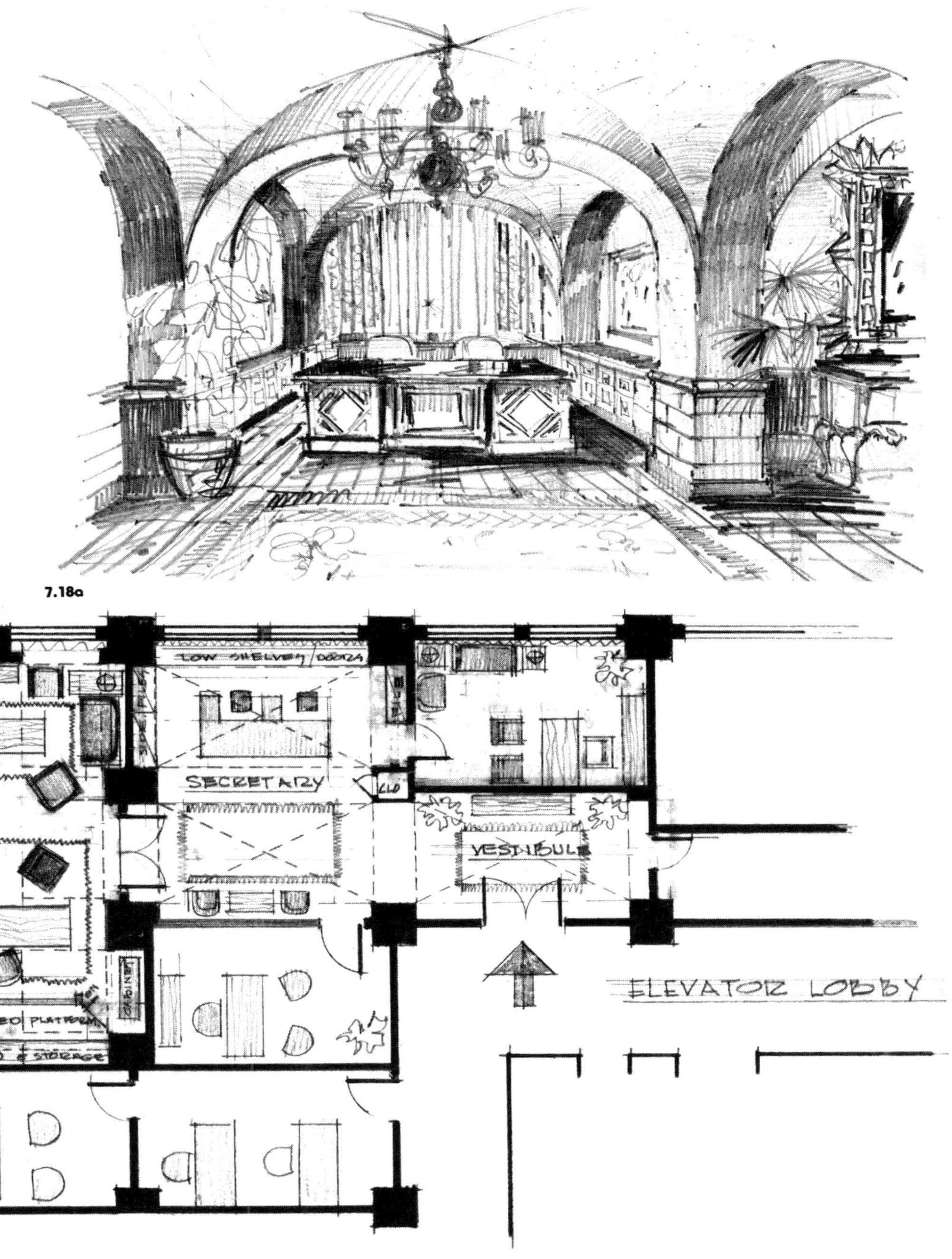

FIGURE 7.18a and b This original design sketch and the floor plan were created to sell the concept and functional layout only. It was felt that a three-dimensionally accurate model (Figure 7.18d) was needed to aid in the creation of the presentation drawing seen in Figure 7.18g. The vaulted-ceiling office suite was constructed on the sixth floor of a concrete and steel office building. The plan shows the base area encompassed by the new plaster work as well as a suggestion of furniture, rugs, and floor coverings.

The Plaster Model from a Styrofoam Core

1. To create an accurate, three-dimensional, plaster of paris model similar to the one shown in Figure 7.18d, a Styrofoam form in the shape of all negative space in the connected vaulted spaces is required. This negative volume is first carved from a larger volume of Styrofoam (Figure 7.18c), placed inside a cardboard box, and covered with plaster of paris.

Remove the Styrofoam core

2. After the plaster has hardened, the box is turned upside down, and the bulk of the Styrofoam is scraped out. Next, lacquer thinner is poured into the cavity to dissolve any remaining Styrofoam.

3. Door openings are cut with a coping saw, and the model is placed on a painted cardboard "floor."

Paint the model

4. The wainscot tile can be roughly painted onto the plaster, if desired, before the interior space is photographed.

Photograph the Model

5. Shine a bright light into the space through the cut openings.

6. Point a close-up lens of a 35-mm camera through the door openings. Using the smallest lens opening available, that is, f/16 or f/22, and a 1- or 2-minute exposure (depending on the amount of light in the space), take photographs of the volume from as many angles as possible. (See Figure 7.18d.)

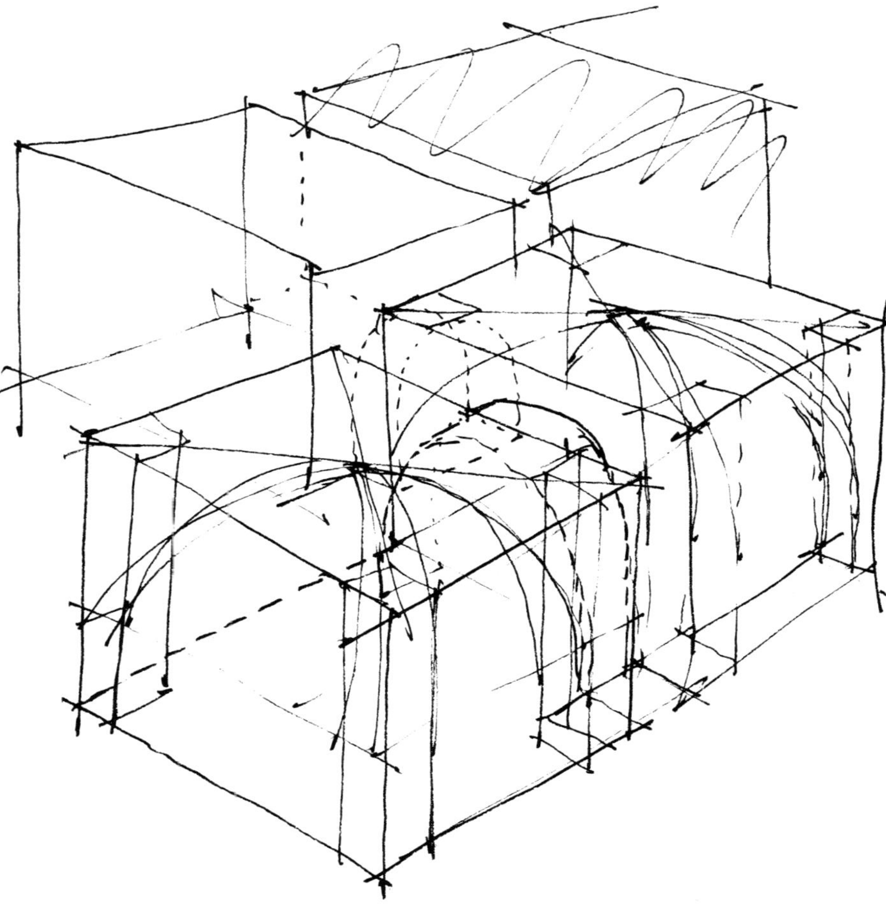

FIGURE 7.18c The line drawing shown here illustrates a positive volume of Styrofoam to be carved into shapes that will represent the negative space of the vaulted-ceiling offices shown in Figure 7.18d, the completed plaster model.

First 2″ slabs of rigid Styrofoam were cemented together with water-base contact cement. Next these blocks were rasped and sanded into their respective "negative" vaulted three-dimensional shapes. The resulting carving was placed in a cardboard box and covered with a soupy mixture of plaster of paris. (*Note:* The Styrofoam core must be secured before covering it with plaster of paris so that it does not float.)

The Styrofoam was then scooped from the overturned block after the plaster had set. Lacquer thinner was used to melt the remaining Styrofoam particles from the cavity, to create the casting shown in Figure 7.18d.

Trace the Photograph of the Model to Create a Drawing

The resulting shots can be traced on an overlay. Find the vanishing point (Figure 7.18e). Then draw all proposed items into the space; use frosted Mylar or Clearprint 1000H tracing paper.

The completed installation (Figure 7.18f) and the presentation sketch (Figure 7.18g), when compared to the design sketch (Figure 7.18a), are remarkably similar. When Figure 7.18g is compared to the finished installation in Figure 7.18f, the two views are almost identical.

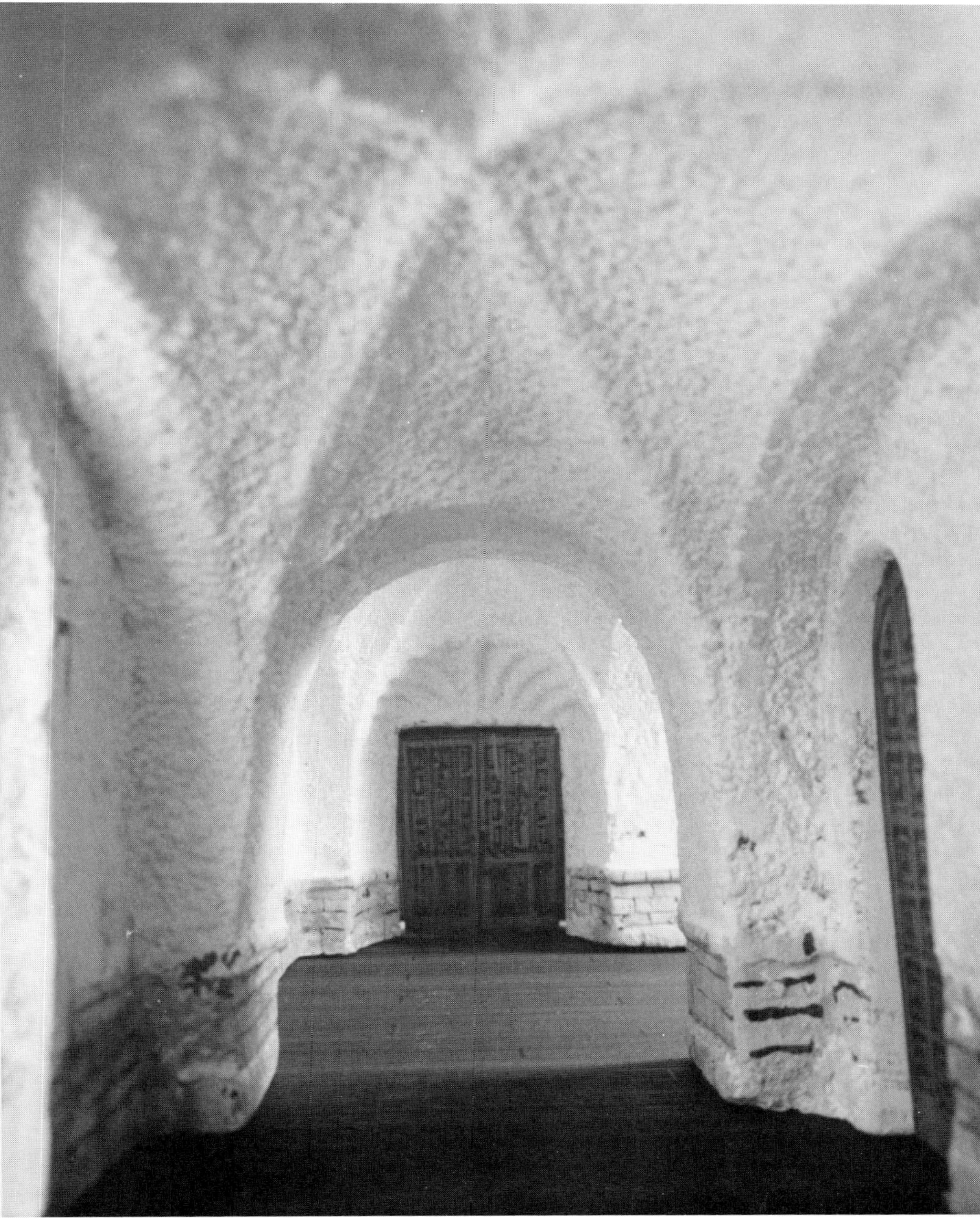

FIGURE 7.18d After painting and the addition of a "wood" floor, the realistic textured plaster of paris casting shown here has been photographed with a 55-mm to 62-mm automatic Macro 1:2.8 Vivitar lens mounted on a Nikon F. E. 35-mm camera. A 200-W bulb illuminated the subject from an opening that was cut for the purpose of photographing (not seen in the photograph).

The extremely small f/16 lens opening and an extremely long shutter speed allowed a depth of field great enough within the space to create a relatively sharp image with an acceptable distortion factor.

FIGURE 7.18e This line tracing of the photograph of the model in Figure 7.18d has been adjusted for verticality. Wall-floor lines, baselines, and wainscot lines have been traced to find the single vanishing point at the rear wall, i.e., primary plane *A*. The pair of doors also lies on primary plane *A*, and each successive parallel *A* plane forward will be noted as A^1 and A^2; *parallel* planes *B*, B^1, and B^2 are noted in a similar manner for this one-point perspective.

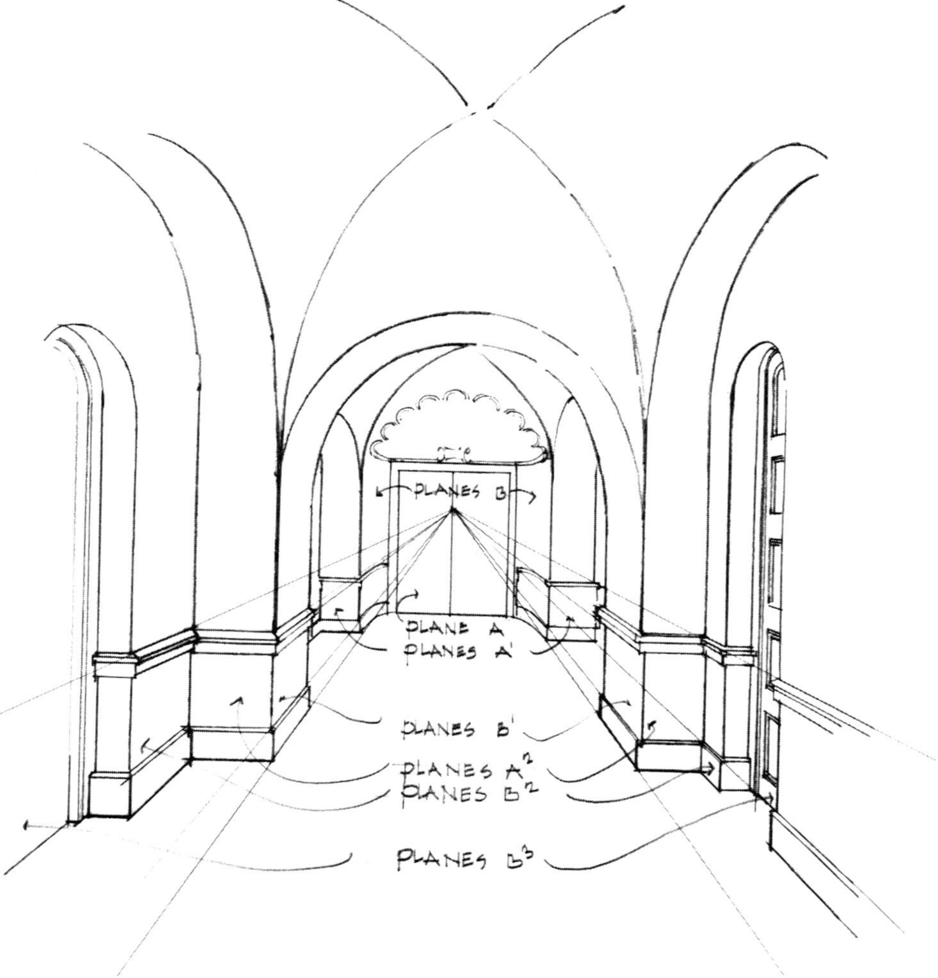

FIGURE 7.18f This photograph shows the completed installation of the reception area based on the model in Figure 7.18d.

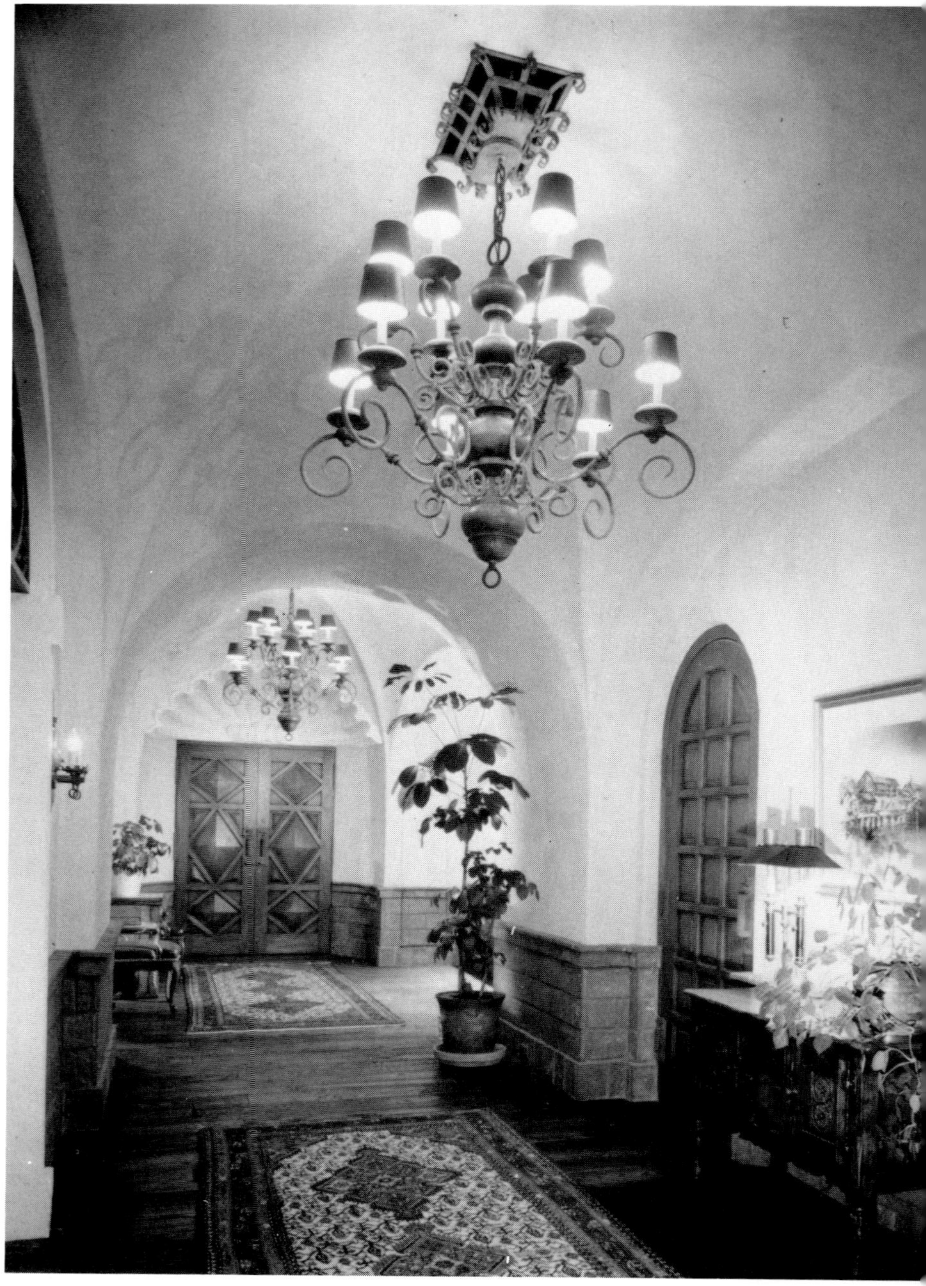

Jeremiah O. Bragstad

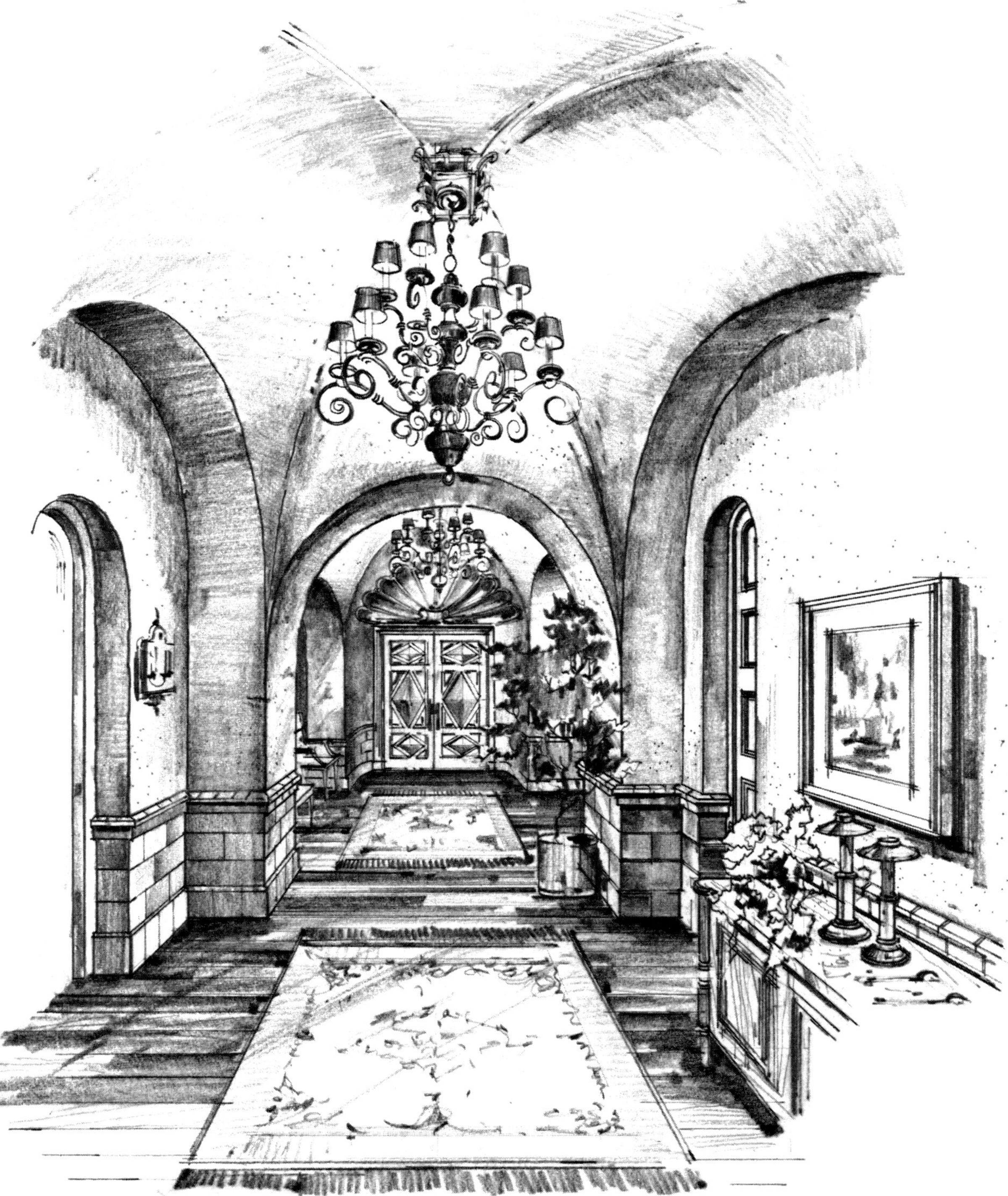

FIGURE 7.18g The completed presentation drawing has been rendered on Clearprint 1000H tracing paper with 2H, H, and F lead pencils. A small version of the chandelier shown here and in Figure 7.18f was first photographed at the manufacturer's showroom. Because of its extremely complicated shape, the resulting photographs, taken from approximately the same viewing angle as this sketch, were enlarged, and then the chandeliers were traced onto the final drawing. Chandeliers and doors were drawn full size before fabrication.

This presentation drawing, which has been based on a three-dimensional model, when compared to the completed installation is acceptable as a realistic selling tool for this traditional vaulted-ceiling space.

PROJECT: Corporate offices, San Francisco
ARCHITECTURAL DESIGNER: the author
INTERIOR DESIGNER: the author
PRODUCTION ARCHITECT: Robert M. Morris Jr., AIA

CHAPTER 8

PRACTICAL APPLICATION OF THE PHOTOLINEAR PERSPECTIVE: A RESORT HOTEL

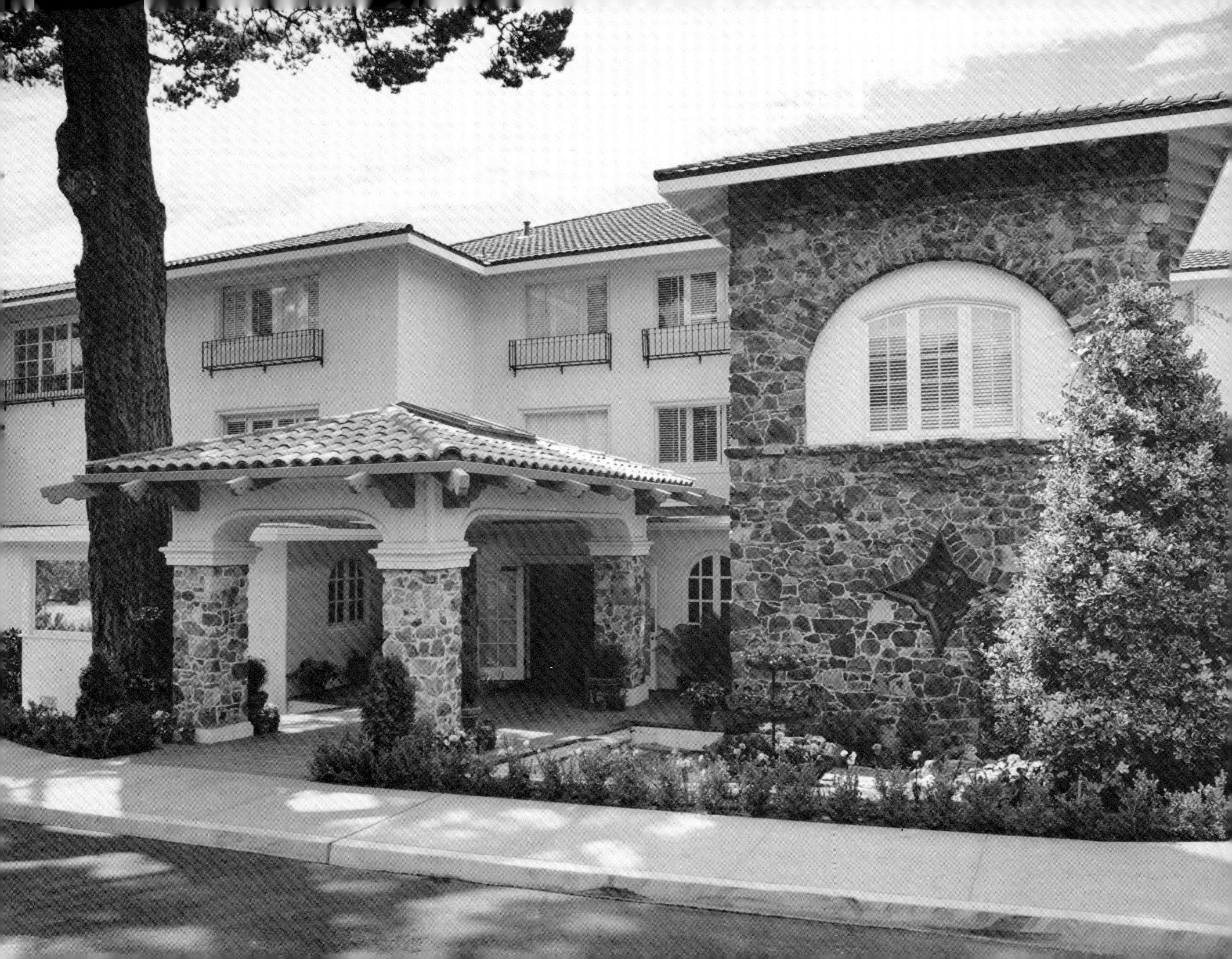

CHAPTER 8

PRACTICAL APPLICATION OF THE PHOTOLINEAR PERSPECTIVE: A RESORT HOTEL

Overview

It is important to realize that the techniques shown in previous chapters all contribute to *accurate pictorial representations of design concepts and three-dimensional rendering techniques that give line drawings dimension.*

Projects shown have ranged from the very simple to the complex. Care has been taken to make the reader aware that even though the concepts are very basic, the magnitude of the benefit derived from their use in design presentation and job communication is very great.

Illustrated in this final chapter are original photographs, presentation drawings, and final installation photographs of a resort hotel. The photographs, tracings, and final drawings for this project were used to visually inspire the client and aid the design team in the many difficult decisions in the design process. Equally important was their use in demonstrating design concepts to city design review officials and on-site construction teams.

Photographs of the final project, when compared with the original concept sketches, show how accurate drawings can be when the photolinear perspective method is used. No matter how complex the project, if the principles explained in this book are used along with the photolinear perspective theory, value studies, shade and shadow applications, proper pen-and-pencil techniques, three-dimensional elevations, and detail rendering concepts, then the drawings that emerge will exhibit remarkable accuracy and pictorial clarity. Of course, the practice of all these techniques and the learned ability to take accurate photographs are most important in the creation of accurate and pleasing presentation drawings.

PROJECT: La Playa Hotel, Carmel by the Sea, California
PROJECT DESIGNER: the author
PRODUCTION ARCHITECT: Keeble & Rhoda
INTERIOR CONSULTANT: Elizabeth Bernhardt
ILLUSTRATOR: the author

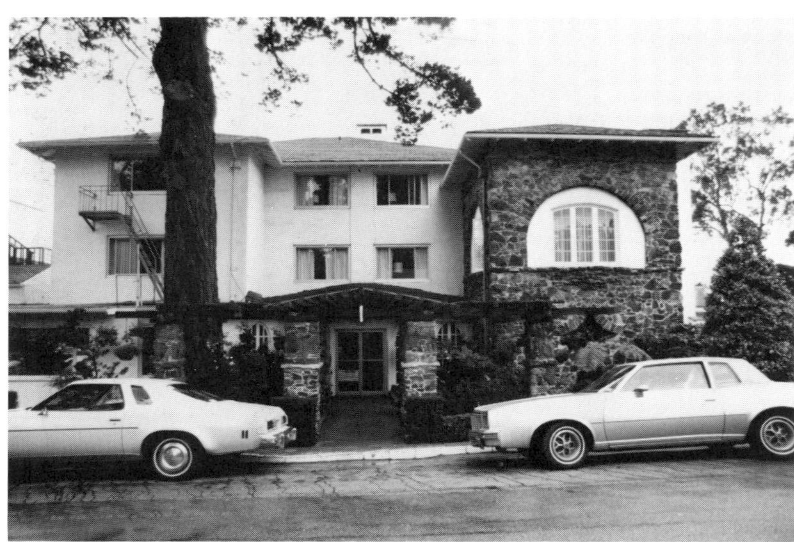

8.1a

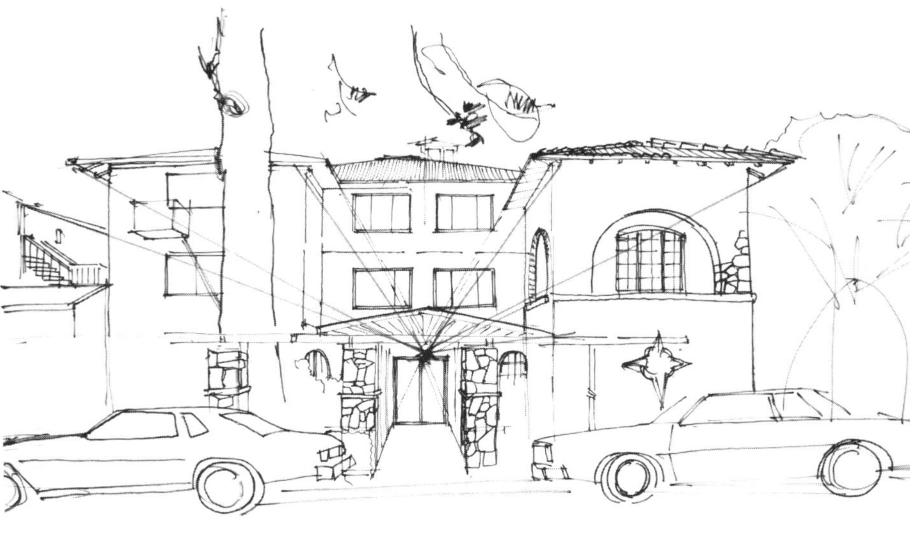

8.1b

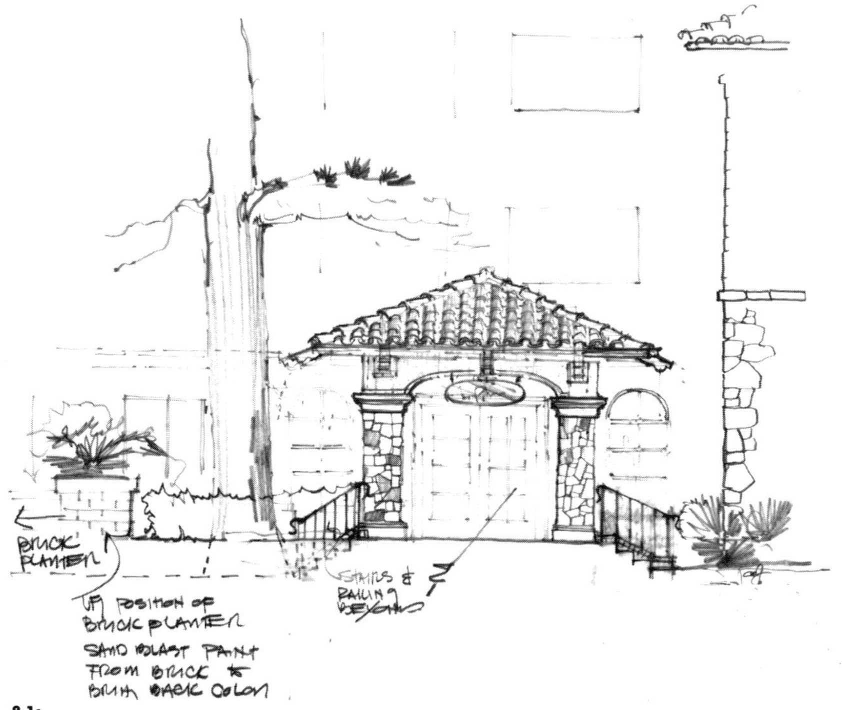

8.1c

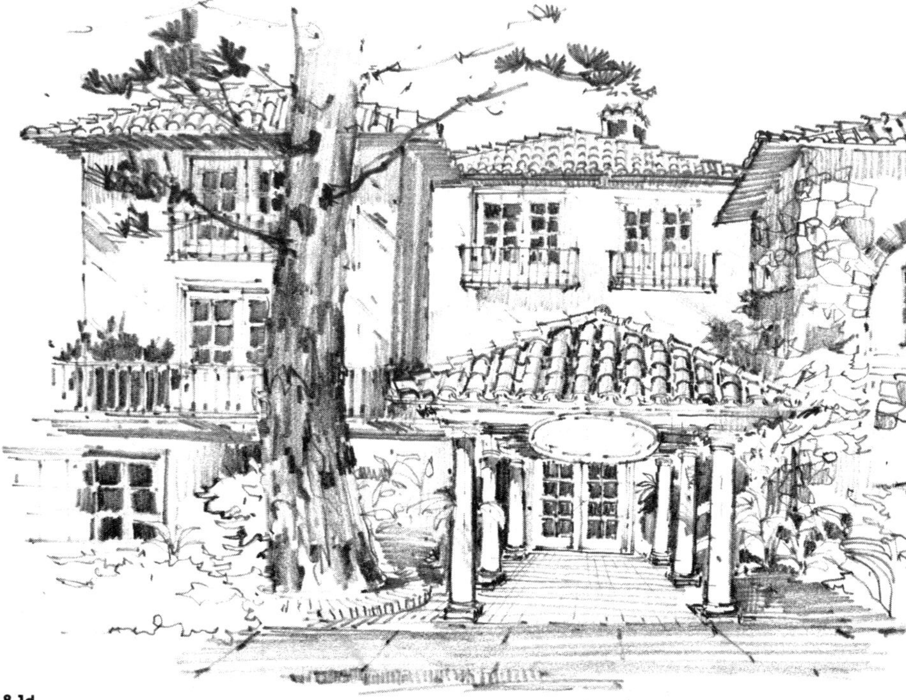

8.1d

FIGURE 8.1a through d These initial concept sketches were traced from the original black-and-white photograph in Figure 8.1a. Figure 8.1d depicts an entry with a covered walkway. This concept was later reused, as seen in the elevation (Figure 8.1c) and the completed installation (overleaf).

FIGURE 8.1e The completed first concept presentation drawing was illustrated on drafting vellum with new and semidry felt-tip pens of the drugstore variety. It is important to save used pens of this type, for they can be used to lay down the 2 and 3 values to create variation in line and value.

The car, tree, and major building line work were traced from Figure 8.1a.

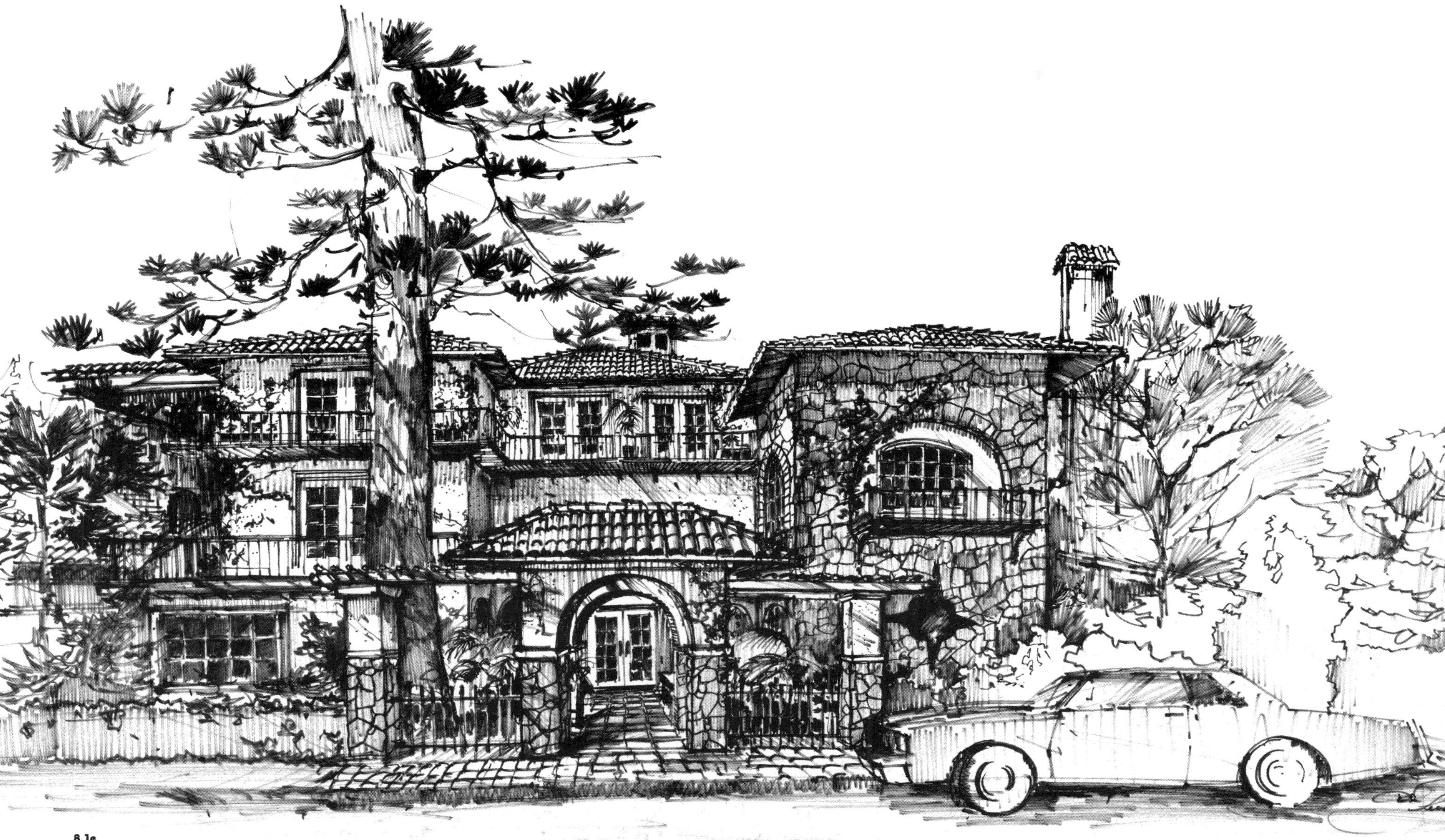

8.1e

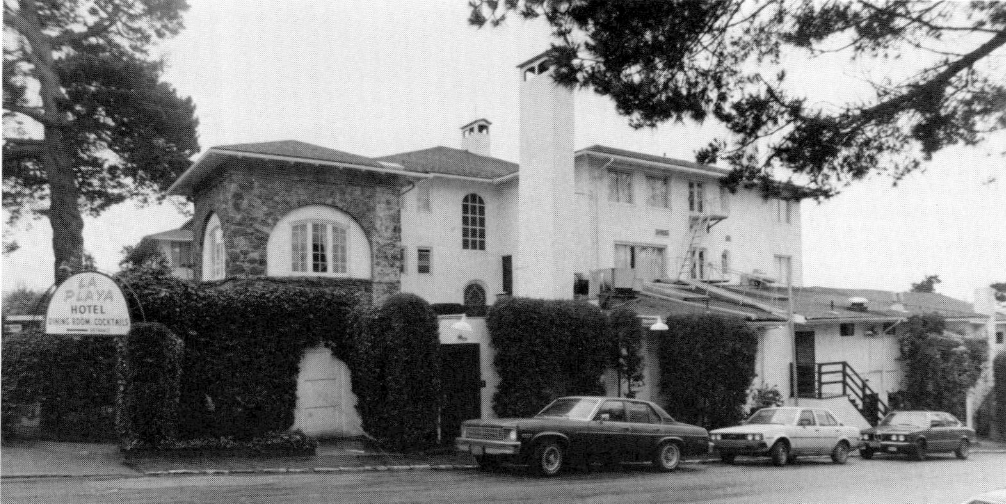

8.2a

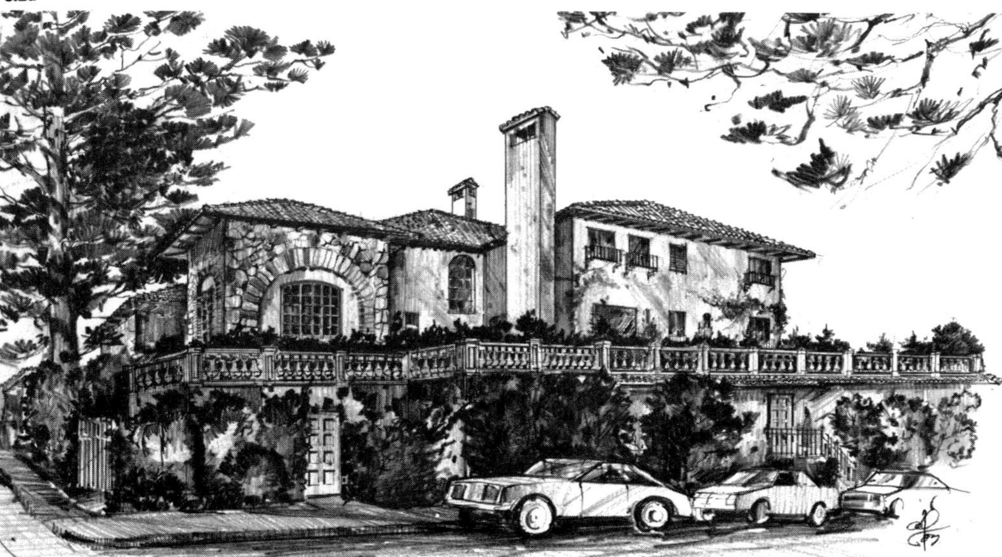

8.2b

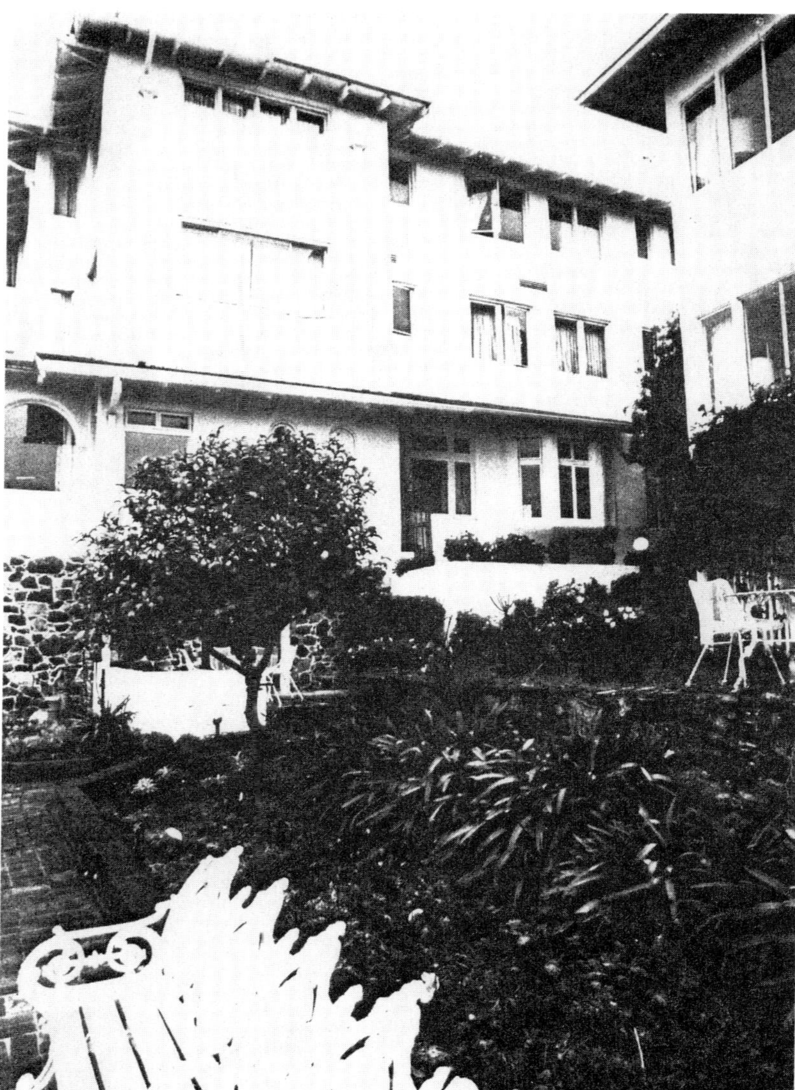

8.3a

FIGURE 8.2a and b The cars and building elements were included in this sketch along with this fully rendered Monterey pine. And 2B, B, and H pencils were used to create the drawing on Clearprint 1000H tracing paper.

A balustrade with planting behind is used in this concept sketch to hide mechanical equipment mounted on this hotel kitchen roof. The cars, trees, and major building lines were faithfully produced in pencil on Clearprint 1000H tracing paper. H, 2B, and 4B pencils were used.

FIGURE 8.3a and b The black-and-white photograph in (a) has been enlarged on a photocopy machine. Note how the window areas, planting, and other details have been washed out by the high contrast that is typical of this type of photocopy print.

Figure 8.3b has been screened with a fine photograph dot screen that is integral to some laser

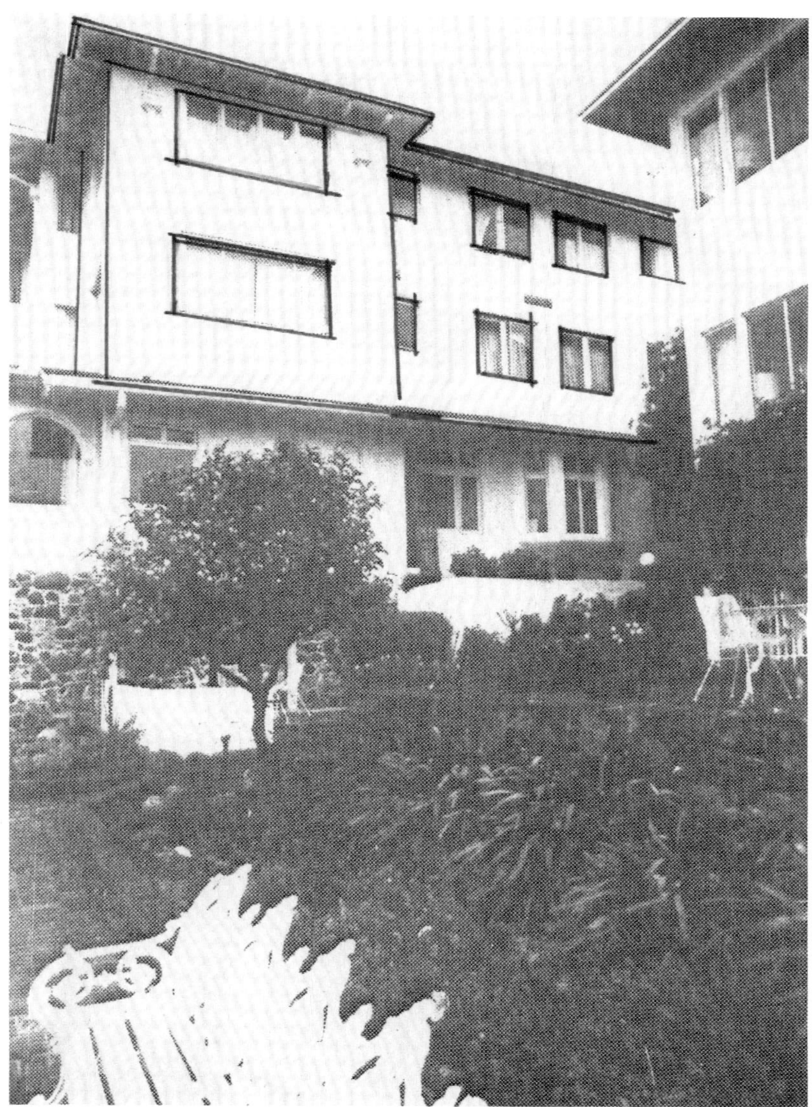

8.3b

photocopy machines. The process changes the tones and values of a photograph into a series of dots, much as in newspaper print. This allows the details to remain in the enlarged print. Note that the windows have been outlined to aid in the photograph tracing process.

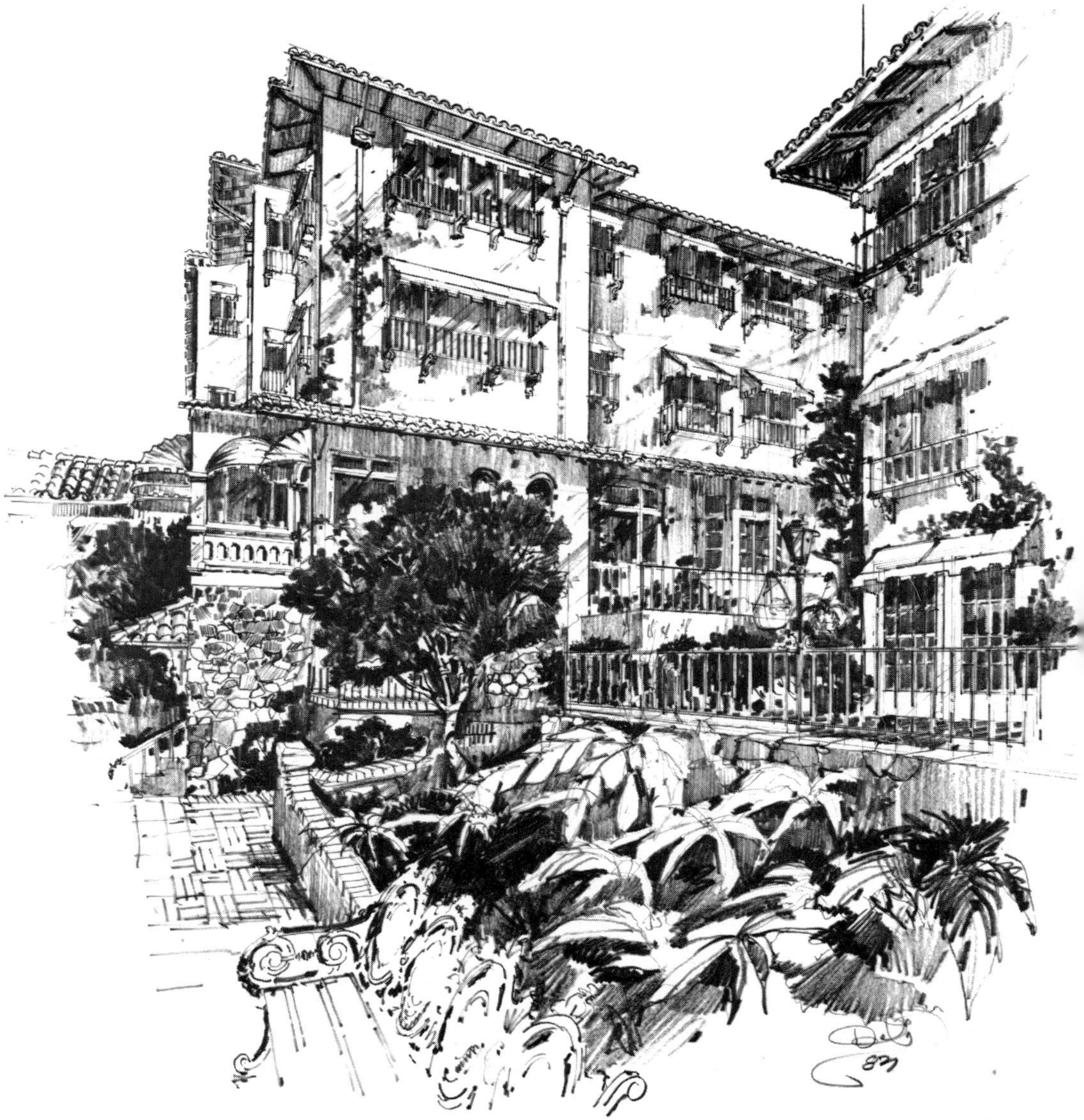

8.3c

FIGURE 8.3c This completed illustration was drawn on double-weight acetate that had been frosted on both sides. The crispness of line on this drawing surface is surpassed only by the capacity of the tooth of the drafting medium to remove graphite from 2H and H pencils and thus create almost black values, if desired.

PROJECT: La Playa Hotel, Carmel by the Sea, California
PROJECT DESIGNER: the author
PRODUCTION ARCHITECTS: Keeble & Rhoda
ILLUSTRATOR: The author

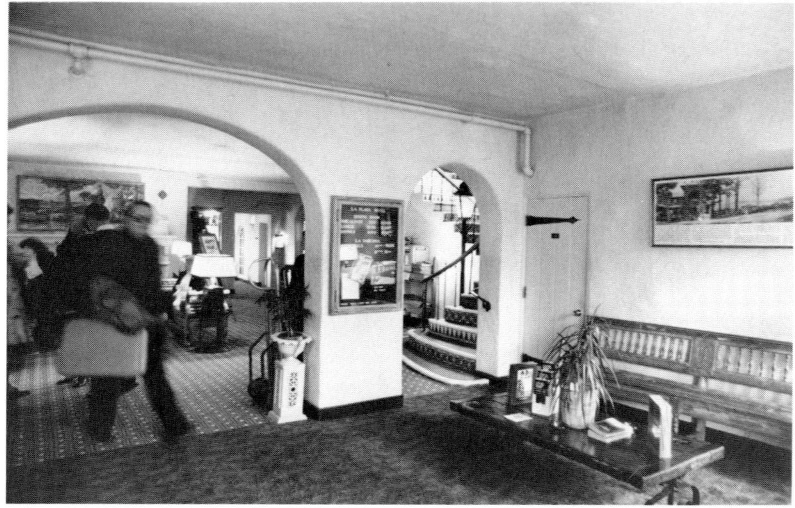

8.4a

FIGURE 8.4a through c The interior lobby of this hotel was refurbished within an existing space. This concept sketch (b) was traced directly from the photograph in (a).

The final installation in (c) shows the addition of mill work, tile, and the chimneypiece, previously seen in Figure 4.2a through c.

PROJECT: La Playa Hotel, Carmel by the Sea, California
DESIGNER: the author
PRODUCTION ARCHITECTS: Keeble & Rhoda
INTERIOR DESIGN CONSULTANT: Elizabeth Bernhardt
ILLUSTRATOR: the author

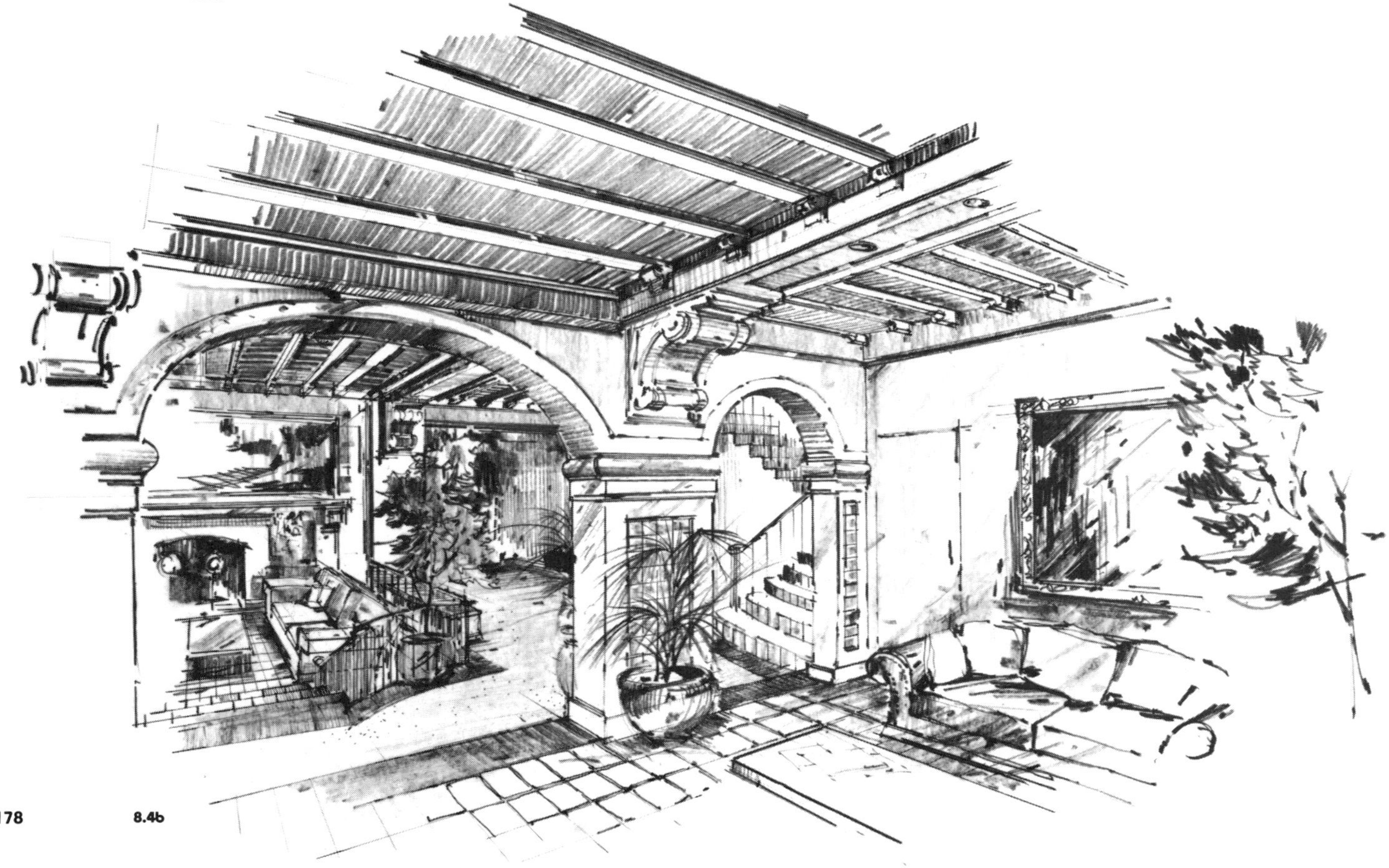

8.4b

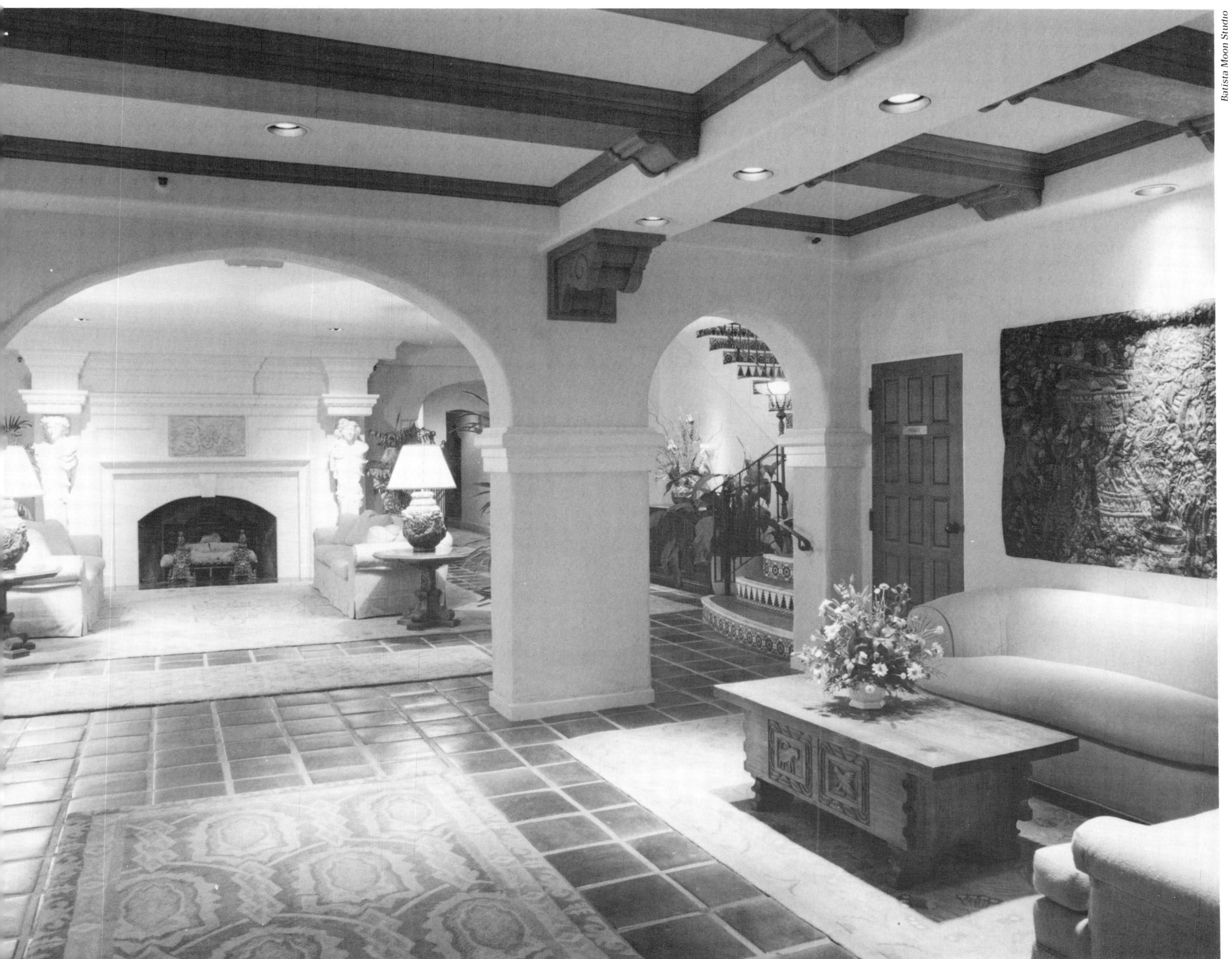

Batista Moon Studio

8.4c

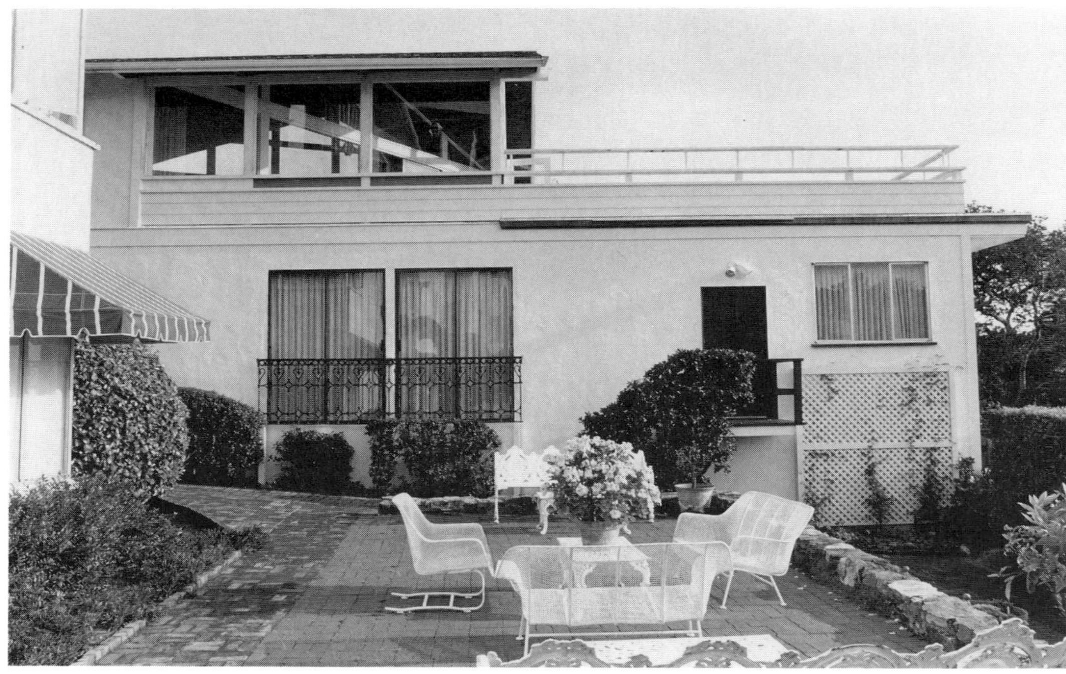

FIGURE 8.5a and b The flat, two-dimensional facade was traced to find the single vanishing point, as shown in (b). The final concept sketch in (c) shows a balustrade at the roof deck and a traditional tile roof "eyebrow" over the new French doors.

8.5a

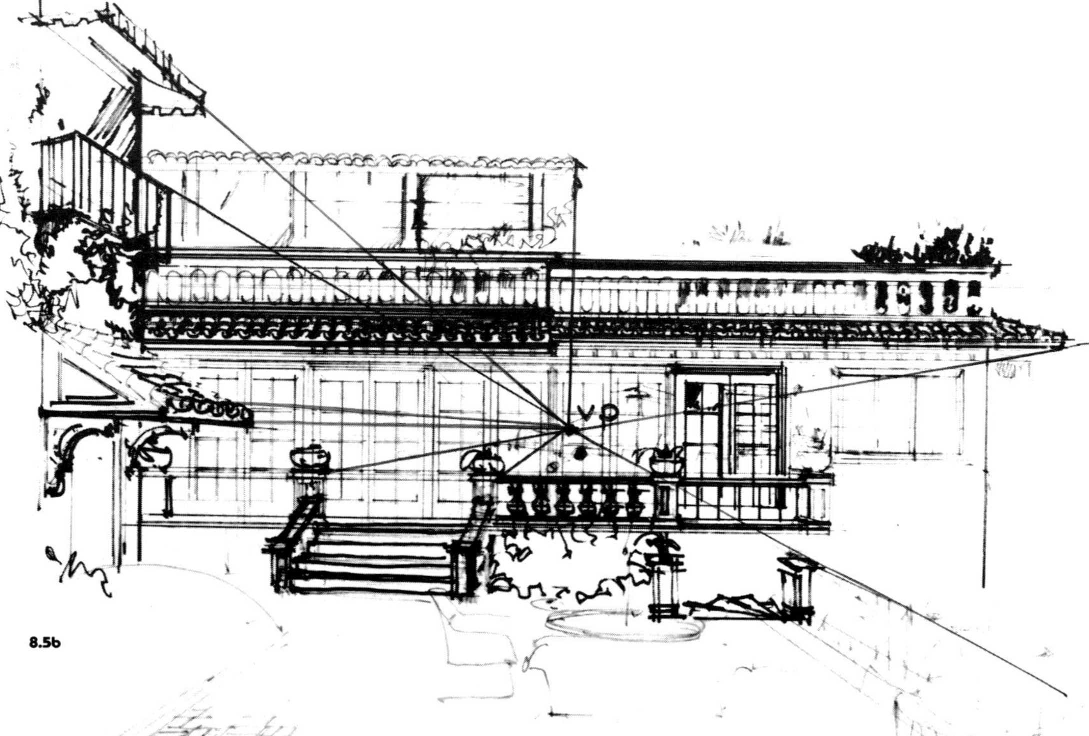

8.5b

FIGURE 8.5c This completed sketch was drawn on Clearprint 1000H tracing paper with 2B and H lead pencils. A 4B-¼" graphite stick was used to fill in some of the dark planting values.

Note the vignette of this drawing. This technique is an excellent method of visual matting because the lines and values trail off to nothing in all directions before coming to the edge of the paper. This allows the eye to concentrate on the central area of the sketch.

PROJECT: La Playa Hotel, Carmel by the Sea, California
PROJECT DESIGNER: The author
PRODUCTION ARCHITECTS: Keeble & Rhoda

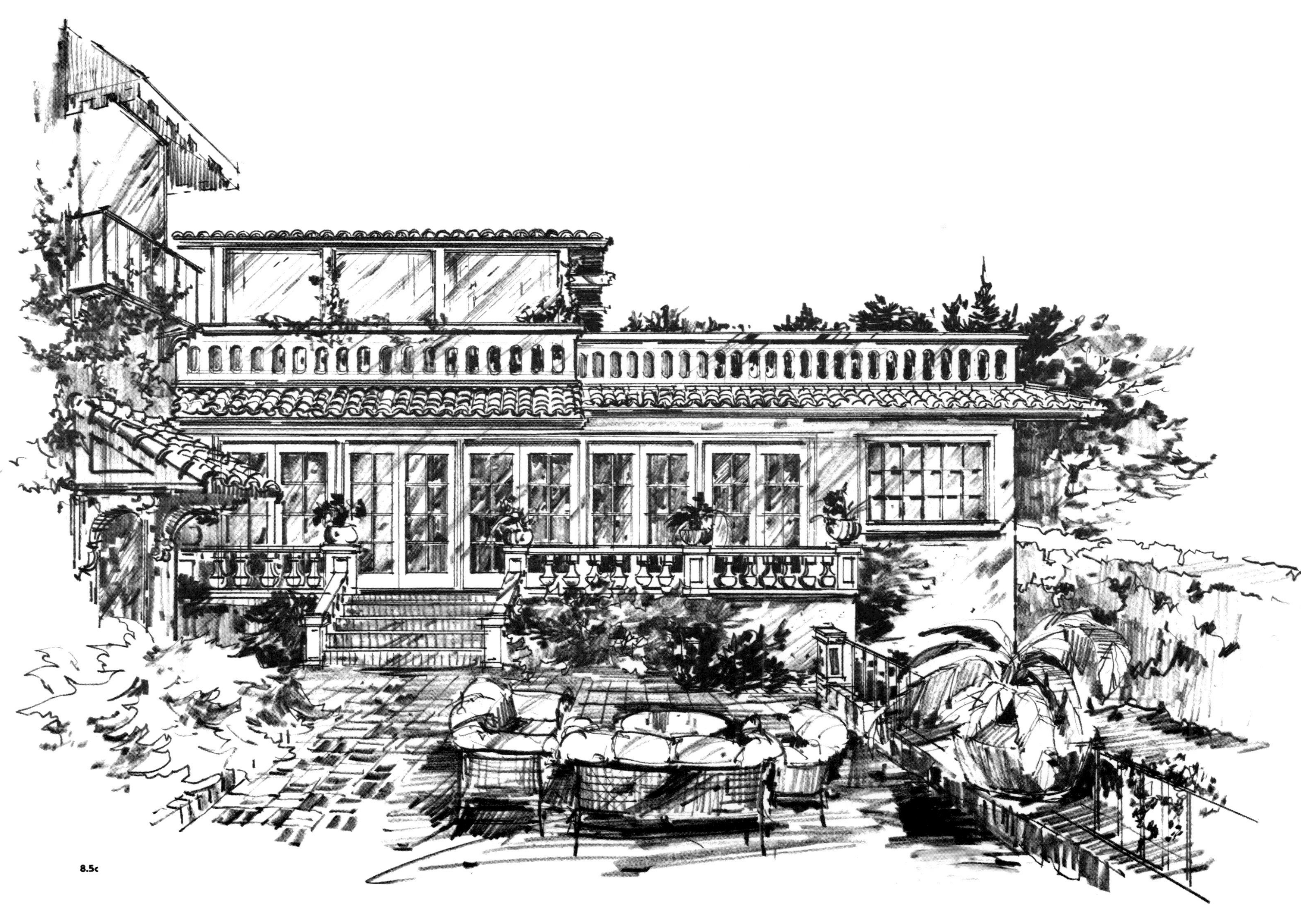

8.5c

FIGURE 8.5d through h Another view of the building in Figure 8.5c is taken from a lower vantage point. The TMC has been established in this two-part perspective underdrawing (Figure 8.5e) as the leading edge of the upper building, creating *A* and *B* planes.

The doors in (f) were divided by the intersecting-diagonals method of Chapter 2. A canvas awning was introduced in this concept sketch (Figure 8.5g) but was later discarded for the tile-covered shed "eyebrow" shown in the final installation (Figure 8.5h).

Full-size rendered drawings were required for the stone balustrades because they were precast at another location.

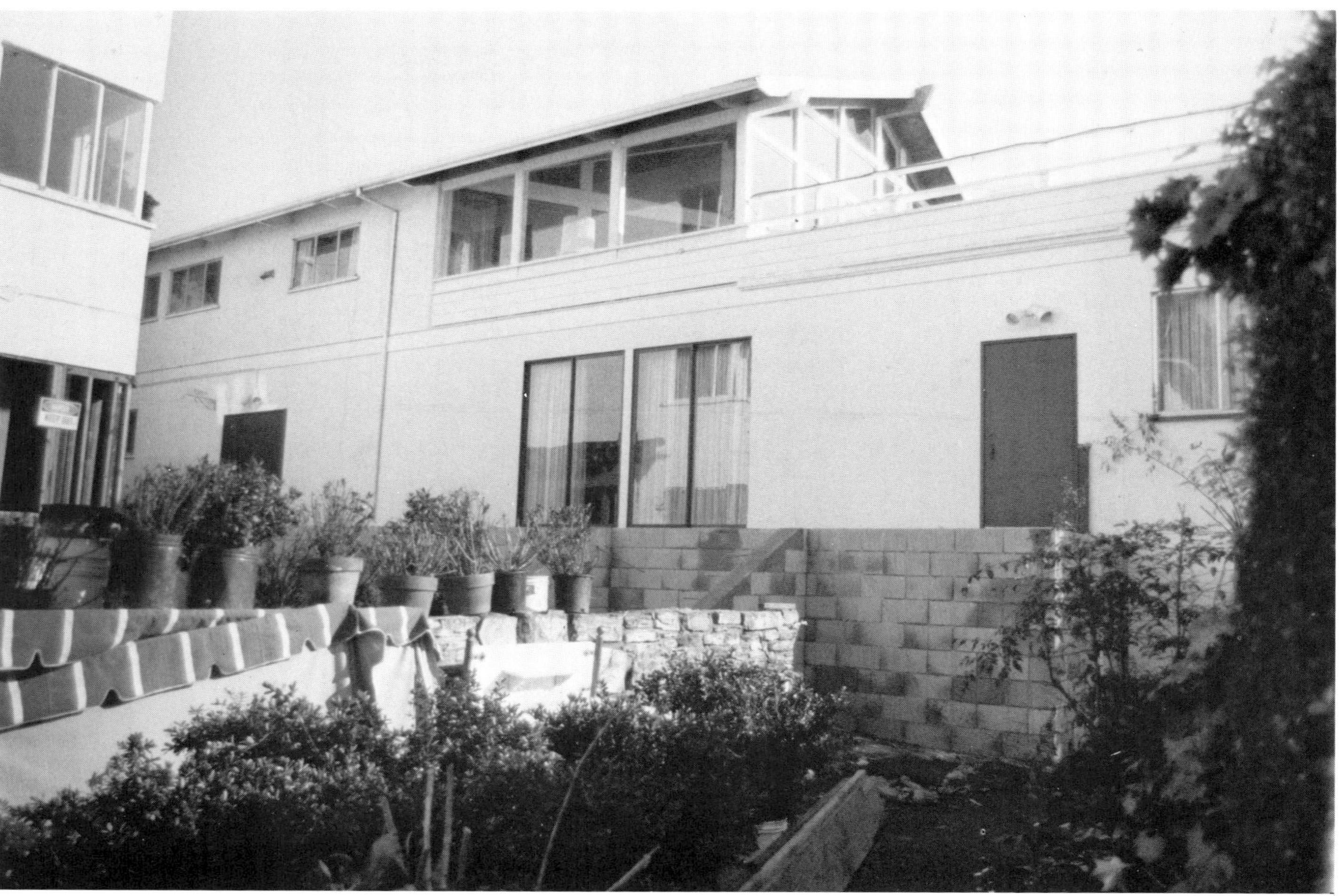

8.5d

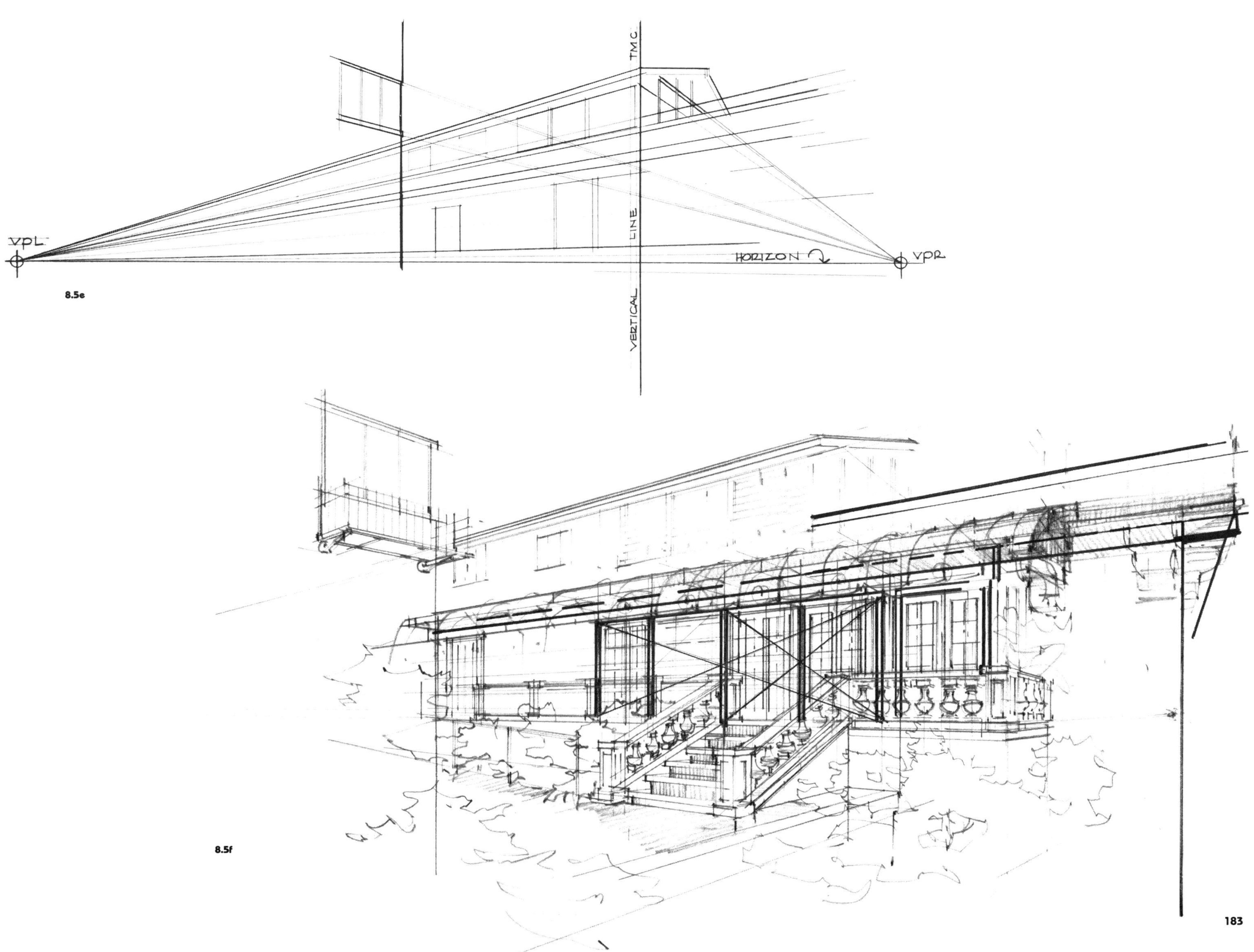

8.5e

8.5f

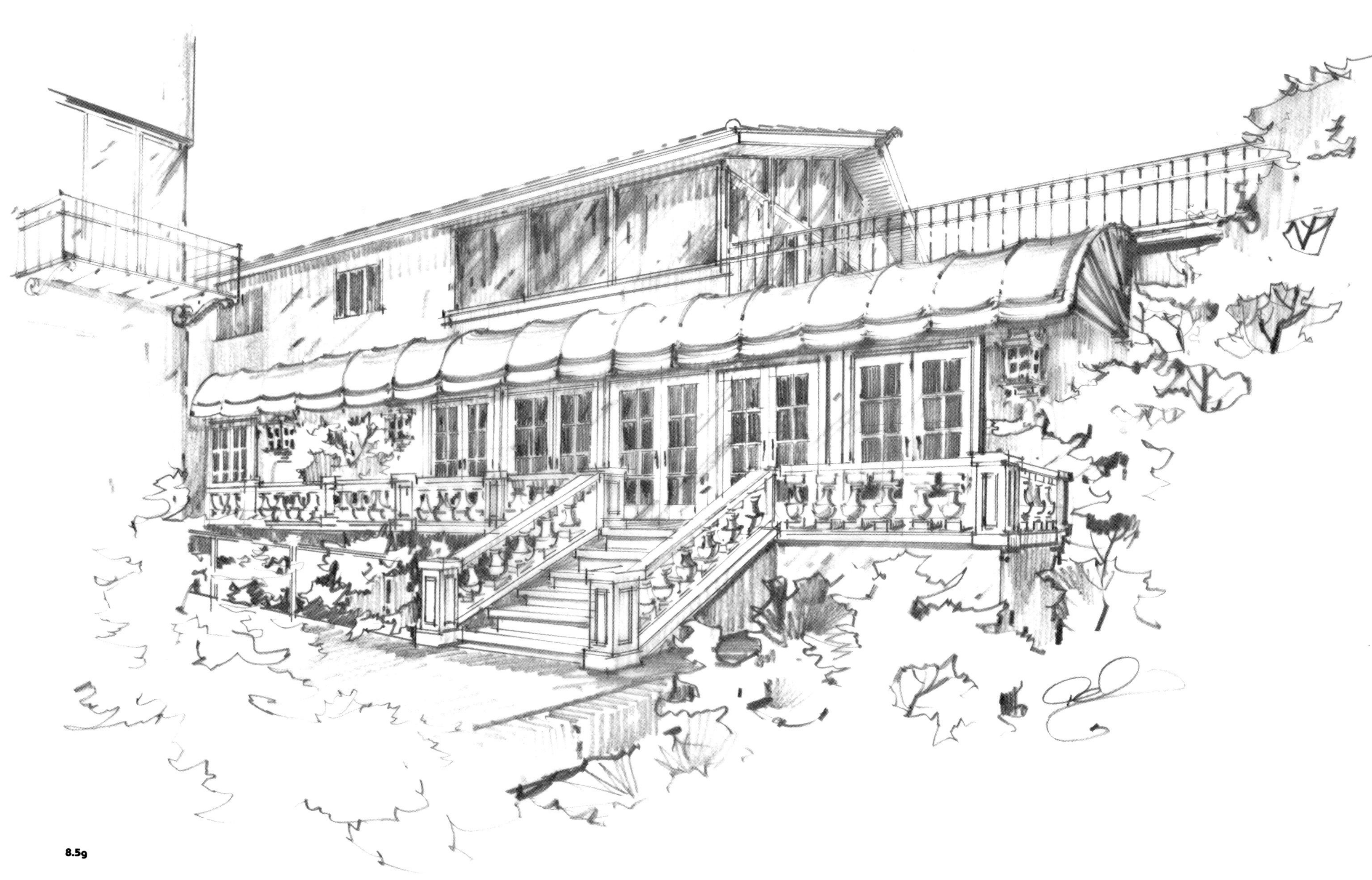

8.5g

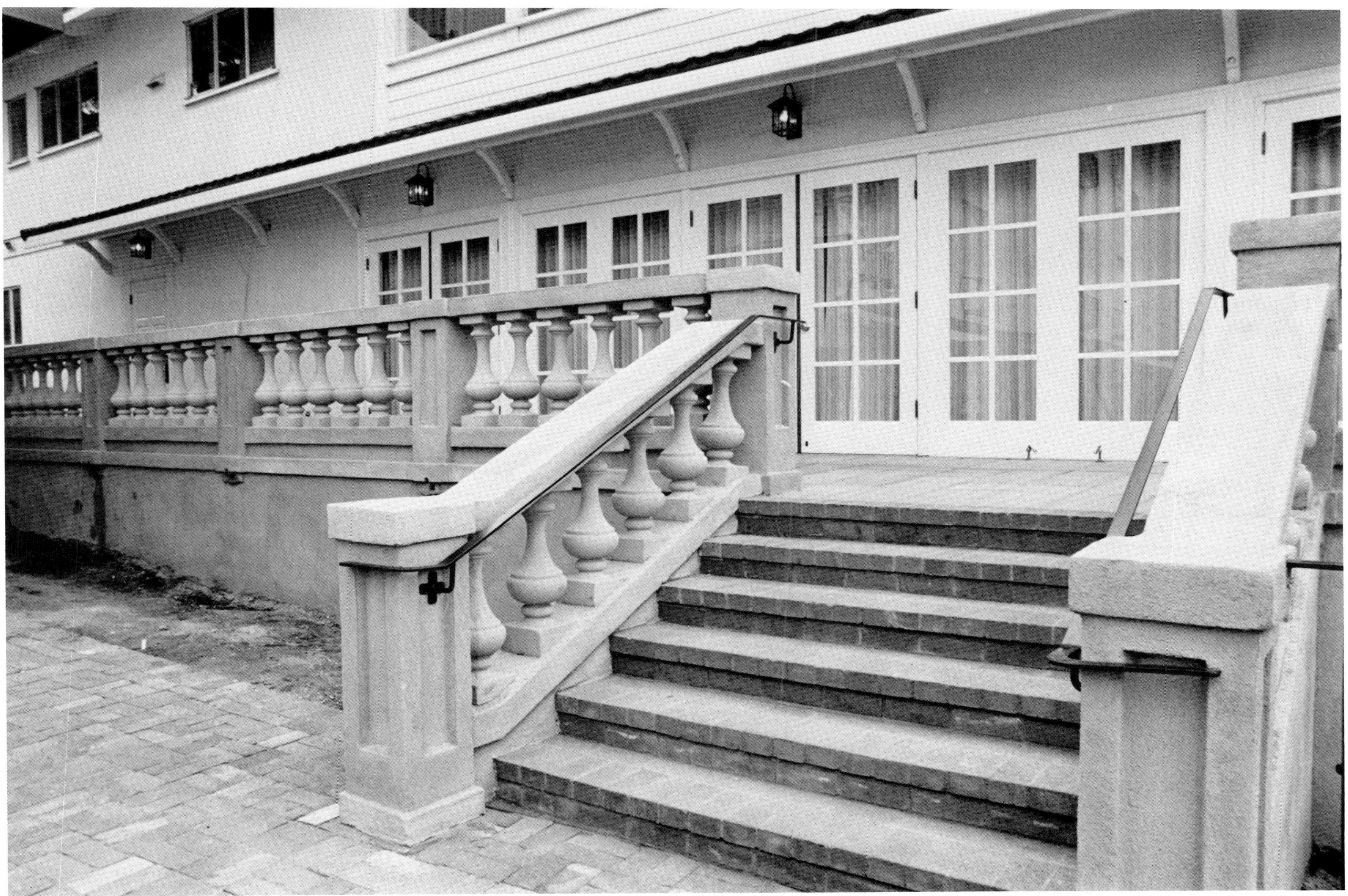

8.5h

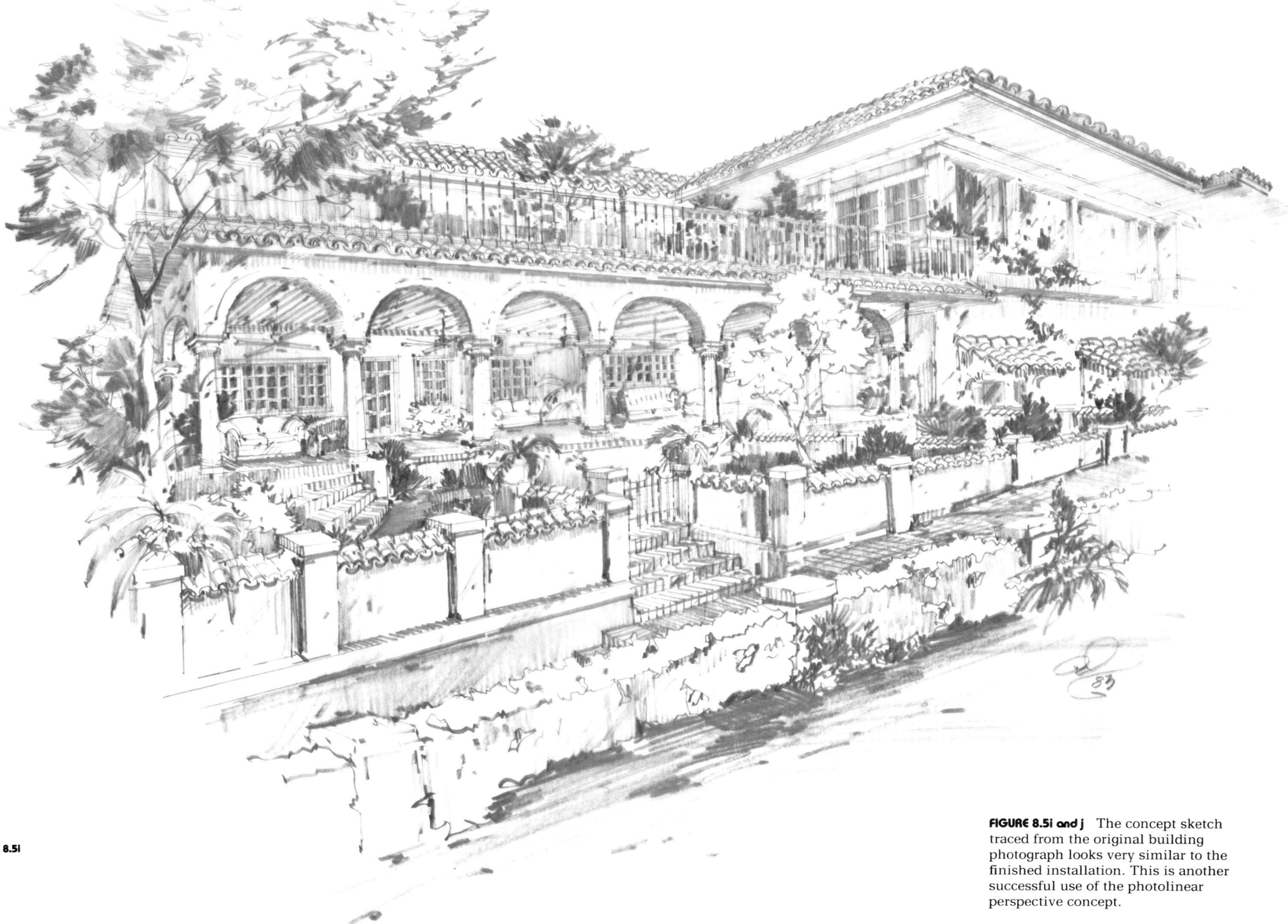

8.5i

FIGURE 8.5i and j The concept sketch traced from the original building photograph looks very similar to the finished installation. This is another successful use of the photolinear perspective concept.

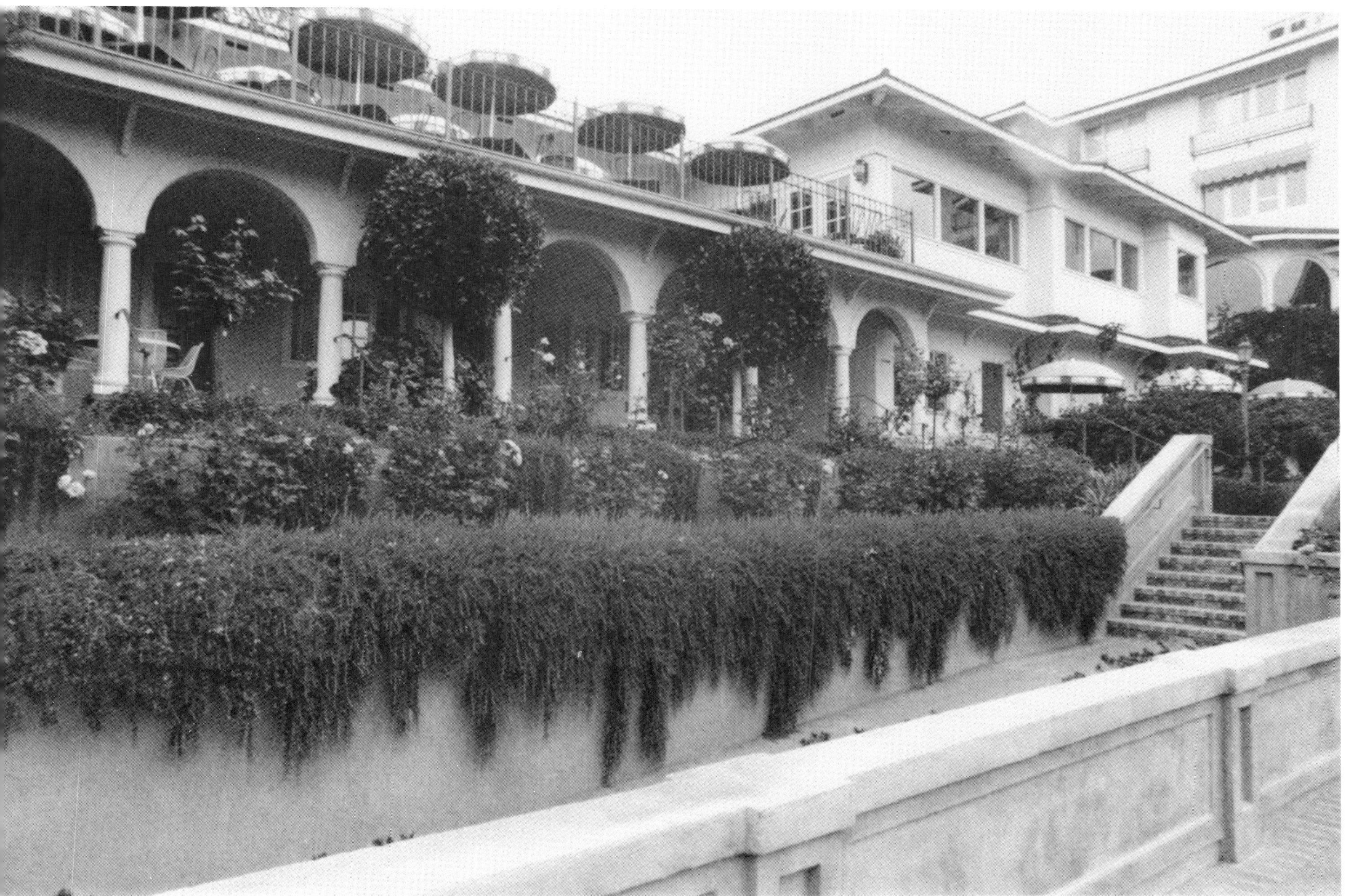

8.5j

INDEX

Page numbers in *italic* indicate illustrations.

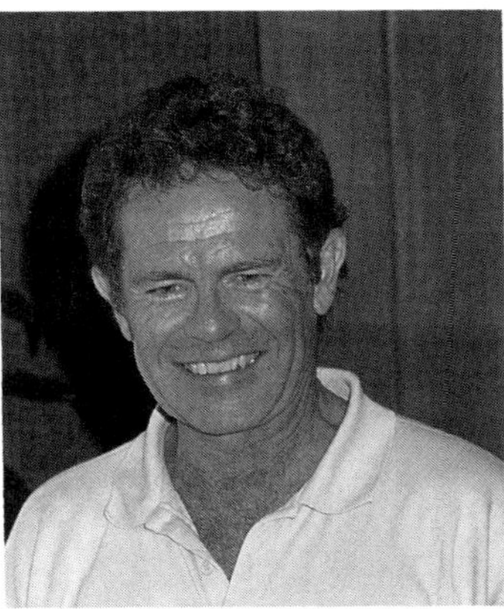

ABOUT THE AUTHOR

Sid DelMar Leach, ASID, is an architectural interior designer and illustrator and a builder. He is widely celebrated as a designer of fine architectural woodwork and appointments in houses of architectural and historical importance. Mr. Leach served as director of the interior design department at the Fashion Institute of Interior Design and Merchandising in San Francisco, California. He is the author of *Techniques of Interior Design Rendering and Presentation,* published by McGraw-Hill.